Quantitative Archaeology and Archaeological Modelling

More information about this series at http://www.springer.com/series/14342

Oliver Nakoinz • Daniel Knitter

Modelling Human Behaviour in Landscapes

Basic Concepts and Modelling Elements

Springer

Oliver Nakoinz
University of Kiel
Kiel, Germany

Daniel Knitter
Excellence Cluster Topoi
Freie Universität
Berlin, Germany

ISSN 2366-5998 ISSN 2366-6005 (electronic)
Quantitative Archaeology and Archaeological Modelling
ISBN 978-3-319-29536-7 ISBN 978-3-319-29538-1 (eBook)
DOI 10.1007/978-3-319-29538-1

Library of Congress Control Number: 2016931615

Printed on acid-free paper

This Springer imprint is published by Springer Nature
The registered company is Springer International Publishing AG Switzerland

This book is dedicated to Peter Haggett and the memory of David L. Clarke, who established a prolific interdisciplinary exchange between geography and archaeology

Series Foreword

Quantitative approaches and modelling techniques have played an increasingly significant role in archaeology over the last few decades, as can be seen both by their prominence in published research and in university courses. Despite this popularity, there remains only a limited number of book-length treatments in archaeology on these subjects (with the exception perhaps being general-purpose GIS). 'Quantitative Archaeology and Archaeological Modelling' is a book series that therefore responds to this need for (a) basic, methodologically transparent, manuals for teaching at all levels, (b) good practice guides with a series of reproducible case studies, and (c) higher-level extended discussions of bleeding edge problems. This series is also intended to be interdisciplinary in the analytical theory and method it fosters, international in its scope, datasets, contributors and audience, and open to both deliberately novel and wellestablished approaches. We look forward to developing a series of books, which support and promote a fast growing sub-discipline in archaeology and invite authors to join us. We are grateful to Springer and in particular to Teresa Kraus for making this series possible and would like to thank members of our wider editorial board for their support so far: Caitlin Buck, Dmitry Korobov, Kenneth Kvamme, Laure Nunninger, Silvia Polla, Luke Premo, Karim Sadr and Hai Zhang.

Oliver Nakoinz, Andrew Bevan

Preface

For landscape archaeology, modelling spatial aspects of human behaviour became an essential topic in the recent years. Located at the disciplinary border between geography and archaeology, modelling human behaviour in landscapes attracts contributions from both sides and is based on an integration of both disciplines. Although there is many research published on this topic and both geography and archaeology possess some textbooks, there is no textbook addressing the specific topic of modelling human behaviour in landscapes. This book attempts to fill this gap.

The authors suffered from this lack of a textbook during university courses and summer and winter schools in Kiel and Berlin. This was motivation enough to turn the course scripts into a textbook, which offers some basic techniques and concepts.

The institutions at which we held our courses are an inspiring environment to develop our concept. The Graduate School Human Development in Landscapes (GSHDL) at the Christian-Albrechts-University of Kiel is a multidisciplinary graduate school, focussed on the change of societies in the context of landscape. The GSHDL judges modelling as an important approach for interdisciplinary communication and meta-disciplinary research. The GSHDL aims to intensify quantitative modelling in research as well as in teaching. This concept is well embedded in the Christian-Albrechts-University of Kiel with its extensive expertise in modelling in many disciplines, including the prehistoric archaeology where quantitative modelling is in focus. The expertise in modelling in Kiel is bundled in two areas. The first modelling focus is the GSHDL. The GSHDL approaches will be continued in the Johanna Mestorf Academy of the Christian-Albrechts-University of Kiel. The second one is a group of specialists around Bernd Thalheim from computer sciences which develops a specific discourse, concepts and practices of modelling.

The Excellence Cluster Topoi investigates the transformation of space and knowledge in ancient civilisations. Its research is based on the expertise concentrated in Berlin: besides the two universities Freie Universität Berlin and Humboldt-Universität zu Berlin, the institutions Berlin-Brandenburgische Akademie der Wissenschaften, Deutsches Archäologisches Institut, Max-Planck-

Institut für Wissenschaftsgeschichte and Stiftung Preußischer Kulturbesitz are taking part in the cluster. Different research areas, consisting of a broad range of scientists from physics and geosciences to archaeology, art and philosophy, target the central terms space and knowledge from very different perspectives. In the course of the Excellence Cluster Topoi, the Berliner Antike Kolleg and its graduate school the Berlin Graduate School for Ancient Studies (BerGSAS) were founded. Thanks to the funding of Topoi, it is possible to teach students the topics covered in this book, e.g. in the doctoral programme 'landscape archaeology and architecture' of the graduate school.

This volume is designed as a 12-lecture textbook which can serve as a course companion, self-teaching guide and handbook for basic concepts. Each lecture has around 20 pages. The main concepts of the book can be summarised as:

- Focussed on principles and methods.
- Applied: the readers are enabled to execute the case studies themselves. The code for open source software is provided in each chapter. The web page of the book provides a digital version of the code as well as the data for the case studies (http://dakni.github.io/mhbil/). While some analyse produce good results, other examples sensitise for common trap falls. This is possible in a textbook, but cannot be provided in research.
- Minimalistic: the content is presented as concise text in short chapters focussing on the main points, with few details but extensive illustrations. This supports an efficient understanding. The book focuses on rather simple methodological concepts and principles which are located between simple statistics and advanced modelling applications. A minimal exemplary data set which the reader gets to know and understand very quickly helps focus on the concepts.
- Sustained and efficient by focusing on principles and methods: the relations between different concepts and methods are described to ensure deeper understanding. Terminology from different traditions, concepts and paradigms helps make connections. By focusing on concepts, we enable the reader to develop more complex models by themselves. The book provides a basic modelling terminology and tool kit to construct coherent modelling concepts. The code is not efficient for computing but for didactic purposes. The text does not get stuck in technical details but tries to convey the concepts with a didactic approach.
- Interdisciplinary: the content derives from different disciplines—mainly archaeology, geography, mathematics and statistics—and is seamlessly integrated in a generalised introduction into spatial modelling. We persistently try to offer an interdisciplinary perspective.

In addition to the didactic concept, we wish to address three points prior to reading the book.

We are dedicated to an *integrative paradigm*. The past decades have been dominated by a discussion about basic scientific paradigms. In archaeology among other terms, 'processual' and 'post-processual' archaeology are opposed. We believe in the complementarity of both approaches and try to integrate them as much as possible. Although the concepts of modelling stand in a processual tradition, the introduction of post-processual ideas increases the applicability and consistency of the content considerably. From an analytical point of view, this integration is seamless, but not from a terminological point of view, at least until today.

Proper research has a good *balance of objective, data, theory and method* (ODTM balance). This book has didactic purposes and hence is allowed to focus on methods and concepts only. Valid case studies have to consider data, source criticism and methodological details. Theory and method have to be justified, and methods have to be based on theory. This is neither possible nor required in a textbook. Otherwise, we could not deal with simple methods, but have to adapt methods to objective, data and theory. This would result in more complicated methods, more extensive code and much more text which does not contribute to the understanding of concepts. Please be aware of the different requirements of didactic purposes and research.

The *choice of methods is not arbitrary* and should not be based on scientific fashions. As indicated in the last paragraph, the choice of method has to be based on objective, data and theory. In particular, theory and method have to be tightly connected and adapted. This involves an adjustment to objectives. Let us imagine two methods which produce different results of the same type. Since the two methods produce different results, they solve different problems. If you cannot decide which method is more suitable, the objective is not precise enough. You have to propose a question that can be answered using the appropriate method and which allows specific interpretations. If two methods apply, the question does not allow a specific interpretation.

To make more sense of this, we invite you to read our book and share your thought with us.

Kiel, Schleswig-Holstein, Germany — Oliver Nakoinz
Berlin, Germany — Daniel Knitter
October 2015

Acknowledgements

Oliver Nakoinz is grateful to the DFG for supporting the work on this volume with a Heisenberg fellowship (NA 687/1-1, NA 687/1-2) and for supporting the project *Modellierung und Rekonstruktion ältereisenzeitlicher Interaktions- und Distributionssysteme in Südwest- und Westdeutschland sowie im Elsass* (NA 687/3-1) which contributed to Chap. 10 of this book. Furthermore, he wants to thank the GSHDL for supporting my work on this topic.

Daniel Knitter is grateful to the Excellence Cluster Topoi—The Formation and Transformation of Space and Knowledge in Ancient Civilizations for supporting this study.

The authors also want to thank Michael Meier, Johannes Müller, Brigitta Schütt and Mara Weinelt for enabling us to give the courses, on which this volume is based.

They received some feedback, useful hints and valuable ideas from colleagues, to which we are grateful: Laurie Tremblay Cormier, Clara Filet, Franziska Faupel, Martin Hinz, Kerstin Kowarik, Carsten Lemmen, Undine Lieberwirth, Dominik Lukas, Cătălin Popa, Christoph Rinne, Bernd Thalheim, Urszula Zawadzka and Gabriel Wurzer.

Some participants of the courses also gave us some valuable feedback: Norbert Anselm, Tilman Baum, Elisa Dalla Longa, Helen Dawson, Martine Gussone, Arie Kai-Browne, Katrin Kermas, Jan Kolar, Jan Kolář, Luise Lorenz, Julia Meister, Moritz Menenga, Tina Michel, Moritz Nykamp, René Ohlrau, Mohamed Osman, Georg Roth, Chiara Schoch, Martin Schumacher, Andrea-Fleur Schweigart, Johanna Seidel, Hendaya Serrano Gil, Michael Thelemann, Barbora Weissova and Arne Windler.

For language editing we are grateful to Carl Evers and Richard Forsythe.

Contents

About the Author

Oliver Nakoinz is associate professor and Heisenberg fellow in Prehistoric Archaeology at Christian-Albrechts-University at Kiel. He received his Diploma in Prehistoric Archaeology (1998). His Ph.D. (2004) dealt with the reconstruction of cultural areas, while his advanced Ph.D. (Habilitation, 2010) applied the methodology on central place research. His research interests are quantitative archaeology, landscape archaeology, interdisciplinary modelling and Iron Age. In particular, he is interested in integrating theory and method and approaches from different disciplines.

Daniel Knitter is PostDoc in the Excellence Cluster Topoi at the Freie Universität Berlin, Department of Earth Science, Institute of Geographical Sciences, Physical Geography. He received a B.Sc. and M.Sc. in Geography. In his Ph.D. (2013) on "Central Places and the Environment – Investigations of an Interdependent Relationship" he investigated how the environmental setting of cities and places influenced the concentration of interactions. In his PostDoc, Daniel Knitter is especially interested in interdisciplinary collaboration in the field of landscape archaeology and geography. His research is focused on human-environmental interactions, (pre)historic landscape development under human influence, theoretical geography as well as spatial analyses with a focus on computational methods and approaches.

Chapter 1
Introduction and Mathematics

1.1 Modelling in Archaeology and Geography

This introduction focuses on spatial models and concepts from geography that can be applied in archaeology. The term model became important in the course of the quantitative revolution in the late 1950s and 1960s. In geography, it was during the old days of 'New Geography' that modelling and quantitative techniques were components of the leading paradigm. One of the most important protagonists of New Geography was Peter Haggett (e.g. [29]). Haggett introduced some of his ideas about modelling to David L. Clarke (e.g. [11]), who became the most important protagonist of the New Archaeology, which was the corresponding paradigm in archaeology. Both New Geography and New Archaeology were terminated by post-modern paradigms in the 1980s, since when no new paradigms have been proposed. However, if we explore in details, we find a creeping paradigm change towards an integrative approach that combines concepts from New Archaeology/Geography with the post-modern approach. At present, quantitative analysis and modelling is a prospering sub-discipline in geography as well as archaeology. The success of Geographical Information Systems (GIS) [15] obviously plays an important role in this process. In recent years, many articles and books have been produced on quantitative analysis and modelling, including a book series 'Quantitative Archaeology and Archaeological Modelling', started with the present volume [5, 23, 40–42, 76].

The history of modelling in different disciplines is visible in the occurrence of the keyword 'model' in the Library of Congress (Fig. 1.1). We find that the disciplines have a different yet interrelated history. Although, there is a difference in the starting points of modelling, the impact of post-modern concepts and the intensity of the current fashion of modelling in the different disciplines, there is a general pattern.

O. Nakoinz, D. Knitter, *Modelling Human Behaviour in Landscapes*, Quantitative Archaeology and Archaeological Modelling, DOI 10.1007/978-3-319-29538-1_1

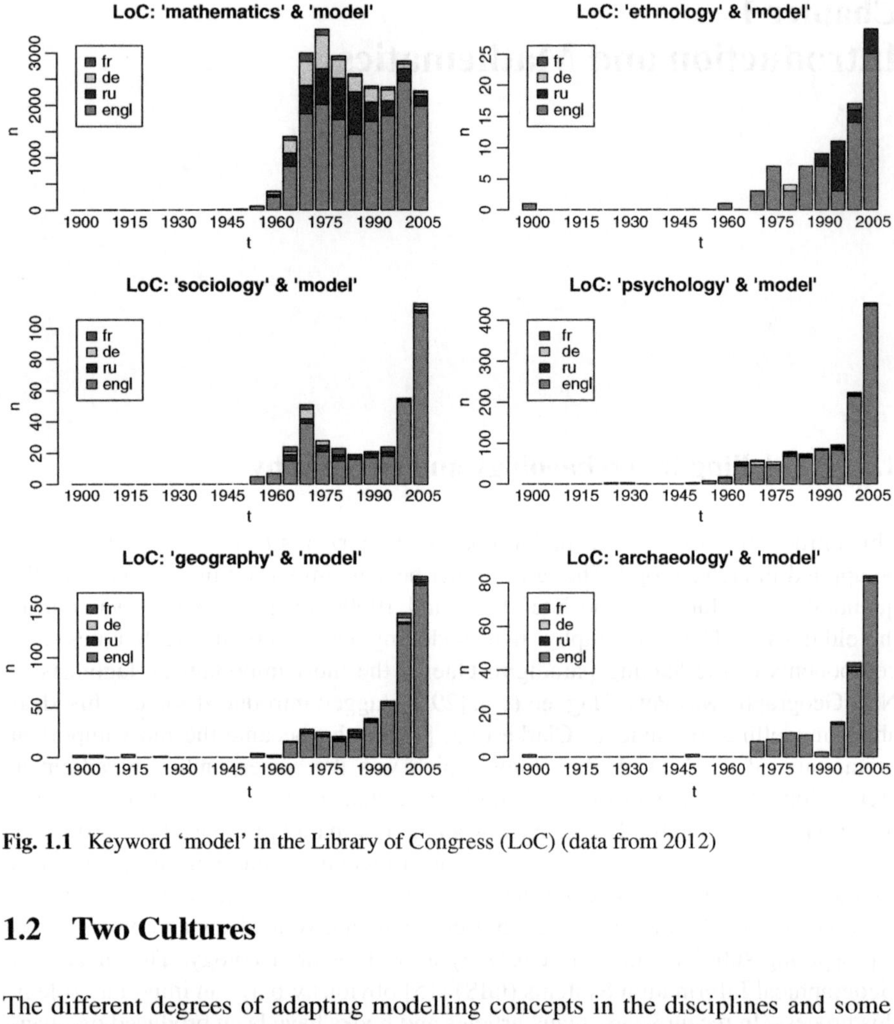

Fig. 1.1 Keyword 'model' in the Library of Congress (LoC) (data from 2012)

1.2 Two Cultures

The different degrees of adapting modelling concepts in the disciplines and some theoretical wars are manifestations of the dynamics in the fields between the two cultures. Since the Middle Ages, two main types of scholarly culture have emerged. In the late nineteenth century, Dilthey [17] developed the concept of science ('Naturwissenschaften'), explaining the subject of research, as well as humanities ('Geisteswissenschaften'), understanding the subject of research. The subject of research of the humanities is the acting human. Snow [72] showed that the different methods and subjects of research are embedded in two cultures, whereby people belonging to these different cultures are hardly able to communicate to each other.

An up-to-date concept of the two cultures based upon semiotics [60] finds that humanities are disciplines dealing with the interpretation of pre-defined meaning. It is acknowledged that subjects such as texts and drawings have a certain meaning. The research process is a negotiation of the existing meaning to produce a new one. Natural sciences are disciplines that formally analyse objects without pre-defined meaning and construct a frame of explanation. The research process constructs meaning for the subjects, which can be particles or velocity, trees or cells. Using these definitions of science and humanities, it is obvious that some disciplines are indigenous inhabitants of both science and humanities; indeed, mathematics, geography and archaeology belong to these hydride- or bridge-disciplines. For example, archaeology deals with finds to which no meaning is attached; rather, the original meaning is lost and in many cases it involves mere fantasy to reconstruct the original meaning by hermeneutic contemplation. Hence, archaeology requires scientific methods to answer questions from humanities. Quantitative methods and New Archaeology of the 1960s and 1970s focused on the scientific part while post-processual archaeology is focused on the humanities part. Since both concepts are natural parts of one discipline in the border zone of science and humanities, it is obvious that there is no paradigm change in the sense of Kuhn [45] but rather a mere shift of the main focus. This fact levels some of the critiques in the war of theories concerning these two perspectives.

1.3 Data

What data shall we use for our case studies? In the literature, there are many case studies with different data. Some of the data are available, whereas others are not. We prefer to use one set of data for all case studies. The advantage of this approach is that we learn about many facets of the data sets and do not have to become familiar with many sets of data. The disadvantage is that only one data set is not optimal to exemplify different methods. Some strange results emerge. It is up to the reader to apply the methods to more suitable data of their own. The case studies in this introduction are minimal examples that do not always make sense for interpretation but are demonstrative for the modelling concept and technique. This introduction does not aim to present useful models but rather to show modelling concepts and components that allow constructing elaborated models. In this sense, we do not deliver a house but rather the bricks to build one.

As the area of interest, we choose the surrounding of the first Modelling Summer School in Noer. This landscape at the shore of the Baltic Sea between Kiel and Eckernförde in Schleswig-Holstein is called Dänischer Wohld. This landscape was formed by glacial sediments during the Ice Age. In the early Middle Ages, this area was in the border zone of the Danish empire. In fact, it was a kind of no-man's land south of the border at the Danevirke. Later, the Dänischer Wohld was located at the southern part of the dukedom of Schleswig at the border to the dukedom of Holstein. In general, the dukedom of Schleswig belonged to Denmark and the dukedom of Holstein to Germany. Defining this area as a border zone in the late Middle Ages and Modern Times is rather difficult due to the dynamic history of Schleswig-Holstein. For example, during some times the dukedom of Holstein belonged to the king of Denmark, who was simultaneously the duke of Holstein in the German empire.

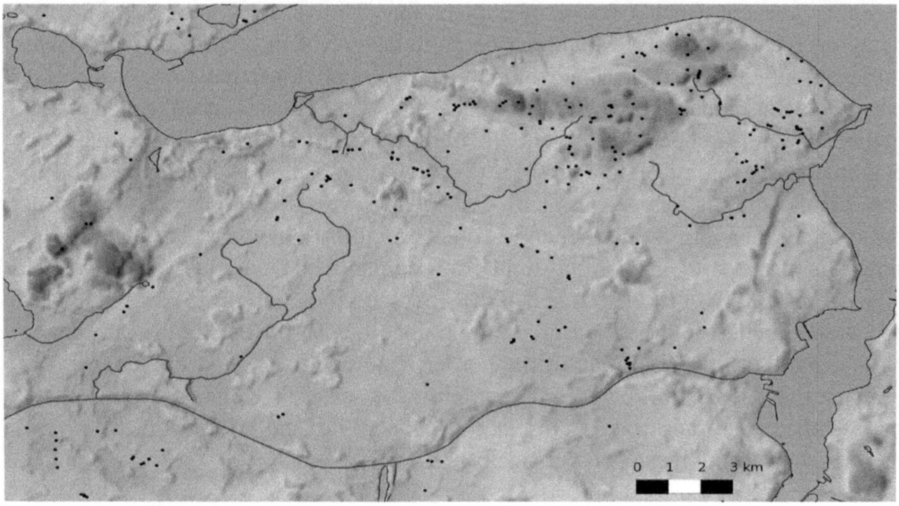

Fig. 1.2 Megalithic tombs from the Funnel Beaker culture in Dänischer Wohld

The data for the case study are from a *Graduate School Human Development in Landscapes* (GSHDL) project. For our first two data sets, we do not have information of the history of this area. These data sets contain monuments from the Stone and Bronze Age [25, 58]. First, we have megalithic tombs from the Funnel Beaker culture, which mainly date during the period between 3500 BC and 3000 BC (Fig. 1.2). The second data set contains Bronze Age burial mounds, which date in the period from 1800 BC to 1100 BC (Fig. 1.3). These two data sets contain nothing but locations of the monuments and hence they are represented by a set of points. The third data set contains the dates of settlement foundation in the Middle Ages. While details can be found in the literature [33, 47, 62], a list can be found in the internet (www.de.wikipedia.org/wiki/Dänischer_Wohld). Here, an additional information is attached to the location of the villages.

1.4 Source Criticism

The first question arising after the preparation of the data is whether the data are suitable for the intended purpose. When analysing data, we make certain implicit or explicit assumptions. Accordingly, we have to consider whether the data meet these assumptions [20, pp. 255–258]; [36, pp. 98–101]; [57, Fig. 2]; [63, pp. 33–41].

Since all archaeological data collections are samples of the original objects, it is important to establish whether the data are representative for the phenomenon that they should represent. Are the samples randomly distributed? Are there filters working that destroy the representativeness? The question whether finds were buried

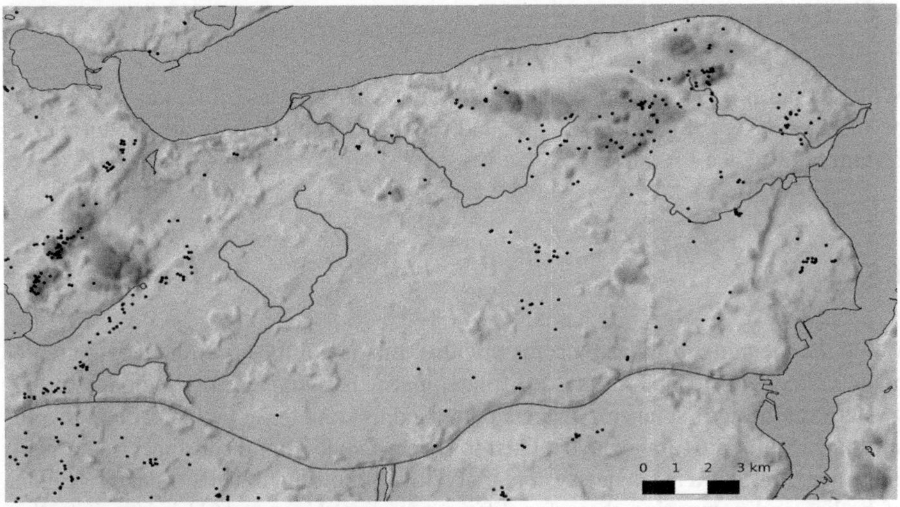

Fig. 1.3 Bronze Age burial mounds in Dänischer Wohld

and building structures decayed to soil structures addresses the first step in the reduction process of potential archaeological information. The burial practice and building techniques have an important influence on the creation of archaeological structures. Does the preservation of the finds and structures produce patterns that are problematic for the intended investigation? Organic finds are usually not preserved at dry conditions and they accumulate on wetland sites. Erosion can destroy settlement structures at dynamic coasts, as well as hill-slopes. Was there an alteration of the objects and structures caused by natural forces or cultural practice? Corrosive processes and grave-robbery may be such examples. Which archaeological finds and structures are discovered? There is a private collector in one area who collects stone tools and a research project about fortified settlement in an other area. What does the distribution of stone tools and fortifications tell us? Settlements in floodplains are covered with colluvial layers. How likely is it to find such a settlement? The next step relates to the data. Are all data recorded? Are there errors in the recordings and how precise are those measurements? Do abstractions and classification cause problems? What about the localisation? How exact are the coordinates? The authenticity is also important. Objects, structures or data can be forged. Is the information true? Another problem is dating: did the objects exist at the same point in time or are they simply from the same period? Is the area of interest suitable for our purpose? Are there different conditions? Settlements may concentrate on good soil because intense work in this area revealed them or on bad soils because agricultural activity has already destroyed them. In both cases the settlements may have a distribution completely unrelated to the soil or contrary to the observations. Are there edge effects? Do the borders of the research area cut important entities?

1.5 Key Terms

While the term ‘model’ will be addressed in the Chap. 2, some other key terms shall be discussed here. Space, landscape and landscape archaeology appear to bear a certain importance for our topic.

1.5.1 Space

While the meaning of ‘space’ seems obvious, this is not the case; indeed, there are many concepts of space in use. ‘Absolute space’ is a concept that belongs to the western tradition of science. Space is perceived as something that is different from substance but bodies are always related to space. Even without substance space is in existence. Space is a reference system that allows recording the place and movement of bodies and comparing them for different bodies. Newton [61] brings it to the point:

> II. Absolute space, in its own nature, without relation to anything external, remains always similar and immovable.

Space is a feature shared by all bodies, forces and many other physical quantities. In fact, together with time, space is considered one of the most basic properties of objects. In addition to the simple usage as a system of reference, space can be used to connect entities; for example, we can use a map of soil types and plot settlements on this map. Perhaps we find that settlements prefer a certain soil type. In this case, we use space to establish a connection between the soil and settlement location. This relationship is based upon the observation that both phenomena occur together at the same place. Space ‘in its own right’ is not of interest, although it is essential to establish the connection between two phenomena.

The concept of absolute space is formalised in mathematics. Aleksandrov [2] defines it as follows:

> A logical conceptual form (or structure) serving as a medium in which other forms and some structures are realized.

There is a hierarchy of spaces. A topological space is constructed by a topology that defines continuity, connectedness and neighbourhood, for example. Distances are not defined. Topological spaces are the most general spaces in mathematics. Metric spaces are constructed with a metric that defines distances. The metric is often realised with a norm, which is the length of a vector and induces a vector space. Hence, normed spaces (= vector spaces) are a subset of metric spaces, which themselves are a subset of topological spaces [7].

The relative or relational space emerges with the objects populating the space. This space is not ‘similar and immovable’ since it is constructed based upon the relationship of ‘points’ in the space. Among the protagonists of a relative space, Leibniz and Einstein seem to be the most famous. Einstein [21, 22] proposed the idea that there is a time–space continuum in which fast-moving objects can cause a curved space. Newton's relative space is not relative in this sense, since it is considered part of the absolute space.

Both concepts of space are useful for certain purposes. Absolute space is the basis for many analytical applications. Relational space is important when we are interested in the meaning of spatial aspects. Here, again the dichotomies of the "two cultures" take effect. Although both concepts are used in both cultures, there is a certain preference. This preference is not by chance but rather is caused by the research objectives, the research objects and the theories used. Some examples may illustrate the adoption of concepts of space to disciplinary needs. In anthropology and archaeological anthropology, a concept of space focused on humans is preferred. Leroi-Gourhan [50] states that a human space is constructed during a domestication of space:

> Le fait humain par excellence est peut-etre moins la creation de l'outil que la domestication du temps et de espace, c'est-a-dire la creation d'un temps et d'une espace humaine.

The philosopher and sociologist Lefebvre [48] proposed three interwoven kinds of space:

- L'espace perçu: practical space in daily use,
- L'espace conçu: space of maps and orientation and
- L'espace vécu: space of imagination and symbols.

In architecture, the movement of people is important. Hillier and Hanson [32] stressed that the organisation of space is based upon axial lines of movement and reflects social structures. The space syntax theory is based upon this idea.

The geographical space emerges based upon of a certain property of objects and their location, which allows defining relationships between these objects. Hence, space is a parameter used to connect other parameters. Although geography is not limited to this concept of absolute space, this concept establishes the basic assumption of geography: objects are generally not randomly dispersed in space; rather, they have a certain location, which induces a relationship to other objects. Geography is interested in the wide range of spatial relationships that can be established on differences in locations on the earth and in a certain scale range. The objects that can be connected by space stem from the human sphere as well as the natural sphere. The geographical space develops special potentials when both spheres come together. One of the most influencing ideas was launched by Herder in the eighteenth century. His idea was that cultural areas are connected to certain ethnicities and culture in this area is influenced by natural conditions. This kind of environmental determinism was further developed by Ritter and Ratzel. Vidal de la Blanche stresses that humans shape their environment. From the perspective of geographical space, both concepts are based upon a strong correlation of different parameters connected by space, whereby only the cause and effect have changed.

There is a certain relationship between spatial structures and social structures, which influences each other. Simmel [71] describes that social structures of power are projected to space. For example, borders with their associated territories represent socio-political entities that exist a priori. In recent years, the dynamic interrelationship has dominated the discussion. Löw [51, p. 167] even states that:

> ... spatial structures are, ..., kinds of social structures.

We can adapt ideas from systems theory to understand the relationship between society and space. Spacing is a technique to reduce social complexity, whereby a complicated social structure is mapped on a simple yet suggestive spatial structure. The spatial structure serves as a model or tool to manage the social world (see Chap. 2 for modelling theory).

In fact, it is not as simple as stating that only structures of power are mapped to space; rather, the mapping involves overlapping spheres whose spatial representations superpose each other. In addition, the spatial representations may be used in different spheres and hence they can be ambiguous. The social sphere is concerned with power in the actual community. The historical sphere contains ancestors and historical events. The practical sphere with traditions and habits is focused on stability and the reproduction of knowledge. The ritual sphere produces meaning and the cultural sphere is concerned with standardisations and similarities. This list is not complete, although it shows the different interests in spatial representations.

According to mathematical theories, spaces are spanned by certain functions defining mathematical structures that are valid for the space in question. The definition of distances is the dominant function used for this purpose. Based upon this idea, we can define:

Definition 1.1. Disciplinary spaces are constructed by specific disciplinary distances:

A **social space** is constructed by social distances.
An **economic space** is constructed by economic distances.
A **cultural space** is constructed by cultural distances.
A **geographic space** is constructed by geodetic distances.

The geographic space plays a special role. Geography is a discipline working on the spatial aspect of objects that is also used in other disciplines; for example, the construction of social spaces is an important topic in geography. After all, the geographical map remains the connecting element. Hence, we use the geodetic distance to define the geographical space, not to disqualify social and economic spaces in geography, but rather to minimise confusion. For example, economical spaces can be superimposed on geographical spaces. We will use this powerful concept in Chap. 8.

We now have a rough idea how to construct spaces, but what is in the space? Which elements populate the space? There are as many answers as disciplines and sub-disciplines dealing with space. Some formal characterisations of spatial representations stand out among the multitude of spatial representations. In cartography, point, line and area are the main elements [53]. From a GIS perspective, a geometric characterisation based upon absolute space in which coordinates reference locations is vital [79]. There are vector data, which can be points, lines and polygons, as well as raster data, which superimpose a pre-defined grid on the area of interest, defining the spatial units to which information is assigned. Raster data can contain binary data such as presence/absence data. These can be used for a rough representation of vector data. In addition, rasters can represent fields that assign an interval-scaled number to each grid cell. Vector data can roughly represent these fields with contour lines. Up to a certain degree albeit not perfectly vector data and raster data can represent each other. Additionally, it is important to mention networks, which represent mathematical graphs and comprise edges and nodes. Although edges and nodes are simply lines and points, a network employs certain topological rules.

Mark [53] uses three categories for the spatial relations of spatial entities:

- distance,
- direction and
- reference frame.

We have already discussed that distances—defined by norms and realising a metric—are used for spanning a space in mathematics. From a geographic perspective this concept is adapted to the need of a relative concept of space, which is essential for social geography and spatial sociology. In addition, a distance is the basic concept to describe the relationship between two objects. To compare two objects from the perspective of a third object, direction emerges in a relational space as an other fundamental concept. Distances and directions have to be embedded in a certain reference frame. This includes information about the measurements and units of the disciplinary space as well as sometimes guides that are used as a standard for referencing objects. These categories can be perceived as a relation between spatial elements or a relational definition of space.

1.5.2 Landscape

Landscape is a complicated term, since it is a common term in both everyday language and science. In a scientific sense, it is used especially by geographers of the early twentieth century as a unity concept to characterise the interrelations of certain phenomena or facts in a certain section of space. This understanding is equivalent to terms like 'area' and 'region'. Accordingly, landscape can be defined as [68, p. 98]

> (…) an area made up of a distinct association of forms, both physical and cultural.

This concept determines the work of the geographer [68, p. 98]:

> The geographer may describe the individual landscape as a type or possibly as a variant from type, but always he has in mind the generic, and proceeds by comparison.

The term 'landscape' has an etymology dating back to the Middle Ages. The old German 'lantschaft'—first mentioned in 830 AD—had the meaning of a political territory independent from the surrounding environment [49, p. 39]. In more recent history, this meaning changed from the politically defined region to a more limited, geographically defined area without political implications. The other meaning is a technical one, etymologically related to the Dutch term 'landschap' as a *terminus technicus* for painters [24, p. 5]. In general, the term means a portion of land that the eye can comprehend at a glance. Due to its roots in arts, the term did not mean the view itself but rather the picture of it, i.e. the artist's interpretation [8, p. 154]. Throughout time, the term has changed its meaning from a picture of the view to the view itself.

In geography, it is usual to distinguish between physical and cultural landscape. Gray [28] defines a landscape as the interrelation of a geological, biological and cultural layer [28, p. 267]. This is closely related to Bobek and Schmithüsen's [6] perspective, perceiving landscape as a logical, hierarchically organised system [6]. Such a perspective allows thinking of a physical landscape as the ground where society/humans/culture occurs. GIS technology caused a boom in this branch of thinking and analysis since it allowed easy correlations and causation based upon the layer concept (see [12, 46, 54] for more information and critical discussion). All of those concepts are etic concepts with a scientific view from outside on the landscape, which is perceived by people. Another concept, an emic concept, states that a landscape is the result of people's perception [4]. Following this approach, we find that different procedures of processing the perception influence the result and hence landscapes are highly context sensitive and depend upon the preceptor who supplies the landscape elements with meaning.

The term cultural landscape dates back to Friedrich Ratzel and was introduced to the English-speaking world by Carl O. Sauer in 1925, when it became central in the work of the Berkeley school of geography [39, p. 21]; [78]. Sauer [68, p. 100] characterises this approach as being process-oriented and holistic:

> There is a strictly geographic way of thinking of culture; namely, as the impress of the works of man upon the area. We may think of people as associated within and with an area, as we may think of them as groups associated in descent or tradition, in the first case we are thinking of culture as a geographic expression, composed of forms which are a part of geographic phenomenology. In this view there is no place for a dualism of landscape.
>
> ...
>
> The works of man express themselves in the cultural landscape. There may be a succession of these landscapes with a succession of cultures. They are derived in each case from the natural landscape, man expressing his place in nature as a distinct agent of modification.

In contrast to the old school of cultural geography, the 'New Cultural Geography' [56] has a focus on sociology and politics rather than the relationship between people and landscape.

1.5.3 Landscape Archaeology

Landscape archaeology is a fancy term and one of the main interfaces between archaeology and geography. 'Landscape-archaeology' is a very ambiguous term that covers several meanings and is superimposed on a field of research with a long tradition. We will discuss different facets and ultimately aim to ascertain a definition. First, we will address the term settlement archaeology, which has two meanings. In a first place, it is the investigation of single settlements. While this is not the place to resume this kind of research, some milestones may be mentioned, including the first was the recognition of small stratigraphic structures. In 1909, Schuchhardt [69] published the observation of post-holes in Haltern. In the 1930s, an extensive exploitation of sources began with the large-scale excavations in Maiden Castle [80] and Haithabu [38]. Other disciplines like botany and zoology were included in the investigations. The achievements of aerial photography and geophysical prospection methods have also enhanced settlement archaeology, while the refinement of stratigraphic methods was another enhancement [31]. The recent decades have brought significant changes in documentation techniques, with GIS and structure from motion (SFM).

The other type of settlement archaeology is concerned with the investigation of settlement patterns and dynamics. This approach had to struggle with the term 'Siedlungsarchäologie', which was occupied by Kossinna [44] for rather an ethnographic method. Nevertheless, the investigation of settlement patterns took place and emancipated itself from the old term after Second World War. Eggers edited the journal *Archaeologia Geographica* from 1950 to 1963, which was dedicated to geographical methods in archaeology. The focus was on cartographic methods and the interpretation of maps [19]. Source criticism for which Eggers remains famous played an important role. The journal was stopped because in those days the research focus was on large-scale excavations and the editing catalogues of archaeological evidence rather than critical interpretations. It is not by accident that the protagonists of settlement archaeology—which investigates single settlements on a large scale—became dominant in the investigation of settlement patterns. For example, Jankuhn [37] combined both concepts in his book on settlement archaeology. With its tight connections to geography and modelling approaches, the New Archaeology brought new concepts to settlement archaeology [11]. Christaller's [14] central place theory and Thünen's [75] theory were introduced into archaeology in this context. Indeed, modelling approaches including predictive modelling still play an important role in settlement archaeology. Geo-archaeology is also an ambiguous term. It can be interpreted as a discipline that investigates the history of the interrelationship between humans and the environment [34]. For this variant, the term 'environmental archaeology' is increasingly used [1]. The other variant is an application of methods from geology, soil science and physical geography [10, 66], with a focus on landscape reconstruction. It is obvious that both variants are closely connected.

Despite in principle being a part of cultural geography, the geography of cultures is not a usual object of it. Research on spatial aspects of culture is integrated in archaeological and ethnological research. The aforementioned 'Siedlungsarchäologie' from Kossinna [44], adapted by Childe [13], and the 'Kulturkreislehre' [26] are famous yet problematic examples. Both are based upon wrong assumptions, including the equating of culture and race [59]. Strongly influenced by ideologies, politics and different scholarly perspective, the topic of spatial organisation of cultures remained a virulent topic during the twentieth century. The formalistic concept

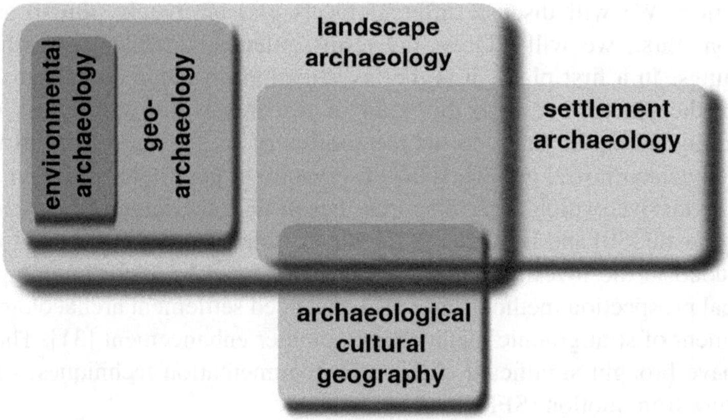

Fig. 1.4 Venn diagram of terms

from Clarke [11]—in which culture is nothing but a certain level of classification—solved some problems but neglected others. In particular, the connection to cultural studies which became a dominating discipline during the cultural turn is barely possible with this approach. The term 'Archaeological Cultural Geography' was coined in 2013 [59] and refers to the investigation of spatial aspects of culture in prehistoric times. It is understood as research focused on investigating structures of interaction [60]. In contrast to previous research on this topic, some assumptions are no longer used; for instance, concepts based upon the theory of culture from Hansen [30] which allows integrating semiotic and formal approaches (see Chap. 8 for details).

Like most of the other terms, landscape archaeology is also an ambiguous term (Fig. 1.4). The first variant is nothing but regional settlement archaeology. In Germany, this terminology was introduced by Lüning [52]. 'Landscape archaeology' is a fashionable term and hence replaced the term 'settlement archaeology', which is reduced to investigating single settlements. This kind of landscape archaeology mainly uses an absolute space. The second type of landscape archaeology is focused on the cultural landscape as a meaningful object. This is a concept based upon semiotics which understands the cultural landscape as text [27]. This variant is closely connected to ideas of the cultural turn [67] and 'New Cultural Geography' [56]. A relational space plays an important role in this concept. A Venn diagram may visualise this rather complicated terminological field of landscape archaeology.

Landscape archaeology covers a field with many facets. The term is fuzzy, although we could define crisp boundaries between the fields of research denoted by aforementioned terms. The overlapping of terms maps the strong interrelationship between different components and encourages real interdisciplinarity. All facets themselves are highly interdisciplinary, although bricking up new borders between landscape archaeologists and geo-archaeologists would contradict this effect. Overlapping terminology encourages connecting different approaches on a conceptual level. In this volume, we will find some examples of different terminological frames that can be applied to certain phenomena. Each approach is concerned with a certain facet of the phenomenon and hence each has its strengths and weaknesses. However, a certain degree of precision in terminology is necessary, otherwise the terms would not be able to carry any meaning [55]. There are some ideas for more concise terminology, that do not abandon the benefits of overlapping. For example, Ingold [35] defines 'landscape' as an introspective view (=emic) and 'environment' as an external view (=etic) of the world.

At this point, we propose a holistic definition of landscape archaeology, which respects the use of this term as umbrella for a wide range of applications. In order to find a term for the emic landscape archaeology approach, we introduce the term 'semiotic landscape archaeology'.

Definition 1.2. Landscape archaeology investigates the interrelationship of animated, inanimated, cultural, social and economic objects on a regional level in space.

Specialised yet overlapping sub-disciplines are geo-archaeology, environmental archaeology, settlement archaeology and semiotic landscape archaeology.

1.6 Mathematics

This is not an introduction to mathematical basics but rather a reminder of knowledge that you already have or can obtain from sources cited in this text. Hence, this section contains no explanations, proofs or applications of mathematical structures or even explanations of all variables, but rather a brief list of the most important mathematical structures and topics. As a general reference, we provide [9], which is used if no other reference is given. If you find something that you do not understand, please consult a textbook on the specific topic to learn more about it.

1.6.1 Logic and Sets

Most implicitly and sometimes explicitly used, logic is the common basis of science. Mathematical logic is a logic formalised according to mathematical rules, which is the case for most logical systems. Among the logical systems, the predicate logic is most popular. Quine [64, 65] may serve as a reference.

Propositions can be connected with the operators *not*, *and*, *or*, *then* and *if and only if*.

$$\neg A \qquad A \vee B \qquad A \wedge B \qquad A \Rightarrow B \qquad A \Leftrightarrow B \tag{1.1}$$

Fig. 1.5 Truth table

A	B	$\neg A$	$A \vee B$	$A \wedge B$	$A \Rightarrow B$	$A \Leftrightarrow B$
0	0	1	0	0	1	1
0	1	1	1	0	1	0
1	0	0	1	0	0	0
1	1	0	1	1	1	1

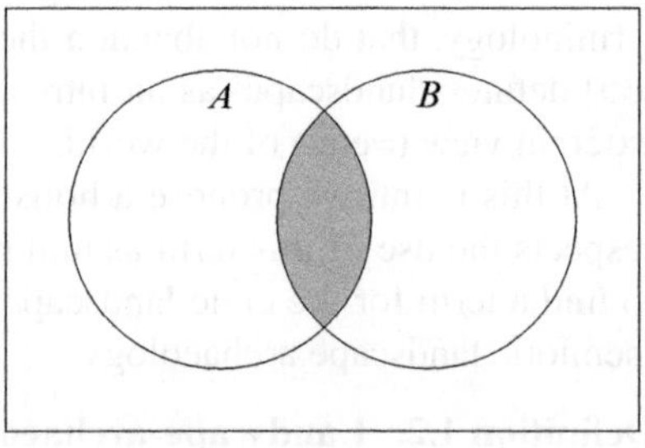

Fig. 1.6 $A \cap B$

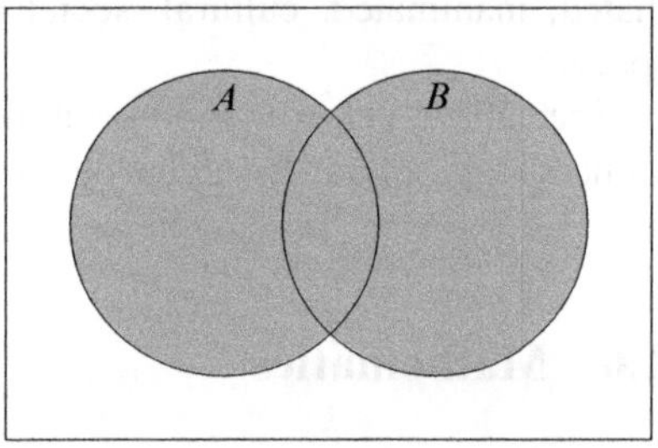

Fig. 1.7 $A \cup B$

Since the truth of the compositions of propositions only depends on the truth of the compositions, truth tables (Fig. 1.5) for all operators can be used. In this table, 0 is used for false and 1 for true.

Quantifiers define for which objects a proposition is valid. $\forall$ means for all elements while $\exists$ means that there exists at least one element for which the proposition is valid.

Since its development in the nineteenth century, set theory has become one of the most essential tools in mathematics. A set is a collection of different objects, which are called elements. The operators stating whether an element belongs to a set A are

$$a \in A \qquad a \notin A \tag{1.2}$$

An explicit and implicit definition of members is possible:

$$A = \{a, b, c\} \qquad B = \{a | a > 5\} \tag{1.3}$$

Venn diagrams (Figs. 1.6 and 1.7) can be used to visualise the intersection and union of subsets, for example. Figure 1.4 is also a kind of Venn diagram; rather, it is simply the shape of the set representation, which is different from the following example.

1.6.2 Linear Algebra

Linear algebra is used in many branches of mathematics and other disciplines. It is concerned with vector space and objects in vector spaces. One of the most central topics in linear algebra is a system of linear equations. A linear equation is something like

$$a_1x_1 + a_2x_2 + \cdots + a_nx_n = b \tag{1.4}$$

While a's $(a_1, a_2, \ldots)$ are the coefficients and x the variables. The number of additive terms is the degree of the equation. With one equation, it is possible to solve one variable. In general, the degree of a system of linear equations gives the number of equations necessary to solve the system. The solution can be found with algebraic operations, which eliminate the variables step by step: a concept that Gauss formalised in the early nineteenth century.

Another important construct used in linear algebra is the matrix, which is a rectangular array of numbers:

$$A_{m,n} = \begin{pmatrix} a_{1,1} & a_{1,2} & \cdots & a_{1,n} \\ a_{2,1} & a_{2,2} & \cdots & a_{2,n} \\ \vdots & \vdots & \ddots & \vdots \\ a_{m,1} & a_{m,2} & \cdots & a_{m,n} \end{pmatrix} \tag{1.5}$$

Several types of matrices and operators for the calculation with matrices are defined. Addition, scalar multiplication and transposition are specially defined operations for matrices. In addition, row operations can be used. A vector is a matrix with one column:

$$\mathbf{a} = \begin{pmatrix} a_1 \\ a_2 \\ \vdots \\ a_m \end{pmatrix} \tag{1.6}$$

With these tools, we can simplify the notation of systems of linear equation. A is the matrix of coefficients, x the vector of variables and b the vector containing the results of the single calculations.

$$\mathbf{Ax} = \mathbf{b} \tag{1.7}$$

A vector space is a set of vectors and some operations that satisfy some axioms, such as associativity and commutativity of addition. Vectors can be considered as containing coordinates. Although, the geometrical interpretation of vectors and vector space is obvious, it is not limited to geometry. In this interpretation, the norm of a vector is the geometrical length of the vector. A norm has to satisfy the norm axioms:

$$\|\mathbf{x}\| \geq 0; \quad \|\mathbf{x}\| = 0 \text{ if and only if } \mathbf{x} = 0 \tag{1.8}$$

$$\|\lambda \mathbf{x}\| = |\lambda| \|\mathbf{x}\| \tag{1.9}$$

$$\|\mathbf{x} + \mathbf{y}\| = \|\mathbf{x}\| + \|\mathbf{y}\| \tag{1.10}$$

As mentioned above, a norm is used to define a vector space. A frequently used norm is the Euclidean norm:

$$\|\mathbf{x}\| = \sqrt{\sum_{i=1}^{n} x_i{}^2} \tag{1.11}$$

Matrices can hold information, which is used for a transformation—e.g. translation and rotation—of the coordinate system. In the case of such transformations, eigenvectors are the invariant lines of the system.

1.6.3 Graph Theory

Many problems can be reduced to structures comprising points and lines. This is the domain of graph theory [16]. A graph is a mathematical structure comprising vertices (points) v and edges (lines) e (Figs. 1.8, 1.9, and 1.10).

$$G_1 = (V, E) \qquad V = \{v_1, v_2, v_3, v_4, v_5, v_6, v_7\} \qquad E = \{e_1, e_2, e_3, e_4, e_5, e_6, e_7\} \tag{1.12}$$

The edges connect two vertices and hence can be described as

$$E = \{\{v_1, v_2\}, \{v_1, v_3\}, \{v_2, v_4\}, \{v_5, v_2\}, \{v_3, v_6\}, \{v_3, v_7\}\} \tag{1.13}$$

A path is a sequence of edges. A path is called a circle when the starting point and the end point of a path with at least three edges is the same point. A graph without circles is a tree. Final vertices in a tree are leafs. A path with edges where the direction matters is a directed graph. In the case of a weighted graph, the edges are qualified with values.

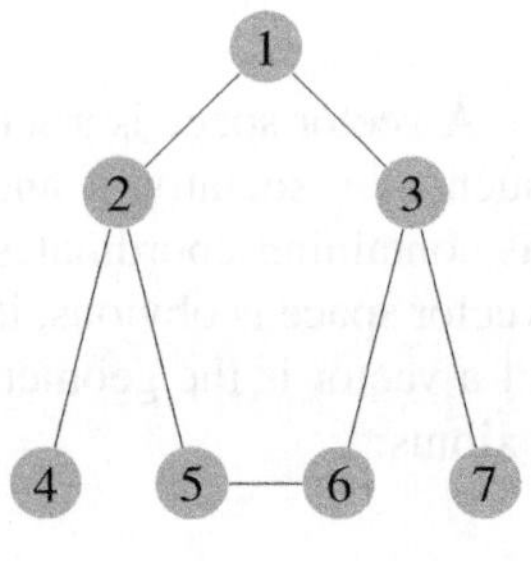

Fig. 1.8 G1: Graph with circle

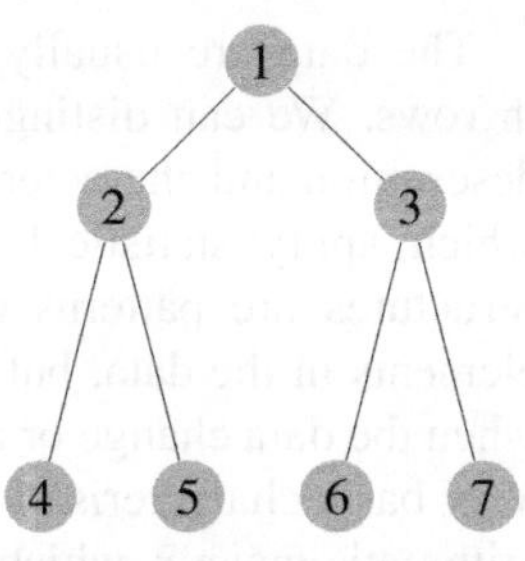

Fig. 1.9 G2: Tree

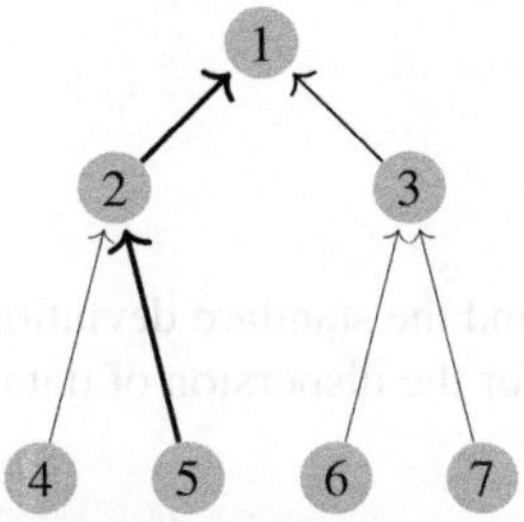

Fig. 1.10 G3: Weighted and directed graph

A graph is sufficiently defined with an edge list. Another representative of a graph is an adjacency matrix. Each value in the matrix characterises an edge. For directed graphs, the matrix is asymmetric and for weighted graphs, the values are not restricted to 0 and 1.

$$G_1 = \begin{pmatrix} 0\,1\,1\,0\,0\,0\,0 \\ 1\,0\,0\,1\,1\,0\,0 \\ 1\,0\,0\,0\,0\,1\,1 \\ 0\,1\,0\,0\,0\,0\,0 \\ 0\,1\,0\,0\,0\,1\,0 \\ 0\,0\,1\,0\,0\,1\,0 \\ 0\,0\,1\,0\,0\,0\,0 \end{pmatrix} \tag{1.14}$$

1.6.4 Statistics and Stochastic

Statistics is interested in the structures that are inherent in data [3, 18, 43, 70, 77]. The structures are represented by the distribution of values, which can belong to different levels of measurement [73].

Nominal-scaled variables: Attributes are only names (red, blue)
Ordinal-scaled variables: Attributes can be ordered (A, B, C)
Interval-scaled variables: Distance is meaningful (1.5, 7.3)
Ratio-scaled variables: Absolute zero (0, 4.5)

The data are usually given as tables with variables in columns and objects in rows. We can distinguish two basic types of using statistics: the exploration, description and characterisation of data is a very important task; while inferences—which apply statistical tests—are used to establish certain structures in data. Structures are patterns of the data that represent certain relationships between elements in the data, but do not depend on specific data. The structure can remain when the data change or a certain structure can be observed in different sets of data. Very basic characterisations of univariate data comprising only one variable are the arithmetic mean $\bar{x}$, which is the expected value of a set of data values

$$\bar{x} = \frac{1}{n}\sum_{i=1}^{n} x_i \tag{1.15}$$

and the standard deviation σ, which is the square root of the variance and a measure for the dispersion of data values.

$$\sigma = \sqrt{\frac{1}{n-1}\sum_{i=1}^{n}(x_i - \bar{x})^2} \tag{1.16}$$

For bivariate data the correlation is a parameter that tells us how similar the relative values of two variables for all objects are. The correlation coefficient according to Pearson is

$$\rho_{X,Y} = \frac{\mathrm{cov}(X, Y)}{\sigma_X \sigma_Y} \tag{1.17}$$

Note that this coefficient is valid for populations and not for samples for which an other variant is in use. If there is a correlation between two variables, the relationship can be described by regression (see Chap. 5).

Variables may be representations of original variables, obscured by noise and mixed relationships. In this case, it is important to know which original variables are inherent in the data and which variance in data is produced by which variables. Principle component analysis, correspondence analysis and factor analysis address this problem, where we deal with the grouping, sorting and weighting of variables.

Methods for grouping objects can be found under the label of 'cluster analysis'. Partitioning cluster analyses produce different sets of objects that hierarchical cluster analyses produce hierarchies of objects which can be split into sets of objects. Fuzzy cluster analysis gives a degree of membership for the groups.

Inference statistics is interested in the probability of a certain event; hence, probability is a key term in this field of statistics. In particular, the probability of the data belonging to a certain distribution is an important topic. Empirical distributions are compared to theoretical distributions whose properties are known. Normal or Gaussian distribution are well-known theoretical distributions. The probability density of the normal distribution is

$$\varphi(x, \mu, \sigma) = \frac{1}{\sigma\sqrt{2\pi}} e^{-\frac{(x-\mu)^2}{2\sigma^2}} \tag{1.18}$$

A special type of statistics—Bayesian statistics—is build upon the foundation of the Bayes theorem:

$$P(A|B) = \frac{P(B|A)\,P(A)}{P(B)} \tag{1.19}$$

The Bayes statistic implies the notion that probability is a certain expression of knowledge. This term of probability is different from the classical definition of probability in statistics, which is the relative frequency of random events.

1.7 Problems

1.1. How would you characterise your work in the field between the two cultures?

1.2. Please locate the area of our case study on a global map.

1.3. Which aspects have to be considered in source critiques?

1.4. Can you find types of spaces that are not mentioned in this brief summary?

References

1. Albarelle, U. (Ed.). (2001). *Environmental archaeology*. Dordrecht: Kluwer Academic Publishers.
2. Aleksandrov, A. D. (2002) Space. In M. Hazewinkel (Ed.), *Encyclopaedia of mathematics*. Berlin: Springer.
3. Baxter, M. J. (2003). *Statistics in archaeology*. London: Wiley.
4. Bender, B. (1993). Introduction: Landscapes - meaning and action. In B. Bender (Ed.), *Landscape: politics and perspectives* (pp. 1–18). Oxford: Berg.
5. Bevan, A., & Lake, M. (Eds.). (2013). *Computational approaches to archaeological spaces*. Walnut Creek: Left Coast Press.
6. Bobek, H., & Schmithüsen, J. (1967). Die Landschaft im logischen System der Geographie. In W. Storkebaum (Ed.), *Zum Gegenstand und zur Methode der Geographie. Wege der Forschung* (Vol. 58, pp. 257–276). Darmstadt: Wissenschaftliche Buchgesellschaft.
7. Bourbaki, N. (1994). *Elements of the history of mathematics*. Berlin: Springer.
8. Brinckerhoff Jackson, J. (2008). The world itself. In T. Oakes, & P. Price (Eds.), *The cultural geography reader* (pp. 154–158). London: Routledge.
9. Bronstein, I. N., Semendjajew, K. A., Musiol, G., & Muehlig, H. (2007). *Handbook of mathematics*. Berlin: Springer.

10. Canti, M. (2001). What is geoarchaeology? Re-examining the relationship between archaeology and earth. In U. Albarelle (Ed.), *Environmental archaeology* (pp. 103–112). Dordrecht: Kluwer Academic Publishers.
11. Clarke, D. L. (1968). *Analytical archaeology*. London: Methuen.
12. Chesworth, W. (2010). A semantic introduction. In I. P. Martini, & W. Chesworth (Eds.), *Landscapes and societies* (pp. 19–24). New York: Springer.
13. Childe, V. G. (1925). *The dawn of european civilization*. London: K. Paul.
14. Christaller, W. (1933). *Die Zentralen Orte in Süddeutschland*. Jena: Fischer.
15. Conolly, J., & Lake, M. (2006). *Geographical information systems in archaeology*. Cambridge: Cambridge University Press.
16. Diestel, R. (2000). *Graph theory*. New York: Springer.
17. Dilthey, W. (1883). *Einleitung in die Geisteswissenschaften*. Leipzig: Duncker & Humblot.
18. Drennan, R. D. (2010). *Statistics for archaeologists*. New York: Springer.
19. Eggers, H. J. (1950). Die vergleichende geographisch-kartographische Methode in der Urgeschichtsforschung. *Archaeologia Geographica, 1*, 1–3.
20. Eggers, H. J. (1986). *Einführung in die Vorgeschichte* (3rd ed.). München: Piper Verlag.
21. Einstein, A. (1908). Über das Relativitätsprinzip und die aus demselben gezogenen Folgerungen. *Jahrbuch der Radioaktivität und Elektronik, IV*, 411–462.
22. Einstein, A. (1916). Die Grundlage der allgemeinen Relativitätstheorie. *Annalen der Physik, 354*, 769–822.
23. Fletcher, M., & Lock, G. (2005). *Digging numbers*. Oxford: Oxbow.
24. Förster, F., Großmann, R., Iwe, K., Kinkel, H., Larsen, A., Lungershausen, U., et al. (2012). What is landscape? Towards a common concept within an interdisciplinary research environment. Landscape archaeology conference (LAC 2012), eTopoi. *Journal for Ancient Studies, Special Volume 3*, 169–179.
25. Fritsch, B., Furholt, M., Hinz, M., Lorenz, L., Nelson, H., Schafferer, G., et al. (2010). Dichtezentren und lokale Gruppierungen - Eine Karte zu den Großsteingräbern Mittel- und Nordeuropas. *Journal of Neolithic Archaeology, 12*, 1–4. doi: http://dx.doi.org/10.12766/jna.2010.56.
26. Graebner, F. (1911). *Methode der ethnologie*. Heidelberg: Winter.
27. Gramsch, A. (2003). Landschaftsarchäologie - ein fachgeschichtlicher Überblick und ein theoretisches Konzept. In J. Kunow, & J. Müller (Eds.), Archäoprognose Brandenburg 1. *Forschungen zur Archäologie im Land Brandenburg* (Vol. 8, pp. 35–54). Wünsdorf: Brandenburgisches Landesamt für Denkmalpflege und Archäologisches Landesmuseum.
28. Gray, M. (2009). Landscape: The physical layer. In N. J. Clifford, S. L. Holloway, S. P. Rice, & G. Valentine (Eds.), *Key concepts in geography* (pp. 265–285). Newbury Park: SAGE.
29. Haggett, P. (1965). *Locational analysis in human geography*. London: Arnold.
30. Hansen, K. P. (2003). *Kultur und Kulturwissenschaft*. Tübingen/Basel: A. Francke.
31. Harris, E. (1989). *Principles of archaeological stratigraphy*. London: Academic.
32. Hillier, B., & Hanson, J. (1984). *The social logic of space*. Cambridge: Cambridge University Press.
33. Hoffmann, E. (1981–1990). Spätmittelalter und Reformationszeit. In O. Klose (Ed.), *Geschichte Schlewig-Holsteins* (Vol. 4). Neumünster: Wachholtz Verlag.
34. Hoffmann-Wieck, G., & Nakoinz, O. (2003). Die Schlei als ein bedeutendes geoarchäologisches Archiv der Landesgeschichte Schleswig-Holsteins. In A. Daschkeit, & H. Sterr (Eds.), *Aktuelle Ergebnisse der Küstenforschung [20. AMK Tagung Kiel 2002] Ber. Forsch. u. Technologiezentr. Westküste der University Kiel* (Vol. 28, pp. 215–224). Büsum: University of Kiel.
35. Ingold, T. (1993). Globes and spheres. The topology of environmentalism. In K. Milton (Ed.), *Environmentalism: The view from anthropology*. London: Routledge.
36. Jacob-Friesenm, K. H. (1928). *Grundfragen der Urgeschichtsforschung*. Hannover: Helwingsche Verlagsbuchhandlung.
37. Jankuhn, H. (1977). *Einführung in die Siedlungsarchäologie*. Berlin/New York: De Gruyter.
38. Jankuhn, H. (1986). *Haithabu - Ein Handelsplatz der Wikingerzeit*. Neumünster: Wachholtz.

39. Jones, M. (2003) The concept of cultural landscape: Discourse and narratives. In H. Palang, & G. Fry (Eds.), *Landscape interfaces* (p. 21–51). Dordrecht: Springer.
40. Kohler, T. A., & Gumerman, G. J. (2000). *Dynamics in human and primate societies: Agent-based modeling of social and spatial processes*. Oxford: Oxbow.
41. Kohler, T. A., & van der Leeuw, S. E. (Eds.). (2007). *The model-based archaeology of socionatural systems*. Santa Fe: SAR Press.
42. Kohring, S., & Wynne-Jones, S. (Eds.). (2007). *Socialising complexity: Approaches to power and interaction in archaeological discourse*. Oxford: Oxbow.
43. Koopmans, L. H. (1987). *Introduction to contemporary statistical methods*. Boston: Duxbury.
44. Kossinna, G. (1911). Die Herkunft der Germanen. *Zur Methode der Siedlungsarchäologie. Mannus-Bibliothek* (Vol. 6). Würzburg: Kabitzsch.
45. Kuhn, T. S. (1962). *The structure of scientific revolutions*. Chicago: University of Chicago Press.
46. Kunow, J. & Müller, J. (Eds.). (2003). Archäoprognose Brandenburg 1. *Forschungen zur Archäologie im Land Brandenburg* (Vol. 8). Wünsdorf: Brandenburgisches Landesamt für Denkmalpflege und Archäologisches Landesmuseum.
47. Laur, W. (1992). *Historisches Ortsnamenlexikon von Schleswig-Holstein*. Neumünster: Wachholtz.
48. Lefebvre, H. (1974). La production de l'espace. L Homme et la société, **31–32**. Sociologie de la connaissance marxisme et anthropolgie (pp. 15–32).
49. Legler, K. (2012). Der archäologische Landschaftsbegriff aus wissenschaftsgeschichtlicher Perspektive – ein Überblick. *Archäologische Informationen, 35*, 39–52.
50. Leroi-Gourhan, A. (1964). *Le geste et la parole*. Paris: Michel.
51. Löw, M. (2001). *Raumsoziologie*. Frankfurt am Main: Suhrkamp.
52. Lüning, J. (1997). Landschaftsarchäologie in Deutschland - Ein Programm. *Archäologisches Nachrichtenblatt, 2*, 277–285.
53. Mark, D. M. (1999). Spatial representation: A cognitive view. In D. J. Maguire, M. F. Goodchild, D. W. Rhind, & P. Longley (Eds.), *Geographical information systems: Principles and applications*. (2nd ed. Vol. 1, pp. 81–89). Chichester: Wiley
54. Mehrer, M. W., & Wescott, K. L. (Eds.). (2006). *GIS and archaeological site location modeling*. Boca Raton: CRC.
55. Meier, T. (2012). 'Landscape', 'environment' and a vision of interdisciplinarity. In S. Kluiving, E., & Guttmann-Bond, (Eds.), *Landscape archaeology between art and science* (pp. 503–514). Amsterdam: Amsterdam university press.
56. Mitchell, D. (2000). *Cultural geography*. Malden: Blackwell Publishing.
57. Nakoinz, O. (2001). Die Siedlungsgeschichte der südlichen Vulkaneifel. *Trierer Zeitschrift, 64*, 9–48.
58. Nakoinz, O. (2012). Ausgewählte Parameter der Lage von Wegen und Monumenten als Proxy für soziale Prozesse prähistorischer Gesellschaften. In: M. Hinz, & J. Müller (Eds.), *Siedlung, Grabenwerk, Großsteingrab. Studien zu Gesellschaft, Wirtschaft und Umwelt der Trichterbechergruppen im nördlichen Mitteleuropa. Frühe Monumentalität und soziale Differenzierung* (Vol. 2, pp. 445–456). Bonn: Habelt.
59. Nakoinz, O. (2013). Archäologische Kulturgeographie der ältereisenzeitlichen Zentralorte Südwestdeutschlands. *Universitätsforsch. prähist. Arch.* (Vol. 224). Bonn: Habelt.
60. Nakoinz, O. (2014). Fingerprinting iron age communities in south west Germany and an integrative theory of culture. In C. Popa, & S. Stoddart (Eds.), *Fingerprinting the Iron Age* (pp. 187–199). Oxford: Oxbow.
61. Newton, I. (1687). *Philosophiae naturalis principia mathematica*. London: Societatis Regia.
62. Oldenkop, H. (1906). *Topographie des Herzogtums Schleswig*. Weissenheim: Hein.
63. O'Sullivan, D., & Unwin, D. (2003). *Geographic information analysis*. Hoboken: Wiley.
64. Quine, W. V. (1962). *Set theory and its logic*. Cambridge: Belknap Press.
65. Quine, W. V. (1965). *Mathematical logic*. Cambridge: Harvard university press.
66. Rapp, G. R., & Hill, G. L. (1998). *Geoarchaeology - the earth-science approach to archaeological interpretation*. New Haven: Yale University Press.

67. Rorty, R. (Ed.). (1967). *The linguistic turn*. Chicago: University of Chicago.
68. Sauer, C. O. (2008). The morphology of landscape. In T. Oakes, & P. Price (Eds.). *The cultural geography reader* (pp. 96–104). London: Routledge.
69. Schuchhardt, C. (1909). Die Römerschanze bei Potsdam nach den Ausgrabungen von 1908 und 1909. *Prähistorische Zeitschrift, 1*, S. 209–238
70. Shennan, S. (1997). *Quantifying archaeology*. Edinburgh: University Press.
71. Simmel, G. (2003). Über räumliche Projektionen sozialer Formen. *Zeitschrift für Socialwissenschaft, 6/7*, 287–302.
72. Snow, C. P. (1960). *The two cultures*. Cambridge: Cambridge University Press.
73. Stevens, S. S. (1946). On the theory of scales of measurement. *Science, 103/2684*, 677–680.
74. Stewart, J. Q. (1950). The development of social physics. *American Journal of Physics, 18*, 239–253.
75. Thünen, J. H. v. (1875). *Der isolirte Staat in Beziehung auf Landwirtschaft und Nationalökonomie*. Berlin: Wiegand, Hempel und Parey.
76. VanPool, T. L., & Leonard, R. D. (2010). *Quantitative analysis in archaeology*. Hoboken: Wiley.
77. Venables, W. N., & Ripley, B. D. (2002). *Modern applied statistics with S*. New York: Springer.
78. Wagner, P. L., & Mikesell, M. W. (Eds.). (1962). *Readings in cultural geography*. Chicago: The University of Chicago Press.
79. Wheatley, D., & Gillings, M. (2002). *Spatial technology and archaeology: The archaeological applications of GIS*. London: CRC.
80. Wheeler, M. (1935–1937) The excavation of Maiden Castle, Dorset. *First, second and third interim reports*. London: Society of Antiquaries of London. (Sonderabdrucke aus: The antiquaries journal. 15, July 1935, 3, ISSN 0003-5815, S. 265–275; 16, July 1936, 3, S. 265–283; 17, July).

Chapter 2
Theory of Modelling

2.1 Models Are Everywhere

Models are rather frequent tools in science and even daily life. Models are a representative of the reality with certain purposes: in children's games, model cars represent real cars and thus break down the concept of street traffic to a scope that is manageable for children. There is an obvious difference between the use of the word 'model' in this example and that in the term 'climate model'. There is a confusingly wide range of models; indeed, the same word is used for a confusingly wide range of concepts. Clarifying what is referred to as a model in this book is thus necessary first step in our discussion of archaeological modelling. For this purpose, we will provide some examples from geography and archaeology.

In 1798, Malthus [6, 14, 35, 57] proposed his theory of population growth. According to his idea, populations will double every 25 years if provided with perfect conditions. Nonetheless, Malthus also described certain limits; for instance, war and disease reduce the population. Moreover, the food supply is limited and if the population increases a certain extent called carrying capacity, a part of the population will starve. The model postulates an exponential population growth with a threshold at the carrying capacity. Verhulst's logistic equation represents this model [14]:

$$\frac{\partial d}{\partial t} = rP(1 - \frac{P}{C}) \tag{2.1}$$

In this equation, C stands for carrying capacity, r is the rate of population growth and P represents the population.

Innovations can increase the carrying capacity. Although this model has been criticised over the last two centuries, it proves a good basis for predicting population dynamics.

O. Nakoinz, D. Knitter, *Modelling Human Behaviour in Landscapes*, Quantitative Archaeology and Archaeological Modelling, DOI 10.1007/978-3-319-29538-1_2

In the carrying capacity model, the location of people is important: if the population size exceeds the carrying capacity, the population will cease to grow further. Trade can compensate this effect to a certain degree, with urbanization reflecting a good example. Nonetheless, urbanisation also reveals another flaw in the model, namely that people are mobile and attracted to certain places. This problem is addressed by the gravity model, which was adapted from physics to geography and finally to archaeology. In 1686, Newton [39] defined the law of gravitation with which the mutual influence of bodies of matter in motion can be explained and predicted. Newton discovered that two bodies attract each other and that the force of attraction is determined by their mass and the distance between them. For the geographical problem of migration, Ravenstein [44] developed a similar model, formulated as a proper socio-geographical law of gravitation by Stewart [47] in 1948. The idea is that two populations attract each other according to the number of individuals belonging to the populations (p_1, p_2) and the distance (d) between them, with the attraction F.

$$F = \frac{p_1 p_2}{d^2} \tag{2.2}$$

Gravitational laws cover a wide range of applications in geography-related fields of research. Reilly's [45] retail gravitational law is an example for economics, while the work from Diachenko and Menotti [13] is an example of an archaeological application.

There are many other models dealing with location and distance; for instance, Christaller's [11] central place model or Thünen's model [51] is also interested in distances. V. Thünen's does not investigate the attraction but rather the influence of land use in relation to the distance of the market places (Fig. 2.1). The land use depends on the costs of bringing the products to the markets. For each place, the landowner decides for the land use that allows the highest land rate. The land rate (R) is defined by the equation

$$R = Y(p - c) - YTd \tag{2.3}$$

where Y is the yield per unit of land, p is the market price per unit of commodity, c is the production expenses per unit of commodity, T the freight rate and d the distance to the market. For each product with specific yields, prices and costs within a certain range of distances can be found, where the rents are optimal. For example, market gardening has an optimal distance to the market that is lower than the optimal distance for field crops. If the characteristic land use for different distances are on a map like a graph, the famous Thünen rings emerge.

In contrast to the explicit models mentioned above, many implicit or latent models are also used, whereby we will provide some further examples from archaeology and geography. Latent models are used as models, although they are rather hidden. They are very powerful and influential but explicit discussions can seldom be found. We will mention the four main latent models in archaeology [38].

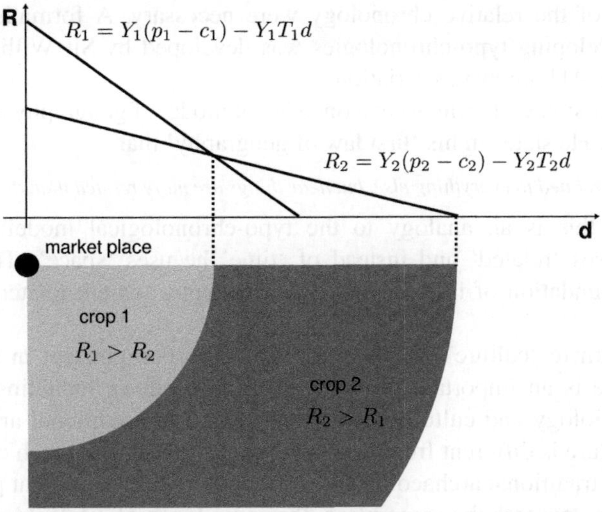

Fig. 2.1 Land rent (R) and land (crop 1 and crop 2) use in relation to the distance of the market place (d), based upon Thünen

Objects with similar diagnostic features are subsumed under a certain type. This classification allows making general statements like 'all finds of type 1 date to phase 4' or 'all finds of type 2 served function b'. However, a type is more than a class; rather, it implies a certain interpretation, such as a chronological or functional interpretation. For all objects of a certain type we assume a certain dating, function, provenance or meaning. This is a simple yet powerful conceptual model.

Upon first glance, it does not seem to involve quantitative aspects. However, this model is a very general one, used to develop other models with more specific elements. For example, the types can be defined using numerical classification. Subsequently, we can reduce the range of interpretations to chronological categories, for example. Finally, we obtain the latent typo-chronological model, which assumes that objects of the same type date to the same time and that similar objects date to phases close to the original one. This model implies a metric for object similarity and time. The measurement of similarity is based upon common features and allows constituting a scale, a typological series. The most simple temporal metric uses relative phases and the number of phases between two points in time as a measure of the temporal distance. The different phases are defined by the presence of different diagnostic types. Using the diagnostic-type-based chronology, the features of the objects condensed in types can be plotted against time. The typo-chronological model is nothing but a regression model with ordinal numbers, which maps the relationship of two parameters. This model, which was developed in the nineteenth century, has subsequently proved very successful—then uses the description of finds only. It is a very sophisticated concept of how to turn formal descriptions of material culture into history. The resulting chronologies proved very good, although some modifications of the relative chronology were necessary. A formalisation of the process of developing typo-chronologies was developed by Sir William Matthew Flinders Petrie [41], known as seriation.

A brief excursion will bring us to a once latent model of geography made explicit by Tobler [52]. He states in his 'first law of geography' that

Everything is related to everything else, but near things are more related than distant things.

Obviously, this is an analogy to the typo-chronological model: rather than 'similar' he uses 'related' and instead of 'time' he uses 'space'. This model is the implicit foundation of interpolation—for example—where related also means similar.

Now we turn to 'culture' which is another important concept in archaeology. In fact, culture is an important term for many disciplines, including geography, ethnology, sociology and cultural studies, although, the traditional archaeological concept of culture is different from that in cultural studies. The much criticised, yet still pervasive, traditional archaeological concept of culture states that people living in a certain area possess the same ideas, the same types of artefacts and the same style of decorations. The area delimited by the cultural border is thought to be homogeneous. The traditional archaeological concept is obviously a simplification that does not fit to reality and is incompatible with the term 'culture' in some other disciplines. Despite this problem, this model can serve certain purposes; for example, it allows observing a pattern in a vast amount of archaeological data and connecting it to certain research questions. One example is the concept of Kossinna [26] and Childe [7], who perceive cultures as actors of history. If you accept some theoretical assumptions of this approach—although we do not—the traditional archaeological concept of culture is a useful model. Another example is Lüning's [32] concept, which interprets cultures as zones of validity for chronological systems. In this concept, the very simple model of culture makes sense; thus, the degree of simplification fits perfectly to the task.

Despite being problematic, the traditional archaeological concept of culture is implicitly present in many archaeological works, even of those who explicitly reject the concept. It is very tempting to structure archaeological observations using this concept as a first step of research. Sometimes the traditional concept is modified to serve certain purposes; for instance, Clarke [9] accepts the cultural model as a mere classification of a set of archaeological observations, although he insists upon heterogeneity and fuzzy borders. While the traditional archaeological concept of culture assumes homogeneity within cultural borders and particularly in small areas and single settlements, another latent model assumes heterogeneity.

The social rank model assumes that the social rank in a certain community corresponds to the wealth expressed by artefacts in a grave. Likewise, as a simplification, this model allows exploring prehistoric societies by constructing hypothetical social structures.

The latent models mainly comprise relationships between basic categories. These relationships are described in a very simplified way which involves unrealistic

Fig. 2.2 Bohr model of hydrogen and nitrogen

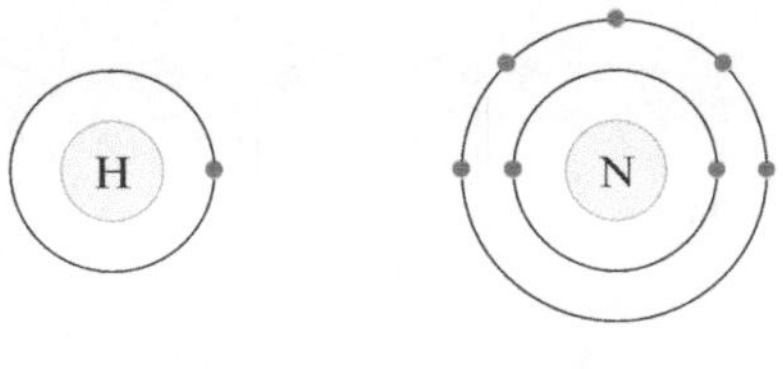

assumptions and does not fit reality. However, the latent models are useful and powerful due to the simplicity of the model, allowing a preliminary structuring of the data. The threat lies in the fact that we mostly use latent models without being aware of it and hence we cannot be cognizant of the natural limits of these models.

Explicit models of different disciplines form a contrast to the latent and implicit models. Physics provides very instructive examples for understanding explicit models. There are two models used to deal with light: one model describes light as an electromagnetic wave, thus explaining interference, for instance; whereas the other model describes light as a particle and is able to explain reflection and diffraction. While these models can be used for different purposes, according to quantum mechanics both particles and waves are possible at the same time, called the wave-particle-duality of light. Hence, a universal model of light involves two complementary parts, each of which describes certain properties of the phenomenon but fails to describe others. It has recently been possible to observe both effects of light at the same time [42].

Another well-known type of model in physics is atom models; for instance, the Dalton model expresses that the element comprises similar small particles that are called atoms and cannot be sub-divided any further. By contrast, the Bohr model shows that atoms comprise of electrons, protons and neutrons and that protons and neutrons form the nucleus, while the electrons are on certain orbits surrounding the nucleus, representing different energy levels (Fig. 2.2). A change of orbit means a change in energy level.

This rather simple model can explain many properties of matter. Despite the fact that models with a higher predictability exist, it remains in use owing to its simplicity.

In chemistry, the mechanical molecule model—introduced by Hofmann [23]—is an example of a very influential chemical model. This model connects to the atom model yet has its focus on another scale. Molecules are visualised using balls and sticks: the balls represent the single atoms—which are coloured differently according to the different elements—while the sticks represent the bonds. Structure formulae like the balls-and-sticks model and chemical formulae in the same manner as simple empirical formulae represent certain aspects of chemical compounds. Different graphical representations of benzene—including the balls-and-sticks model—exemplify models of chemical compounds (Fig. 2.3).

While the atom and the molecule models are focused on small details, climate models deal with objects ranging between the regional and global [24, 29]. In fact, this is a rather marginal difference. More importantly, climate models do not comprise the description of simple relationships of some elements that allow defining a structure very precisely. Climate models involve an enormous amount

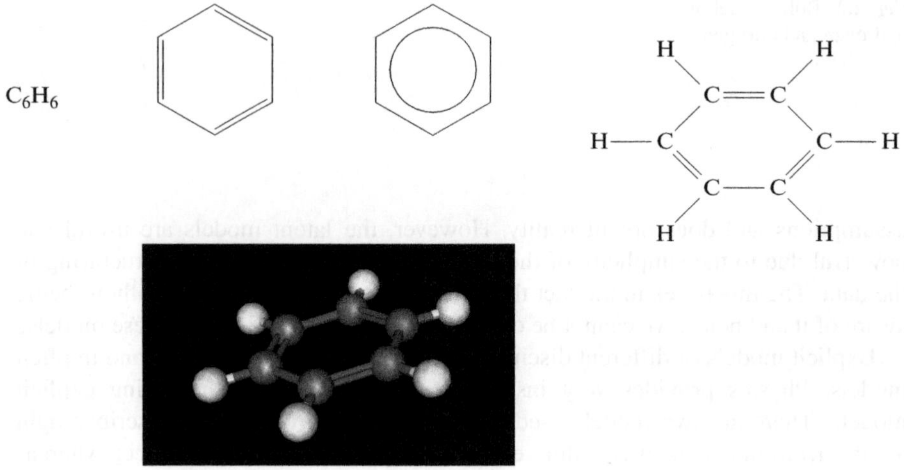

Fig. 2.3 Chemical benzene models

of data and some rules that define the behaviour of the climate system. Even with this amount of data, climate models are less dependable than molecular models. Nonetheless, this does not mean that molecular models are more precise. Simple molecular models do not care for scales and angles, but they are suitable for describing the chemical bonds between different types of atoms.

Differential equations define the interrelationship between different parameters in climate models. Hence, it is possible to calculate the effect of a changing parameter. A set of differential equations and certain initial conditions allow calculating the state of the climate system for any point in time. Numerical simulations are used in climate models, whereby the result depends on the initial conditions. In complex models like climate models, non-linear relationships, emergence from certain patterns and *butterfly effects*—or more precisely, the sensitive dependence on initial conditions—are possible. This means that the probability of the simulation result declines with the increasing temporal distance to the starting point in time. We know this effect from the daily weather forecast, which is not convincing for a longer period, owing to butterfly effects. Initial conditions differing in small details can cause completely different states of the system after a short period. One example of climate models is atmospheric general circulation models (AGCM), which comprise a number of differential equations.

Now we move on from the climate component of environment to a geological component. Process-based models of coasts model the morphological change of coastal areas [36]. These models couple different components concerned with currents, waves and sediment transport. The models are simulations based upon initial states and differential equations and are used similarly to the climate models.

Another example of simulations is *cellular automata*. The idea is to define a grid and rules for the behaviour of the grid cells, whereby the value of a cell depends on the value of other cells. In an iteration, the values of all cells are calculated. The complex interrelationship between cells can lead to a dynamic pattern, which changes in every step of iteration. The famous 'game of life' is an application of cellular automata developed by J. H. Conway in 1970 [10, 18]. Cells can be dead or alive, whereby the state of a cell depends on the state of the surrounding cells. During the simulation, characteristic patterns can emerge that cannot be deduced from the rules. This is a characteristic of a complex system.

Agent-based modelling [16, 40] is related to cellular automata, though they allow agents that preserve their identity while moving. We can think of cellular automata as being a special kind of agent-based models where the agents are not allowed to move but need to have different states. Agent-based models are defined by the rules of behaviour of the individual agents and can produce emerging patterns. In case of cellular automata as well as agent-based models, the study of complex systems is the most interesting application. The bottom-up approach allows connecting certain system properties and patterns to individual behaviour. In the case of simulations that use system parameters, this is much more difficult.

The rules defined within an ABM are not a statement about the goals of the agent; rather, they concern how the agent acts to reach a goal under specific conditions. The *homo economicus* will purchase the cheapest good from a set of similar goods. This principle is applied even if the goal is getting some rain by offering goods to certain gods: if the gods possess the same power, the homo economicus will offer to the god with the most moderate demands.

Despite the fact that the homo economicus is rather unrealistic as a general concept, it remains in use for understanding economic mechanisms such as markets. Indeed, certainly the homo economicus certainly remains a component of the description of more realistic actors.

In biology, the development of populations is a common topic in which modelling approaches are applied. In particular, the interrelationship between the populations of two species is addressed by models and simulations. In this case, the behaviour of coupled systems is estimated using differential equations. The most famous example is the predator–prey model to which the Lotka–Volterra equations [31, 55] are applied. The idea is that there is a growing population of prey, mostly exemplified as rabbits, and a growing population of predators, such as wolves. The growth of rabbits depends on the number of wolves, since the rabbits are the wolves' food. On the other hand the wolves' growth depends on the number of rabbits: the more wolves there are, the lower the growth of the rabbit population, while the more rabbits there are, the higher the growth of the wolf population. This interrelationship can be modelled with two differential equations:

$$\frac{\partial x}{\partial t} = ayx - bx \tag{2.4}$$

$$\frac{\partial y}{\partial t} = cy - dxy \tag{2.5}$$

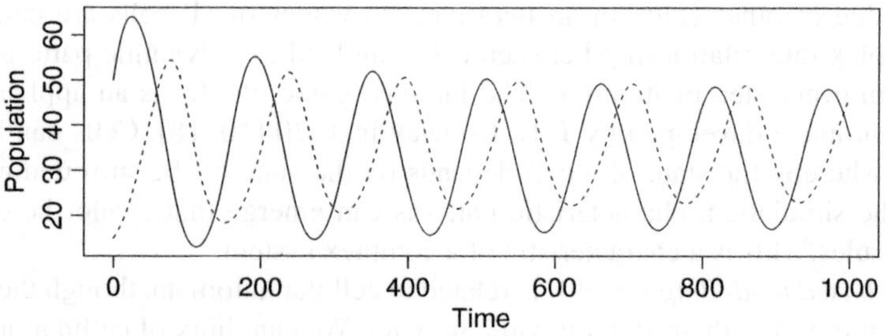

Fig. 2.4 Typical development of the population of two species in the predator–prey model. Prey: *solid line*; predator: *dashed line*

In the equations, x is the population of the predator and y the population of its prey. The other parameters control the behaviour of the system. A usual system behaviour is an alternating up and down of the populations where the predator shows a certain delay (Fig. 2.4).

Epidemic models [50, 53] can serve as an example from medicine. The models of animal epidemics have two main components: first, the process of the disease, which includes—for instance—infected, infectious and diagnosed as characteristics and second, the network of contact, which includes the paths of spread.

The final example is taken from social science and has been transferred to many other disciplines. The concept of *ideal types* was proposed by Max Weber [56]. Ideal types are models of certain facts or objects that represent the extreme or pure application of a single property or principle. Ideal types do not exist in reality but are useful to understand the mechanisms and relationships of some phenomena. They are based upon the one-sided accentuation of a certain point of view.

It seems that the term 'ideal type' is something very similar to the term 'model'. Ideal types appear to be a special type of model embedded in another terminological framework.

While this brief collection of some models is naturally incomplete it offers a notion of the range of different types of models. Obviously, there are many terms of models in use. Is 'model' a fancy term without real content or a fuzzy 'term' covering a field of meanings rather than one actual meaning, or is there a general term of 'model' that is varied in the different disciplines? The choice of successful and traditional examples indicates that fanciness is at least not the major aspect of the term 'model'. After providing an overview of some models from different disciplines, it is time to explore the meaning of the term 'model'. Subsequently, we will be able to apply the modelling concept in a scientific framework and discuss basic methods used in landscape modelling.

2.2 What Is a Model?

The term 'modelling' is becoming increasingly fashionable. An exploration of the keyword 'modelling' in the Library of Congress reveals that modelling became popular in the 1960s. We should mention that 'model' was introduced into mathematics (mathematical logic) in 1933 by the Polish logician Alfred Tarski [48]. His theory became important in the 1950s during the course of the work on artificial languages (for example, programming languages). Tarski's English papers from the 1950s certainly helped to distribute his ideas. In addition, one related process increased the importance of the term 'modelling', namely the quantitative revolution that took place in the 1950s and 1960s, which was enabled by the development of computer systems.

In many disciplines, a peak in the 1970s marked the first hype of quantitative modelling. In the 1980s, there was a break induced by post-modern theories. Since the 1990s, the importance of 'modelling' has continuously increasing again.

We now know that the term 'model' is very fashionable, although we do not know what a model is. Accordingly, we have to explore the meaning of 'model'. Tarski [48, pp. 11–12] defines it as:

A possible realisation in which all valid sentences of a theory T are satisfied is called a model of T.

This is a definition from the mathematical logic and it hardly applies to all disciplines. A very pragmatic and useful characterisation of 'model' comes from Herbert Stachowiak [46], who claims that a model:

- is a mapping;
- is a reduction and
- is pragmatic.

We can use this as a first simple standard definition of model which might be sufficient for some contexts and can be replaced by a more sophisticated definition, if required:

Definition 2.1. A **model** is a simplified mapping for a special purpose.

The entire concept of Stachowiak—including his definition of 'model'—is embedded in system theories. Stachowiak explicit definition [46, pp. 322–323] is:

O_1 and O_2 are objects and O_2 is a model of O_1 for k in the time interval t regarding a certain purpose Z if in $t\,k$:

1. is L-rational
2. performs a description P_1 of O_1
3. performs a description P_2 of O_2
4. performs a mapping of P_1 on P_2
5. performs a transcoding of P_1 in P_2
6. performs the substitution of O_1 by O_2

7. performs certain operations on O_2 in order to fulfil the purpose Z and which transfer O_2 to O_2*
8. performs a description P_2* of O_2*
9. performs the reverse mapping of P_2* on P_1*
10. accepts P_1* as the description of O_1*
11. accepts the substitution of O_1* by O_2*
12. performs a recoding of P_1 in P_2 regarding P_1* and P_2*

Obviously, his characterisation seems more comprehensive than the formal definition with the twelve conditions of determination.

Balzer [5] formulated a definition related to Tarski's original definition from the field of philosophy of science. Accordingly, a model:

- is a structure of a theory;
- complies with a set of hypotheses and
- is not a simple statement.

For Richard Chorley and Peter Haggett, a model is a 'simplified and intelligible picture of the world' [8, p. 22]. This picture allows an overview by decomposing the original into details and merging selected details again for a certain purpose. Due to the selection, models have a limited range of applications. Chorley and Haggett characterise models with some key terms. We have already mentioned the selectiveness of models, which allows focusing on certain aspects, while they are not valid for others. In addition, models are structured because they exploit the connection between significant aspects of the real world. This also means that models are an approximation of reality and an analogy of the real world. They are suggestive because they suggest extension of the model and re-applicable because they can be applied to other subsystems of the real world. The main function of models can be seen in bridging between observation and theory. The validation of models is based upon the fact that models are able to predict reality. Certain models with a very high probability are called laws. Since models have a limited probability and a limited range of application, validation based upon prediction becomes a key feature.

In archaeology, David Clarke [9] was the first to deal with models explicitly. He followed the ideas of his friend—the geographer Peter Haggett [8]—but focused particularly on the models' ability to predict. Clarke claims that models are best characterised by:

- comprehensiveness;
- predictiveness;
- efficiency and
- accuracy.

It is obvious that the origin of this characterisation is the quantitative revolution of the 1960s. In this context, models are a mapping of real-world processes, which allows predicting system states for another moment.

In the concept of Mahr [33, 34], the usage of models is the key to understanding their nature. Mahr states that any object can be used as model if it is assumed that it represents another object in terms of certain aspects. He speaks of 'models for' if the models are used as a template for another object and 'models of' if they map or picture an other object. The virtual model is represented by one or more model objects. In addition, this distinguishes between the perspective of producing and applying a model. Mahr connects the viewpoint of induction with that of deduction. The cargo of a model is the information, which is transferred from the inductive component to the deductive component.

Frigg and Hartmann [17] distinguish between representational models of phenomena and data and models of theory. Rather than providing a definition, they describe certain types of models, among which are fictional objects, physical objects and equations. It seems that these types of models are completely different things. The conclusion of Frigg and Hartmann's article [17] might serve as an example of wide-spread opinion about the confused nature of models:

> Models play an important role in science. But despite the fact that they have generated considerable interest among philosophers, there remain significant lacunas in our understanding of what models are and of how they work.

Björn Kralemann and Claas Lattmann [27, 28] adopt a semiotic approach, claiming that models are a specific kind of sign, namely the icon. Charles Peirce classifies signs into icons, symbols and indices: while an icon refers to its object through similarity, an index refers through factual connection and a symbol through a norm. This concept picks up the mapping function from Stachowiak.

According to Thalheim and Nissen [49], *models are artefacts, representing a part of the real world*. These artefacts are used as tools for a certain purpose. The relationship between the model and original is an analogy. A model is connected to a community of practice, which developed and uses the model. This practice-based concept of a model was developed with a bottom-up approach, using a large number of specific modelling approaches in Kiel. The Kiel term of a model is intended to cover a wide range of interdisciplinary applications. The process of developing models and negotiating their use and meaning is perceived as something like Wittgenstein's language games. The community of practice defines the criteria that enable the model to be accepted and used. The model as an instrument has to be adequate, dependable and well-formed, whereby the latter term means that an artefact serving as a model should obey some formal rules. Adequate models serve the purpose defined by the objective. The analogy used in a model is significant for the objective and the representation is more simple, clear, abstract, focused, usable or intelligible than the original. For dependable models we have valid reasons to believe that they will serve the purpose, whereby empiric evidence, coherency, fallibility and stability are criteria for dependability.

Models can have different functions, most prominently including description, explanation, optimisation, verification, representation, reflection and documentation. Application scenarios are distinguished from function, although they are obviously related. Possible scenarios are explanation, designing, prediction and description. The background of a model is formed by paradigms, theories and principles, which are called bases, on the one hand, as well as principles, culture and common sense—called foundations—on the other. The science and art of modelling is divided into three facets. A model itself—to repeat the definition—is an artefact used as tool for a certain purpose. To model is an activity that covers the model development, including the optimisation, merging, specialisation, generalisation and presentation of models, as well as their usage. This facet is the practice embedded in a certain culture. Modelling is a technique based upon certain principles and tightly connected to the purpose. Although, this concept cannot be condensed in one definition sentence, we will use this as the second—more elaborated—standard concept of model.

2.3 Types of Models

There is a multitude of model classifications; accordingly, we can only discuss a small, yet very important selection of classifications here. We will start with a dichotomy that runs like a thread through the history of science: theory and empiricism. It is necessary to distinguish between theoretical and empirical models (Fig. 2.5). Theoretical models—also known as *models for*, ideal models, constructions or templates—apply principles. Observations are only used to set up the model's outline. The model is formed based upon theoretical considerations. Theoretical models are related to the method of deduction. A theoretical model allows determining what would be good, rather than what is really the case.

Empirical models map observations and they are also known as *models of*, real models, reconstructions or mapping. Empirical models are related to the method of induction and they allow us to describe what is, while we not understand why.

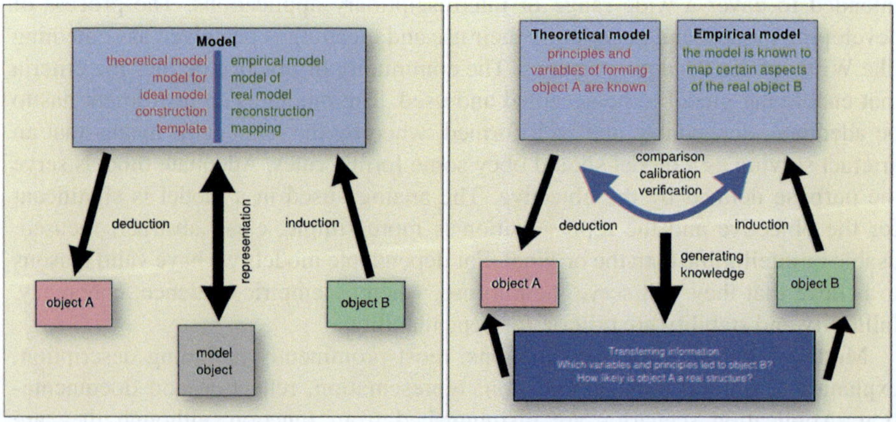

Fig. 2.5 Two main types of models and model comparison

In most cases, a model is represented by a model object. This is a material representation like a model railway, a constructional drawing or a person who sits for a painter. Sometimes the model object simplifies the decision concerning whether it is a theoretical or empirical model. In some cases, this is not so easy because it depends on the degree of empirical and theoretical input, as well as the purpose of the model. A model object can be used as a theoretical model for one purpose and an empirical model for another. Regardless, we have to establish that our model can be used in the intended way and thus serve the intended purpose. This is very important because a misclassification leads to misinterpretation. A model that has to be used as theoretical model due to the limited input of empirical data cannot be used as an empirical model. We would misinterpret the model as a description of an observation. A classical example is the usage of Thiessen polygons to find borders, which is not possible since the method allows establishing where borders should be drawn to minimise distances between related points, but not to establish the position of real borders.

At this point, it seems that models have a very limited account of explanation. Theoretical models are only a mapping of some ideas and empirical models do nothing but duplicating the original with reduced characteristics. Knowledge emerges when models are compared. If we find that a theoretical model fits to an empirical model, then we can transfer the knowledge about principles and variables from the theoretical model to the empirical model. We can denote the resulting model as *conclusive model* or *interpreted model*. An interpreted model provides us with the requirements to understand the object that we have modelled. This step of comparison can be realised as direct comparison, calibration, verification or validation.

We will only mention some of the other classifications. Models can be static or dynamic, depending on time, as possible a variable. Moreover, models can be discrete or continuous. Stochastic models deal with probability and contingency, while deterministic models aim to be exact or unique. Models can aim at optimisation or equilibrium. Models can be classified by mathematical techniques, namely linear equations, non-linear equations or differential equations.

Kai Velten [54] developed the more elaborated three-dimensional SQM classification of models, whereby S, Q and M represent dimensions of the model classification. We only mention the criteria of the dimensions:

S: system

- physical–conceptual
- natural–technical
- stochastic–deterministic
- continuous–discrete
- dimension
- field of application

Q: objectives

- phenomenological–mechanistic
- stationary–instationary

- lumped–distributed
- direct–inverse
- research–management
- speculation–design
- scale

M: mathematical structure

- linear–non-linear
- analytical–numerical
- autonomous–non-autonomous
- continuous–discrete
- differential equations
- integral equations
- algebraic equations

Finally we have to deal with complexity. Models involve mapping a part of a complex reality. Developing complexity is a research process stepping towards more complex models. Higher complexity means:

- a better mapping of complex cases;
- sensitive measures of correspondence of empiric and theoretic models;
- an increasing amount of new knowledge and
- a pretentious demand for data and methods.

Reducing complexity is the concept of extracting relevant information from models (Fig. 2.6). Models with reduced complexity can represent the significant relations of a complex reality and hence have an analogical meaning as eigenvectors for a square matrix.

We can distinguish between five types of models in a chain of developing complexity.

1. Mapping models do nothing other than map an object. An example is archaeological documentation.
2. Emergent models allow producing new knowledge by comparing models.
3. Quantitative models introduce mathematical methods.
4. Cybernetic models allow reciprocal effects.
5. Complex models allow non-linear interdependency, memory-effects, emergent phenomena in systems and other features.

Which degree of complexity is appropriate for a model depends on the research question as well as the data. We have to find this optimal degree of complexity for each application. In principle, one would develop a high degree of complexity first and subsequently reduce the complexity until the optimal degree is reached. In practice, the effort involved for this is often too great, whereby the researcher stops at the assumed optimal degree of complexity.

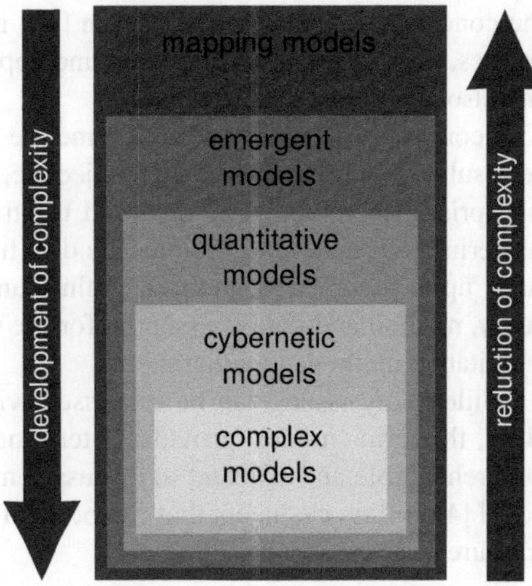

Fig. 2.6 Developing and reducing complexity

2.4 Usage of Models

Modelling provides us with a specific terminological and conceptual framework that is able to significantly reduce the complexity of the research process. Moreover, models offer further benefits:

- increasing knowledge;
- transferring of knowledge;
- practising interdisciplinary research;
- handling complex data and problems and
- working at the cutting edge of research.

For the usage of models there are some rules of thumb that we denote as directions of modelling. These guidelines aim to avoid pitfalls and increase the quality of modelling, stating that one should consider:

- the purpose of models;
- the limit of model types;
- the complementarity of model types;
- the empirical verification of theoretical models and
- purposive developing and reducing complexity.

2.5 Models Between Theory and Method

Sometimes modelling is understood as the mere application of certain techniques, although, we reject this perspective. Like all other methods—to keep this restriction for a moment—a model is based upon a certain theory that serves to solve a problem.

The concept of Thalheim and Nissen [49] makes clear that models include certain theories, methods (for development and application) and objectives. In many cases, data also has to be considered.

Theories are necessary to determine the parameters of the method and interpret the results. The method connects objective, theory and data. The method has to be appropriate for the specific data and the theory of the investigation and has help answering the research question. The data has to be helpful for solving the problem based upon theory and method. A fine-tuning of the four elements of objective, theory, method and data is essential for the successful usage of methods, as well as quantitative methods in general [43].

While many issues can be discussed without a reference to models and modelling, the term 'model' provides a terminological framework that makes it more comprehendible and efficient to discuss some points. In particular, the Kiel term of model [49] offers a concept that can be used to develop a consistent background and structure of an application.

2.6 Examples

We started this chapter by providing some examples to offer a potential notion of models. Now we end this chapter with some examples to show the potential of models in archaeology and geography. Some examples are directly linked to those at the beginning of this chapter, although, by now the reader should have some background knowledge on modelling and hence be able to interpret the examples in a different way.

One of the most virulent topics in archaeology is the process known as neolithisation. From a local to regional perspective, this is the transition from the mesolithic to the neolithic way of life [22], which can be caused by external and internal factors or a combination of both. From a supra-regional perspective, the relationship between the time and location of the transition can be investigated and modelled. The process is perceived as a diffusion. Diffusion models can describe the movement of both people and cultural traits and they are used to describe different phenomena. Fisher [15] developed the concept of *the wave of advance* for modelling the spread of advantageous genes. Accordingly, Fisher published an equation that has to be satisfied:

$$\frac{\partial p}{\partial t} = k\frac{\partial^2 p}{\partial x^2} + mp(1-p) \tag{2.6}$$

In this equation, p is the frequency of a mutant gene, t the time, x a spatial coordinate, m the intensity of selection and k the diffusion coefficient. A similar equation was developed by Kolmogoroff et al. [25] and hence the equation is known as the Fisher–Kolmogoroff–Petrovsky–Piscounoff or FKPP equation. Many other authors have used this concept and in archaeology Ammerman and Cavalli-Sforza [2, 3] adapted the idea to model neolithisation, proposing a similar equation:

$$\frac{\partial p}{\partial t} = kp(1 - \frac{p}{c}) \tag{2.7}$$

In this equation, k is the growth rate and c the maximal p-value, also known as the *carrying capacity*.

The mentioned works allow an analytical solution that provides the frequency of the new feature at a certain place and time. More recent articles employ simulations, Bayesian inference or additional information like variable coefficients [1, 4, 30].

A similar diffusion process was developed by the geographer Torsten Hägerstrand [19, 20], who dedicated some of his work to modelling the diffusion of innovation. Although the basic mechanism was similar to the wave-of-advance model, Hägerstrand focused on other aspects. In particular, he does not assume a uniform wave; rather, he also considers diffusion in networks. His work comprises three major parts: empirical models of the diffusion of innovation, Monte Carlo simulations and conceptual models of the process of diffusion. In contrast to the wave-of-advance model, Hägerstrand is not interested in the arrival or dominance of a certain innovation, but rather in the dynamics of the spread of innovation. Which factors influence the spatial and temporal patterns of the diffusion of innovation? Hägerstrand's diffusion model still serves as the basis for further development [12].

The next example is based upon the predator–prey model and in fact it is an extension of this classical model. The HANDY (human and nature dynamics) model [37] aims to understand crises of populations and cultures. It starts with a re-interpretation of the original predator–prey model. The human population is interpreted as a predator while nature is interpreted as prey. In addition to this ecological component, HANDY has an economical component, whereby the population is divided into two parts: commons and elites. The elites are defined by wealth and both groups have different consumption rates. In contrast to the predator–prey model, HANDY comprises four differential equations:

$$\frac{\partial x_C}{\partial t} = \beta_C x_C - \alpha_C x_C \tag{2.8}$$

$$\frac{\partial x_E}{\partial t} = \beta_E x_E - \alpha_E x_E \tag{2.9}$$

$$\frac{\partial y}{\partial t} = \gamma y(\lambda - y) - \delta x_C y \tag{2.10}$$

$$\frac{\partial w}{\partial t} = \delta x_C y - c_C - c_E \tag{2.11}$$

In these equations, x is the human population, y the nature, w the wealth and c the consumption. The indices E for elites and C for commons can qualify x and c. Different scenarios can be applied to the model; for example, an egalitarian society, equitable society and unequal society. These models—particularly when applied in simulations—teach us about the relationships between the parameters used under conditions of crises as well as stability.

We return to the Thünen model to exemplify some of the details discussed above. According to Stachowiak, a model is a reduced mapping for a certain purpose. The purpose is obviously to discuss the main parameters that influence the land use in relation to the distance to the market. The relationship between the land use and distance is mapped and mainly comprises some equations concerning the rent for different products and the maximisation of the rent. The reduction is the selection of only a few parameters that seem to be significant for the topic. For instance, topography which influences the transportational costs is excluded as well as other markets.

From Haggett and Clarke's perspective the Thünen model allows predicting land use. Owing to the reduction, the accuracy of this model is rather low. The quality of the Thünen model for prediction also depends on the scale employed. It might produce a rough picture that is sufficient for some purposes, but it will definitely not be useful for other purposes. From this perspective, the Thünen model seems to be a weak model. However at this point we are making a mistake; namely, the purpose of this model is not prediction but rather to 'discuss the main parameters which influence the land use in dependence of the distance'. We would be misusing the model in applying it for prediction.

We can learn from Mahr [34] that it is a theoretical model. It might be based upon empirical observations, although the model itself comprises a simple theoretical rule concerning how to optimise land use. If we find that the theoretical model matches the empirical observations, we learn that the theoretical rules also apply to the empirical case; otherwise, parameters not included in the model might be important or the optimisation is not intended, which is rather strange. In addition, Mahr shows us that a model is represented by a model object. In the Thünen case, the equations or the ideas that they express are the model, while the map with the Thünen rings is the model object. It should be mentioned that using another metric that uses another definition of distance is also possible; for instance, we could define a distance that respects topography. The model would be the same, as would the map of Thünen rings in the space spanned by the metric in use. However, we could also plot the rings on a geographical map, whereby they would no longer be circles. This example stresses the importance of the definition of space; indeed, we will connect to this idea at several places in this volume.

From Thalheim and Nissen's [49] perspective, the model is an artefact that involves a set of equations. This artefact is used to represent the relationship between land use and distance. From the above discussion, we have learned that it is an adequate and well-formed model. Moreover, it is also dependable because the usage in many textbooks shows that it successfully serves the aforementioned purpose. Obviously, the Thünen model is more simple, clear, abstract, focused, usable and intelligible than the original relationship of parameters of land use. We have already seen that the function of a model matters, whereby the Thünen model holds limited use for prediction. The major critique of this model can be explained by a shift in function: while the original model was developed to explain a relationship, most of the more recent geographical literature implicitly assumes that the model should predict. The Thünen model is not accepted for use in prediction by the community of practice. At the same time the model is used for explaining a relationship, albeit likewise not explicitly. The Thünen model is mostly described as the history of research, serving in a hidden way to explain some basics and it is finely criticised as being insufficient for prediction [21]. This phenomenon shows that models are created in a kind of language game by a community of practice. Function, paradigms, evaluation and other parameters can change, and a new version of a model can be completely different to the original one. Sometimes it is useful to return to the original version, given that the changing perspective may offer new perspectives of the original model, which can help to better understand the topic.

2.7 Problems

2.1. Please discuss:

(a) Which is your preferred definition of model and why?
(b) What is the difference between an empirical and theoretical model?

2.2. Please classify some models that you already know according to the following classes:

(a) empirical model, theoretical model
(b) SQM classification
(c) stochastic model, deterministic model, simulation
(d) five degrees of complexity

2.3. Please identify the models among the following list of objects and classify them according to the classes from the last problem:

(a) chronological scheme with relative and absolute dates
(b) plate of types of ceramic vessels
(c) thin section of ceramic sherds
(d) gypsum reconstruction of a ceramic vessel
(e) digital 3D reconstruction of the same vessel
(f) digital 3D reconstruction of a landscape (elevation)
(g) seriation matrix of finds
(h) drawing of a profile of an excavation trench
(i) photography of the same profile
(j) soil sample from the same profile
(k) stratigraphic Harris-matrix of the layers of the same profile
(l) map of the ancient road system of a certain region
(m) agent-based model of ancient trade

2.4. Please outline the benefits of models from the examples in this chapter from your perspective.

2.5. Please list some properties of complex systems.

2.6. Can you find an example of the need for balancing theory, method, data and research question based upon your own experience.

References

1. Ackland, G. J., Signitzer, M., Stratford, K., & Cohen, M. (2007). Cultural hitchhiking on the wave of advance of beneficial technologies. *Proceedings of the National Academy of Sciences, 104*, 8714–8719.
2. Ammerman, A. J., & Cavalli-Sforza, L. L. (1973). A population model for the diffusion of early farming in Europe. In C. Renfrew (Ed.), *The explanation of culture change*. London: Duckworth.
3. Ammerman, A. J., & Cavalli-Sforza, L. L. (1979). The wave of advance model for the spread of agriculture in Europe. In C. Renfrew, & K. L. Cooke (Eds.), *Transformations - mathematical approaches to culture change* (pp. 275–293). New York: Academic.
4. Baggaley, A. W., Sarson, G. R., Shukurov, A., Boys, R. J., & Golightly, A. (2012). Bayesian inference for a wavefront model of the Neolithisation of Europe. *Physics Review, E 86*, 016105.
5. Balzer, W. (2009). *Die Wissenschaft und ihre Methoden*. Freiburg: Karl Alber.
6. Birdsell, J. B. (1953). Some environmental and cultural factors influencing the structuring of Australian Aboriginal populations. *The American Naturalist, 87/834*, 171–207.
7. Childe, V. G. (1925). *The dawn of European civilization*. London: Kegan Paul.
8. Chorley, R., & Haggett, P. (1967). *Models in geography*. London: Edward Arnold.
9. Clarke, D. L. (Ed.). (1972). *Models in archaeology*. London: Methuen.
10. Clarke, K. C. (2013). Cellular automata and agent-based models. *Handbook of regional science*, (pp. 1217–1233). Springer Berlin Heidelberg.
11. Christaller, W. (1933). *Die Zentralen Orte in Süddeutschland*. Jena: Fischer.
12. Daudé, E. (2004). Apports de la simulation multi-agents à l'étude des processus de diffusion, Cybergeo. *Revue européenne de géographie, 255*. http://cybergeo.revues.org/3835; doi: 10.4000/cybergeo.3835
13. Diachenko, A, & Menotti, F. (2012). The gravity model: Monitoring the formation and development of the Tripolye culture giant-settlements in Ukraine. *Journal of Archaeological Science, 39*, 2810–2817.
14. Diachenko, A., & Zubrow, E. B. W. (2015). Stabilization points in carrying capacity: Population growth and migrations. *Journal of Neolithic Archaeology, 17*, 1–15.
15. Fisher, R.A. (1937). The advance of advantageous genes. *Annals of Eugenics, 7*, 335–369.
16. Fonstad, M. A. (2006). Cellular automata as analysis and synthesis engines at the geomorphology/ecology interface. *Geomorphology, 77*, 217–234.
17. Frigg, R., & Hartmann, S. (2012). Models in science. In E. N. Zalta (Ed.), *The Stanford encyclopedia of philosophy* (Fall 2012 ed.). Stanford, CA: The Metaphysics Research Lab, Center for the Study of Language and Information (CSLI), Stanford University. http://plato.stanford.edu/archives/fall2012/entries/models-science/
18. Gardner, M. (1970). Mathematical games – The fantastic combinations of John Conway's new solitaire game "life". *Scientific American, 223*, 120–123.
19. Hägerstrand, T. (1952). *The propagation of innovation waves. Lund studies in geography* (Vol. B4). Lund: Lund University.
20. Hägerstrand, T. (1967). *Innovation diffusion as a spatial process*. Chicago: University of Chicago Press.

21. Haggett, P. (1965). *Locational analysis in human geography*. London: Arnold.
22. Hartz, S., Lübke, H., & Terberger, T. (2007). From fish and seal to sheep and cattle: New research into the process of neolithisation in northern Germany. *Proceedings of the British Academy, 144*, 567–594.
23. Hofmann, A. W. (1865). On the combining power of atoms. *Proceedings of the Royal Institution of Great Britain, 4*, 401–430.
24. Intergovernmental Panel on Climate Change 2013: The Physical Science Basis (2013). *IPCC Working Group I Contribution to AR5*. Cambridge: Cambridge University Press.
25. Kolmogoroff, I. P., & Piscounoff, N. (1937). Etude de léquation de la diffusion avec croissance de la quantité de matière et son application a un probléme biologique. *Bulletin de lUniversité détat à Moscou Série Internationale Section A Mathématiques et Mécanique, 1*, 1–25.
26. Kossinna, G. (1911). *Die Herkunft der Germanen*. Würzburg: Zur Methode der Siedlungsarchäologie.
27. Kralemann, B., & Lattmann, C. (2012). Models as icons: Modeling models in the semiotic framework of Peirce's theory of signs. *Synthese, 190*, 3397–3420.
28. Kralemann, B., & Lattmann, C. (2013). The semantics of models: A semiotic philosophy of science approach. In K.-D. Schewe, & B. Thalheim, (Eds.), *Semantics in data and knowledge bases. Lecture notes in computer science* (Vol. 7693, pp. 50–69). New York: Springer.
29. Latif, M. (2015). Klimamodelle. In B. Thalheim, & I. Nissen (Eds.), *Wissenschaft und Kunst der Modellierung. Kieler Zugang zur Definition, Nutzung und Zukunft. Philosophische Analysen* (Vol. 64, pp. 281–306). Berlin: De Gruyter.
30. Lemmen, C., Gronenborn, D., & Wirtz, K. W. (2011). A simulation of the Neolithic transition in Western Eurasia. *Journal of Archaeological Science, 38*, 3459–3470.
31. Lotka, A. J. (1925). *Elements of physical biology*. Baltimore: Waverly Press.
32. Lüning, J. (1972). Zum Kulturbegriff im Neolithikum. *Prähistorische Zeitschrift, 47*, 145–173.
33. Mahr, B. (2004). *Wissen in Modellen*. KIT Report 150. Berlin: KIT.
34. Mahr, B. (2008). Ein Modell des Modellseins. Ein Beitrag zur Aufklärung des Modellbegriffs. In U. Dirks, & E. Knobloch (Eds.), *Modelle* (pp. 187–218). Lang, Frankfurt am Main.
35. Malthus, T. R. (1798). *An essay on the principle of population as it affects the future improvement of society with remarks on the speculations of Mr. Godwin, M. Condorcet and other writers*. London: Johnson.
36. Mayerle, R., & Zielke, W. (2005). Predictions of medium scale morphodynamics: Promorph project overview. *Die Kueste, 69*, 1–23.
37. Motesharrei, S., Rivas, J., & Kalnay, E. (2014). Human and nature dynamics (HANDY): Modeling inequality and use of resources in the collapse or sustainability of societies. *Ecological Economics, 101*, 90–102.
38. Nakoinz, O., & Hinz, M. (2015). Modelle in der Archäologie. In B. Thalheim, & I. Nissen (Eds.), *Wissenschaft und Kunst der Modellierung. Kieler Zugang zur Definition, Nutzung und Zukunft. Philosophische Analysen* (Vol. 64, pp. 281–306). Berlin: De Gruyter.
39. Newton, I. (1687). *Philosophiae Naturalis Principia Mathematica*. London: Societatis Regia.
40. Parker, D. C., Manson, S. M, Janssen, M. A., Hoffmann, M. J., & Deadman, P. (2003). Multi-agent systems for the simulation of land-use and land-cover change: a review. *Annals of the Association of American Geographers, 93*, 314–337.
41. Petrie, F., & W. M. (1899). Sequences in prehistoric remains. *The Journal of the Anthropological Institute of Great Britain and Ireland, 29*, 295–301.
42. Piazza, L., Lummen, T. T. A., Quin, E., Murooka, Y. Reed, B. W., Barwick, B., et al. (2015). Simultaneous observation of the quantization and the interference pattern of a plasmonic near-field. *Nature Communications*. doi:10.1038/ncomms7407
43. Popa, C. (2016). Modelling identities. *Late iron age identity in South-East Europe*. QAAM 2. New York: Springer.
44. Ravenstein, E. (1889). The laws of migration. *Journal of the Royal Statistical Society, 52*, 241–305.
45. Reilly, W.J. (1931). The law of retail gravitation. New York: Knickerbocker.
46. Stachowiak, H. (1973). *Allgemeine Modelltheorie*. Wien: Springer.

47. Stewart, J. Q. (1948). Demographic gravitation: Evidence and application. *Sociometry, 11*, 31–58.
48. Tarski, A., Mostowski, A., & Robinson, R. M. (1953). *Undecidable theories*. Amsterdam: North-Holland.
49. Thalheim, B., & Nissen, I. (2015). Ein neuer Modellbegriff. In B. Thalheim, & I. Nissen, (Eds.), *Wissenschaft und Kunst der Modellierung. Kieler Zugang zur Definition, Nutzung und Zukunft. Philosophische Analysen* (Vol. 64, pp. 491–547). Berlin: De Gruyter.
50. Thrusfield, M. (1995). *Veterinary epidemiology*. Hoboken: Wiley-Blackwell.
51. Thünen, J. H. v.: *Der isolirte Staat in Beziehung auf Landwirtschaft und Nationalökonomie*. Berlin: Wiegand, Hempel und Parey.
52. Tobler W. (1970). A computer movie simulating urban growth in the Detroit region. *Economic Geography, 46*(2), 234–240.
53. Traulsen, I. (2015). Modellierung von Tierseuchen. In B. Thalheim, & I. Nissen, (Eds.), *Wissenschaft und Kunst der Modellierung. Kieler Zugang zur Definition, Nutzung und Zukunft. Philosophische Analysen* (Vol. 64, pp. 475–488). Berlin: De Gruyter.
54. Velten, K. (2009). *Mathematical modeling and simulation*. Weinheim: VLC.
55. Volterra, V. (1926). Variazioni e fluttuazioni del numero dindividui in specie animali conviventi. *Mem. Acad. Lincei Roma, 2*, 31–113.
56. Weber, M. (1904). *Die Objektivität sozialwissenschaftlicher und sozialpolitischer Erkenntnis*. Tübingen: J.C.B. Mohr.
57. Zubrow, E. B. W. (1975). Prehistoric carrying capacity: A model. Menlo Park: Cummings Publishing.

Chapter 3
Software

3.1 Working with Command-Line Programs

Since this is an introduction to the basic ideas of modelling, we are bound to use flexible yet simple software. Software with a scripting language offers the most flexibility. Among several suitable software packages, R has the most simple language and the largest repository of ready-to-use algorithms. Although there are some graphical user interfaces, we will use the command-line approach, since this approach allows using the full power of R and is not restricted by the interface, which is sometimes seen as disadvantage. In fact, it has some important advantages; for instance, we have already mentioned that it provides access to the full power of R, allows a very efficient and flexible working process and is a perfect tool for didactic purposes. However, for an effective usage, one has to be familiar with some basic concepts and rules. We begin this chapter with these concepts to provide the reader a seamless start with R.

Sometimes it is assumed that working with command-line programs involves remembering commands, typing commands into the console and obtaining results. While this is possible, it contradicts scientific principles. The results are not reproducible because there is no exact documentation of the analysis. A better concept is to use scripts, which offer many advantages:

- Scripts are an exact documentation of the work.
- Scripts allow reproducing the analysis.
- Scripts allow reusing commands, algorithms and whole analyses.
- Scripts allow sharing code because it is very easy to hand a text file to colleagues.
- Scripts allow the automation of complex analyses.
- Scripts allow the automation of report generation; for instance, in R with the packages `knitr` or `sweave`.

O. Nakoinz, D. Knitter, *Modelling Human Behaviour in Landscapes*, Quantitative Archaeology and Archaeological Modelling, DOI 10.1007/978-3-319-29538-1_3

- Scripts allow rerunning and testing code snippets.
- Scripts make it easy to create complex solutions.
- Scripts allow limiting the active knowledge of the researcher to the most important aspects.

One should obey some rules to maximise the advantages of scripts. These rules require slightly more effort while applying them but result in much less work later. Anyone who has experienced working with old scripts that do not apply these rules knows how time-consuming and frustrating this can be.

- Each analysis has its own script.
- Each script has a header containing important information such as title, topic, purpose, author, date, etc.
- For each command, you should learn the usage only once. Supplement the command with comments so that you can re-use the command for similar purposes without reading the manual again. Copy, paste and adapt the commands from old scripts.
- Use standardised names and denotations to ease the re-use of code.
- Use detailed comments to understand your analysis years later.
- Use a proper structuration of the script to ease the reading of the script. Use indentation, headers and comments according to your style guide.
- It is useful to think that you should hand over the script to a colleague with limited knowledge to optimise comments and structure.
- Use versioning of the scripts by adding a version number to the file name (-v01.xxx) or a version control system.
- Avoid special characters in file names, variable names, etc. Moreover, it is a good idea to encode the file in UTF8.
- Use a convenient yet standardised folder structure for scripts, data, results and reports.

3.2 R

3.2.1 What Is R?

At present, `R` [1–4, 6, 8, 10–12] is the leading statistic software package. `R` is the free and open source implementation of `S`, which was developed by John Chambers, Rick Becker and Allan Wilks in 1976 and aimed to be a unified statistical language. S developed to become a very useful piece of software, prompting Ross Ihaka and Robert Gentleman to start working on a free and open source alternative in 1992.

`R` comprises of three components: scripting language, core packages with basic statistical routines and additional packages. The scripting language is very flexible. It is a functional programming language with object-oriented additions. The fact that vectors are the main data structure is very convenient for statistical analysis.

Common statistical algorithms are available as ready-to-use functions in the core packages. Many additional packages on the CRAN-server provide R-users with a multitude of further algorithms. Most packages are implemented directly with R, C or Fortran.

3.2.2 *Using R*

The bare usage of R is possible with the console. As mentioned above, using a script is a much better way than typing commands in the console. Hence, in addition to the R installation with console access, we need a text editor. Notepad++ or gedit are very convenient text editors that also provide an extension connecting the text editor with R. Specialised IDEs like RStudio (http://www.rstudio.com), ESS (http://www.http://ess.r-project.org/) and TinnR (http://http://www.sciviews.org/Tinn-R/) have a little better integration of R and the script editor. Graphical user interfaces such as RKWard (http://rkward.kde.org) and Statistiklabor (http://www.http://www.statistiklabor.de/) allow executing the analysis using graphical buttons but restrict the analysis to only a few algorithms. We recommend RStudio.

Typically, the first steps using R involve exploring its capabilities as a calculator. All basic operators are available. Here are some examples. Lines starting with > are the interactive command prompt that waits for input. > or similar symbols are displayed but not inserted by the user. Lines starting with [1] or similar contents are output from R. Later we will see a + at the beginning of a line, which indicates that the text is originally in one line and broken up for the book layout. A + also occurs when a command is broken into different lines or not yet finished, e.g. due to a missing bracket.

```
> 5+3
[1] 8
> 5-3
[1] 2
> 5*3
[1] 15
> 5/3
[1] 1.666667
> 5 %% 2
[1] 2
> 5^2
[1] 25
> sqrt(25)
[1] 5
> sin(3.14)
[1] 0.001592653
> 3.14 * (180 / pi)
```

```
[1] 179.9087
> log(25)
[1] 3.218876
> log10(25)
[1] 1.39794
> abs(-23.45)
[1] 23.45
> round(2.454324,2)
[1] 2.45
> ceiling(2.5)
[1] 3
> floor(2.5)
[1] 2
```

For all scripting languages variables are an important feature. While $< -$ is the traditional way of assigning variables $=$ is also allowed nowadays.

```
> x <- 5
> x
[1] 5
> sqrt(x)
[1] 2.236068
> y = 7
> y
[1] 7
```

It also works the other way around. Think of the symbol $< -$ as an assigning symbol.

```
> 5 -> x
```

R provides different data structures, the most important of which are vectors.

```
> x <- c(3,5,2,2,5,8,5,2)
> y <- c(6,7,2,4,5,2,9,1)
> z <- seq(1:5)
> z2 <- seq(along=y)
> z3 <- rep(3,5)
> min(x)
[1] 2
> range(x)
[1] 2 8
> length(x)
[1] 8
> xs <- sort(x)
> xr <- rev(x)
> xrs <- rev(sort(x))
> xr <- sort(x, decreasing = T)
```

```
> x[4]
[1] 2
> x[c(2,4)]
[1] 5 2
> x[3:6]
[1] 2 2 5 8
> x[x>4]
[1] 5 5 8 5
```

Vectors can be combined to data frames and matrices. A data frame is something like a table with row and column names, while a matrix is a multi-dimensional mathematical structure.

```
> df <- data.frame(x,y)
> df$x
[1] 3 5 2 2 5 8 5 2
> df[,1]
[1] 3 5 2 2 5 8 5 2
> df[1,]
  x y
1 3 6
> which(x == 2)
[1] 3 4 8
> z <- seq(5:77)
> z <- seq(along=x)
> zx <- matrix(x,2,4)
> zy <- matrix(y,2,4)
> zx+zy
     [,1] [,2] [,3] [,4]
[1,]    9    4   10   14
[2,]   12    6   10    3
```

Using R means applying functions in most cases. The function name is followed by the parameters in round brackets. The result of functions can be assigned to a variable in most cases.

```
> sum(x)
[1] 32
> m <- mean(x)
> m
[1] 4
> sd(x)
[1] 2.13809
> quantile(x)
  0%  25%  50%  75% 100%
   2    2    4    5    8
```

New functions can easily be defined. Like the >-symbol, the + at the beginning of the lines is not part of the code; rather this symbol indicates that the command continues in the line starting with +.

```
> f1 <- function(x1,x2){
+       y <- (x + y) / 2
+       return(y)}
> f1(3,7)
[1] 4.5 6.0 2.0 3.0 5.0 5.0 7.0 1.5
```

Control structures allow more complex algorithms. The basic control structures known from programming languages are implemented in R. Here are some examples:

```
> if(4==7) {z <- 27} else {z <- 3}
> z
[1] 3
> for(i in seq(1:5)){z=z+4}
> z
[1] 23
```

Tools to support the development process are very helpful. You should use these functions very frequently. The function `help()` calls the manpage for the function, which is passed as an argument. A shorter form that does the same is `?`. While `?` searches for help content of a known function from a loaded package, `??` can be used to search for a pattern or functions in all installed packages. The content of the workspace can be shown using `ls()`. The internal structure of an object can be revealed by `str()`, while `summary()` provides the main information. We strongly recommend the extensive usage of these functions.

```
> help(sin)
> ?sin
> ls()
 [1] "df"  "f1"   "i"   "m"   "x"  "xr"  "xrs"  "xs"
[10]  "y"   "z"   "z2"   "z3"   "zx"   "zy"
> str(x)
 num [1:8] 3 5 2 2 5 8 5 2
> str(m)
 num 4
> summary(x)
   Min. 1st Qu.  Median    Mean 3rd Qu.    Max.
      2       2       4       4       5       8
```

A strong advantage of R is the very flexible graphic system. Some functions to produce graphics are given below (Fig. 3.1). Try the following commands.

```
> plot(x)
> barplot(x)
> hist(x)
```

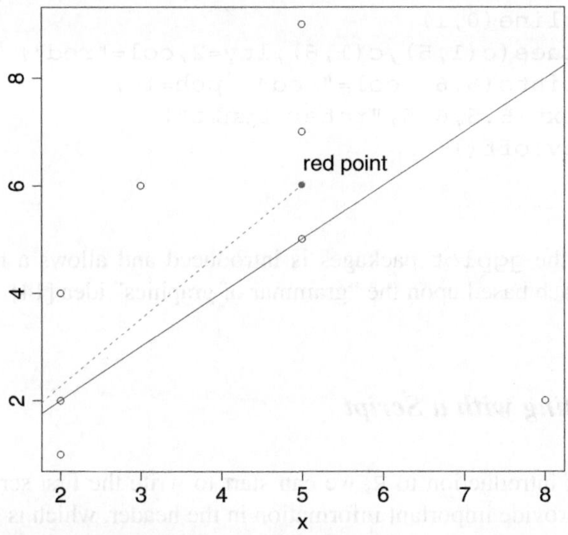

Fig. 3.1 Result of the last code chunk

```
> hist(y)
> plot(x,y)
> abline(0,1)
> lines(c(1,5),c(1,6),lty=2,col="red")
> points(5,6, col="red", pch=16)
> text(5.5,6.5,"red point")
```

Graphic commands produce results on the screen. To export graphics, special devices are available. After opening the device, the plots do not appear on the screen but are exported to a file. Finally, the device needs to be closed. The "+" indicates that the command continues in the next line.

```
> postscript("test.eps", paper="special", height=6,
+   width=6, onefile=F, horizontal=F)
>       plot(x,y)
>       abline(0,1)
>       lines(c(1,5),c(1,6),lty=2,col="red")
>       points(5,6, col="red", pch=16)
>       text(5.5,6.5,"roter Punkt")
>       dev.off()

pdf
  2

> png("test.png", height=10, width=10, units="cm",
+   res=300, bg = "white")
>       plot(x,y)
```

```
>       abline(0,1)
>       lines(c(1,5),c(1,6),lty=2,col="red")
>       points(5,6, col="red", pch=16)
>       text(5.5,6.5,"roter Punkt")
>       dev.off()
pdf
  2
```

In Chap. 6 the ggplot packages is introduced and allows a more elaborated plotting approach based upon the "grammar of graphics" idea [14].

3.2.3 *Starting with a Script*

After the brief introduction to R, we can start to write the first script. One should remember to provide important information in the header, which is realised as a list of comments where the comment sign is the first character in each row.

```
> ################################################
> ## Didactic R-Script for Modelling Summer School
> ## ============================================
> ## Project: GSHDL/TOPOI Modelling Summer School
> ## Author: Oliver Nakoinz & Daniel Knitter
> ## Version: 06
> ## Date of last changes: 03.05.2015
> ## Data: srtm, monuments
> ## Author of data: gshdl
> ## Purpose: didactic
> ## Content: 1. preparation, 2. data import, ...
> ## Description: The script include ...
> ## Licence data: -
> ## Licence Script: GPL
> ##     (http://www.gnu.org/licenses/gpl-3.0.html)
> ################################################
```

Before we fill the script with commands we have to define a style guide. Some style guides are available, for instance: http://google-styleguide.googlecode.com/svn/trunk/google-r-style.html and http://stat405.had.co.nz/r-style.html or http://www.r-bloggers.com/r-style-guide/. It does not matter which style guide one uses, but it is important to be consistent. Here are some examples of points in a style guide:

- Use short meaningful names
- To combine parts of the name, you can use points, hyphens or underscores. It does not matter which symbol you use, but use the same symbol every time.
- Limit the line length to 80 characters.

- Use spaces before and after operators like +, =, >.
- Try to align similar parts in different rows. You can insert as many spaces as you like.
- Curly braces never start in their own line but end in their own line.
- Use four spaces for indentation.
- Use <- for assignment.
- Use comments in a consistent way.

The first thing we have to do in the script is to define a working directory. Within the working directory, you can use different folders. We define a variable with the path to the working directory and subsequently set the working directory. The reader has to adapt the path to the own system. On a Linux system, the variable could be

```
> wd <- "/home/xxx/qaam1/modproj"
> setwd(wd)
```

and alternatively for Windows:

```
> wd <- "D:\\xxx\\qaam1\\modproj"
> setwd(wd)
```

Sometimes, it is a good idea to use some sub-folders in the project folder. We are using the following:

- 1data
- 2geodata
- 3script
- 4ws
- 5result
- 6pictures
- 7report

Content in folder "2geodata" can be accessed with "./2geodata/xxx"

Now we should define variables with the main file names. "meg..." are the megalithic tombs, "tum..." the tumuli. "coast..." is a shapefile with coastlines. For the coastline, we try two versions: one with and one without file extension. "dw_gk3_50_ag.asc" are the SRTM-data [7, 9] re-sampled to a 50 m grid and transformed to the local coordinate system. The last file contains the foundation of villages as Excel file.

```
> file_meg    <- "1data/meg_dw.csv"
> file_tum    <- "1data/tum_dw.csv"
> file_coast1 <- "2geodata/coast_gk3.shp"
> file_coast  <- "coast_gk3"
> file_srtm   <- "2geodata/dw_gk3_50_ag.asc"
> file_vil    <- "1data/villages.xls"
```

For the work with spatial data, we should define a coordinate reference system (crs). Geographical coordinate systems are not trivial. Latitude, Longitude and

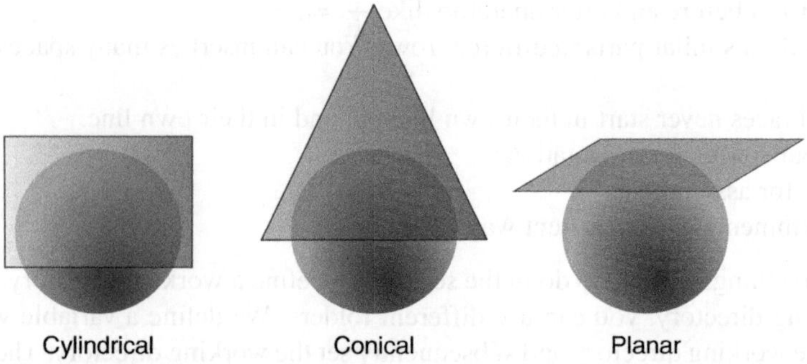

Fig. 3.2 Three basic geodesic projection types

Altitude allow giving a reference to every location on earth, although there are two problems: First, how can you define the exact position of the coordinate system? Second, how can we map the three-dimensional information in two dimensions? A solution for the first problem is to choose a reference ellipsoid that is defined by origin and orientation. Subsequently, this ellipsoid has to be anchored by some base points. This system is called geodetic datum, a well-known example of which is WGS84. The solution for the second problem is to define a projection from 3d to 2d. Imagine a simple sheet of paper or cones and cylinders formed from plain sheets of paper near a globe or rather an ellipsoid (Fig. 3.2). The principle of projection can be imagined by a beam of light, originated in the centre of the globe. The beam connects a point on the globe to a point on the paper and hence maps a point on a three-dimensional object on a two-dimensional sheet of paper. These solutions usually work well for a certain area but are not useful for other areas. Hence, in practice, geographical reference systems such as UTM use adapted projections for different zones.

There are many different geodetic datums and projections in use. The `proj4` package—which connects to the proj4 library—handles this information and uses specific text strings to characterise coordinate reference systems. In the following example of such a crs-string, the command is too long for the page. Accordingly, we put the second part of the command in a second line.

```
> crs1 <- "+proj=tmerc +lat_0=0 +lon_0=9 +k=1
+   +x_0=3500000 +y_0=0 +ellps=bessel +towgs84=598.1,
+   73.7,418.2,0.202,0.045,-2.455,6.7 +units=m +no_defs"
> crs2 <- "+proj=longlat +ellps=WGS84 +datum=WGS84
+   +no_defs"
```

Here, we have two different csr. The second one—`crs2`—features unprojected lat/long coordinates with the Bessel geodetic datum. The first one is a projected one, which also uses the WGS84 geodetic datum. Here, a transverse Mercator projection is used. The *x*-coordinate is shifted by 3,500,000 m to obtain positive values in the whole zone. The central meridian is 9 (indicated by the 3 in the *x*-shift) and the scaling factor k is 1. In addition, the map units and some transformation information is provided. It is possible to write this string by hand, although it is usually more convenient to query the EPSG database with the package rgdal or copy the values from web services like http://spatialreferences.org. The EPSG database is a widely used compilation of information concerning almost 4000 csr definitions and it offers an id for each csr.

The next step is to define some constants and variables used in the analysis. The idea is that one can run the whole analysis with a different set of parameters simply by modifying this section in the script. Thus far, we have no constants and variables, so we will skip this part for the moment.

What we have to do is load additional software components that are available via packages. Here, we only provide a few examples because we do not know which packages are needed before working on the concepts and the theory. The command install. packages('xxx') installs a package from the internet or a local source. library(xxx) loads an already-installed package.

```
> install.packages('sp')
> library(sp)
> library(proj4)
> library(rgdal)
> library(spatstat)
> library(RSQLite)
> library(gdata)
```

Please find out what we can do with these packages.

The last step in our preparation section is to load some data. Spatial data belong to two categories: points, lines and polygons are categorised as vector data, whereas grid or raster data are something like an image. For every point in a regular grid, a value is provided. Among the many available formats, we will use csv tables, Excel files, shape files and ascii raster files. The csv import is very simple.

```
> df_meg <- read.table(file_meg, sep=';', header=TRUE)
> df_tum <- read.table(file_tum, sep=';', header=TRUE)
```

If we want to conduct spatial analysis, we have to produce a SpatialPointsData Frame [2, 3]. The system needs information about the coordinates, which is provided by the coordinates command from the sp package. Here, *x* and *y* are identified as the variables with coordinates.

```
> spdf_meg <- read.table(file_meg, sep=';',
+   header=TRUE)
> spdf_tum <- read.table(file_tum, sep=';',
+   header=TRUE)
> coordinates(spdf_meg)=~x+y
> coordinates(spdf_tum)=~x+y
```

The shape file import is a little difficult if you use an internal folder structure due to the multi-file structure of a shape file. Please compare the two import commands.

The comment indicates some problems with the first variant, whereas the second version defines a path, that is used for shape files. This path is used to open the file with the readOGR command, which uses the OGR library to read spatial data.

```
> #coast <- readOGR(arbverz, p4s=NULL, file_coast1)
> avs <- paste(arbverz,"/2geodata",sep="")
> coast <- readOGR(avs, p4s=NULL, file_coast)

OGR data source with driver: ESRI Shapefile
Source: "/home/fon/daten/lehre/ss2013/mod/modproj/
    2geodata", layer: "coast_gk3"
with 20 features and 5 fields
Feature type: wkbPolygon with 2 dimensions
```

For the import of Excel files, there are several concepts and functions all relying on non-base libraries. In this case, we also have to produce a SpatialPointsDataFrame to enable spatial analysis.

```
> df_vil_wgs84 <- read.xls(file_vil, 1)
> spdf_vil_wgs84 <- df_vil_wgs84
> coordinates(spdf_vil_wgs84)=~x+y
```

The digital terrain model is available as an ascii raster file. We can use a specialised function for the import, which produces a SpatialGridDataFrame.

```
> sgdf_srtm <- read.asciigrid(file_srtm)
```

Having shown the access of elements in vectors, data frames and matrices above, now we try to access coordinates in spatial objects.

```
> spdf_vil_wgs84@coords[,1]
 [1]  9.974427  9.855466 10.165958 10.126798
 [5]  9.951253 10.054271 10.164521 9.906342
 [9]  10.059958  9.995842 10.102165 10.078712
 [13]  10.159854
> spdf_vil_wgs84@coords[,"x"]
 [1]  9.974427  9.855466 10.165958 10.126798
 [5]   9.951253 10.054271 10.164521  9.906342
 [9]   10.059958  9.995842 10.102165 10.078712
 [13]   10.159854
> spdf_vil_wgs84@coords[,2]
 [1] 54.40829 54.40040 54.41925 54.42469 54.34823
 [6]  54.47711 54.45785 54.38614 54.41003 54.36086
 [11]  54.37465 54.38088 54.40968
```

Unfortunately, we have different crs for the imported data. Most data were given as projected Gauss–Krueger zone 3 coordinates. The villages have unprojected WGS84 coordinates. Now we project the coordinates, which we extract from the spatial object. Subsequently, we produce a data frame with the new coordinates and the attached information and generate a SpatialPointsDataFrame:

```
> df_vil_coord <- project(cbind(spdf_vil_wgs84
 @coords[,1]
+    , spdf_vil_wgs84@coords[,2]), crs1)
> df_vil_k <- cbind(x=df_vil_coord[,1],
+  y=df_vil_coord[,2])
> df_vil <- data.frame(id=df_vil_wgs84[,1], villa
+   ge=as.character(df_vil_wgs84[,2]),
+    AD=df_vil_wgs84[,3])
> spdf_vil <- SpatialPointsDataFrame(df_vil_k, as.
+   data.frame(df_vil),
+   proj4string=CRS(as.character(crs1)))
```

Another approach would be to use the spTransform command to project the coordinate's information from one variable to a different crs. If you look at the structure of coast and spdf_vil, you will see that the crs is stored in the spatial object. This information is not available in the objects spdf_meg, spdf_tum and sgdf_srtm. We can add the crs to the objects.

```
> proj4string(spdf_meg)   <- CRS(as.character(crs1))
> proj4string(spdf_tum)   <- CRS(as.character(crs1))
> proj4string(sgdf_srtm)  <- CRS(as.character(crs1))
```

Finally, we should produce point pattern objects that we use in later analysis. First, the bounding box is extracted and used to define a window of the area of interest. Subsequently, duplicates are removed and the point pattern object is generated with the ppp command ([1] from the spatstat package).

```
> bb = bbox(sgdf_srtm)
> win <- owin(xrange=c(bb[1,1],bb[1,2]), yrange=c(
+   bb[2,1],bb[2,2]), unitname="m")
> spdf_meg <-remove.duplicates(spdf_meg, zero=0,
+   remove.second=TRUE)
> spdf_tum <-remove.duplicates(spdf_tum, zero=0,
+   remove.second=TRUE)
> spdf_vil <-remove.duplicates(spdf_vil, zero=0,
+   remove.second=TRUE)
> ppp_meg <- ppp(spdf_meg@coords[,1], spdf_meg@coo
+   rds[,2], window=win)
> ppp_tum <- ppp(spdf_tum@coords[,1], spdf_tum@coo
+   rds[,2], window=win)
> ppp_vil <- ppp(spdf_vil@coords[,1], spdf_vil@coo
+   rds[,2], window=win)
```

There are several solutions for plotting geographical maps. The package GISTools provides some GIS functionality for R. The package ggplot (see Chap. 5) offers a certain plotting environment, which is also applicable for spatial data. In the sp package, there is a generic plotting and image command and a special spplot command. The raster package—which provides functions for raster objects—has also a generic plotting command. We use sp and raster as an example. The first step is to prepare the hill-shade layer and a topographical colour ramp:

```
> library(raster)
> srtm_slope  <- terrain(raster(sgdf_srtm), opt='slope')
> srtm_aspect <- terrain(raster(sgdf_srtm), opt='aspect')
> srtm_shade  <- hillShade(srtm_slope, srtm_aspect, 40,
+   270)
> top.colors = colorRampPalette(c("#618CB5", "#23B0EE",
+   "#81BB7C", "#E5CE98", "#B89E83", "#9E5D4C"), bias=1.2)
```

Subsequently, the different components of the map are plotted step by step (Fig. 3.3). The generic plotting command uses a raster object and the prepared colour ramp as arguments. The raster object is produced in line with the raster command from a SpatialGridDataFrame. For the hill-shade, a semi-transparent grey colour ramp is used. Rather than the real coast line, we use the 0.2 m contour line. Although the contemporary relief is used with modern elements like the Kiel channel, the line is more adapted to the relief than the real coast line. Thereafter, the tumuli, megaliths and villages are inserted as point symbols with different colours and a legend. A scale bar and some text complete the map.

```
> par(mai = c(0, 0, 0, 0.2), mar = c(0, 0, 0, 0.2))
> plot(raster(sgdf_srtm), col = top.colors(25))
> plot(srtm_shade, col=grey(seq(from=0,to=1,by=0.02),
+   alpha=0.60), legend=FALSE, add=TRUE,  cex=0.8)
> contour(raster(sgdf_srtm), levels=c(0.2), labcex=0.001,
+   cex=1, add=TRUE)
> points(spdf_tum,pch = 19, cex = 0.4, col = "#D0043A")
> points(spdf_meg,pch = 17, cex = 0.5, col = "#074A9D")
> points(spdf_vil,pch = 15, cex = 0.8, col = "black")
> legend("bottomright", cex=0.7, legend=c("Bronze Age
+   Barrows", "Neolithic Megaliths","Mediaeval Villages"),
+   pch=c(19,17,15), col=c("#D0043A","#074A9D","black"))
> scalebar(d = 5000, cex=0.7, divs = 2, below="m", type =
+   "bar", xy=c(3573500, 6026500), label= c("0","2.5","5"),
+   adj = c(.5,-1.3))
> text(3581600, 6025000, "Altitude (m)", cex=0.8)
> text(3565000, 6039600, "Baltic Sea", cex=0.8,  font=3)
> text(3562000, 6030000, "Daenischer Wohld", cex=0.8,
   font=3)
```

3.2.4 Helpful Functions, Techniques and Packages

We have already compiled some basic functions in general and for spatial data in particular. These functions make R a powerful tool, although they represent a very small subset of its abilities. Now we will discuss some additional functions provided

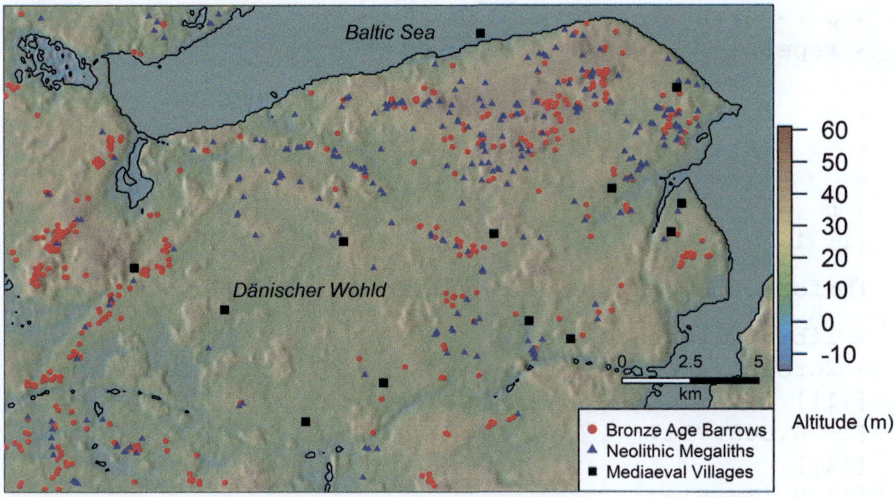

Fig. 3.3 A map of the area of interest with the monuments

by the core packages and some specialised ones. The intention of this sub-section is to offer a notion of the power of R and some concepts in R, rather than to provide a list of useful functions.

We will start this sub-section with loops. We have seen the `for` command, which applies some commands a certain number of times. Sometimes we do not know how many times we want to apply the commands, whereby a `while()` loop is useful:

```
> a <- 5; b <- 0; c <- 100; i=0
> while (i < c) {
+     b <- b + 1
+     i <- i + a
+ }
> b
[1] 20
```

This example undertakes an integer division. The number `a` fits `b` times into `c`. For this particular purpose, we can certainly find code that is more simple. However since it works, it is acceptable. Simple and efficient code is preferable but what really matters is whether the code works. This small code fragment has some other points that we could optimise. Writing several commands in one line—separated by `;`—is bad style, because it reduces the readability of the code. In this book, we will allow this sometimes to save space, although we use different assignment symbols in the same line. = works as well as `<-`, but you should use the same symbol for the same purpose. In R, `<-` is usually preferred.

Returning to the loops, we assume that we have rather complicated conditions for ending the loop. In this case, the `repeat()` loop can be used, where `break` ends the loop:

```
> a <- 6; b <- 0; c <- 100; i <- 0
> repeat{
+     b <- b + 1
+     i <- i + a
+     if (i==c | i>(c-a)) {break}
+     }
> b
[1] 16
```

The foreach package provides an alternative approach for for loops:

```
> library(foreach)
> foreach(a=c(0.05,0.24,0.3), b=1:3) %do% (sin(a) / b)
[[1]]
[1] 0.04997917
[[2]]
[1] 0.1188513
[[3]]
[1] 0.09850674
```

The foreach command allows going through all instances of one, or in our case more variables and applying certain calculations. The binary %do% operator is followed by the calculation commands, resulting in a list. We have to use a certain option to produce a vector:

```
> foreach(a=c(0.05,0.24,0.3), b=1:3,
 .combine='c') %do%
+    (sin(a) / b)
[1] 0.04997917 0.11885131 0.09850674
```

Loops in R are usually not very fast. A real advantage of using the foreach package is that parallel execution of the different steps in the loop is possible. For this purpose, we have to load the doMC package, register the number of cores and use %dopar% rather than %do%:

```
> library(doMC)
> registerDoMC(cores=4)
> foreach(a=c(0.05,0.24,0.3), .combine='c') %dopar%
+    (sin(a))
[1] 0.04997917 0.23770263 0.29552021
```

The classical R approach for repetitive computations is to use functions from the apply family. These are vectorised functions and since R is a system optimised for vectors, they are very fast. The arguments for the apply command an array like a data frame or matrix, the margin and the function that has to be applied. The margin indicates whether the function has to be applied to rows (1) or columns (2).

```
> a1 <- c(2,5,4,7,5,9,7)
> a2 <- c(1,2,3,4,5,6,7)
> a3 <- c(8,4,6,2,3,7,8)
```

```
> a  <- cbind(a1,a2,a3)
> apply(a,1,sum)
[1] 11 11 13 13 13 22 22
```

The function `lapply` can be used for lists, applies on rows and returns a list. The functions `sapply` and `vapply` are variants of `lapply` with specific default values. The function `mapply` is a multivariate version of `sapply` while `rapply` is a recursive version of `lapply`. The `apply` family—we have not presented all members—has many members specialised for certain purposes. We strongly recommend using these functions extensively due to their efficiency. In this book, we often prefer loops, since they give a better impression of the algorithm.

Now we move on to the next topic. An issue that frequently occurs is data organisation and layout. Before we can start to analyse the data, we have to tidy it [13]. This includes transposing, merging and transforming the data, filling gaps and renaming vectors. Data mainly comprises

- object labels and/or identifications;
- feature labels and/or identifications and
- values.

The objects—often called “observations”—connect the different variables at certain meaningful entities. The features, attributes or variables combine observations of the same category. The values are the actual observations or measurements. Values can be numbers, text strings, dates or boolean values. This information can be stored in objects or in relation, which are the most important data storing paradigms. The object-oriented concept stores together information belonging to the same object. An xml file is an example of this type. In statistics, relations are dominant and hence tables are frequently used. In `R`, tables are data frames, but matrices and vectors can be assumed to be a special type of tables.

`R` offers some packages and functions for tidying data. Let us first introduce an example:

```
> id <- c(1,2,3,4,5,6)
> diameter <- c(3,6,4,4,2,9)
> lengtth <- c(23,32,12,22,16,77)
> colour <- c("red","red","blue","red","blue","green")
> finds <- rbind(id,diameter,lengtth,colour)
> finds
          [,1]  [,2]  [,3]   [,4]  [,5]   [,6]
id        "1"   "2"   "3"    "4"   "5"    "6"
diameter "3"    "6"   "4"    "4"   "2"    "9"
length   "23"   "32"  "12"   "22"  "16"   "77"
colour   "red" "red" "blue" "red" "blue" "green"
```

This is a rather messy table. There is a convention to place observations in rows and variables in columns. If this is inappropriate—like in our example—we can transpose the data.frame:

```
> finds <- t(finds)
> finds
     id  diameter lengtth colour
[1,] "1" "3"      "23"    "red"
[2,] "2" "6"      "32"    "red"
[3,] "3" "4"      "12"    "blue"
[4,] "4" "4"      "22"    "red"
[5,] "5" "2"      "16"    "blue"
[6,] "6" "9"      "77"    "green"
```

Perhaps we should rename the third column:

```
> colnames(finds)[3]  <- "length"
```

The next problem is that all values are text strings. We should convert the first three columns to numbers using the `as.numeric` function. Using colour names as text is fair, but numbers indicating certain strings are also useful in some cases. R offers the data type factor that stores numbers in the data frame and displays and uses the text in functions.

```
> finds <- data.frame(id=as.numeric(finds[,1]),
+   diameter=as.numeric(finds[,2]),
+   length=as.numeric(finds[,3]), colour=factor(finds
  [,4]))
> str(finds)
'data.frame':    6 obs. of  4 variables:
$ id       : num  1 2 3 4 5 6
$ diameter: num  3 6 4 4 2 9
$ length   : num  23 32 12 22 16 77
$ colour    : Factor w/ 3 levels "blue","green",..: 3
   3 1 3
+     1 2
> finds
  id diameter length colour
1  1        3     23    red
2  2        6     32    red
3  3        4     12   blue
4  4        4     22    red
5  5        2     16   blue
6  6        9     77  green
```

Now we have the data with the layout that is useful for most analyses, although this layout is not optimal for storing data in databases. For databases, a set of rules is in use, which allows optimising the data structure for storing. The application of these rules is the normalisation of a database [5]. In a normalised database, one would avoid many columns with the same type of values. A table with an id, the variable name and the value would be preferred in a database. The `reshape` and `reshape2` packages offer a function for converting tables:

```
> library(reshape)
> finds_m <- melt(finds, id.vars="id")
> finds_m
   id variable value
1   1 diameter     3
2   2 diameter     6
3   3 diameter     4
4   4 diameter     4
5   5 diameter     2
6   6 diameter     9
7   1   length    23
8   2   length    32
9   3   length    12
10  4   length    22
11  5   length    16
12  6   length    77
13  1   colour   red
14  2   colour   red
15  3   colour  blue
16  4   colour   red
17  5   colour  blue
18  6   colour green
```

In most databases, columns with different types of data are not possible. In our case, we have to use two tables: one for numbers and one for factors:

```
> finds_m_f <- subset(finds_m, variable=="colour")
> finds_m_n <- subset(finds_m, variable=="diameter"
+ | variable=="length")
```

An inspection of the data reveals that the numerical values are stored as text because the `melt` function was forced to produce text, since a factor was involved.

```
> str(finds_m_n)
'data.frame':    12 obs. of  3 variables:
 $ id      : num  1 2 3 4 5 6 1 2 3 4 ...
 $ variable: Factor w/ 3 levels "diameter",
  "length",..:
 +  1 1 1 1 1 1 2 2 2 2 ...
 $ value   : chr  "3" "6" "4" "4" ...
```

We already know that a conversion is rather simple:

```
> finds_m_n$value <- as.numeric(finds_m_n$value)
```

A direct export from a normalised database can produce a layout similar to the one we have produced now. Here, we have multiple variables in one column, which is called a long layout. Let us try to reverse the conversion. We can convert a long layout into a wide layout with the `cast` function:

```
> finds_w_n <-cast(finds_m_n)
> finds_w_n
  id diameter length
1  1        3     23
2  2        6     32
3  3        4     12
4  4        4     22
5  5        2     16
6  6        9     77
> finds_w_f <-cast(finds_m_f)
```

Subsequently, we can merge the two data frames again:

```
> finds_w <- merge(finds_w_n, finds_w_f)
> finds_w
  id diameter length colour
1  1        3     23    red
2  2        6     32    red
3  3        4     12   blue
4  4        4     22    red
5  5        2     16   blue
6  6        9     77  green
```

The difference between wide and long data is just one aspect of comparing database data structures and statistical data structures. Both are optimised for a certain purpose and specific tools exist for both. A combination of a database and analysing framework is often useful. For instance, you can use R as a procedural language inside PostgreSQL databases. By contrast, the RPostgreSQL package provides access to the PostgreSQL database from R. Sometimes, it is also useful to use a tool from one framework in the other. People who are familiar with databases and the SQL language for querying data would prefer SQL to the R tools, which is possible. The package sqldf provides SQL for data frames:

```
> library(sqldf)
> sqldf('select diameter, length from finds_w where
   colour
+   is "red"')
  diameter length
1        3     23
2        6     32
3        4     22
```

Even joins are possible:

```
> sqldf('select id, diameter, length, colour from
   finds_w_n
+   natural join finds_w_f where colour is "blue"')
  id diameter length colour
1  3        4     12   blue
2  5        2     16   blue
```

The `data.table` packages offer an other approach for subsetting, grouping, updating and joining data. The advantage of this packages is concise and consistent syntax and fast execution.

Now we will save the workspace of the initial session.

```
> save.image("4ws/ws03.rws")
```

We can reload the workspace with

```
> load("4ws/ws03.rws")
```

Subsequently, all objects—including variables—are restored, although packages usually have to be loaded manually.

3.3 Problems

3.1. Please use the help-function for some of the functions, that are used in the R introduction.

3.2. Please calculate with R the square root of the mean number of pages of this book's chapters.

3.3. You certainly used a vector to solve the last problem. Please construct an other vector with the number of figures of each chapter and one with the chapter numbers. Combine both vectors to a data frame.

3.4. Please plot the number of pages and figures for each chapter as points and lines.

3.5. Please develop a script in which you collect all useful commands, functions and algorithms with simple examples. Use comments.

3.6. Please compare the structure of `df_meg` and `spdf_meg`. Are there differences in accessing elements of the data structure?

3.7. Please explore the spatial village's objects. Can you produce a copy of the village's point pattern object where all points are shifted 1500 m to the East? Try a vector-based approach and a loop.

3.8. Please explore functions for tidying data in the reshape, reshape2, plyr, dplyr and stats packages.

References

1. Baddeley, A., & Turner, R. (2005). Spatstat: an R package for analyzing spatial point patterns. *Journal of Statistical Software*, *12*, 1–42.
2. Bivand, R. S., Pebesma, E. J., & Gómez-Rubio, V. (2008). *Applied spatial data analysis with R*. New York: Springer.

3. Brundsdon, C., & Comber, L. (2015). *An introduction to R for spatial analysis and mapping* Los Angeles: Sage.
4. Chambers, J. M. (2008). *Software for data analysis* New York: Springer.
5. Codd, E. F. (1990). *The relational model for database management*. Reading: Addison-Wesley.
6. Everitt, B. S., & Hothorn, T. (2010). *A handbook of statistical analysis using R*. Boca Raton: Chapman & Hall.
7. Jarvis, A., Reuter, H. I., Nelson, A., & Guevara, E. (2008). *Hole-filled seamless SRTM data V4*. International Centre for Tropical Agriculture (CIAT). http://srtm.csi.cgiar.org.
8. Murrell, P. (2011). *R graphics*. Chapman & Hall/CRC the R Series, 2nd edn. Boca Raton: Chapman & Hall/CRC Press.
9. NASA (2008). SRTM 90m Digital Elevation Data from the CGIAR-CSI Consortium for Spatial Information. CGIAR Consortium for Spatial Information (CGIAR-CSI). http://srtm.csi.cgiar.org/
10. Stowell, S. (2012). *Instant R: An introduction to R for statistical analysis*. Jotunheim Publishing.
11. Teetor, P. (2011). *R cookbook*. Sebastopol: O'Reilly.
12. Venables, W. N., & Ripley, B. D. (2002). *Modern applied statistics with S*. New York: Springer.
13. Wickham, H. (2014). Tidy data. *Journal of Statistical Software*, *59*(10). doi:10.18637/jss.v059.i10
14. Wilkinson, L. (2006). *The grammar of graphics*. New York: Springer.

Chapter 4
Density

4.1 One-Dimensional Data

Usually, the first task in an investigation is to seek structure in the data, which emerges from the relations of the single elements in the data set. The most simple data set in which we may find a structure is a set of values. In R, the most basic data type is a vector that contains the values in a certain order. We assume a random order. This vector (Fig. 4.1a) represents a one-dimensional coordinate system in which we record nothing but occurrences (Fig. 4.1b). Each coordinate in the data set indicates that something is at this point. The first example does not use spatial but rather temporal coordinates, since we use the founding dates of villages. The task is to find a structure of the colonisation process modelled by the founding years of villages. At present, we do not possess other data than the founding years, whereby we can extract the years from the data frame df_vil into a vector of village foundations vil_fd.

```
> vil_fd <- df_vil[,3]
```

However, the vector naturally includes more information. The order of values indicated by the index of the values represents a second reference system of the data. In this chapter, we assume that the index of the original data is arbitrary. If we sort the values, the index becomes a meaningful parameter. At present, we ignore the index but attach another axis to the time axis, which represents the counts of points (Fig. 4.1c). In the next chapter, we will use a configuration with a meaningful index for interpolation (Fig. 4.1d). This rather confusing comment highlights that the configuration of the information in a system of coordinate systems, occurrences and derived parameters is closely connected to the research objective and the methods. Accordingly, a slight reconfiguration might have an effect on new perspectives for the analysis.

O. Nakoinz, D. Knitter, *Modelling Human Behaviour in Landscapes*, Quantitative Archaeology and Archaeological Modelling, DOI 10.1007/978-3-319-29538-1_4

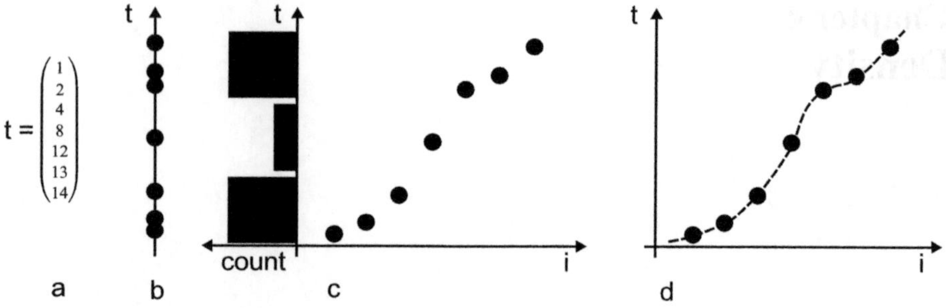

Fig. 4.1 Points and reference systems; *t*: time and *i*: index

Two pieces of information are required to describe a structure in the data. First, there is a characteristic value, which (a) describes something related to the objective of the analysis and (b) serves to discriminate different entities. It is called the "dependent variable" in statistical terminology. "How much?" is a usual category for this value. Second, there is a parameter that structures the space in which we are looking for a structure and hence allows defining the entities that carry different characteristic values. Statistically, it is called the "independent variable". This is a kind of coordinate system that depends on the perspective of the analysis.

In case of a single vector, there is not much choice: the vector or something derived from the vector has to serve as both a characteristic value and coordinate system. While this sounds strange, it is nevertheless a very common and successful approach. We will discuss three realisations of this approach.

4.1.1 Histogram

Density values or related parameters can serve as a characteristic value or dependent variable. Density is defined as the measure of *something* in a certain *amount* of space. In our example, it is the number of newly established villages in a certain time interval.

A simple timeline would be the first choice for the time axis. However, how can densities be calculated on an interval scale: namely, how many village foundations are there in which time interval? There are two solutions: we can transform the interval scale into an ordinal scale of several time intervals with certain borders, whereby we can count the village founding dates in the time intervals and assign the sum to the `id` of the time intervals, the median year or the interval name. First, we define the breaks of the intervals with the variable `cb` and prepare the variable `count` for the results. The dates are filtered in a loop through all intervals, whereby those above the lower border are stored in the variable `higher` and those below the upper border in the variable `lower`. The intersection contains only the villages found in the *i*th time interval. However, something is wrong with the code (Problem 4.2).

```
> cb <- c(1200,1250,1300,1350,1400)
> count <- 1:4
> for (i in 1:4) {
+   higher <- which(df_vil[,3] > cb[i])
+   lower  <- which(df_vil[,3] < cb[i+1])
+   hl <- intersect(higher,lower)
+   length(hl)
+   count[i] <- length(hl)
+   }
> years <- c("1200-1250","1250-1300","1300-1350",
+   "1350-1400")
> data.frame(years,count)
      years count
1 1200-1250     0
2 1250-1300     5
3 1300-1350     6
4 1350-1400     0
```

A histogram is a graphical representation of these values. The process of colonisation can be described by the number of village foundations per year, decade or century. Our code for this model is `EM-Vil-1`, which means an "empirical model for villages founding dates one". Later on, we will use "EM" for empirical models and "TM" for theoretical models. There is a built-in function in R that undertakes both the calculation and the visualisation (Fig. 4.2).

```
> hist(x = df_vil[,3], breaks = 6,
+   col = "gray", border = "white", xlab = "Time
  A.D.",
+   main = "Histogram of village foundations
+   in different periods")
```

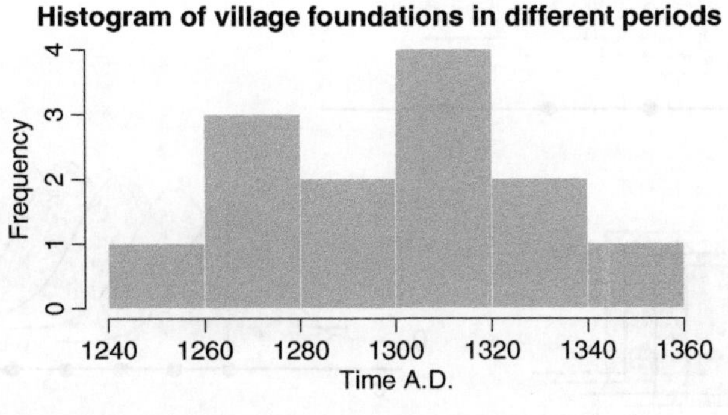

Fig. 4.2 Histogram (`EM-Vil-1`)

To obtain proper density values, we should divide the number of events in the time interval by the length of the time interval. In case of intervals with equal length, this holds minor importance if the label of the axis is correct. In case of intervals with different length, this is important because otherwise the values are not comparable.

4.1.2 Density

A certain problem with the histogram approach is the decision concerning distinct borders. The borders strongly influence the result, although we do not have any reason to draw a border between certain values. One subjective or arbitrary choice shapes the result. A solution is to replace the crisp classes by fuzzy classes in the sense of fuzzy set theory [11]. In addition, two other ideas feature this concept; namely, we might have errors and gaps in the data. In the case of errors, it can be difficult to decide to which of two crisp classes a point belongs. A fuzzy border maps this fact. Furthermore, densities can be used to predict additional points. Although fuzzy memberships are not probabilities, they allow a kind of prediction of additional points, which is more likely in high density areas than in low density areas. This concept does not correspond to the idea of crisp classes. The concepts of prediction usually involve the assumption of a continuous density values.

In case of the histogram approach, we have a rectangular membership function (see Chap. 1 and Fig. 4.3) that decides whether a village belongs to a certain interval. In the case of fuzzy classes, there is no crisp border between classes. The degree of membership decreases with increasing distance to the centre value of the class, which has several implications. The counting intervals are decoupled from the

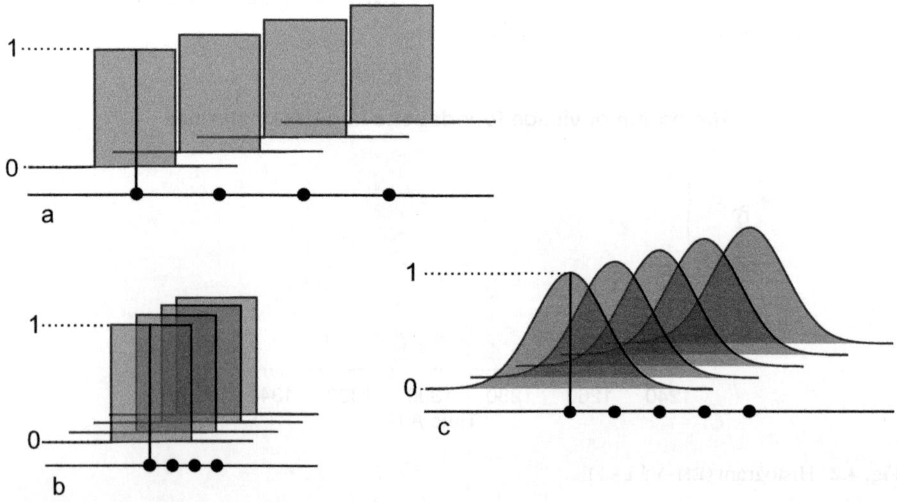

Fig. 4.3 Membership functions as moving kernels

display intervals. In Fig. 4.3a displays disjunct class ranges like in histograms, while Fig. 4.3b, c feature overlapping class ranges. Figure 4.3b shows fuzzy set membership functions of crisp yet overlapping classes, while Fig. 4.3c shows fuzzy classes.

A density value is assigned to a certain value of the independent variable, which allows us to use an interval scale and assign density values to all available years. The classes are not separated by borders and the borders of all classes are the same, namely the defined interval for the membership functions.

The shape of the membership function is called a `kernel` and the approach described above is called "kernel smoothing" or "kernel density estimation" (KDE; [6, 9, 10]). For this approach, we need to define a kernel that influences the result but not as strongly as class borders. The kernel is defined by the shape and bandwidth. A common shape type is the normal distribution density function, which is nothing but the Gaussian function or bell curve. The bandwidth is the main parameter of this function, which is the standard deviation. High bandwidth values produce more smoothed results than small values. The kernel function is applied to each point in the defined interval.

Kernel smoothing does not count the number of events but rather sums all weights of events per sample point. The kernel function assigns the weighting, whereby the events are weighted according to the distance to the point where the density is estimated. For proper density values, the integral of the kernel function has to be 1 (Fig. 4.4).

```
> library("KernSmooth")
> ks_vil <- bkde(df_vil[,3], kernel="normal",
+   bandwidth=5, gridsize=201, range.x =
+   c(1200,1400))
> plot(ks_vil, pch=20, col = "gray", xlim =
  c(1240,1360),
+   xlab = "Time A.D.", ylab = "density of
+   village foundation",
+   panel.first = grid())
> lines(ks_vil)
```

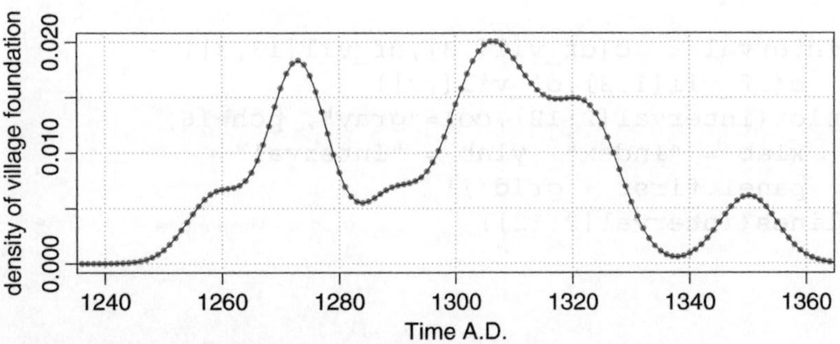

Fig. 4.4 Smoothed density of village founding dates (`EM-Vil-2`)

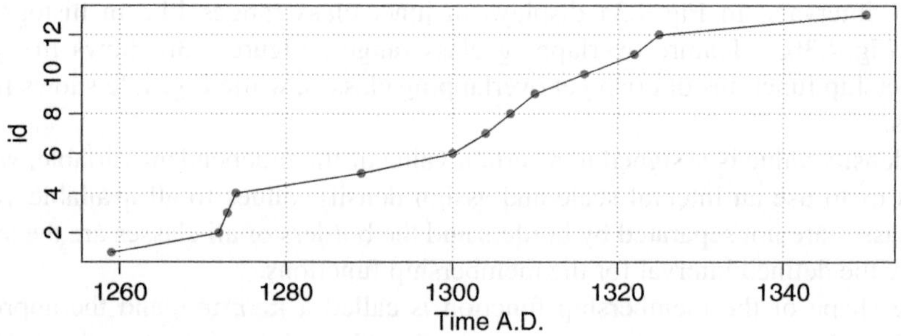

Fig. 4.5 Empirical model of village foundings (EM-Vil-3)

4.1.3 Distance Between Events

We can denote the histogram and the density approaches as *number of events concept*. Now, we come to an alternative and more straightforward concept, which we can denote as the *distance between events concept*.

Given that we have very few dates, the interval between the village foundations seems more significant than the number of events. This information is inherent in the sorted list of dates. The value that makes the connection is obviously the index of dates. We have one vector with indices and one with dates. Now, we can build a model that maps the relation between these two variables. A graphical representation of an empirical model is easy gained (Fig. 4.5).

```
> plot(df_vil[,3],df_vil[,1], col="gray", pch=16,
+   xlab = "Time A.D.", ylab = "id",
+   panel.first = grid())
> lines(df_vil[,3],df_vil[,1])
```

If the villages were founded continuously, we would obtain a straight line with a certain gradient. We can transform the data to derive a more simple model. If we consider at the intervals (Fig. 4.6), the straight line with a gradient becomes a horizontal line (gradient = 0).

```
> interval <- c(df_vil[,3],df_vil[13,3]) -
+   c(df_vil[1,3],df_vil[,3])
> plot(interval[2:12],col="gray", pch=16,
+   xlab = "Index", ylab = "Interval",
+   panel.first = grid())
> lines(interval[2:12])
```

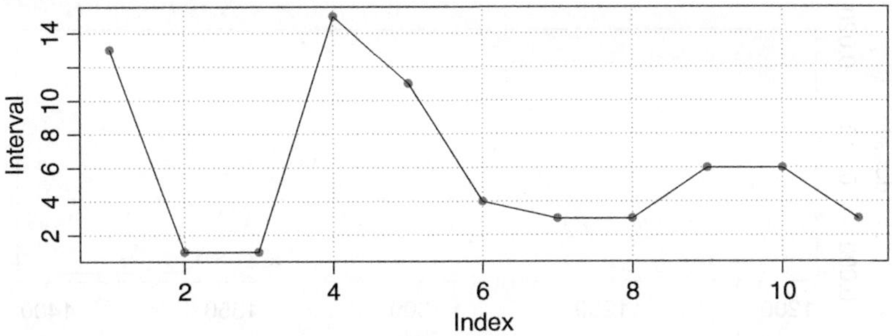

Fig. 4.6 Empirical model of village foundations using intervals between village foundations (EM-Vil-4)

Is it a truly useful concept to plot intervals or event values over an index? The index is not a proper scale and changes with additional data. If we remember ideas like the rank-size rule [12], it seems a useful concept since the index represents an internal order of the data set. Additional data may change the values, although it can preserve the structure inherent in the data.

Through the idea of founding dates at equal intervals, we have introduced a theoretical model, although the comparison shows that this theoretical model does not fit the empirical model. Other theoretical models could use the Poisson distribution or the binomial distribution, for example. We will proceed with this example in the next chapter on regression.

4.1.4 Time Series

Since we have events on a time scale, time series analysis [2–5, 10] may yield additional insights that help to understand the process of colonisation. For time series analysis, values at equal intervals are most suitable, which are exactly what we have produced with the kernel smoothing technique. Now, we can produce a ts-object representing the time series.

```
> ts_vil <- ts(ks_vil$y, start=c(1200), end=c(1400),
+   frequency = 1)
> plot(ts_vil, ylab = "density",
+   panel.first = grid())
```

The visualisation (Fig. 4.7) looks like the kernel smoothing and in fact it is the same. The difference is the internal representation in R, which is optimised for time series analysis. Among the methods of time series analysis, the analysis of second-order properties is very important. Second-order properties describe the interdependency of values at different points. If values are always similar to the previous point, it is assumed that they depend on the value of the previous point, which means they are autocorrelated. The auto-correlation is estimated by [4]:

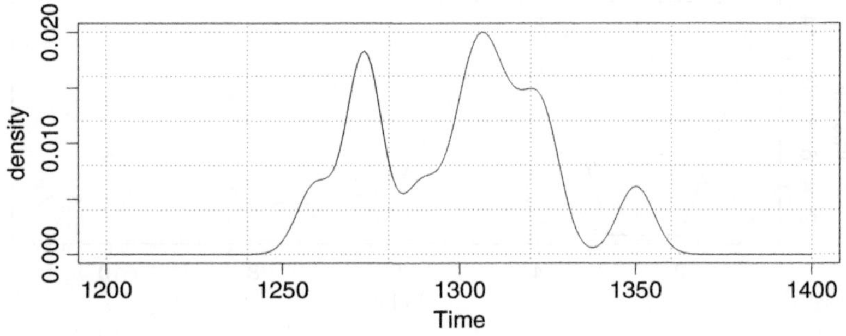

Fig. 4.7 Time series (`TS-Vil-1`)

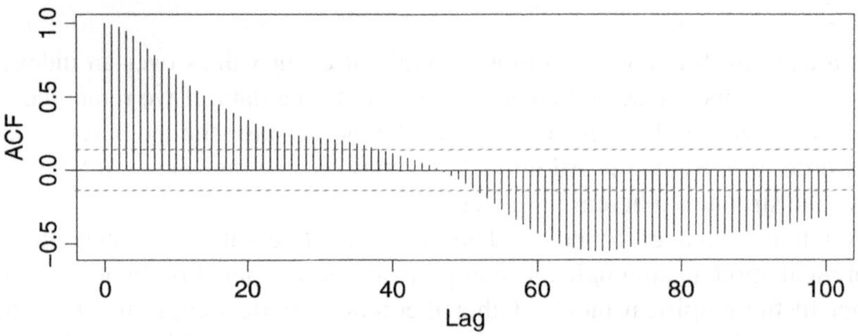

Fig. 4.8 Auto-correlation of `TS-Vil-1` calculated with `acf`

$$r_k = \frac{\sum_{i=1}^{N-k}(X_i - \bar{X})(X_{i+k} - \bar{X})}{\sum_{i=1}^{N}(X_i - \bar{X})^2} \tag{4.1}$$

In fact, this is a formula for correlation in which only one vector is used, rather than two. The function calculates the correlation of the vector with itself, or more precisely the correlation of different parts of the vector. `X` are the observations in the vector—in our case, the years when the villages were founded—while `k` is the lag, which is observed and plotted as horizontal axis in the result. The `c4acf` function computes the auto-correlation in R and plots the results (Fig. 4.8).

```
> acf(ts_vil, lag.max = 100, main = "")
```

For lower lag-values, we find a strong auto-correlation. The shape of the lag/acf-diagram shows the same shape in the left part as the Gaussian kernel that we have used. Of course, this is not by accident; rather, we have applied this kernel to produce the `ks_vil`-data. This means that we have auto-correlation in the `ks_vil`-data, but not necessary in the original `df_vil`-data.

Time series can be decomposed into a trend, a seasonal component and noise. A moving average is used to calculate a trend. Subtracting the trend from the time series leaves the seasonal component and the noise, which allows isolating certain information.

4.2 Two-Dimensional Data

Many concepts that we have applied to one-dimensional data can also be conducted on two- or three-dimensional data. We will concentrate on density calculation applied to the monuments (see Chap. 1). In general, density (d) is point-count (p) by area (a):

$$d = \frac{p}{a} \tag{4.2}$$

We can directly apply this equation to a square area as represented by the bounding box of our points and calculate the density (EM-Meg-1). A point pattern object is used, which was introduced in Chap. 3. The variable dx corresponds to the East–West extension and dy corresponds to the South–North extension of the area. The original coordinates are in metres, which would result in very small density values. Accordingly dividing by 1000 produces a result of points per square kilometre.

```
> library(spatstat)
> count <- ppp_meg$n
> dx <- (ppp_meg$window$xrange[2] -
+ ppp_meg$window$xrange[1]) / 1000
> dy <- (ppp_meg$window$yrange[2] -
+ ppp_meg$window$yrange[1]) / 1000
> density_1 <- count/ (dx*dy)
> density_1
     max
0.5212502
```

It would presumably be better to adjust the area to the spread of points (EM-Meg-2), because the points may not cover the entire bounding box. The first step is to calculate the area of the convex hull around the points.

```
> library(spatstat)
> ch <- convexhull.xy(ppp_meg$x, ppp_meg$y)
> fl <- area.owin(ch)
```

Again, we can apply the formula for density calculations, which gives a different result (see density_2). The final step is to compare the two density values by calculating the ratio. For this purpose, we have to transform density_2 to points per kilometre by multiplying by 1,000,000.

```
> fl <- area.owin(ch)
> density_2 <- count / fl
> (density_2 * 1000000) / density_1
     max
1.421855
```

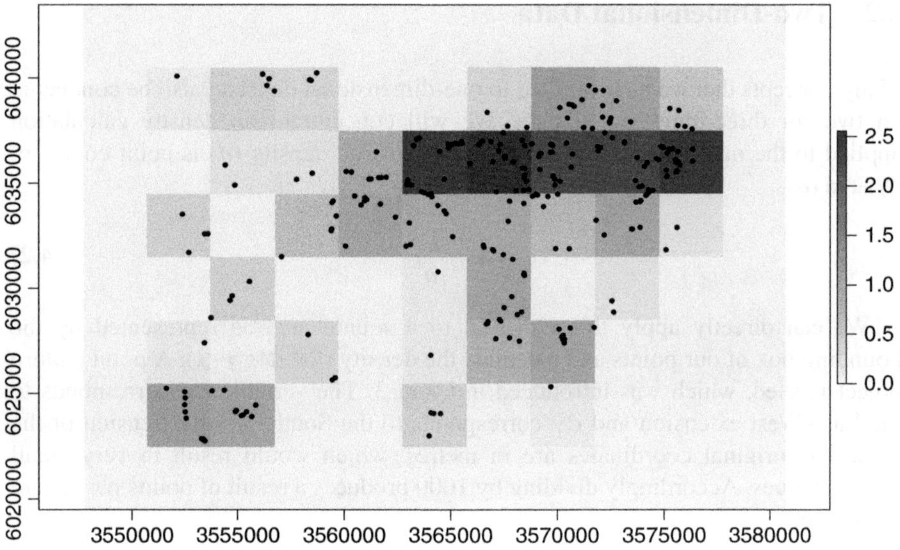

Fig. 4.9 Megaliths, density with chess board method (EM-Meg-3)

The problem is that we are interested in local variations of density rather than a single value, in most cases. A single density value might be useful for population estimation, but even then local variations are an important information. Single density values do not reveal these structures. One way to overcome this is to calculate the local density for many squares (EM-Meg-3, Fig. 4.9), similar to the histogram approach. First, we define the grid and prepare a vector containing values for all grid cells:

```
> rw      <- 3000
> xmin    <- ppp_meg$window$xrange[1] - rw/2
> xmax    <- ppp_meg$window$xrange[2] + rw/2
> ymin    <- ppp_meg$window$yrange[1] - rw/2
> ymax    <- ppp_meg$window$yrange[2] + rw/2
> rows  <- round((ymax-ymin)/rw, 0) + 1
> columns <- round((xmax-xmin)/rw, 0) + 1
> z <- cbind(1:(columns*rows))
> df <- data.frame(z)
```

We subsequently use the prepared information to generate a GridTopology-object (gt), which is a formal grid description in the sp package.

```
> gt  <- GridTopology(cellcentre.offset=
+   c(xmin,ymin), cellsize=c(rw,rw),
+   cells.dim=c(columns,rows))
> sgdf <- SpatialGridDataFrame(gt, df, proj4string
+   = CRS(as.character(crs1)))
```

In a loop, we extract the coordinates of all grid cells and look for the points that are inside. This is conducted separately for `x` and `y` coordinates, before we intersect the results and count the points. The density is calculated as the number of points by area of the grid cell.

```
> for (i in seq(along=coordinates(gt)[,1])){
+     x <- coordinates(gt)[i,1] - rw/2
+     y <- coordinates(gt)[i,2] - rw/2
+     xi <- which(ppp_meg$x>x & ppp_meg$x<x+rw)
+     yi <- which(ppp_meg$y>y & ppp_meg$y<y+rw)
+     pz <- length(intersect(xi,yi))
+     sgdf@data$z[i]<- pz / (rw/1000)^2
+     }
```

Finally, we can plot the result. The `raster package` is used to `plot` this `SpatialGridDataFrames`.

```
> library(raster)
> plot(raster(sgdf), col = gray.colors(25, start
  = 0.97,
+   end = 0.4),
+     cex.axis = .9)
> points(ppp_meg$x, ppp_meg$y, pch=20)
```

Now, we have a spatial density model that describes how many points are located in a certain area and hence the probability of the occurrence of points in this area. The first part of the last sentence describes an empirical model of the point distribution in the data, while the second part describes a calibrated theoretical model. The theoretical model allows predicting the location of additional points.

4.2.1 Kernel-Based Density

The quadrant count method has some flaws, for instance, if we want reliable density values we need large squares and thus we lose spatial resolution. However, of course, we want to have both. The first thing that we could do is separate areas for calculation and areas for visualisation in the same way as for one dimension, although we get overlapping calculation squares. Another drawback is that points in the corner of a square have the same influence as those in the middle. To overcome this, we can use the above-discussed kernel techniques, which realise the separation of areas for calculation and areas for visualisation. The method that we use is a two-dimensional kernel density estimation ("KDE"; [9]; Fig. 4.10).

```
> sgdf_kde <- sgdf
> sd       <- 3000
> for (i in seq(along=coordinates(gt)[,1])){
```

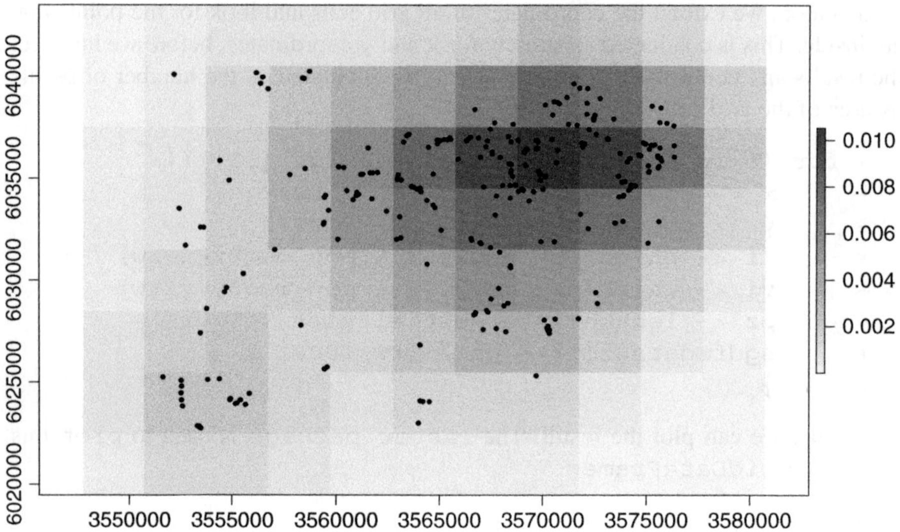

Fig. 4.10 Megaliths, KDE (EM-Meg-4)

```
+       x <- coordinates(gt)[i,1]
+       y <- coordinates(gt)[i,2]
+       g2 <- 0
+       for (j in seq(along=ppp_meg$x)){
+           distance <- sqrt((ppp_meg$x[j] - x)^2 +
+     (ppp_meg$y[j] - y)^2)
+           g1 <- dnorm(distance, mean=0, sd=sd)
+           g2 <-g2 + g1
+           }
+       sgdf_kde@data$z[i]<- g2
+       }
> plot(raster(sgdf_kde), col = gray.colors(25, start
  = 0.97,
+     end = 0.4), cex.axis = .9)
> points(ppp_meg$x, ppp_meg$y, pch=20)
```

The last code chunk is a KDE calculation without a specialised function. It makes the principle of KDE clear, although it is easier and faster to use a built-in KDE function. The function `density` provides us with a simple-to-use KDE function. We use a smaller bandwidth and a smaller cell size (Fig. 4.11). It is very instructive to compare several parameter settings. Since a detailed comparison exceeds the scope of this book, this is left to the reader.

```
> library(spatstat)
> rw <- 1000
> sd <- 2000
```

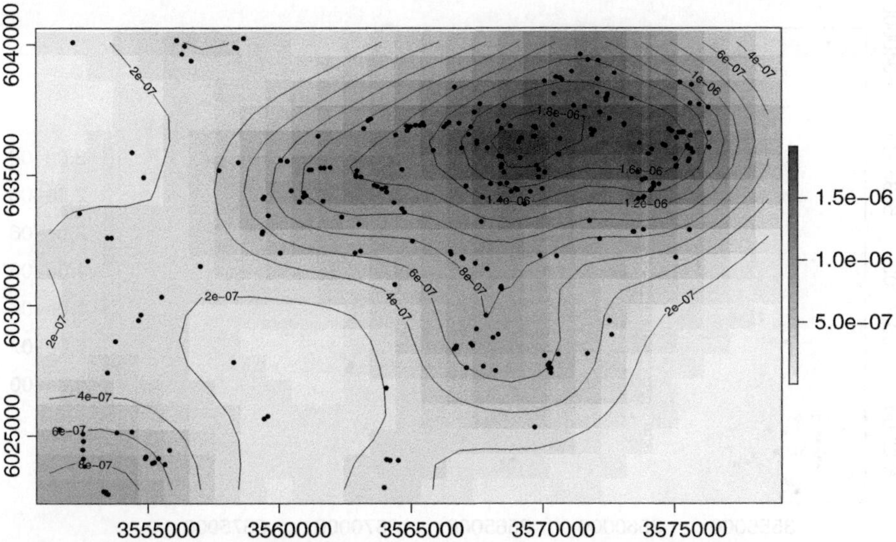

Fig. 4.11 Megaliths, KDE (EM-Meg-5)

```
> dens_p <- density(ppp_meg, sd, edge=TRUE,
+ at="points")
> dens_r5 <- density(ppp_meg, sd, eps=rw,
+   edge=TRUE, at="pixels")
> plot(raster(dens_r5), col = gray.colors(25,
+   start = 0.97, end = 0.4))
> contour(dens_r5, add=T)
> points(ppp_meg$x, ppp_meg$y, pch=20)
```

The question remains how to determine the bandwidth. The value depends on the research objective, and thus it must be discussed in each case. If you are interested in the general trend, a high value is appropriate, whereas in case you are interested in details, a small value is more suitable. There are some rules of thumb, including that it should be about three times the mean distance to the nearest neighbours and at least the distance to the nearest neighbours itself. This results in a rather detailed density model (Fig. 4.12).

```
> sdev <- 3*mean(nndist(ppp_meg))
> dens_r6 <- density(ppp_meg, sdev, eps=rw,
+   edge=TRUE, at="pixels")
> plot(raster(dens_r6), col = gray.colors(25,
+   start = 0.97, end = 0.4))
> contour(dens_r6, add=T)
> points(ppp_meg$x, ppp_meg$y, pch=20)
```

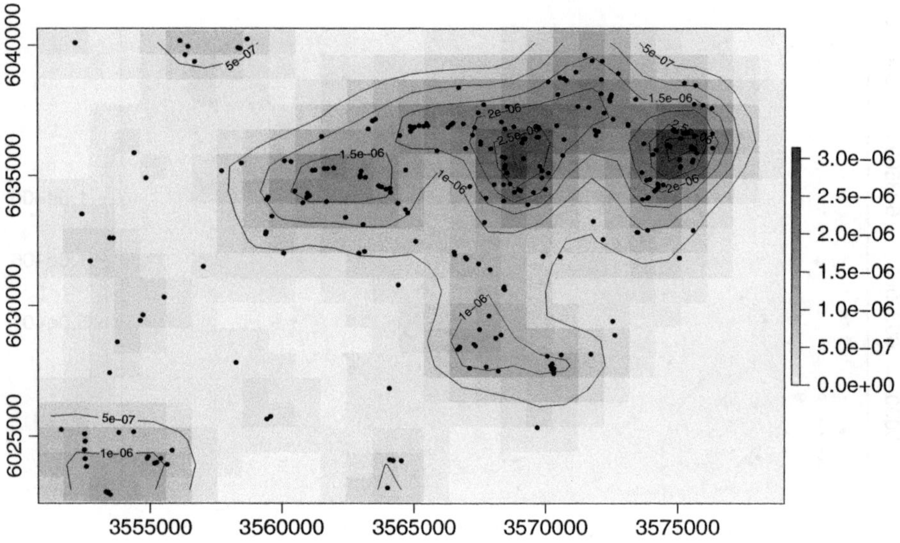

Fig. 4.12 Megaliths, KDE (`EM-Meg-6`)

A built-in function is based upon Silverman's suggestion [1]. According to the manual, "it defaults to 0.9 times the minimum of the standard deviation and the interquartile range divided by 1.34 times the sample size to the negative one-fifth power". Scott [8] suggests a factor of 1.06. This method results in a coarse density model (Fig. 4.13). It should be noted that both rules differ in definition, whereby the structure of data has an influence. Therefore, again an individual discussion is necessary in each case.

```
> dens_r <- density(ppp_meg, bw = "nrd", eps=rw,
+   edge=TRUE, at="pixels")
> plot(raster(dens_r), col = gray.colors(25,
+   start = 0.97, end = 0.4))
> contour(dens_r, add=T)
> points(ppp_meg$x, ppp_meg$y, pch=20)
```

We applied a Gaussian kernel, although many others are available [see help: `help(density)`], each with their own advantages and disadvantages. Maximal gradient, footing and shape of the top are relevant characteristics. The kernel has to fit the theoretical considerations of the research project. Although the Gaussian kernel is appropriate in most cases, it will not suffice to use a standard kernel for all purposes.

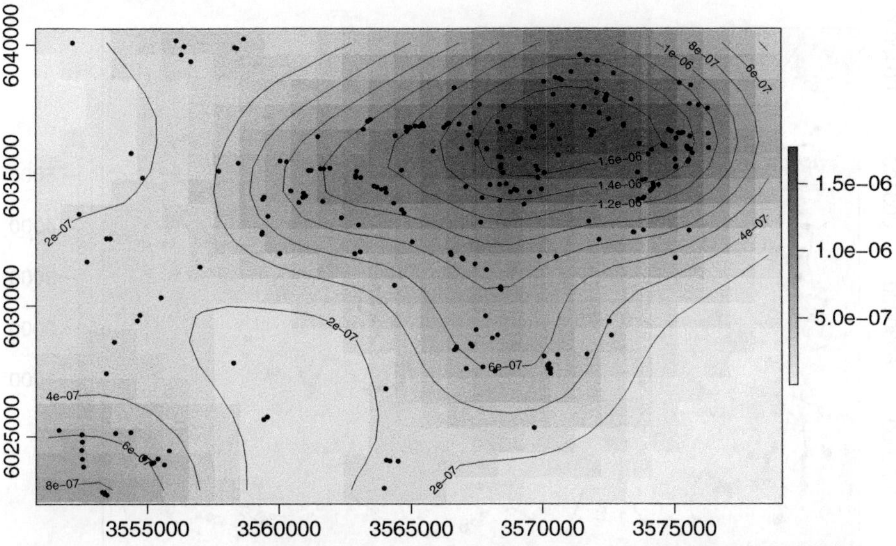

Fig. 4.13 Megaliths, KDE (EM-Meg-7)

4.2.2 Distance-Based Density

While KDE produces a smoothed density model, it does not allow investigating the general trend and details at the same time. This can be achieved with the method of the largest empty circle ("empty circle density" (ECD); [7, 13, 14]), although it is sensitive for location errors and cannot handle multiple points at the same place. The idea is that the radius of the largest empty circle in the point pattern is an inverse proxy for the local density (Fig. 4.14). We start with the preparation of a grid:

```
> rw <- 1000
> fs <- cbind(x=spdf_meg@coords[,1],
+    y=spdf_meg@coords[,2])
> rows   <- round((bbox(spdf_meg)[2,2]-
+    bbox(spdf_meg)[2,1])/rw, 0) + 2
> cols <- round((bbox(spdf_meg)[1,2]-
+    bbox(spdf_meg)[1,1])/rw, 0) + 2
> z     <- cbind(1:(rows*cols))
> df    <- data.frame(cbind(1:((round(
+   (bbox(spdf_meg)[2,2]-bbox(spdf_meg)[2,1])/rw, 0)
+    + 2)*(round((bbox(spdf_meg)[1,2]-
+    bbox(spdf_meg)[1,1])/rw, 0) + 2))))
> gt    <- GridTopology(cellcentre.offset=
+    c(bbox(spdf_meg)[1,1] - rw/2,bbox(spdf_meg)[2,1] -
+    rw/2), cellsize=c(rw,rw), cells.dim=c(cols,rows))
```

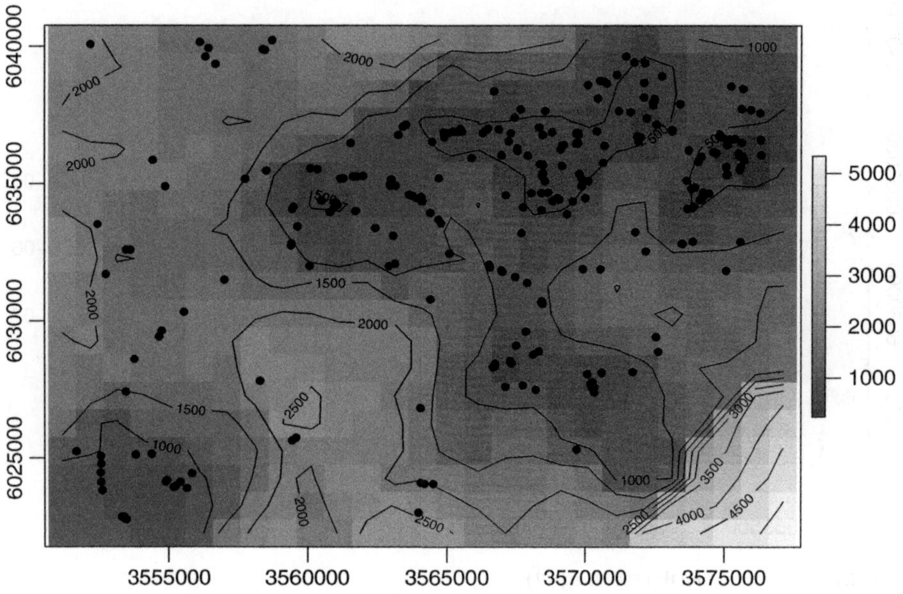

Fig. 4.14 Megaliths, empty circle as inverse proxy for density (EM-Meg-8)

```
> sgdf <- SpatialGridDataFrame(gt, df, proj4string =
+    CRS(as.character(crs1)))
```

The function voronoi.mosaic from the tripack package calculates both the centres of the largest empty circles which are the corners of the Voronoi graph and the diameter of the largest empty circles. These data are transformed to a SpatialPointsDataFrame-object.

```
> library(tripack)
> fsv   <- voronoi.mosaic(spdf_meg$x, spdf_meg$y,
+   duplicate = 'remove')
> rad <- fsv$radius
> fsvsp <- SpatialPointsDataFrame(cbind(fsv$x, fsv$y),
+   as.data.frame(rad), proj4string=
+   CRS(as.character(crs1)))
> fspv  <- ppp(fsvsp@coords[,1], fsvsp@coords[,2],
+   window=win)
> fs_vd <- cbind(fspv$x,fspv$y,nncross(fspv,ppp_meg)
  $dist)
> fs_vd_spdf <- SpatialPointsDataFrame(cbind
  (fs_vd[,1],
+   fs_vd[,2]), as.data.frame(fs_vd[,3]),
+   proj4string=CRS(as.character(crs1)))
```

We interpolate the calculated points using a kriging method from the `gstat` package (see Chap. 5). We subsequently prepare a grid that will hold the density values. Now, we have inverse proxies for the density at the location of the edges of the Voronoi graph.

```
> library(gstat)
> g <- gstat(formula=fsvsp@data$rad ~ 1, data=fsvsp,
+   nmin = 5, maxdist = 10000, nmax = 15)
> vt <- variogram(g)
> v.fit <- fit.variogram(vt, vgm(1, "Gau", 10000, 1),
+   fit.sills = TRUE, fit.ranges = TRUE,fit.method
  = 1)
> g <- gstat(g, id="var1", model=v.fit )
> k <- predict(g, model=v.fit, newdata=sgdf_srtm)
```

Finally, we need to plot the result in the already-known way:

```
> image(raster(k), col = gray.colors(25, start = 0.4,
+   end = 0.97))
> contour(k, add=T)
> points(ppp_meg$x, ppp_meg$y, pch=16, cex=0.4)
```

The methods of density estimation can be distinguished between *counting methods* and *distance-based methods*. Among the former, KDE is the best choice for most applications, whereas the empty circle method is best among the distance-based methods (Fig. 4.15).

Use KDE when:

- gaps in data or samples
- location errors
- multiple points on one position
- searching for trends

Use ECD when:

- data are complete and exact
- searching for detailed results
- needing details in low and high density areas

4.2.3 Decomposition

Finally, we try a simple decomposition of a density model. `EM-Meg-5` and `EM-Meg-6` are KDEs with different bandwidth. The coarse model can be seen as the general trend. To focus on details, we can subtract `EM-Meg-5` from `EM-Meg-6`.

```
> diff6_5 <- dens_r5
> diff6_5$v <- dens_r6$v - dens_r5$v
```

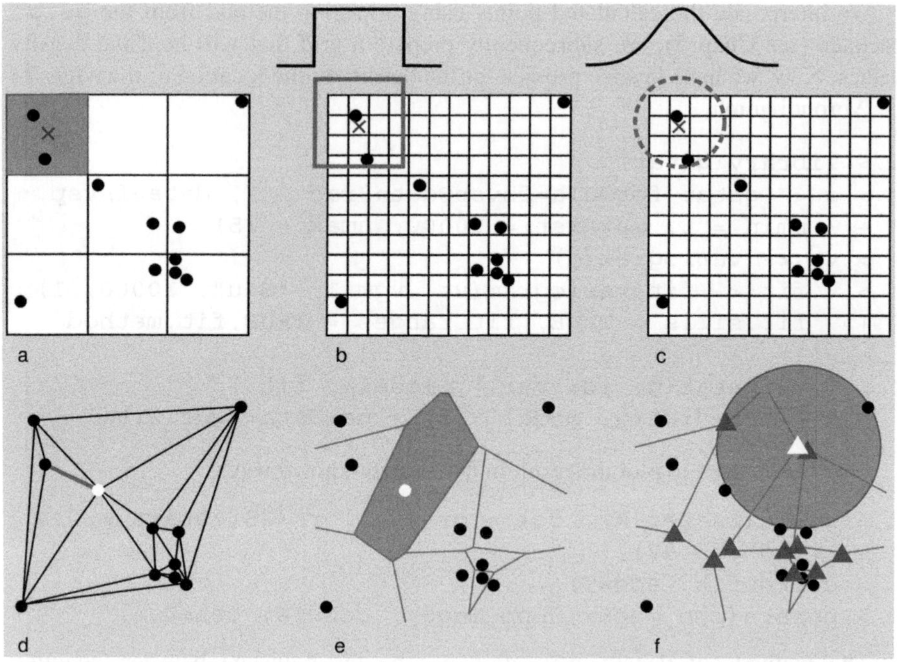

Fig. 4.15 Some methods for density estimation; (**a**)–(**c**): counting approaches; (**d**)–(**f**): distance-based approaches

It is always a good idea to save new versions of the workspace.

```
> save.image("4ws/ws04.rws")
```

4.3 Problems

4.1. Collect all words in this chapter that are related to the dependent variable and all words related to the independent variable including "event", "density", etc. Discuss the context to which these words refer. Do you have any idea why this chapter does not use consistent terminology?

4.2. Please find the mistake in the code for counting the villages for different time intervals and write a correct version of the code.

4.3. Why is `EM-Vil-1` an empirical model?

4.4. Please change the number of classes of the histogram and ascertain how to use intervals with a different length.

4.5. Which kernel types are available?

4.6. Please discuss the advantage and disadvantages of different kernels.

4.7. Under what conditions do you prefer the *number of events concept* and the *distance between events concept*?

4.8. Please explain the details in the code for manual KDE calculation.

4.9. Compare different parameters (cell size, bandwidth) for different density methods.

4.10. Compare the density maps of megaliths and Bronze Age tumuli.

4.11. Please explore the difference between `dens_p` and `dens_r`.

4.12. Which values are printed near the contour lines in `EM-Meg-8`?

References

1. Baddeley, A., & Turner, R. (2005). spatstat: An R package for analyzing spatial point patterns. *Journal of Statistical Software, 12*, 1–42.
2. Box, G. E. P., & Jenkins, G. M. (1970). *Time series analysis, forecasting and control*. San Francisco: Holden-Day.
3. Everitt, B. S., & Hothorn, T. (2010). *A handbook of statistical analysis using R*. Boca Raton: Chapman & Hall.
4. Huitema, B. E., & McKean, J. W. (1991). Autocorrelation estimation and inference with small samples. *Psychological Bulletin, 110*, 291–304.
5. Kleiber, C., & Zeileis, A. (2008). *Applied econometrics with R*. New York: Springer.
6. Parzen, E. (1962). On estimation of a probability density function and mode. *The Annals of Mathematical Statistics, 33*, 1065–1076.
7. Preparata, F. P., & Shamos, I. S. (1988). *Computational geometry. An introduction*. New York: Springer.
8. Scott, D. W. (1992). *Multivariate density estimation. Theory, practice and visualization*. New York: Wiley.
9. Silverman, B. W. (1986). *Density estimation for statistics and data analysis*. Boca Raton: Chapman & Hall/CRC.
10. Venables, W. N., & Ripley, B. D. (2002). *Modern applied statistics with S*. New York: Springer.
11. Zadeh, L. A. (1965). Fuzzy sets. *Information and Control, 8*, 338–353.
12. Zipf, G. K. (1949). *Human behavior and the principle of least effort*. Cambridge: Addison-Wesley.
13. Zimmermann, A., Richter, J., Frank, T., & Wendt, K. P. (2004). Landschaftsarchäologie II - Überlegungen zu Prinzipien einer Landschaftsarchäologie. *Ber. RGK, 85*, 37–95.
14. Zimmermann, A., Hilpert, J., & Wendt, K. P. (2009). Estimations of population density for selected periods between the Neolithic and AD 1800. In J. Steel, & S. Shennan (Eds.), *Demography and cultural macroevolution* (pp. 357–380). Special Issue Human Biology.

Chapter 5
Regression and Interpolation

5.1 Regression

Regression is the most classical type of quantitative models. Regression models occur in many different contexts, disciplines and applications. Due to the importance and wide range of applications, there are many variants and methodical details concerned with regression. In this section, we can provide no more than a very basic idea and some simple applications. Please refer to the literature on regression for more details [1, 5, 6, 9, 14].

In this section, we again use the data of village foundation. Anticipating some terminology, the year of foundation is the independent variable X and the order of founding the dependent variable E or T. In order to simplify the R-script, we will rename the two vectors in this chapter.

```
> library(gdata)
> file_vil <- "1data/villages.xls"
> df_vil <- read.xls(file_vil)
> X <- df_vil[,3]
> E_vil <- df_vil[,1]
```

5.1.1 The Concept of Regression

Variables that depend on each other are much more exciting and instructive for researchers than completely independent variables. The dependence of two variables and even the degree of dependence can be established with correlation tests, the most prominent of which is the Pearson correlation:

O. Nakoinz, D. Knitter, *Modelling Human Behaviour in Landscapes*, Quantitative Archaeology and Archaeological Modelling, DOI 10.1007/978-3-319-29538-1_5

$$\rho_{X,Y} = \frac{\text{cov}(X,Y)}{\sigma_X \sigma_Y} \tag{5.1}$$

with

$$\text{cov}(X,Y) = E[(X - \mu_X)(Y - \mu_Y)] \tag{5.2}$$

where X and Y are vectors of two variables, μ the mean, σ the standard deviation, ρ the correlation coefficient and E the expectation.

```
> cor(cbind(X,E_vil), method="pearson")
              X     E_vil
X     1.0000000 0.9782945
E_vil 0.9782945 1.0000000
```

Naturally, we find a correlation. Nonetheless, how does the dependent variable depend on the independent variable? This is the key question, which is solved by the method of regression based upon some data. This data are points in space, induced by the independent and dependent variable. In other words, regression is a method to construct a theoretical model that maps the relationship of an independent and a dependent variable and fits it to the empirical model.

Definition 5.1. Regression is a mathematical mapping of the relationship of two correlated variables.

The relationship between the variables is modelled by a function that assigns a value to the dependent variable for each value of the independent variable. The general idea is that the regression function has to be as close as possible to the data points. The regression process comprises of two steps: first, we have to decide upon a regression model that defines the general shape of the regression curve, such as a kind of linear or non-linear model; and second, we have to find the coefficients of the regression function that produce the best fit. For the second step, the least square method was developed by Legendre and Gauss as an algorithm that minimises the sum of the squares of the residues S. The residues r are the difference between data points and the regression curve:

$$S = \sum_{i=1}^{n} r_i^2 \tag{5.3}$$

The maximum likelihood method is a similar approach that offers some advantages but requires assuming a certain distribution.

The first step is much more difficult than the second one. The choice of the regression model depends on the theory about the data, as well as on the data itself. Restricting the regression models based upon theory and trying some regression models based upon experience seems to be a good approach.

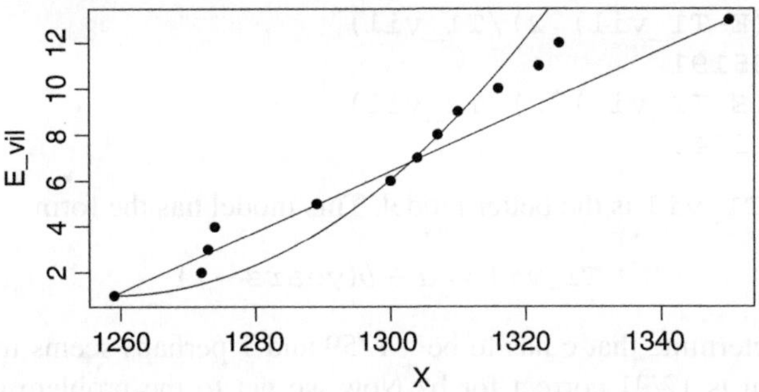

Fig. 5.1 Theoretical models of village foundations (T1_vil and T2_vil)

5.1.2 Linear Models

Now we apply regression to the village foundation data. Our first and very primitive theoretical model (T1_vil) is a straight line between the first and last point (Fig. 5.1). The second model is a quadratic function (T2_vil), which begins in the first point (Fig. 5.1). Although a quadratic function is not linear fitting, a quadratic function or a polynomial is considered a linear regression problem.

```
> plot(X,E_vil,col="black", pch=16)
> lines(c(df_vil[1,3],df_vil[13,3]),c(df_vil[1,1],
+   df_vil[13,1]) )
> years <- 1259:1350
> y <- 1 + 0.003* (years-1259)^2
> lines (years,y)
```

Our first comparison method is the autopsy. Both models are not very good but which is the better one? It is difficult to say. In the middle part T2_vil is very good but for all points T1_vil seems better. We have to find a measure for the quality of the model fit. The goodness of fit can be measured with the classical Chi Square test. T are values in the theoretical model and E values in the empirical model.

$$\chi^2 = \sum \frac{(E-T)^2}{T} \tag{5.4}$$

Low values of χ^2 mean a good fit of models. The test is not sufficient to decide whether a model is good although it is sufficient to decide whether one model is better than another one. At this point, we only aim to measure the goodness of fit to compare models. In statistics, you can find more elaborated tests.

```
> E <-  E_vil
> T1_vil <- 1 + (12/91)*(X - 1259)
> T2_vil <- 1 + 0.003* (X-1259)^2
```

```
> sum(((E-T1_vil)^2)/T1_vil)
[1] 1.955191
> sum(((E-T2_vil)^2)/T2_vil)
[1] 12.12744
```

Obviously `T1_vil` is the better model. This model has the form

$$\texttt{T1\_vil} = a + b(\texttt{years} - c) \tag{5.5}$$

It is easy to determine that c has to be −1259 and 1 perhaps seems to be the right value for a, but is 12/91 correct for b? Now we get to the problem of estimating the parameters. Of course, we can try several values but there has to be a better way of doing it. Indeed, this way is nothing but the mathematical concept of regression. In the terminology of modelling we can say that we have selected a model and now we have to calibrate this model, or that we know the right class of the theoretical model and need to know the precise theoretical model that fits to the empirical model. Whether we exercise model comparison or model calibration using regression depends on the research layout as well as available methods. In very complicated models, the calibration may be difficult.

In a first step, we deal with c to simplify the process by transforming the data so that $c = 0$.

```
> yr <- X - 1259
> T3_vil <- lm(E ~ yr)
> coef(T3_vil)
(Intercept)          yr
  0.9467163   0.1473646
> plot(X- 1259,E_vil,col="black",
+   pch=16)
> abline(T3_vil)
```

`T3_vil` is the linear regression model produced by the R-function `lm` (Fig. 5.2). The `R` function `coef` will return the coefficients. The first one (a) is the intercept, which is not 0 because the first point in the data has the coordinates (0, 1) since the number of the first point is 1. The second value (b) is the gradient.

The `R`-function `fitted` gives us access to the fitted values. Again, we check χ^2 and find that this model is better than those with guessed parameters. This model has the best fit.

```
> fT3_vil <- fitted(T3_vil)
> sum(((E-fT3_vil)^2)/fT3_vil)
[1] 1.128076
```

In regression analysis, another coefficient than χ^2 is in use, which is similar to χ^2 but not the same. This so-called *coefficient of determination* (R^2) is defined as

$$R^2 = \frac{\sum_i (E_i - T_i)^2}{\sum_i (E_i - \bar{E})^2} \tag{5.6}$$

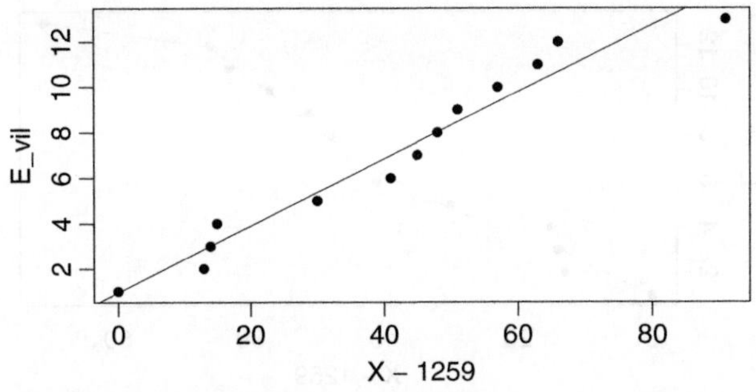

Fig. 5.2 Calibrated linear model of village foundation (`T3_vil`)

where $\bar{E}$ is the mean of E. This coefficient can be obtained directly from the `lm`-object. The value ranges between 0 and 1. The best fit is with a value of 1.

```
> summary(T3_vil)$r.squared
[1] 0.9570601
```

Perhaps a quadratic model with calibrated parameters is significantly better than `T2_vil`.

```
> T4_vil <- lm(E ~ I(yr^2))
> coef(T4_vil)
(Intercept)      I(yr^2)
3.484030442 0.001525825
> fT4_vil <- fitted(T4_vil)
> sum((E-fT4_vil)^2)/fT4_vil)
[1] 4.708115
> summary(T4_vil)$r.squared
[1] 0.8283887
```

Model `T3_vil` continues to have the best fit. However we will not give up. We can try a polynomial. Let us try a polynomial of degree 4:

```
> T5_vil <- lm(E ~ poly(yr, 4, raw=TRUE))
> coef(T5_vil)
   (Intercept) poly(yr, 4, raw = TRUE)1
   9.442846e-01            2.146162e-01
   poly(yr, 4, raw = TRUE)2
   -6.889610e-03
   poly(yr, 4, raw = TRUE)3
   1.659085e-04
   poly(yr, 4, raw = TRUE)4
   -1.100231e-06
> fT5_vil <- fitted(T5_vil)
```

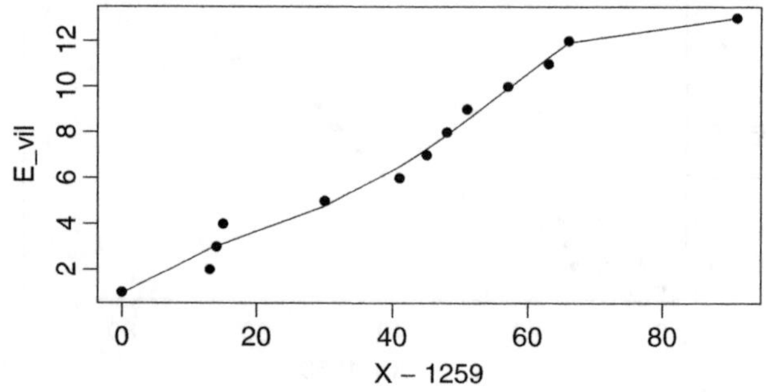

Fig. 5.3 Calibrated polynomial (degree = 4) model of village foundations (`T5_vil`)

```
> sum(((E-fT5_vil)^2)/fT5_vil)
[1] 0.6261346
> summary(T5_vil)$r.squared
[1] 0.9874966
```

The fit is fairly good, so we should have a look at the graphic (Fig. 5.3).

```
> plot(X- 1259,E_vil,col="black",
+ pch=16)
> lines(yr,fT5_vil)
```

Multiple regression allows using more than one parameter to estimate the variable of interest. The *logit model* is a linear model that has a binary variable as the variable of interest. Logit models can be calculated with `glm()`, which is a function to apply generalised linear models (see Chap. 6). Furthermore, the `gam()` function for generalised additive models is useful function for regression.

Thus far, we have not considered that we are dealing with temporal data. In this case, time series analysis with autoregressive integrated moving average (ARIMA) models comes into focus.

5.1.3 Model Choice, Overfitting and Decomposition

Polynomial regression models of different degrees offer the opportunity to produce a very good fit for most data. However is the degree of the polynomial appropriate for the phenomenon mapped by the data? A first estimation has to be based upon theoretical considerations. If the theory requires a linear relationship, a polynomial model of degree 5 makes absolutely no sense. If the data still follow the shape of curve, we have to search for systematic errors rather than adapting the regression model. Subsequently, we can try to establish the optimal degree based upon the data. The first question concerning the degree to which an increase of degree produces a reasonable better fit. We have to try several degrees and then we can apply a

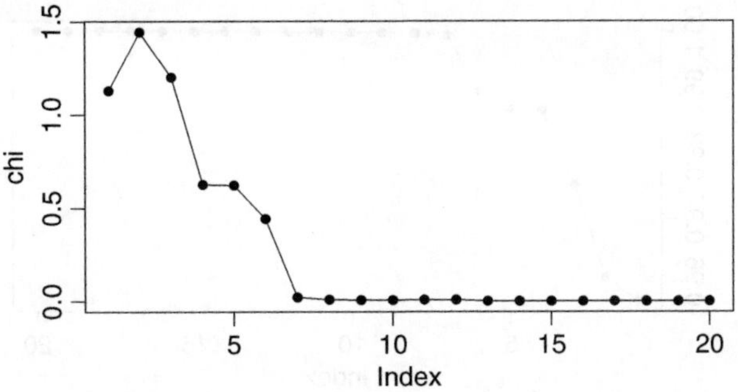

Fig. 5.4 χ^2 for some polynomials of different degrees

kind of elbow criterion (Fig. 5.4). In our example, a degree of more than 8 does not make sense. The degrees 2, 3 and 5 are poor compared with their forerunner or fore-forerunner. Accordingly, we have to choose between degree = 1, 4, 6 and 7, whereby the choice depends on the necessary goodness of fit for our purpose.

```
> chi <- 1:20
> for(i in seq(1:20)){
+     T6_vil <- lm(E ~ poly(yr, i, raw=TRUE))
+     fT6_vil <- fitted(T6_vil)
+     chi[i] <- sum(((E-fT6_vil)^2)/fT6_vil)
+     }
> chi
 [1] 1.128e+00 1.443e+00 1.199e+00 6.261e-01 6.221e-01
 [6] 4.427e-01 2.072e-02 8.517e-03 6.099e-03 6.099e-03
[11] 6.970e-03 6.970e-03 6.293e-07 6.293e-07 6.293e-07
[16] 6.293e-07 6.293e-07 6.293e-07 6.293e-07 0.000e+00
> plot(chi,col="black", pch=16)
> lines(chi)
```

Finally, we do the same with the coefficient of determination (Fig. 5.5).

```
> r <- 1:20
> for(i in seq(1:20)){
+    T7_vil <- lm(E ~ poly(yr, i, raw=TRUE))
+    fT7_vil <- fitted(T6_vil)
+    r[i] <- summary(T7_vil)$r.squared
+    }
>r
> plot(r,col="black", pch=16)
> lines(r)
```

Here, 4 and 7 seem to be the best choice.

Now we have restricted the set of possible degrees to four possible values, although we still have not solved the problem of whether the degrees 4 and 7 map a

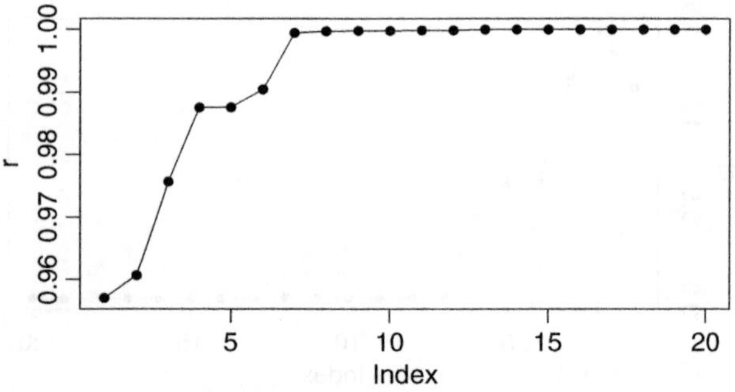

Fig. 5.5 Coefficient of determination for some polynomials of different degrees

real phenomenon or rather some noise. If we could get additional points, would they fit to the regression curve? Does the model represent a random state and change with additional points or is it stable? Since we cannot get additional points, we have to manage with the available data. The idea is to build the model based upon a part of the available points. Subsequently, the other points can be used to test the stability. This process can be repeated for different partitions and is called bootstrapping.

```
> data <- data.frame(x=yr, y=E)
> its <- 100
> dd <- 6
> res <-data.frame()
> for (d in 1:dd) {
+    ei <- numeric(d)
+    eo <- numeric(d)
+    for (it in 1:its)     {
+        sel    <- sample(x=1:13, size=8,replace=F)
+        train  <- data[sel,]
+        seli   <- !(1:13 %in% sel)
+        test   <- data[seli,]
+        T7_vil  <- lm(y~poly(x,d),data=train)
+        ei[it] <- mean(T7_vil$residuals^2)
+        pred <- predict(T7_vil,
+                newdata=data.frame(data[seli,]))
+        eo[it] <- mean((test-pred)^2)
+    }
+    eiv <- mean(ei)
+    eov <- mean(eo)
+    res <- rbind(res,data.frame(d=d,eiv=eiv,
 eov=eov))
+ }
> plot(res$d,res$eiv,col="grey",log="y",ylim=c(min
   (res$eiv
+ ), max(res$eov)), pch=16, type="b")
> points(res$d,res$eov, type ="b", pch=16,
 col="black")
```

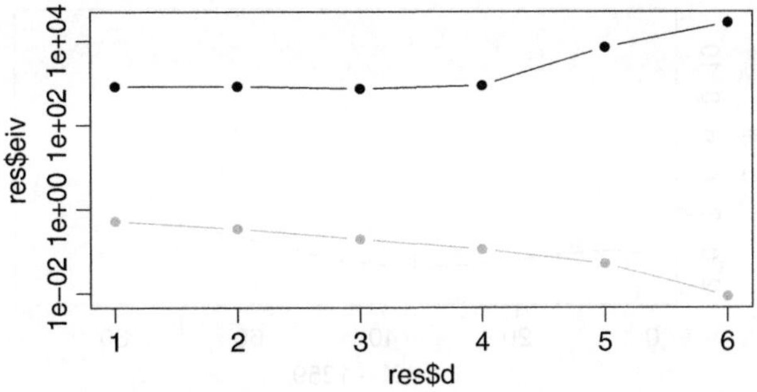

Fig. 5.6 Coefficient of determination for some polynomials of different degrees. *Black*: test data, *grey*: training data

The mean of squared residuals is used for validation (Fig. 5.6). The grey curve shows the mean of this value for the points that were used to develop the model. The black curve shows the same for the points that were not involved in the model development and hence are a kind of additional points. The black curve shows that the error of prediction increases if the degree is larger than 4. This indicates an overfitting starting with a degree of 5. Does this correspond with the archaeological interpretation of the points? Thirteen points in total are certainly not a sound basis for such an analysis. Single points with a high residual can be an outlayer or a single indicator of a real structure. The probability that unexpected details in the structure are represented by more than one point increases with the number of points.

The final step in this section is to discuss the decomposition of models. We can assume that there are different phenomena that contribute to the empirical model. Accordingly, it seems a good idea to decompose the theoretical model into several components that induce different interpretations. Three components can be found in many models:

1. general trend
2. actual modulation of the curve
3. noise

In our example, the general trend is caused by the fact that the dependent variable is the order of village foundations. The values have to increase. This is a trend induced by data preparation and bears no geospatial interest. Subsequently, we can interpret the residues to the polynomial model with the highest degree, albeit without overfitting as noise. In between are modulations that can serve for an interpretation. In our case, this instructive component shows the development of the colonisation process. The instructive component can be decomposed itself. For example, each term in the polynomial forms a component that can—under certain circumstances—induce different levels of interpretation. Different periodicities can be decomposed using the Fourier approach.

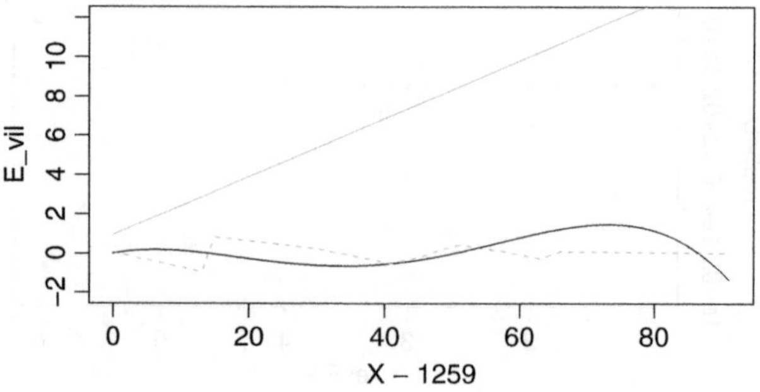

Fig. 5.7 Decomposition of the regression model. *Black, solid*: actual modulation of the curve; *grey, solid*: general trend; *grey, dashed*: noise

We will try a decomposition in the three main parts. First, we calculate the linear trend and remove the trend, which are the predicted values from the data.

```
> T3_vil <- lm(E ~ yr)
> fT3_vil <- fitted(T3_vil)
> pred3 <- predict(T3_vil)
> E3 <- E-pred3
```

We then calculate the model with the optimal degree, which was 4 in our case. Again, we are removing the predicted values from the data.

```
> T8_vil <- lm(E3 ~ poly(yr, 4, raw=TRUE))
> fT8_vil <- fitted(T8_vil)
> pred8 <- predict(T8_vil)
> E8 <- E3-pred8
```

Now, an extremely detailed model with a very high degree is calculated. This represents the noise.

```
> T9_vil <- lm(E8 ~ poly(yr, 12, raw=TRUE))
> fT9_vil <- fitted(T9_vil)
```

Finally, we plot the results (Fig. 5.7).

```
> plot(X- 1259,E_vil,col="white", pch=16, ylim=c
    (-2,12))
> lines(yr,fT3_vil, col="grey")
> curve(coef(T8_vil)[1] + coef(T8_vil)[2]*x + coef
    (T8_vil)
+ [3]*x^2 + coef(T8_vil)[4]*x^3 + coef(T8_vil)[5]*x^4,
+ add = TRUE)
> lines(yr,fT9_vil, col="grey", lty=2)
```

Most of the theoretical models do not fit exactly. They give a trend on which random variations are added to get the empiric model. If this is the case, we are interested in two things: The magnitude of variance and the trend model. We have seen that high degree polynomials can fit empirical models very good. But do we want this? The theoretical model has to be as good to fit the part of the empirical model which is not random. Estimating this threshold is no easy task. In addition it can be useful to differentiate the trend into several components. There might be a general trend which is superposed by a local trend. Which one is of interest depends on our research objective.

5.2 Interpolation

Regression and interpolation are very similar approaches. Regression aims to map the relationship between an independent and dependent variable, whereby the specification of the relationship as a function is the main task. Interpolation aims to predict values of the dependent variable based upon the values of the independent variable. Regression models can be used for interpolation. In fact, we have used a regression model for interpolation in the bootstrapping approach. We have calculated values for the test data set based upon the regression model. Interpolation is not restricted to models with nice functions; rather, it deals with all methods that give hints about the values that we want to predict. In this section, we discuss some general concepts of interpolation and proceed into further details concerning two frequently used interpolation techniques. Having discussed regression with one independent variable, we will now use two independent variables that we can interpret as geographical information [2–4, 7–11]. The interpolation techniques could be applied to elevation as a dependent variable and longitude and latitude as independent variables. Rather than using this standard example, we return to the density data from the previous Chap. 4.

5.2.1 The Concept of Interpolation

Interpolation is a technique to produce predictive models:

Definition 5.2. Interpolation is a regression-based method for predicting values of points where no measures were taken.

The general idea is that the closer a point with measurement, the more similar the value is at the point without measurement. This is nothing but Tobler's [13] first law of geography. While the regression objective is to derive a mathematical description of the trend in the data, the interpolation objective is to obtain the value for points without measurement. If we have a regression model with a good fit, we can use it to perform an interpolation.

We have to distinguish some kinds of interpolation methods (Fig. 5.8). At the sampling points, the interpolated value can be the same as the measured value,

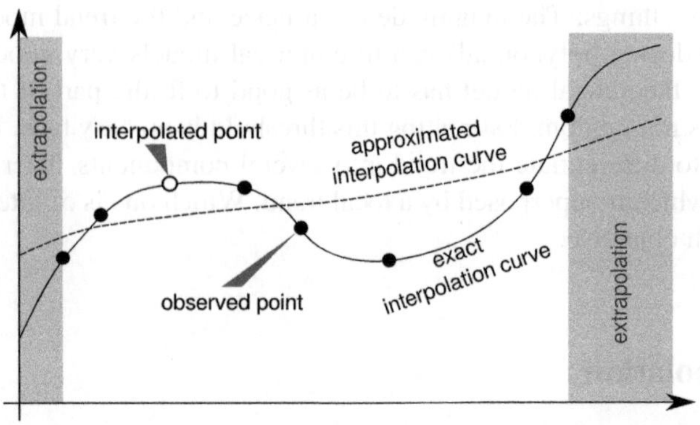

Fig. 5.8 Basic interpolation types

reflecting an exact interpolation. By contrast, an approximated interpolation gives values that are near the measured values but are usually not the same. There are some reasons to use an approximated interpolation, as listed below:

- the data have errors
- we are only interested in the trend
- we want to separate local variations from the trend
- we are happy with a reduced model, which might be easier to handle

A global interpolation uses all sampling points to interpolate. A local interpolation only considers the points from the specified neighbourhood. If you use few points, outliers have a major influence. If you use all points, the local characteristic might be smoothed by distant points.

We will mention two methods before coming to the most important approaches. One method of historic interest is Thiessen polygons. The meteorologist Alfred Thiessen [12] describes a method to construct polygons around sample points where the borders are in the middle of the sample points, whereby the value from the sample point is assigned to the whole polygon. During a times when no computers were available and in a field where quick calculations were necessary, this method proved useful. In fact, Thiessen polygon interpolation is only appropriate for categorical variables rather than numerical variables, although this is seldom considered in practice (Fig. 5.9). From a mathematical perspective, one should refer to Voronois work [15].

Spline interpolation uses regression functions that cover only a few points (Fig. 5.10). The combination of these spline functions allows the interpolation of all points. It is necessary that the spline functions have the same gradient and value where they meet.

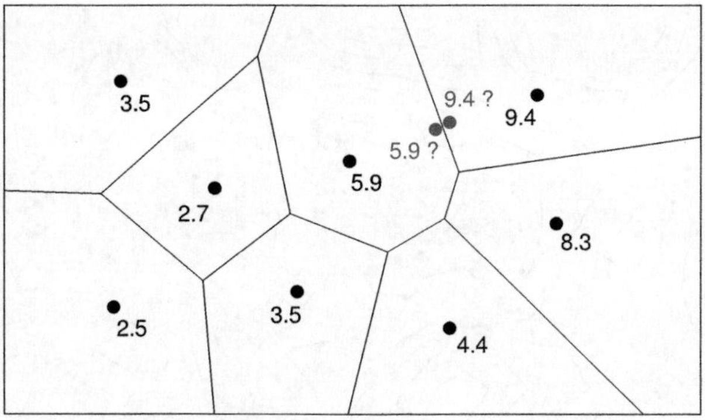

Fig. 5.9 Thiessen polygons as a simple interpolation tool for numerical values. This is obviously not an appropriate method

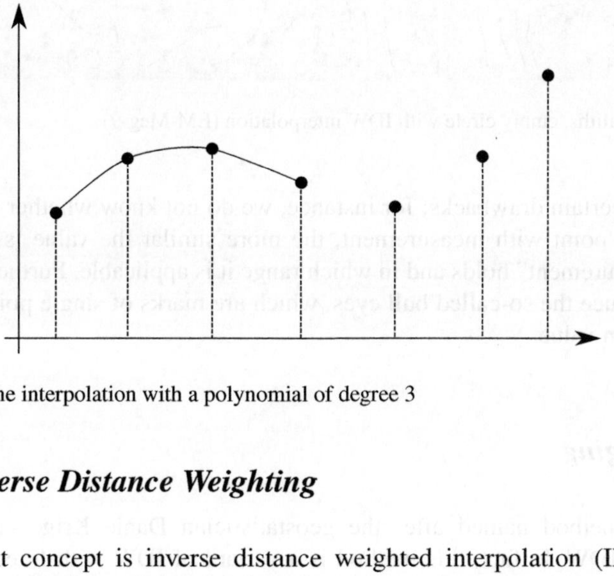

Fig. 5.10 Spline interpolation with a polynomial of degree 3

5.2.2 Inverse Distance Weighting

An important concept is inverse distance weighted interpolation (IDW), which calculates a mean value of several sample points weighted by inverse distance to the unknown point to correspond to Tobler's first law of geography. We use the empty circle density data for the megaliths as an example (see Chap. 4; Fig. 5.11).

```
> library(gstat)
> meg_idw      <- idw(fs_vd_spdf@data$fs_vd ~ 1,
+    fs_vd_spdf, sgdf)
[inverse distance weighted interpolation]
> image(meg_idw, col = gray.colors(25, start = 0.4,
+    end = 0.97))
> contour(meg_idw, add=T)
> points(ppp_meg$x, ppp_meg$y, pch=16, cex=0.4)
```

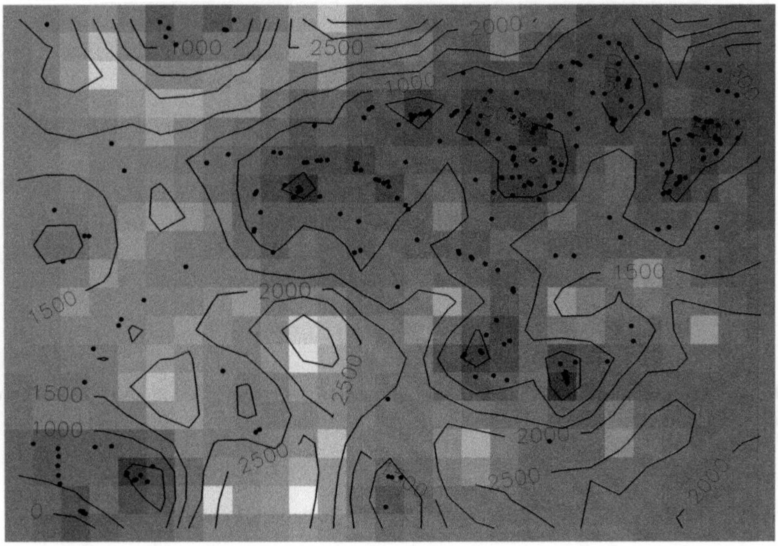

Fig. 5.11 Megaliths, empty circle with IDW interpolation (EM-Meg-9)

IDW has certain drawbacks; for instance, we do not know whether the idea that "the closer a point with measurement, the more similar the value is at the point without measurement" holds and in which range it is applicable. Furthermore, IDW tends to produce the so-called bull eyes, which are marks of single points differing from the mean value.

5.2.3 *Kriging*

Kriging—a method named after the geostatistician Danie Krige—solves some problems of IDW. In fact, this method is a variant of IDW with fitted regression, where the distance-similarity relation is empirically estimated. This is archived with a variogram in which the spatial distance and value distance—i.e. value difference—of all pairs of points are plotted. A regression curve is fitted to the points. A variogram (Fig. 5.12) is typically a monotonic increasing curve, which starts with a value called "nugget", which is the local error. The "sill" is the range of values, while "range" denotes the spatial range of the variogram. Points that are more distant than the range value can no longer be weighted by distance and they can only contribute to a global mean. The variogram is used to weight the points included in the calculation of a mean value of surrounding points.

There are different types of kriging, which vary in the number of known parameters that can be used in the interpolation process. For instance, information

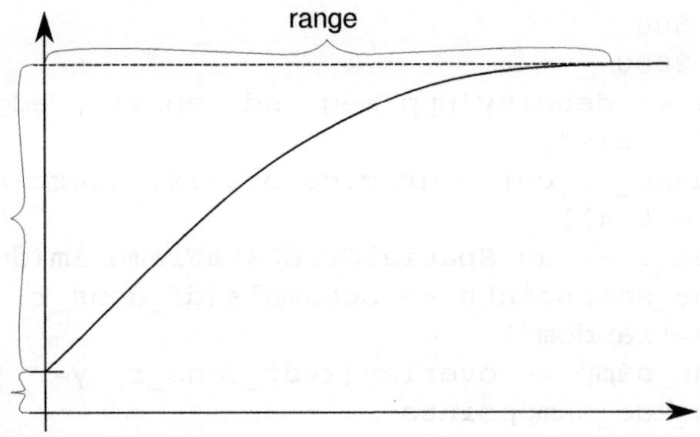

Fig. 5.12 Scheme of a variogram

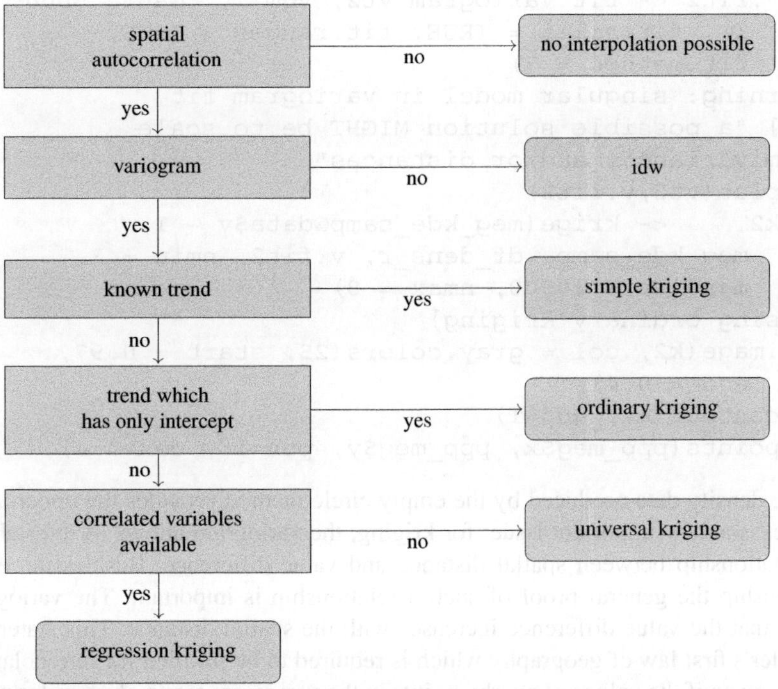

Fig. 5.13 Decision tree for some interpolation methods

about the trend can be used. In the literature [8, 10], some decisions help to find the right method. We provide a very simple decision tree, which gives a first orientation (Fig. 5.13).

Now we return to the code and have a look at the variogram (Fig. 5.14).

```
> library(maptools)
> library(spatstat)
```

```
> rw <- 500
> sd <- 2000
> dens_r <- density(ppp_meg, sd, eps=rw, edge=TRUE,
+   at="pixels")
> plot(dens_r, col = gray.colors(25, start = 0.97,
+   end = 0.4))
> df_dens_r <- as.SpatialGridDataFrame.im(dens_r)
> meg_kde_samppoints <- spsample(df_dens_r, 1000,
+   type="random")
> meg_kde_samp <- overlay(x=df_dens_r, y=
+    meg_kde_samppoints)
> vt2     <- variogram(meg_kde_samp@data$v ~ 1,
+   meg_kde_samp)
> v.fit2 <- fit.variogram(vt2, vgm(1, "Gau", 5000,
+   1), fit.sills = TRUE, fit.ranges = TRUE,
+   fit.method = 7)
Warning: singular model in variogram fit
[1] "a possible solution MIGHT be to scale
semivariances and/or distances"
> plot(vt2,v.fit2)
> k2      <- krige(meg_kde_samp@data$v ~ 1,
+   meg_kde_samp, df_dens_r, v.fit2, nmin = 3,
+   maxdist = 10000, nmax = 8)
[using ordinary kriging]
> image(k2, col = gray.colors(25, start = 0.97,
+   end = 0.4))
> contour(k2, add=T)
> points(ppp_meg$x, ppp_meg$y, pch=16, cex=0.4)
```

The density data produced by the empty circle method provides the opportunity to discuss a very important issue: for kriging, the variogram allows us to establish the relationship between spatial distance and value difference. Besides the exact relationship the general proof of such a relationship is important. The variogram shows that the value difference increases with the spatial distance. This statement is Tobler's first law of geography which is required to be fulfilled for interpolation. This is given if the values of nearby points in the variogram tend to be similar while those of remote points are not. In fact, it is a certain degree of redundancy that proves this law. Points that are not absolutely necessary for a basic prediction show that the values are not changing randomly between two points rather they change from one value to the other when moving along the connection line. Due to the variogram—which includes this information—it is not necessary to apply a test of spatial auto-correlation.

In the case of density data obtained by the empty circle method we have a minimal set of optimal placed points that do not necessarily need to show auto-correlation. However, per definition, the function of the values between two points

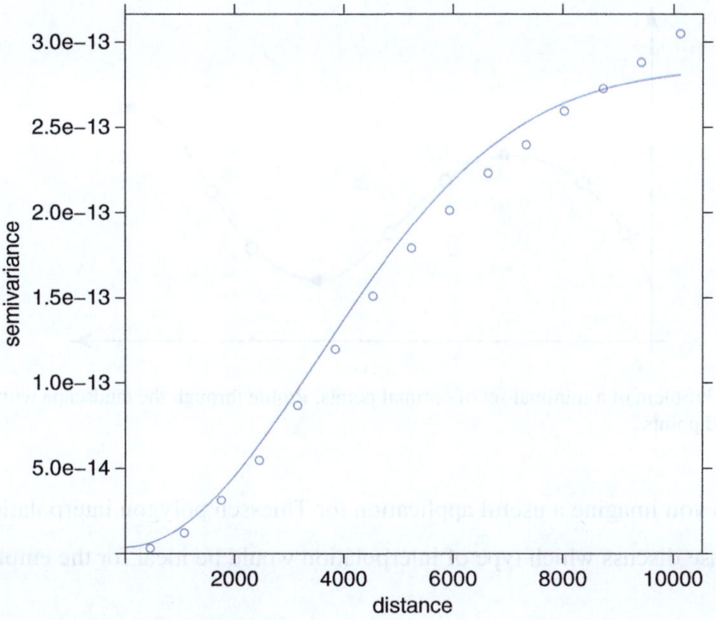

Fig. 5.14 Variogram for KDE samples points

changes in a monotone and continuous manner, whereby the required conditions are given. In this case the variogram would not map the information required for the kriging but rather other properties of the data. In this case it would make sense not to use the regression curve of the variogram for kriging, but rather a manually defined variogram curve based upon the knowledge about the relationship. The reader should be aware that such problems can arise in the course of applying kriging on empty circle density data. In Fig. 5.15, the black points—which are a minimal set of optimal points—would not give the impression of auto-correlated values and would produce a poor variogram. Indeed, the values could be random. The redundant white points contribute rather marginally to the interpolation but allow producing a proper variogram. The white points show that there is a trend between the black points, which is the basis for the interpolation.

5.3 Problems

5.1. Please use the function chisq.test() rather than the explicit equation for calculating and comparing the models.

5.2. Is χ^2 or coefficient of determination the better choice to establish the optimal degree of a polynomial?

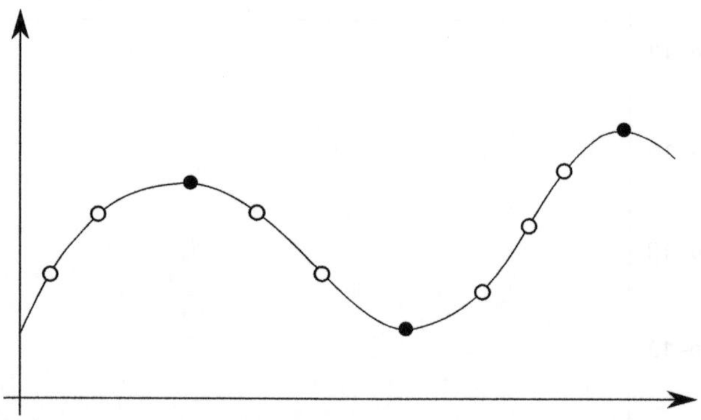

Fig. 5.15 Problem of a minimal set of optimal points. Profile through the landscape with two sets of observed points

5.3. Can you imagine a useful application for Thiessen polygon interpolation?

5.4. Please discuss which type of interpolation would be ideal for the empty circle method.

5.5. Is kriging an approximative or an exact interpolation method?

5.6. Explore different parameter settings for kriging.

5.7. Try to visualise the model decomposition for our case study of the villages and discuss the interpretation of the components.

References

1. Bronstein, I. N., Semendjajew, K. A., Musiol, G., & Muehlig, H. (2007). *Handbook of mathematics*. Berlin: Springer.
2. Brundsdon, C., & Comber, L. (2015). *An introduction to R for spatial analysis and mapping*. Los Angeles: Sage.
3. Cressi, N. A. C. (1991). *Statistics for spatial data*. New York: Springer.
4. Diggle, P. J., & Ribeiro, P. J., Jr., (2010). *Model-based geostatistics*. New York: Springer.
5. Everitt, B. S., & Hothorn, T. (2010). *A handbook of statistical analysis using R*. Boca Raton: Chapman and Hall.
6. Fahrmeir, L., Kneib, T., & Lang, S. (2009). *Regression: modelle, methoden und anwendungen*. Heidelberg: Springer.
7. Gaetan, C., & Guyon, X. (2010). *Spatial statistics and modelling*. New York: Springer.
8. Hengl, T. (2007). *A practical guide to geostatistical mapping of environmental variables*. Luxembourg: Office for Official Publications of the European Communities.
9. Niemeier, W. (2008). *Ausgleichsrechnung*. Berlin: De Gruyter.
10. Pebesma, E. J. (2004). Multivariable geostatistics in S: The gstat package. *Computers and Geosciences, 30*, 683–691.
11. Ripley, B. D. (1981) *Spatial statistics*. New York: Springer.

12. Thiessen, A. H. (1911). Precipitation averages for large areas. *Monthly Weather Review, 39*, 1082–1084.
13. Tobler, W. (1970). A computer movie simulating urban growth in the Detroit region. *Economic Geography, 46*(2), 234–240.
14. Venables, W. N., & Ripley, B. D. (2002). *Modern applied statistics with S*. New York: Springer.
15. Voronoi, G. (1907). Nouvelles applications des paramètres continus à la théorie des formes quadratiques. *Journal für die Reine und Angewandte Mathematik, 133*, 97–178.

Chapter 6
Location and Characterisation

6.1 Characterising Locations

Characterising a location involves recording its characteristics and interpreting them in the light of a specific question. For instance, a city's location can be characterised by the population density, distance to other cities, administrative affiliations, etc. It can also be described by environmental features such as water availability, altitude, distance to streams, etc.

We are interested in the environmental characteristics of the megalithic graves. Do they differ in terms of location? Are they located at specific environmental locations? Given that we are missing environmental information for our focused prehistoric period, we rely on the *general* relief characteristic that can be regarded as comparable, derived from globally available SRTM data.

Before we are going to create these let's check the characteristics of the graves.

First, we load the SRTM and ensure that the spatial references between the raster and the megaliths correspond.

```
> sgdf_srtm <- read.asciigrid(file_srtm)
2geodata/dw_gk3_50_ag.asc has GDAL driver AAIGrid
and has 362 rows and 566 columns
> names(sgdf_srtm@data) <- "srtm"
> is.projected(sgdf_srtm)
[1] NA
> sgdf_srtm@proj4string@projargs <- crs1
> is.projected(sgdf_srtm)
[1] TRUE
> spdf_meg@proj4string@projargs == sgdf_srtm@proj4string
+   @projargs
[1] TRUE
```


O. Nakoinz, D. Knitter, *Modelling Human Behaviour in Landscapes*, Quantitative Archaeology and Archaeological Modelling, DOI 10.1007/978-3-319-29538-1_6

For the subsequent analyses we will use the raster package hence transforming our srtm object from a SpatialGridDataFrame into a raster object and consider at its characteristics

```
> srtm <- raster(sgdf_srtm)
> srtm
class       : RasterLayer
dimensions  : 362, 566, 204892  (nrow, ncol, ncell)
resolution  : 50, 50  (x, y)
extent      : 3550736, 3579036, 6022467, 6040567
+   (xmin, xmax, ymin, ymax)
coord. ref. : +proj=tmerc +lat_0=0 +lon_0=9 +k=1+x_0=3500000
     +y_0=0 +ellps=WGS84 +units=m +no_defs
data source : in memory
names       : srtm
values      : -15.1568, 61.0053  (min, max)

> summary(srtm)
                 srtm
Min.     -15.15680
1st Qu.    6.06045
Median    15.26705152
3rd Qu.   21.46960
Max.      61.00530
NA's     362.00000
```

A plot of the raster with the different points gives a first impression of the locational characteristics (Fig. 6.1)

```
> par(mar=c(2.1, 2.1, 2.1, 2.1))
> plot(srtm, col = gray.colors(n = 25, start = 0.1, end = .9),
+       legend.lab="Altitude (m)", horizontal = FALSE, legend.
+ width = 1,
+       cex.axis=.9, tcl=-.3, mgp = c(3,.2,0))
> points(spdf_tum,pch = 19, cex = .8, col = "black"
+ ,bg="black")
> points(spdf_meg,pch = 22, cex = 1.5, col = "black",
+ bg="white")
> points(spdf_vil,pch = 23, cex = 2.5, col = "black",
+ bg = "white")
> legend("bottomright",legend=c("Bronze Age Barrows",
+ "Megaliths",
+ "Villages"), pch=c(19,22,23))
> scalebar(d = 5000, divs = 2, below="Meter",type =
+ "bar",xy=
+ c(3573500,6025500),adj = c(.5,-1.3))
```

Visually, villages are located at different locations than Bronze Age barrows and megaliths. However, are these locations different in terms of their characteristics? In

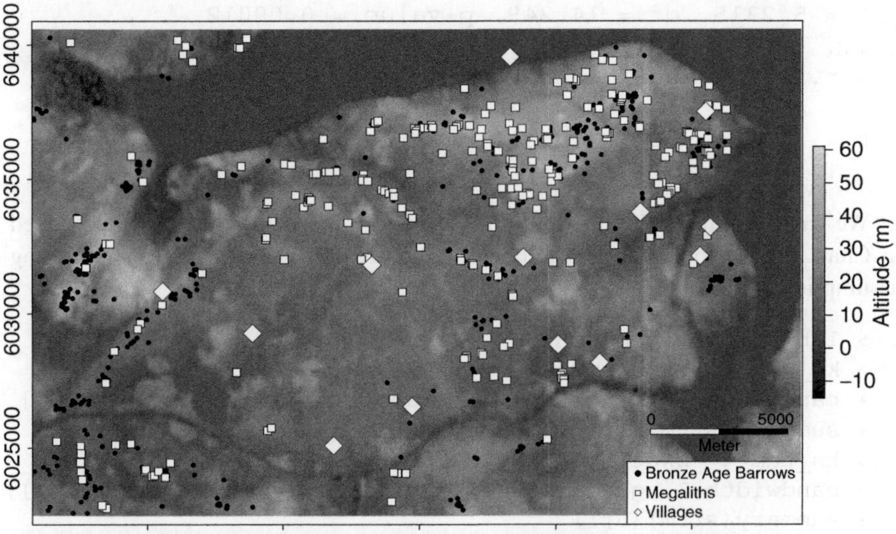

Fig. 6.1 SRTM with sites

order to answer this question we extract the information about the raster at the point locations. A `t.test` shows that the difference in mean is significant.

```
> spdf_meg@data$srtm <- extract(x = srtm, y = spdf_meg,
+ buffer = 200, fun = median)
> spdf_tum@data$srtm <- extract(x = srtm, y = spdf_tum,
+ buffer = 200, fun = median)
> spdf_vil@data$srtm <- extract(x = srtm, y = spdf_vil,
buffer = 200, fun = median)
> t.test(x=spdf_meg@data$srtm, y=spdf_tum@data$srtm)

    Welch Two Sample t-test

data:  spdf_meg@data$srtm and spdf_tum@data$srtm
t = -3.2234, df = 637.51, p-value = 0.001331
alternative hypothesis: true difference in means is
+ not equal to 0
95 percent confidence interval:
 -4.399632 -1.068484
sample estimates:
mean of x mean of y
 22.55336  25.28741

> t.test(x=spdf_tum@data$srtm, y=spdf_vil@data$srtm)
...
```

```
t = 5.2315, df = 14.249, p-value = 0.00012
...
> t.test(x=spdf_meg@data$srtm, y=spdf_vil@data$srtm)
...
t = 3.8586, df = 14.561, p-value = 0.001626
...
```

We can investigate the distributions. Thanks to the kernel methods introduced in Chap. 4 the problems of different sample sizes are avoided, with simplifying assumptions, of course.

```
> library("KernSmooth")
> ks_meg <- bkde(spdf_meg@data$srtm, kernel="normal",
+ bandwidth=3, gridsize=201, range.x = c(summary(srtm)[1],
+ summary(srtm)[5]))
> ks_tum <- bkde(spdf_tum@data$srtm, kernel="normal",
+ bandwidth=3, gridsize=201, range.x = c(summary(srtm)[1],
+ summary(srtm)[5]))
> ks_vil2 <- bkde(spdf_vil@data$srtm, kernel="normal",
+ bandwidth=3, gridsize=201, range.x = c(summary(srtm)[1],
+ summary(srtm)[5]))
```

Now, let us plot the distributions, albeit in this case using another approach realised using the `ggplot2` library. In order to use the strengths of `ggplot`, we need to reshape our data (Fig. 6.2).

```
> srtm_char <- data.frame(ks_meg,ks_tum$y,ks_vil2$y)
> colnames(srtm_char) <- c("altitude","meg","tum","vil")
> library(reshape)
> srtm_char2<- melt(srtm_char, id.vars = "altitude")
```

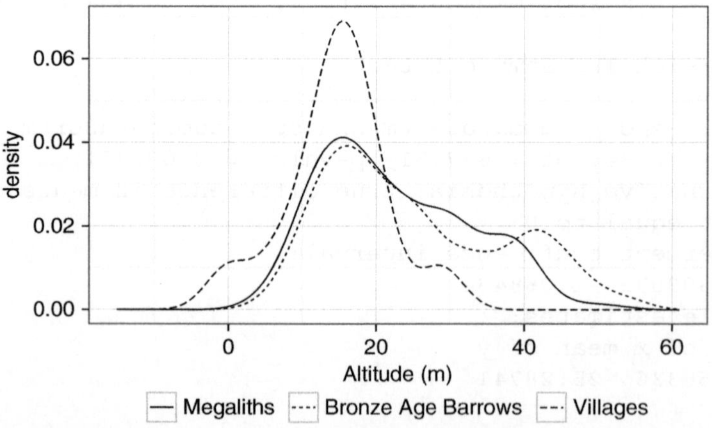

Fig. 6.2 Density distribution of elevation values for the different point classes

```
> head(srtm_char2,3)
  altitude variable        value
1 -15.15680      meg 4.172543e-07
2 -14.77599      meg 5.999285e-07
3 -14.39518      meg 8.132125e-07
> srtm_char2<- melt(srtm_char, id.vars = "altitude")
> srtm_char <- data.frame(ks_meg,ks_tum$y,ks_vil2$y)
> colnames(srtm_char) <- c("altitude","meg","tum","vil")
> library(reshape)
> srtm_char2<- melt(srtm_char, id.vars = "altitude")
> head(srtm_char2,3)
  altitude variable        value
1 -15.15680      meg 4.172543e-07
2 -14.77599      meg 5.999285e-07
3 -14.39518      meg 8.132125e-07
> tail(srtm_char2,3)
    altitude variable        value
601 60.24368      vil 3.469447e-18
602 60.62449      vil 0.000000e+00
603 61.00530      vil 0.000000e+00
> library(ggplot2)
> srtm_char_plot <- ggplot(srtm_char2, aes(x=altitude,
+ y=value)) +
+     geom_line(aes(linetype = variable)) + labs(x="Altitude
+ (m)",y="density",legend="") + theme_bw(base_size = 12)
+ + theme(legend.position="bottom", legend.title=
+ element_blank()) + scale_linetype_discrete(labels =
+ c("Megaliths","Bronze Age Barrows", "Villages"))
> srtm_char_plot
```

Given that a location characterisation solely based upon elevation is not very interesting, we create some terrain parameters using functions collected in a `raster` package. In a real-world example, the reader is advised to calculate terrain attributes using GRASS GIS or SAGA GIS since these tools offer more possibilities, methods, performance and are accessible from `R` via the libraries `spgrass6` and `RSAGA`, respectively.

For the sake of simplicity, we will use our `srtm` scene and derive some terrain attributes directly from R using the `raster` package, as follows:

- slope, i.e. the measure of elevation difference in degree or percent;
- aspect, i.e. the direction of maximum elevation difference, hence exposure and
- topographic position index (TPI), a measure of relative terrain position [5]. The value of the central cell within a moving window is compared to the mean of the window's cells. If the central cell's value is higher, this indicates a more ridge- or hill-like position. A valley-like position corresponds to the situation where the value of the central cell is smaller than mean of the cells of the moving window. A similar value between the mean of the surrounding and central cell is indicative of a straight slope or flat position. TPI is sensitive to scale therefore, we

calculate two different versions of it: one showing the local terrain characteristics and another with a more regional focus.

```
> ter.par <- terrain(x = srtm, opt = c("slope","aspect",
+ "tpi"), neighbors = 4)
> tpi.win <- function(x, w=5) { m <- matrix(1/(w^2-1),
+ nc=w, nr=w); m[ceiling(0.5 * length(m))] <- 0; f <-
+ focal(x, m); x - f }
> tpi.large <- tpi.win(x = srtm, w=15)
> ter.par <- brick(x = c(tpi.large,ter.par))
> colnames(ter.par@data@values)[1] <- "tpi_15"
> colnames(ter.par@data@values)[2] <- "tpi_5"
```

Let us have a look at the characteristics of the resulting raster

```
> summary(ter.par)
              tpi_15         tpi_5          slope     aspect
Min.      -24.222638   -12.6055751      0.0000000     0.0000
1st Qu.    -1.335900    -0.1589120      0.3839363    90.0000
Median      0.000000     0.0000000      0.8980482   153.6286
3rd Qu.     1.090425     0.1473372      1.6616471   261.5069
Max.       20.945616     7.5615871     19.9813567   359.9925
NA's    13144.000000 2212.0000000   2212.0000000  2212.0000
```

Since we are interested in the location of the different sites, TPI is most interesting since it shows us which terrain features—i.e. ridge, valley and plain—have the highest proportion of sites (Fig. 6.3). Before extracting the values from the raster, we plot the sites and the different terrain parameters. To enhance the visual appearance, we add a shading effect to the different raster.

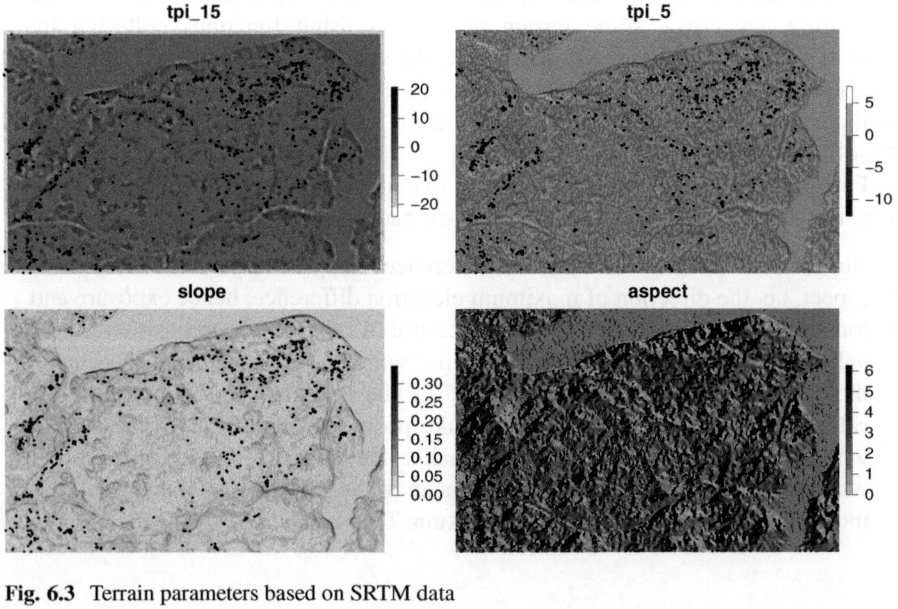

Fig. 6.3 Terrain parameters based on SRTM data

```
> srtm.shade <- hillShade(slope = terrain(srtm,"slope"),
+ aspect = terrain(srtm,"aspect"),angle = 15,direction
+ = 200,normalize = TRUE)
> par(mfrow = c(2,2),mar = c(.5,1,1,1))
> plot(ter.par, 1, col = grey(c(8:0/8)),horizontal =
+ FALSE,legend.width = 1,cex.axis=.9,tcl=-.3,mgp =
+ c(3,.2,0),axes = FALSE, box = FALSE)
> plot(srtm.shade, col = grey(0:200/200,alpha = .3),
+ legend = FALSE,add=TRUE)
> points(spdf_tum,pch = 19, cex = .5, col = "black",
+ bg="black")
> points(spdf_meg,pch = 19, cex = .5, col = "black",
+ bg="white")
> points(spdf_vil,pch = 19, cex = .5, col = "black",
+ bg = "white")
> plot(ter.par, 2, col = grey(c(0:4/4)),horizontal =
+ FALSE,legend.width = 1,cex.axis=.9,tcl=-.3,mgp =
+ c(3,.2,0),axes = FALSE, box = FALSE)
> plot(srtm.shade, col = grey(0:200/200,alpha = .5),
+ legend = FALSE,add=TRUE)
> points(spdf_tum,pch = 19, cex = .5, col = "black",
+ bg="black")
> points(spdf_meg,pch = 19, cex = .5, col = "black",
+ bg="white")
> points(spdf_vil,pch = 19, cex = .5, col = "black",
+ bg = "white")
> plot(ter.par, 3, col = grey(c(10:0/10)),horizontal =
+ FALSE,legend.width = 1,cex.axis=.9,tcl=-.3,mgp =
+ c(3,.2,0),axes = FALSE, box = FALSE)
> plot(srtm.shade, col = grey(0:200/200,alpha = .3),
+ legend = FALSE,add=TRUE)
> points(spdf_tum,pch = 19, cex = .5, col = "black",
+ bg="black")
> points(spdf_meg,pch = 19, cex = .5, col = "black",
+ bg="white")
> points(spdf_vil,pch = 19, cex = .5, col = "black",
+ bg = "white")
> plot(ter.par, 4, col = grey(c(8:0/10)),horizontal =
+ FALSE,legend.width = 1,cex.axis=.9,tcl=-.3,mgp =
+ c(3,.2,0),axes = FALSE, box = FALSE)
> points(spdf_tum,pch = 19, cex = .5, col = "black",
+ bg="black")
> points(spdf_meg,pch = 19, cex = .5, col = "black",
+ bg="white")
> points(spdf_vil,pch = 19, cex = .5, col = "black", bg =
+ "white")
```

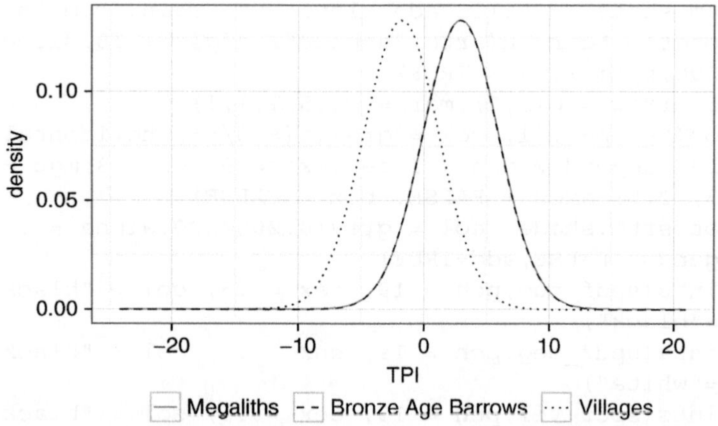

Fig. 6.4 Density estimation for the different sites and TPI with large kernel

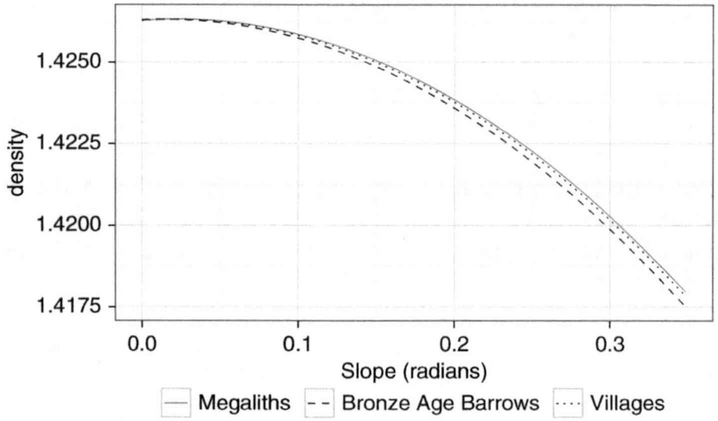

Fig. 6.5 Density estimation for the different sites and slope

We extract the data, write them into different data frames and use kernel smoothing to investigate whether there are potential differences between the sites. Subsequently, we plot the density estimations of two parameters, namely TPI and slope (Fig. 6.4 and 6.5).

```
> tp_meg <- extract(x = ter.par, y = spdf_meg, buffer = 200,
+ fun = median,df=TRUE) [,-1]
> tp_tum <- extract(x = ter.par, y = spdf_tum, buffer = 200,
+ fun = median,df=TRUE) [,-1]
> tp_vil <- extract(x = ter.par, y = spdf_vil, buffer = 200,
+ fun = median,df=TRUE) [,-1]
> library(foreach)
> ks_tp_meg <- foreach (i=1:4) %do% lapply(X = tp_meg[i],
+ FUN = function(x){bkde(x[i], kernel="normal",  bandwidth=3,
```

```
+ gridsize=201, range.x = c(summary(ter.par[[i]])[1],
+ summary(ter.par[[i]])[5]))})
> ks_tp_tum <- foreach (i=1:4) %do% lapply(X = tp_tum[i], FUN =
+ function(x){bkde(x[i], kernel="normal",  bandwidth=3,
+ gridsize=201, range.x = c(summary(ter.par[[i]])[1],
+ summary(ter.par[[i]])[5]))})
> ks_tp_vil <- foreach (i=1:4) %do% lapply(X = tp_vil[i],
+ FUN = function(x){bkde(x[i], kernel="normal",  bandwidth=3,
+ gridsize=201, range.x = c(summary(ter.par[[i]])[1],
+ summary(ter.par[[i]])[5]))})
> ter_char_tpi15 <- data.frame(ks_tp_meg[[1]][[1]],ks_tp_tum
+ [[1]][[1]]$y,ks_tp_vil[[1]][[1]]$y)
> colnames(ter_char_tpi15) <- c("tpi_15","meg","tum","vil")
> ter_char_tpi15_2 <- melt(ter_char_tpi15, id.vars = "tpi_15")
> ter_char_tpi15_plot <- ggplot(ter_char_tpi15_2, aes(x=tpi_15,
+ y=value)) +
+      geom_line(aes(linetype = variable, color = variable)) +
+ labs(x="TPI",y="density",legend="") + theme_bw(base_size =
+ 12) + theme(legend.position="bottom", legend.title=
+ element_blank()) + scale_linetype_manual(values=c("solid",
+ "dashed", "dotted"),
+ labels = c("Megaliths","Bronze Age Barrows", "Villages")) +
+ scale_color_manual(values=c('#999999', '#000000','#000000'),
+ labels = c("Megaliths","Bronze Age Barrows", "Villages"))
> ter_char_tpi15_plot
>
> ter_char_slope <- data.frame(ks_tp_meg[[3]][[1]],ks_tp_tum
+ [[3]][[1]]$y,ks_tp_vil[[3]][[1]]$y)
> colnames(ter_char_slope) <- c("slope","meg","tum","vil")
> ter_char_slope_2 <- melt(ter_char_slope, id.vars = "slope")
> ter_char_slope_plot <- ggplot(ter_char_slope_2, aes(x=slope,
+ y=value))
+      geom_line(aes(linetype = variable, color = variable)) +
+ labs(x="Slope (radians)",y="density",legend="") + theme_bw
+ (base_size = 12) + theme(legend.position="bottom", legend.
+ title=element_blank()) + scale_linetype_manual(values=
+ c("solid", "dashed", "dotted"), labels = c("Megaliths",
+ "Bronze Age Barrows", "Villages")) + scale_color_manual
+ (values=c('#999999','#000000',
+ '#000000'), labels = c("Megaliths","Bronze Age Barrows",
+ "Villages"))
> ter_char_slope_plot
```

It becomes obvious that `slope` as a parameter is not very useful in describing differences in the locations of our different site types. By contrast, TPI shows a pronounced difference in location between graves, i.e. Bronze Age barrows, megaliths and villages. Graves occur more often on hills or ridges—as seen by the larger TPI values—while villages are most frequently found in flat situations or gentle depressions. These observations correspond to the state of the art.

We used the location of the megaliths with a surrounding buffer to obtain information about their median locational characteristics. Of course, other methods might be more suitable or appropriate, such as larger buffers, different functions to extract parameters—like mean or modal values—or approaches that do not focus on the locations itself but rather the catchment characteristics; thus, we encourage the reader to experiment with the different possibilities and discover their strengths and weaknesses.

6.2 Predictive Modelling

Archaeological predictive models—based upon either observed patterns or assumptions about human behaviour—are used to predict the location of archaeological sites or materials in a region [7].

The development of settlement pattern studies has led many archaeologists to understand that settlement locations are influenced by environmental factors, e.g. distance from streams or arable land (see Chap. 7 for a discussion of structured and arbitrary information). This ecological approach was based upon the application of geographical location theory to archaeology, followed by the introduction of site catchment theory [16]. This theory tries to capture the rules that determine human spatial behaviour, focusing on subsistence economy. Hence, the fundamental hypothesis for each predictive modelling is that a causal relationship exists between the spatial behaviour of (pre)historic humans and the natural environment [10]. Archaeological predictive models were developed in the late 1960s as part of the New Archaeology movement and the quantitative revolution [11]. This natural determinant viewpoint is also incorporated into settlement theories based upon concepts of geographical location like those presented by von Thünen [14], Weber [17] and Christaller [4]. Concepts like that of Chisholm [3], who defined settlement locations relative to local resources, were generalised and summarised by Aston [2] or Roberts [13] to fit the archaeological context. These relations depend on the landscape characteristics and the purposes of (pre)historic humans.

It is generally assumed that (a) human location behaviour is patterned [10] and (b) certain parts of the landscape are more attractive for human settlement activity than others [15].

Since the early 1990s there have been several discussions about the logic of prediction, resulting in polarised issues concerning the use of data- (inductive) or theory-driven (deductive) approaches and a discrepancy between environmental-deterministic and social/cognitive models (for more information relating to this topic, see [9, 11, 15]). Despite being useful for describing the different approaches at a methodological level, the dichotomy between data- and theory-driven approaches ignores two important facts: first, the formulation of site location hypotheses is always based upon the knowledge derived from existing data and second, the selection of data sets for inductive modelling is always theory-driven. Therefore, elements of both approaches can be found in many predictive modelling studies [9].

Predictive models can be distinguished according to three categories:

1. Point density approaches: these approaches do not state empirical or theoretical presumptions about the preference of locations; they are not environmentally deterministic (see Chaps. 5 and 7)
2. Inductive approaches: already-known points are considered to have locational characteristics that can be generalised for the population of points; based upon these assumptions, these models are environmentally deterministic.
3. Deductive approaches: we pretend to know why points are located at specific locations; they are based upon prior knowledge and thus—like inductive approaches—deterministic; they are the preferred tools in case of little or unreliable data, where empirical analyses are hampered.

6.2.1 Inductive Models

Predictive models based upon empirical information are called inductive models. In spatial analysis, we can think of location characterisation as a map overlay procedure, whereby different layers are overlain and taken together they describe a location. This location description is used in inductive models as a predictive tool based upon the assumption that unknown places share the same characteristics as already-known places. Accordingly, in filtering the research area for these characteristics, it is possible to identify areas of high potential to find new sites.

Let us apply such an inductive model. Our aim is to identify areas where the potential occurrence of megaliths is high. We will use our calculated terrain parameters and employ two very simple overlay approaches, i.e. binary and weighted binary addition.

Before starting, we will remove the areas covered by the Baltic Sea.

```
> ter.par2 <- ter.par
> srtm[srtm<=0] <- NA
> ter.par2$tpi_15[is.na(srtm)] <- NA
> ter.par2$tpi_5[is.na(srtm)] <- NA
> ter.par2$slope[is.na(srtm)] <- NA
> ter.par2$aspect[is.na(srtm)] <- NA
```

We divide our data into a test and a training set. In order to be reproducible, we undertake this with a specific random seed.

```
> trainSize <- round(nrow(spdf_meg@data) * 0.7)
> testSize <- nrow(spdf_meg@data) - trainSize
> set.seed(333)
> training_indices <- sample(seq_len(nrow(tp_meg)),
+ size=trainSize)
> trainSet <- tp_meg[training_indices,]
> testSet <- tp_meg[-training_indices,]
```

To conduct a binary addition analysis, we need to reclassify the terrain parameter raster into two classes: 1 = characteristics that correspond to the sites and 0 = characteristics that do *not* correspond to the sites. Some sites might be outliers or their characteristics might be very different from the other sites. In order to consider this, we will only select those characteristics that match 90 % of the sites.

```
> q.tpi15 <- quantile(tp_meg$tpi_15, probs = c(.1,.9))
> q.tpi5 <- quantile(tp_meg$tpi_5, probs = c(.1,.9))
> q.sl <- quantile(tp_meg$slope, probs = c(.1,.9))
> q.as <- quantile(tp_meg$aspect, probs = c(.1,.9))
> rcl.tpi15 <- c(-Inf, q.tpi15[1], 0, q.tpi15[1],q.tpi15[2],
+ 1, q.tpi15[2], +Inf, 0)
> rcl.tpi15 <- matrix(rcl.tpi15, ncol = 3, byrow = TRUE)
> ter.par2$tpi_15 <- reclassify(x = ter.par$tpi_15,rcl =
+ rcl.tpi15)
> rcl.tpi5 <- c(-Inf, q.tpi5[1], 0, q.tpi5[1],q.tpi5[2],
+ 1, q.tpi5[2],+Inf, 0)
> rcl.tpi5 <- matrix(rcl.tpi5, ncol = 3, byrow = TRUE)
> ter.par2$tpi_5 <- reclassify(x = ter.par$tpi_5,rcl =
+ rcl.tpi5)
> rcl.sl <- c(-Inf, q.sl[1], 0, q.sl[1],q.sl[2], 1,
+ q.sl[2],+Inf, 0)
> rcl.sl <- matrix(rcl.sl, ncol = 3, byrow = TRUE)
> ter.par2$slope <- reclassify(x = ter.par$slope,rcl =
+ rcl.sl)
> rcl.as <- c(-Inf, q.as[1], 0, q.as[1],q.as[2], 1,
+ q.as[2],+Inf, 0)
> rcl.as <- matrix(rcl.as, ncol = 3, byrow = TRUE)
> ter.par2$aspect <- reclassify(x = ter.par$aspect,
+ rcl = rcl.as)
```

Now we simply sum up the different reclassified raster. Subsequently, we check whether the `testSet` created before is located on the areas of high values, hence giving us an idea about the model's quality (Fig. 6.6).

```
> ba <- overlay(ter.par2, fun=function(w,x,y,z)
+ {return(w+x+y+z)}, unstack = TRUE)
> plot(ba,col = grey(c(7:3/8)),legend.width = 1,
+ cex.axis=.9,tcl=-.3,mgp = c(3,.2,0), axes =
+ FALSE, box = FALSE)
> points(spdf_meg[rownames(testSet),],pch = 19, cex = .3)


> testSet.ba <- extract(x = ba, y = spdf_meg[rownames
+ (testSet),])
> table(testSet.ba)
testSet.ba
 0  1  2  3  4
 5 12 23 22 11
```

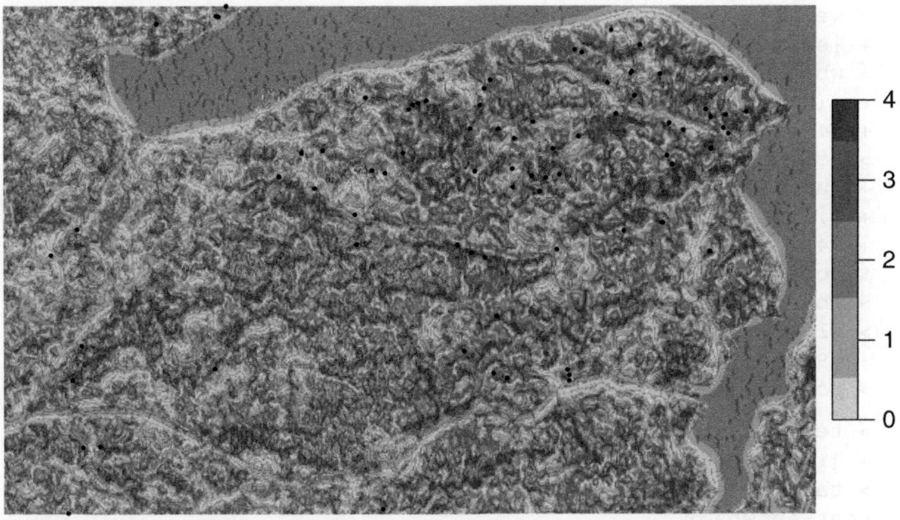

Fig. 6.6 Binary addition predictive model for megaliths

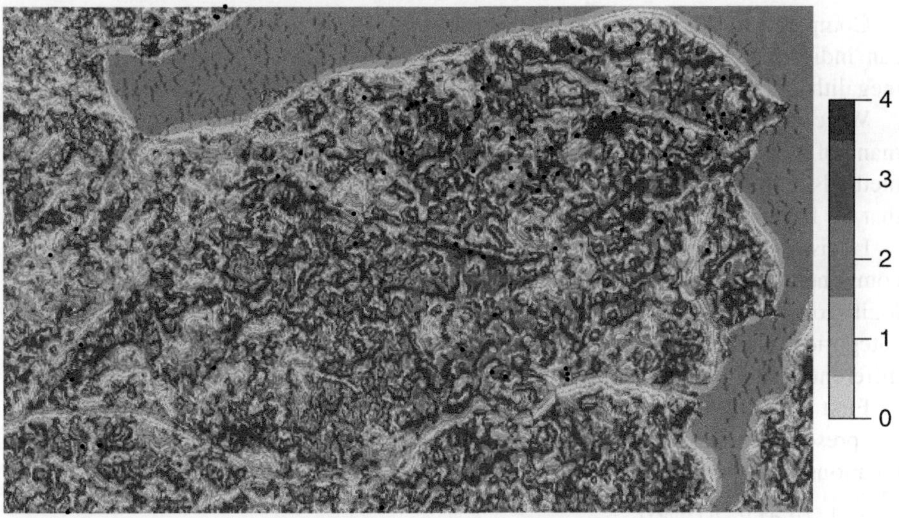

Fig. 6.7 Weighted binary addition predictive model for megaliths

However, this model does not perform well, given that only 11 sites of the `testSet` are actually located on our hypothesised most probable areas. To improve the model, we state another assumption: some parameters are more important than others and this can be measured using standard deviation, whereby the more important a parameter, the smaller the standard deviation in relation to the parameter's range. Using this weighting factor, the classified rasters are weighted and summed up (Fig. 6.7).

```
> weights <- apply(X = tp_meg, MARGIN = 2, FUN = function(x)
+ {sqrt(1/sd(x)*range(x)[2]-range(x)[1])})
> wba <- overlay(ter.par2, fun=function(w,x,y,z){return
+ ((w*weights[1])+(x*weights[2])+(y*weights[3])+(z*weights
+ [4]))}, unstack = TRUE)
> rcl.wba <- c(-Inf, quantile(wba)[1], 0, quantile(wba)[1],
+ quantile(wba)[2], 1, quantile(wba)[2], quantile(wba)[3],
+ 2, quantile(wba)[3], quantile(wba)[4], 3, quantile(wba)
+ [4], quantile(wba)[5], 4)
> rcl.wba <- matrix(rcl.wba, ncol = 3, byrow = TRUE)
> wba.rc <- reclassify(x = wba, rcl = rcl.wba)
> plot(wba.rc,col = grey(c(7:3/8)),legend.width = 1,cex.axis=
+ .9,tcl=-.3,mgp = c(3,.2,0),axes = FALSE, box = FALSE)
> points(spdf_meg[rownames(testSet),],pch = 19, cex = .3)

> testSet.wba.r <- extract(x = wba.rc, y = spdf_meg
+ [rownames(testSet),])
> table(testSet.wba.r)
testSet.wba.r
 0  1  2  3  4
 5 12 16 24 16
```

Compared to the other model, the results again are not very encouraging. This can indicate two things: first, the terrain parameters are inappropriate to model megalith's distribution and second, the methodological approach is too simple.

We cannot resolve the first point so let us try to solve the second. There are many of more advanced predictive modelling approaches. From the broad variety of methods, we only present one example since it is based upon regression approaches that we have already presented, namely logistic regression.

Logistic regression models are generalised linear models with a binomial random component and a logit link function. Logistic regression models are also called logit models [1, 123]. Logistic regression is useful because it is designed to predict categories. The categories in our case are the presence and absence of megaliths on different terrain parameters.

First we need to prepare some random data to represent areas where no sites are present. Subsequently, we create a data set where our empirical and random locations are combined.

```
> library(dismo)
> set.seed(123)
> rand_points <- randomPoints(mask = srtm, p = spdf_meg,
+ n = length(spdf_meg)) # requires dismo
> rand_points <- extract(x = ter.par, y = rand_points,
+ buffer = 200, fun = median,df=TRUE)[,-1]
> emp_ran <- c(rep(1, nrow(tp_meg)), rep(0, nrow
+ (rand_points)))
> geom_data <- data.frame(cbind(as.factor(emp_ran),
+ rbind(tp_meg, rand_points)))
> names(geom_data)[1] <- "emp_ran"
> geom_data <- geom_data[complete.cases(geom_data)==TRUE,]
> head(geom_data,2)
```

```
  emp_ran      tpi_15       tpi_5      slope   aspect
1        1  2.9349788  0.14510626 0.01422135 4.930347
2        1 -0.3939886 -0.03806847 0.02201351 2.475431
> tail(geom_data,2)
    emp_ran      tpi_15       tpi_5      slope   aspect
533       0 -0.9040080  0.10258758 0.02634927 1.003210
534       0 -0.5467961 -0.04793739 0.02091091 4.259732
```

Now we can start with the models. The first one will integrate all parameters that we have.

```
> glm1 <- glm(emp_ran ~ tpi_15+tpi_5+slope+aspect,
+ data=geom_data, family = binomial(link=logit))
> summary(glm1)

Call:
glm(formula = emp_ran ~ tpi_15 + tpi_5 + slope + aspect,
+ family = binomial(link = logit),
    data = geom_data)

Deviance Residuals:
    Min       1Q   Median       3Q      Max
-1.7691  -1.1647   0.7587   1.1252   1.8405

Coefficients:
             Estimate Std. Error z value Pr(>|z|)
(Intercept)   0.21341    0.29634   0.720    0.471
tpi_15        0.18775    0.09662   1.943    0.052 .
tpi_5         0.72409    1.36171   0.532    0.595
slope       -18.17214    7.47427  -2.431    0.015 *
aspect        0.03206    0.06838   0.469    0.639
---
Signif. codes:  0 *** 0.001 ** 0.01 * 0.05 . 0.1 1

(Dispersion parameter for binomial family taken to be 1)

    Null deviance: 736.11  on 530  degrees of freedom
Residual deviance: 713.11  on 526  degrees of freedom
AIC: 723.11

Number of Fisher Scoring iterations: 4
```

What do the results tell us? Thanks to the `summary` function quite a lot. The first thing to notice is the significance codes. As it becomes obvious our model is not very significant. Only `slope` and `tpi_15` show a significant result on the 0.05 and 0.01 level, respectively. Besides this, we can observe a strong negative relation between points' presence and slope, i.e. the probability of the presence of megaliths on the steep slopes is low. For tpi_15, there is a slight positive relationship, i.e. the more ridge-like the terrain, the higher the probability for megaliths, at least in the understanding of this particular model.

Aspect has no real influence and is also not significant. We could conclude that exposition has no influence on location selection, although there is a problem with scale of measurement, which violates the model prerequisites. Hence, aspect cannot be used here.

What about the TPI values? We used two models based upon the idea of deriving local and more regional terrain information. In regression analyses it is problematic when the chosen parameters are correlated. Thus, do the TPI values really show a different thing?

```
> cor(geom_data$tpi_15,geom_data$tpi_5)
[1] 0.8755714
```

The correlation between the TPI with small and large kernel is high; hence, they will explain the same thing. This means that using both in our regression analysis is not useful. Nonetheless, which parameter shall we chose? Well, the significance values of the first model answer this question for us.

Let us create an updated model

```
> glm2 <- glm(emp_ran ~ slope+tpi_15, data=geom_data,
+ family = binomial(link=logit))
> summary(glm2)
...
Coefficients:
             Estimate Std. Error z value Pr(>|z|)
(Intercept)   0.31878    0.18747   1.700   0.0890 .
slope       -18.16541    7.46234  -2.434   0.0149 *
tpi_15        0.22907    0.05116   4.478 7.54e-06 ***
---
Signif. codes:  0 *** 0.001 ** 0.01 * 0.05 . 0.1 1
...
```

This model performs better than the first one and is significant for both parameters. The described relationships are the same as in the first model, although as expected—they are slightly more pronounced.

It is time to evaluate the models predictive utility. We start with a visual inspection (Figs. 6.8 and 6.9) and subsequently perform a gain calculation for all models, including the binary and weighted binary addition (Table 6.1). Gain is calculated as [8, 329]:

$$Gain = 1 - \left(\frac{\%a}{\%s}\right), \tag{6.1}$$

where $\%a$ corresponds to the model's *precision*, i.e. the percentage of total study area covered by the model, while $\%s$ comprises of the percentage of total sites within

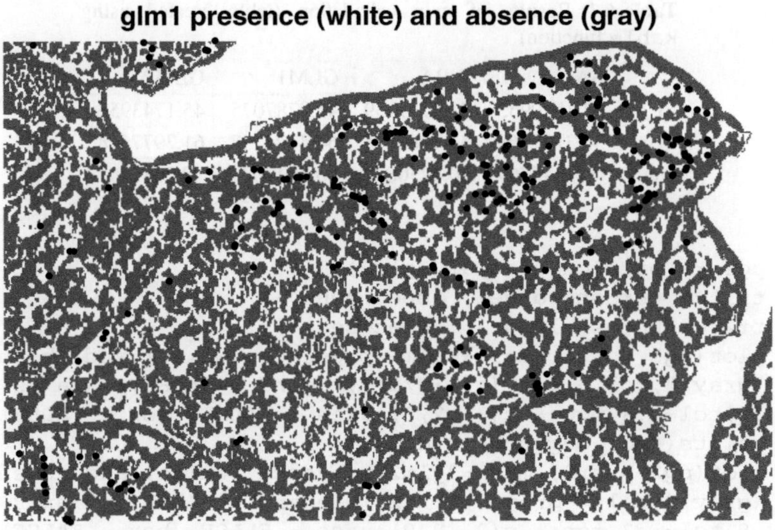

Fig. 6.8 Logistic regression model for megaliths

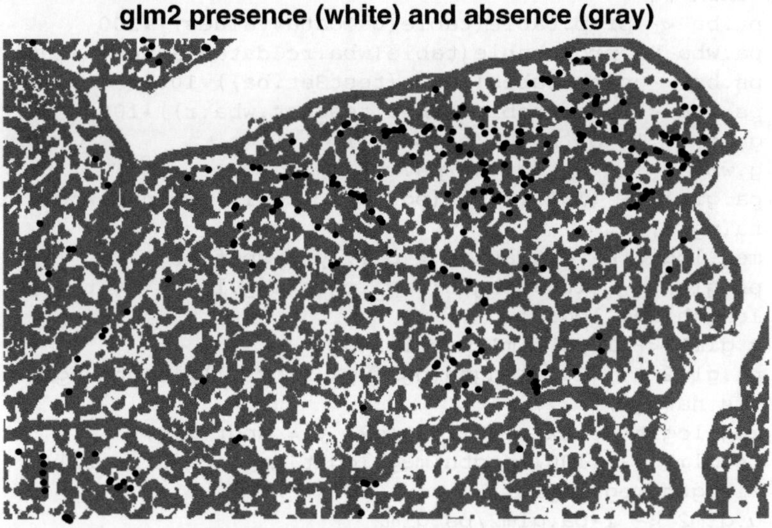

Fig. 6.9 Logistic regression model for megaliths

the modelled area, which represents the model's *accuracy*. Notice that the equation models precision and accuracy as being equally important.

```
> ge1 <- evaluate(p = tp_meg, a = rand_points, model = glm1)
> ge2 <- evaluate(p = tp_meg, a = rand_points, model = glm2)
> pg1 <- predict(ter.par, glm1)
```

Table 6.1 Results of gain calculation (table created using `kable` function)

	BA	WBA	GLM1	GLM2
p_a	7.1520955	21.1777959	46.0787075	45.1743956
p_s	30.3797468	36.7088608	64.4194757	61.7977528
gain	0.7645769	0.4230876	0.2847084	0.2689961

```
> pg2 <- predict(ter.par, glm2)
> tr1 <- threshold(ge1, "spec_sens")
> tr2 <- threshold(ge2, "spec_sens")
> plot(pg1 > tr1, main="glm1 presence (white) and absence
+ (gray)",col = grey(c(1:2/2)),legend = FALSE,cex.axis=
+ .9,tcl=-.3,mgp = c(3,.2,0),axes = FALSE, box = FALSE)
> points(spdf_meg,pch=19,cex=.3)
> plot(pg2 > tr2, main="glm2 presence (white) and absence
+ (gray)",col = grey(c(1:2/2)),legend = FALSE,cex.axis=
+ .9,tcl=-.3,mgp = c(3,.2,0),axes = FALSE, box = FALSE)
> points(spdf_meg,pch=19,cex=.3)

## GAIN ##
> pa.ba <- prop.table(table(ba@data@values))*100
> pa.wba <- prop.table(table(wba.rc@data@values))*100
> ps.ba <- prop.table(table(testSet.ba))*100
> ps.wba <- prop.table(table(testSet.wba.r))*100
> g.ba <- 1-(pa.ba[5]/ps.ba[4])
> g.wba <- 1-(pa.wba[5]/ps.wba[5])
> pa.glm1 <- (100*length(pg1[pg1 > tr1]))/length(pg1[!is.
+ na(pg1)])
> meg.logit <- extract(x = pg1, y = spdf_meg)
> ps.glm1 <- (100*length(meg.logit[meg.logit > tr1]))/
+ length(meg.logit)
> g.glm1 <- 1-pa.glm1/ps.glm1
> pa.glm2 <- (100*length(pg2[pg2 > tr2]))/length(pg2[
+ !is.na(pg2)])
> meg.logit <- extract(x = pg2, y = spdf_meg)
> ps.glm2 <- (100*length(meg.logit[meg.logit > tr2]))
+ /length(meg.logit)
> g.glm2 <- 1-pa.glm2/ps.glm2
> gain <- data.frame(BA=c(pa.ba[5],ps.ba[4],g.ba), WBA=
+ c(pa.wba[5],ps.wba[5],g.wba), GLM1=c(pa.glm1,ps.glm1,
+ g.glm1), GLM2=c(pa.glm2,ps.glm2,g.glm2), row.names =
+ c("p_a","p_s","gain"))
```

Gain values larger than 0.5 have a positive predictive utility while gain values smaller 0.5 have none [12, 215]. Using this threshold, our models do not have predictive utility, aside from the most simple, binary addition model. Nevertheless, the results of the gain calculation tell us a lot about the model structure and the underlying data, although the input data were little and their societal meaning is very low.

6.2.2 Deductive Models

Deductive models are equivalent to our theoretical model. They start with theoretical assumptions about the location of places and test the predictive utility of these ideas based upon known data. An example would be the assumption that megalithic graves prefer elevated locations. Besides, such models can be seen as heuristic tools helping to understand more about the patterns of locations and their characteristics. Examples of deductive predictive models can be found in the literature—such as [6]—although they are less frequent than their inductive counterparts.

Besides its potentials, predictive modelling in general is consistently and actively criticised. The main critiques are (summarised from [9]):

- Many archaeological sites are buried; thus, they cannot be modelled because nothing is known about their real distributions.
- Human behaviour did not occur in discrete bounded areas but rather formed a continuum over the landscape. Therefore, archaeological site distribution cannot be modelled and the site is a non-meaningful concept.
- Past environments were different from present ones; therefore, it is not possible to model the past based upon the present.
- The most interesting sites are those that do not fit the pattern.
- Environmental variables shown to be important to site locations may only be proxies for variables that were actually important.
- Modern soil characteristics are irrelevant to past farming practices because they have changed since the past.
- Grouping sites of many types into a single, site-present class creates too much variability to be modelled.

Furthermore, Verhagen [15] states that predictive models are inappropriate regarding reality owing to

- a biased selection of archaeological data and environmental parameters;
- consequently, they disregard cultural factors in the archaeological data set, as well as;
- in the choice of environmental parameters and
- neglect the changing landscape.

However, the application of archaeological predictive models is useful because human behaviour is patterned with respect to the natural and social environment. It is possible to gain new knowledge by observing relationships between human residues and environmental parameters [9].

6.3 Problems

6.1. We extract raster location information using a buffer: why? Moreover, what new problems arise and what problems have we solved by applying this approach?

6.2. What is the reason why the number of `NAs` of the terrain parameter raster differs in the different layers, despite the input data being the same?

6.3. Please write a function that applies the reclassification procedure for the binary and weighted binary addition method.

6.4. Why is it problematic to use the terrain parameter `aspect` as we used it here? How could this issue be resolved?

6.5. Interpret Table 6.1. Why is the gain for the binary addition model so high? Discuss which model performs best. Do you think that gain calculation where precision and accuracy are equally important is useful?

References

1. Agresti, A. (2002). *Categorical data analysis*. New Jersey: Wiley-Interscience.
2. Aston, M. (1985). *Interpreting the landscape - landscape archaeology and local history*. London: Routledge, Taylor and Francis Group.
3. Chisholm, M. (2007). *Rural settlement and land use*. London: Hutchinson.
4. Christaller, W. (1968). *Die zentralen Orte in Süddeutschland - Eine ökonomisch-geographische Untersuchung über die Gesetzmäßigkeiten der Verbreitung und Entwicklung der Siedlungen mit städtischer Funktion*. Darmstadt: Wissenschaftliche Buchgesellschaft. Reprint of edition 1933, Jena.
5. Guisan, A., Weiss, S. B., & Weiss, A. D. (1999). GLM versus CCA spatial modeling of plant species distribution. *Plant Ecology, 143*, 107–122
6. Kamermans, H., Leusen, M. v., Verhagen, P., Bakels, C., & Kamermans, H. (Eds.) (2009). *Archaeological prediction and risk management: alternatives to current practice*. Leiden: Faculty of Archaeology/Leiden University Press.
7. Kohler, T. A., & Parker, S. C. (1986). Predictive models for archaeological resource location. In Schiffer, M. B. (Ed.), *Advances in archaeological method and theory 9* (pp. 397–452). New York: Academic Press.
8. Kvamme, K. L. (1988). Development and testing of quantitative models. In W. J. Judge, & L. Sebastian (Eds.), *Quantifying the present and predicting the past. Theory, method and application of archaeological predictive modelling* (pp. 325–428). Denver: U.S. Department of the Interior, Bureau of Land Management Service Center.
9. Kvamme, K. L. (2006). There and back again: revisiting archaeological location modeling. In M. W. Mehrer, & K. L. Wescott (Eds.), *GIS and archaeological site location modeling* (pp. 2–34). Boca Raton: Taylor and Francis.
10. Kvamme, K. L. (1999). Recent directions and developments in geographical information systems. *Journal of Archaeological Research, 7*(2), 153–201.
11. van Leusen, M., Deeben, J., Hallewas, D., Kamermans, H., Verhagen, P., & Zoetbrood, P. (2005). A baseline for predictive modelling in the Netherlands. In M. v. Leusen & H. Kamermans (Eds.), *Predictive modelling for archaeological heritage management: a research agenda* (pp. 25–92). Amersfoort: National Service for Archaeological Heritage.

12. Mink, P. B., Stokes, B. J., & Pollack, D. (2006). Points vs. polygons: A test case using a statewide geographic information system. In M. W. Mehrer & K. L. Wescott (Eds.), *GIS and archaeological site location modeling* (pp. 200–219). Boca Raton: CRC Press.
13. Roberts, B. K. (1996). *Landscapes of settlement prehistory to the present*. London, New York: Routledge.
14. von Thünen, J. H. (1910). *Der isolierte Staat in Beziehung auf Landwirtschaft und Sozialökonomie*. Gustav Fischer: Jena.
15. Verhagen, P. (2007). *Case studies in archaeological predictive modelling*. Leiden: Leiden University Press.
16. Vita-Finzi, C., & Higgs, E. (1970). Prehistoric economy in the Mount Carmel Area of Palestine: Site catchment analysis. *Proceedings of the Prehistoric Society*, *36*, 1–37.
17. Weber, A. (1922). *Über den Standort der Industrien - 1. Teil: Reine Theorie des Standorts*. Tübingen: Mohr.

Chapter 7
Point Pattern

7.1 Point Processes

Spatial distributions of points are dominant among the archaeological sources, whereby distribution maps of certain types of finds are just one example. Hence, point distribution producing processes are important models for our topic. We can define (compare [14]):

Definition 7.1. A **point process** is a stochastic model that produces a point pattern under consideration of some parameters.

and

Definition 7.2. A **point pattern** is a set of points in an area interpreted as a realisation of a point process.

Point processes are very useful models when the object location is the main information. For example, this is the case with archaeological distribution maps. The location of finds is not completely arbitrary but also not completely determined; rather, the location can depend on several parameters. Point processes model the emergence of points in a certain area in dependence of different parameters or facts. We can distinguish different influences on the point location that belong to two categories and add up to a determination of the point location.

- *Factors of random point patterns* are not influenced by spatial parameters. These factors are not subject to formal analysis but are addressed in the tradition of post-processual archaeology.
  - Noise. Based upon the current knowledge, the location does not depend on spatial parameters. This component seems to be completely arbitrary.

O. Nakoinz, D. Knitter, *Modelling Human Behaviour in Landscapes*, Quantitative Archaeology and Archaeological Modelling, DOI 10.1007/978-3-319-29538-1_7

  - Individuality. Most cases have a component that is not arbitrary but rather is based upon rational choices in which individual preferences and knowledge are involved. Since no systematic is visible, this component seems to be random.
  - Non-spatial processes. Non-spatial relationships that connect spatial parameters in a non-linear way can influence the point location without producing recognisable patterns. For example, path dependency can be a part of this mechanism.

- *Factors of structured point patterns* are determined by spatial parameters. These factors are subject to formal analysis.
  - Dependence on other factors. For new points certain values of influencing parameters are preferred. For instance, settlements can prefer certain soil types.
  - Dependence on other points. The relationship to other points is considered when new points are located. Villages are usually located at a certain distance to other villages.
  - Dependence on structures. The location of a point is determined because it is part of a larger structure. The whole structure is placed in the landscape and determines the location of the parts. The distance between a settlement and grave yard is usually smaller than a certain threshold.

In the context of point pattern analysis the factors structuring point patterns are called first-, second- and third-order properties (Fig. 7.1):

First-order properties It is assumed that the point location does not depend on other points. The impact of other parameters (covariates) on point location is explored.

Second-order properties It is assumed that the point location depends on other points. The distance to other points is regarded.

Third-order properties It is assumed that the point location depends on other points. Point triples are regarded.

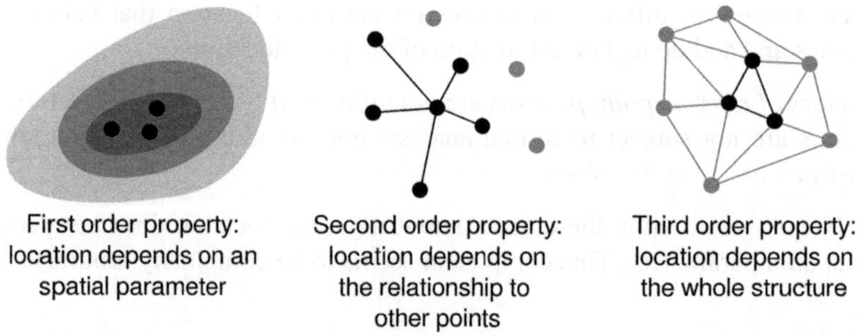

Fig. 7.1 Three classes of spatial dependencies

Point pattern analysis is an interdisciplinary field of research dealing with the determination of the location of points. There are many publications focusing on this topic or including this topic in different disciplines [1–6, 8–12, 14, 17, 18, 21–23]. In archaeology, the publications as well as the applications are rather few [7, 15, 16, 19, 20].

Some terms occurring in the field of point pattern analysis shall be mentioned. The *intensity* of a point process is the probability of being a point in a certain area. The point *density* function is related, as a further important characterisation of a point process. A *simple* point process has no coincident points. A *stationary* point process has a constant point density function. In the case of *isotropy*, the direction does not matter for the point process. *Homogeneous* point processes are stationary and isotropic. A homogeneous *Poisson* point process is completely spatially random in the sense that the point location does not depend on other points. A Poisson point process is stationary and simple and serves as a reference process for many purposes. The *Cox* process is an inhomogeneous Poisson process with a random intensity function. A *Gibbs* process involves influence from other points, which is given by an interaction function. In the case of a *hard core* Gibbs process, points avoid each other up to a certain threshold and they ignore each other. The interaction function has the shape of a step. A *Strauss* process has a constant influence within a certain distance threshold. Finally, *Neyman–Scott* processes are clustered point processes with random cluster centres, which function as a center of intensity functions.

The R-package `spatstat` allows to simulate some of those point processes. Please refer to Chap. 12 for an example of such simulations.

7.2 First-Order Properties

We start with the first-order properties by exploring the dependency of the location of Bronze Age barrows on different parameters. The parameters are the elevation, the location of the Neolithic monuments and the location of medieval villages. We have to compare the quantities of the different parameters at a certain point. Two considerations guide us to the right methodological approach. We cannot directly compare points that are distributed in the same area but not at the same locations. First, we have to transform the point incidents into a field, which can be achieved by density calculations. Densities can be compared at any point in the area of interest. Please refer to Chap. 4 for further details on density calculations.

```
> sdev <- 2*mean(nndist(ppp_meg)+mean(nndist(ppp_tum)))
> bb   <- bbox(sgdf_srtm)
> win  <- owin(xrange=c(bb[1,1],bb[1,2]),
+ yrange= c(bb[2,1],bb[2,2]), unitname="m")
> meg_dens <- density(ppp_meg, kernel="gaussian",
+ sigma=sdev, dimyx=c(36,56), w=win,  > edge=TRUE,
+ at="pixels")
```

```
> tum_dens <- density(ppp_tum, kernel="gaussian",
+ sigma=sdev, dimyx=c(36,56), w=win, edge=TRUE,
    at="pixels")
vil_dens <- density(ppp_vil, kernel="gaussian",
+ sigma=sdev, dimyx=c(36,56), w=win,  edge=TRUE,
    at="pixels")
```

The points where we compare the values should not be the monuments or villages locations, because this could produce a bias. Hence we use random sampling points.

```
> samppt     <- spsample(sgdf_srtm, 500, type="random")
```

Now, we can sample the grid objects. The function `overlay` produces a warning that `overlay` is depreciated and one should use the function `over`. As long as `overlay` works, this is not a problem, although when the function is removed from R one must switch to `over`, which works a slightly differently.

```
> library(maptools)
> sgdf_meg_dens      <- as.SpatialGridDataFrame.im
    (meg_dens)
> meg_dens_samp      <- overlay(x=sgdf_meg_dens,
    y=samppt)
> sgdf_tum_dens      <- as.SpatialGridDataFrame.im
    (tum_dens)
> tum_dens_samp      <- overlay(x=sgdf_tum_dens,
    y=samppt)
> sgdf_vil_dens      <- as.SpatialGridDataFrame.im
    (vil_dens)
> vil_dens_samp      <- overlay(x=sgdf_vil_dens,
    y=samppt)
> dens_samp          <- meg_dens_samp
> names(dens_samp)[names(dens_samp) == 'v'] <- 'meg'
> dens_samp@data     <- cbind(dens_samp@data, tum_dens
    _samp@data$v)
> names(dens_samp)[names(dens_samp) ==   'tum_dens_samp
    @data$v'] <- 'tum'
> dens_samp@data     <- cbind(dens_samp@data, vil_dens
    _samp@data$v)
> names(dens_samp)[names(dens_samp) ==   'vil_dens
    _samp@data$v'] <- 'vil'
> dens_samp@data     <- cbind(dens_samp@data, elev_dens
    _samp@data[,1])
> names(dens_samp)[4] <- 'elev'
```

Now we can run the Pearson correlation test which gives us the correlation between two samples, where x and y are the vectors of the two samples.

$$r_{xy} = \frac{\sum_{i=1}^{n}(x_i - \bar{x})(y_i - \bar{y})}{\sqrt{\sum_{i=1}^{n}(x_i - \bar{x})^2}\sqrt{\sum_{i=1}^{n}(y_i - \bar{y})^2}} \tag{7.1}$$

```
> cor.test(dens_samp@data$meg, dens_samp@data$tum,
+ method="p")
Pearson's product-moment correlation
data:  dens_samp@data$meg and dens_samp@data$tum
t = 9.9529, df = 498, p-value < 2.2e-16
alternative hypothesis: true correlation is not equal to 0
95 percent confidence interval:
 0.3314748 0.4779447
sample estimates:
      cor
0.4073256
> cor.test(dens_samp@data$vil, dens_samp@data$tum,
+ method="p")
Pearson's product-moment correlation
data:  dens_samp@data$vil and dens_samp@data$tum
t = 0.1741, df = 498, p-value = 0.8618
alternative hypothesis: true correlation is not equal
   to 0
95 percent confidence interval:
 -0.07994224  0.09542834
sample estimates:
        cor
0.007803046
> cor.test(dens_samp@data$elev, dens_samp@data$tum,
+ method="p")
Pearson's product-moment correlation
data:  dens_samp@data$elev and dens_samp@data$tum
t = 6.1569, df = 497, p-value = 1.531e-09
alternative hypothesis: true correlation is not equal
   to 0
95 percent confidence interval:
 0.1826994 0.3459043
sample estimates:
      cor
0.2662087
```

Obviously, there is no correlation of megaliths and tumuli, but rather of villages and tumuli. The elevation–tumuli correlation coefficient is small, which is certainly unsurprising. The values for rerunning this test may differ since the sample points are random. A principal component analysis is useful to learn more about the relationship between the variables. The method transforms the data to obtain equally scaled and uncorrelated dimensions.

```
> prcomp(na.omit(dens_samp@data))
Standard deviations:
[1] 1.059019e+01 7.021117e-07 3.849081e-07 2.070099e-08
Rotation:
              PC1           PC2           PC3           PC4
meg  8.116088e-09 -3.355311e-01 -9.418227e-01  1.972217e-02
tum  1.757409e-08 -9.420277e-01  3.354931e-01 -5.306281e-03
vil  1.709456e-10 -1.619074e-03 -2.035925e-02 -9.997914e-01
elev 1.000000e+00  1.927876e-08  1.751410e-09  1.040962e-10
```

The eigenvalues—'Standard deviations' in the console output—show how much of the variance is explained by the new variables. The most important variable is the first one. The principal components ('PC') are the new variables themselves. The loadings—'Rotation' in the console output—give the coordinates of old variables in the coordinate system of the new ones. PC1 is mainly elevation. PC2 and PC3 are different combinations of the density of megaliths and tumuli with a differing influence on the components and PC4 is mainly villages. The values show the degree of dependency between the different variables. In the case of rather complicated interrelationships, this approach provides insights into the dependencies that cannot be obtained by other methods.

In the first-order point pattern analysis, it is sometimes important to establish whether two point patterns have the same preferences concerning certain parameters. Do Neolithic and Bronze Age monuments prefer the same elevation? For this purpose, we have to ascertain whether the distribution of the elevation data of the two point patterns is the same. The Kolmogorov–Smirnov test (KS test) is an appropriate method for this purpose. After sampling the elevation data at the point locations from both point patterns, we can apply the test. The test statistic is

$$d_e = \sup_x |F_e(x) - F_t(x)| \tag{7.2}$$

In this equation, $F_e(x)$ is the empirical cumulative distribution function, while $F_t(x)$ is the theoretical or the other empirical one.

```
> meg_elev_samp     <- overlay(x=sgdf_srtm,  y=spdf_meg)
> tum_elev_samp     <- overlay(x=sgdf_srtm,  y=spdf_tum)
> vil_elev_samp     <- overlay(x=sgdf_srtm,  y=spdf_vil)
> ks.test(meg_elev_samp@data[,1], tum_elev_samp@data[,1])
Two-sample Kolmogorov--Smirnov test
data:  meg_elev_samp@data[, 1] and tum_elev_samp@data[, 1]
D = 0.1426, p-value = 0.002416
alternative hypothesis: two-sided
> ks.test(meg_elev_samp@data[,1], vil_elev_samp@data[,1])
Two-sample Kolmogorov--Smirnov test
data:  meg_elev_samp@data[, 1] and vil_elev_samp@data[, 1]
D = 0.4774, p-value = 0.007034
alternative hypothesis: two-sided
> ks.test(tum_elev_samp@data[,1], vil_elev_samp@data[,1])
```

```
Two-sample Kolmogorov--Smirnov test
data:  tum_elev_samp@data[, 1] and vil_elev_samp@data[, 1]
D = 0.5314, p-value = 0.001605
alternative hypothesis: two-sided
```

We find that none of the pairs of point patterns tested show the same distribution of elevation values and hence have the same preferences for elevation. This does not contradict the correlation previously found. The correlation was about similar values at the same sampling point and the KS test is about similar distributions of values at different places. A note of caution is appropriate at this point, namely that the use of p-values of statistical tests has been strongly criticised in recent years [13, 24]. Accordingly, the reader should apply such methods with sensibility.

7.3 Second-Order Properties

The key question of second-order properties is whether the location of points depends on other points. If the location of new points depends on other points, this is called interaction between points. If not and if no other effects are present, we speak of complete spatial randomness (CSR). Hence, CSR tests are the methodological focus in second-order point pattern analysis. They compare an empirical model of the data with a theoretical model, which represents a complete spatial random Poisson process. The traditional approach is to calculate the point densities in a coarse grid for the empirical data and a theoretical model and apply a test statistics. In spatial statistics, distance-based approaches dominate. If the cumulative distribution of distances between the empirical points matches that of a Poisson process, CSR is established.

However, the usually applied CSR tests are able to produce more information than to detect complete spatial randomness. They are able to distinguish three basic types of point patterns (Fig. 7.2):

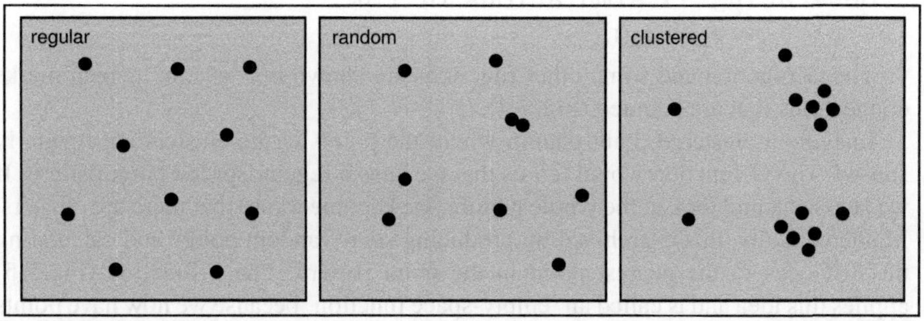

Fig. 7.2 Three types of point patterns

Random points The point location is random and does not depend on other points. Interaction between points is not assumed.

Regular points Regular spaced points are the result of a kind of negative interaction. There is repulsion between the points.

Clustered points Clustered points are the result of a positive interaction. There is attraction between the points.

There are several functions in use as CSR tests. The G-function cumulates the frequency of nearest-neighbour distances. It calculates what fraction of all nearest-neighbour distances $d_{\min}(s_i)$ in the pattern is less than d.

$$G(d) = \frac{\#\{d_{\min}(s_i) \leq d\}}{n} \tag{7.3}$$

If the point pattern is clustered, it is more likely to have another point nearby than in a random point pattern. There are more short distances to the nearest neighbour and the cumulative curve rapidly increases at short distances.

Nonetheless, how different from the theoretical Poisson process curve does the empirical curve have to be to establish a point process that is not completely spatially random? We can assume that some variance around the theoretical model is allowed. Monte Carlo simulations allow calculating an envelope for random points. We can produce several random point patterns and calculate the $G(d)$-values. Subsequently, we can draw an envelope around all values that occur in the simulations of random point processes (grey area in Fig. 7.3). This is undertaken automatically in the R-function `envelope`. In this function y is a ppp-object defined in the `spatstat` package. The function is passed with the fun argument where certain keywords replace the function that will be used. While `nsim` is the number of simulations `nrank` refers to the data for the envelope. A value of 1 means that minimum and maximum values are used. A value of 2 means that the minimum and maximum values are excluded as outliers and the second smallest/highest values are used.

```
> library(spatstat)
> meg_env_g <- envelope(y = ppp_meg, fun = Gest,
+ nrank = 2, nsim = 99)
Generating 99 simulations of CSR ...
> plot(meg_env_g)
```

The G-function and some other functions are shown in a scheme, which marks connections that are counted (Fig. 7.4).

Imagine a clustered point pattern where the points in the clusters are regularly spaced. The G-function would tell us that we have a regular spaced point pattern. If we step back and look at the whole picture, we become aware that there are clusters. Mathematically, this is archived by producing some random points and calculating the distances to the nearest point in the point pattern. The F-function (Fig. 7.5) applies this idea and is called an 'empty-space function' because we now have points in the empty space between the clusters. The F-function behaves differently than the G-function for clustered and even patterns. In a clustered pattern $F(d)$ rises slow at

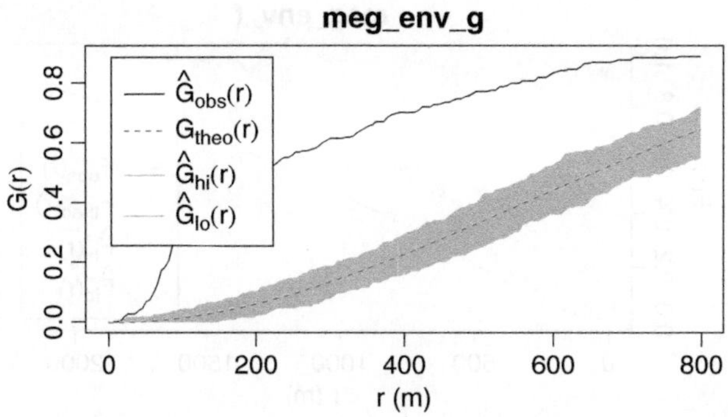

Fig. 7.3 Megaliths, CSR test, G-function (ppa-Meg-g)

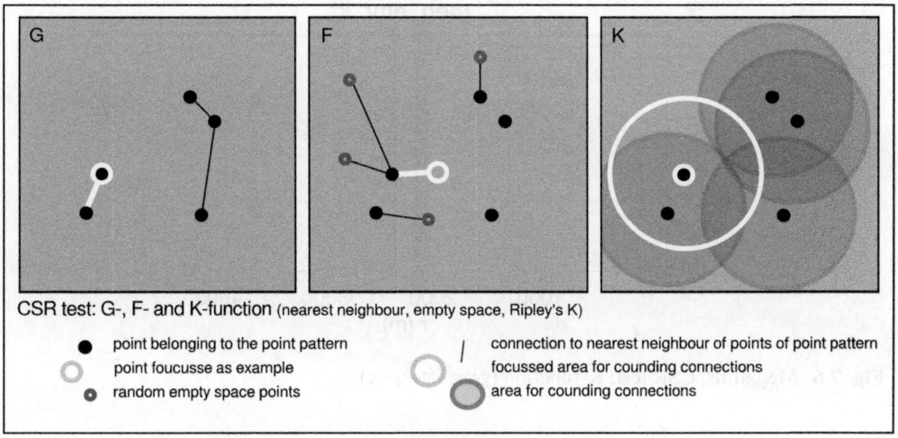

Fig. 7.4 Scheme of some functions for CSR-tests

first but faster at larger distances. This is because it is less likely to have another point nearby the empty space points than in a random point pattern.

$$F(d) = \frac{\#\{d_{\min}(p_i, s) \leq d\}}{m} \tag{7.4}$$

```
> meg_env_f <- envelope(ppp_meg, fun = Fest,
+ nrank = 2, nsim = 99)
Generating 99 simulations of CSR ...
> plot(meg_env_f)
```

Imagine a point pattern that comprises pairs of points in a small yet equal distance. The G- and F-function would tell us that we have a regular point pattern despite the overall point pattern, which might have clusters of point pairs.

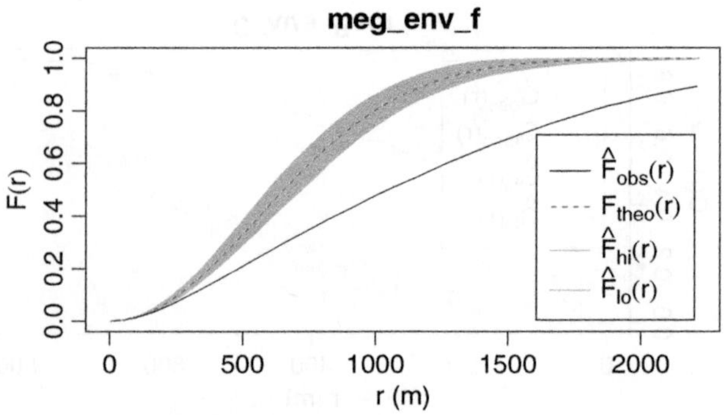

Fig. 7.5 Megaliths, CSR test, F-function (`ppa-Meg-f`)

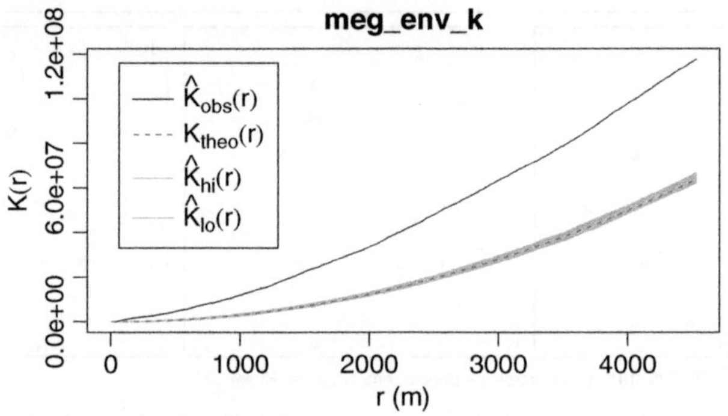

Fig. 7.6 Megaliths, CSR test, K-function (`ppa-Meg-k`)

Ripley's K-function (Fig. 7.6) tries to overcome this problem by looking at all connections of points up to a certain threshold, rather than only the nearest neighbours. This function is assumed to be more stable.

$$K(d) = \frac{\sum_{i=1}^{n} \#(S \in C(s_i, d))}{n\lambda} \tag{7.5}$$

```
> meg_env_k <- envelope(ppp_meg, fun = Kest,
+ nrank = 2, nsim = 99)
Generating 99 simulations of CSR ...
> plot(meg_env_k)
```

In order to stabilize the variance and make visual comparisons easier, it is common in spatial statistics to conduct a square root transformation of the K-function, known as the L-function [14, 95] (Fig. 7.7).

$$L(d) = \sqrt{\frac{K(d)}{\pi}}. \tag{7.6}$$

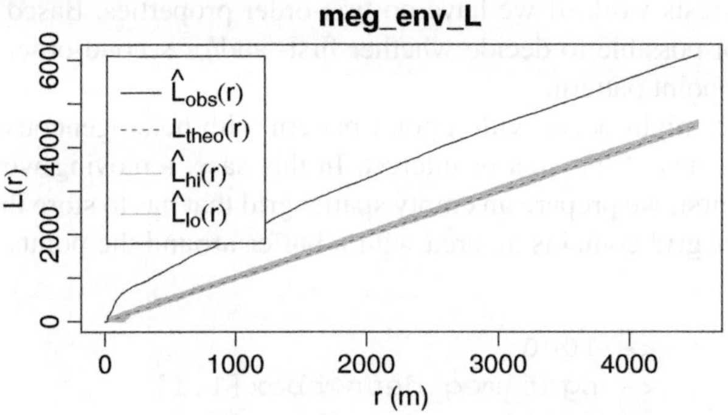

Fig. 7.7 Megaliths, CSR test, L-function (`ppa-Meg-l`)

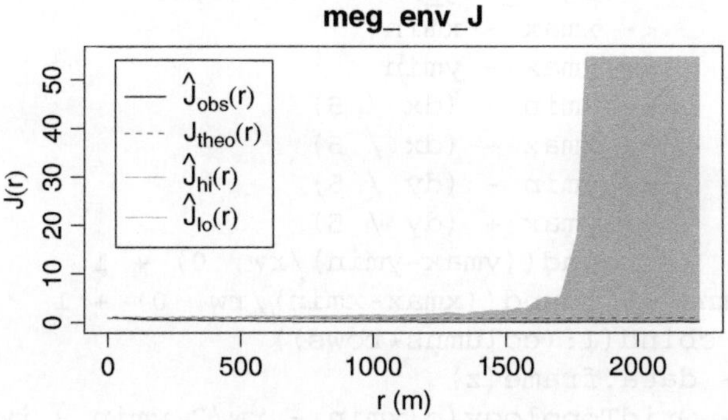

Fig. 7.8 Megaliths, CSR test, J-function (`ppa-Meg-j`)

```
> meg_env_l <- envelope(ppp_meg, fun = Lest,
+ nrank = 2, nsim = 99)
Generating 99 simulations of CSR ...
> plot(meg_env_l)
```

An other function that is usually mentioned in the field of point pattern analysis is the J-function, which is a combination of the G- and F-function (Fig. 7.8).

$$J(d) = \frac{1 - F(d)}{1 - G(d)} \tag{7.7}$$

```
> meg_env_j <- envelope(ppp_meg, fun = Jest,
+ nrank = 2, nsim = 99)
Generating 99 simulations of CSR ...
> plot(meg_env_j)
```

We reject this function especially because it is a combination of the G- and F-function. It is no longer possible to distinguish different phenomena that have a different effect on both functions. The J-function might be useful for CSR-testing but not for point pattern characterization.

The CSR tests work, if we have no first-order properties. Based upon the CSR tests, it is not possible to decide whether first- and/or second-order effects lead to the observed point pattern.

A problem might occur with a point pattern with heterogeneous characteristics in different zones of the area of interest. In this case, a moving window approach might help. First, we prepare an empty spatial grid that has to store the results of our analysis. This grid contains an area with a buffer around the points from the point pattern.

```
> rw       <- 1000
> xmin     <- sgdf_meg_dens@bbox[1,1]
> xmax     <- sgdf_meg_dens@bbox[1,2]
> ymin     <- sgdf_meg_dens@bbox[2,1]
> ymax     <- sgdf_meg_dens@bbox[2,2]
> dx       <- xmax - xmin
> dy       <- ymax - ymin
> xmin     <- xmin - (dx / 5)
> xmax     <- xmax + (dx / 5)
> ymin     <- ymin - (dy / 5)
> ymax     <- ymax + (dy / 5)
> rows   <- round((ymax-ymin)/rw, 0) + 1
> columns <- round((xmax-xmin)/rw, 0) + 1
> z <- cbind(1:(columns*rows))
> df <- data.frame(z)
> gt <- GridTopology(c(xmin - rw/2,ymin - rw/2),
+ c(rw,rw), c(columns,rows))
> ras <- SpatialGridDataFrame(gt, df, proj4string =
+ CRS(as.character(crs1)))
```

The next step is to apply the moving window. We use a loop through all raster cells in the prepared grid. For each cell, the calculation of the G-function is performed with the command `Gest`. In this calculation, the radius of the mowing window defines which points are included in the calculation. A problem occurs when we try to represent the result of such a calculation by one number. The solution is to sum the differences of the theoretical and the empirical curve. This value cannot contain all information expressed by the G-curve, although it is a good representative for the result.

```
> fs_nn <- nndist(ppp_tum)
> radius <- 10000
> r <- seq(0, radius, 250)
> win <- owin(xrange=c(xmin=xmin,xmax=xmax),
+ yrange=
+ c(ymin=ymin,ymax=ymax), unitname="m")
> for (i in seq(along=ras@data$z))  {
+    xr        <- coordinates(ras)[i,1]
```

```
+       yr       <- coordinates(ras)[i,2]
+     distances <- sqrt((ppp_tum$x -xr)^2 +
+ (ppp_tum$y -yr)^2)
+     indiz <- which(distances<radius)
+     if (length(indiz) > 2 ) {
+         x <- ppp_tum$x[indiz]
+         y <- ppp_tum$y[indiz]
+         name <- ppp_tum$x[indiz]
+         fsgf <- SpatialPointsDataFrame
+ (cbind(x, y), as.data.frame(name),
+ proj4string= CRS(as.character(crs1)))
+         fspt <- ppp(fsgf@coords[,1],
+ fsgf@coords[,2], window=win)
+         gfs <- Gest(fspt, r=r,correction="km")
+         value <-  mean(gfs$theo-gfs$km)
+         ras@data$z[i]    <- value
+     }
+     else {ras@data$z[i] <-0}
> }
```

Finally, we plot and store the results (Fig. 7.9). Dark shades of grey and high numbers indicate a regular point pattern, while light shades of grey and low numbers indicate a clustered point pattern. The result mainly shows a clustered point pattern. Dark grey shades can be interpreted as edge effects in this case study.

```
> image(ras, col = gray.colors(20))
> points(ppp_tum$x, ppp_tum$y, pch=16, cex=0.4)
> writeAsciiGrid(ras,  "c7_movingWindowG.asc",
+ attr = 1, na.value = -999999, dec=".")
```

The moving window approach reduces the information available from the functions and hence it is not useful as a default tool. It is a tool specialised in detecting spatial variations in point pattern characteristics and its application is restricted to rather simple point patterns. In case of complicated point patterns, the shape of the whole curve is required.

Which function is best to characterize a point pattern? Why are we discussing more than one function? Obviously, the functions give us different results. They are sensitive for different types of clustered and regular point patterns. The three basic categories of point patterns are not sufficient to describe point patterns. Referring back to our example, we can ask which point pattern type is a regular grid of clusters with random points. The answer is that this depends on the method of CSR test. In the literature, one can sometimes find the advice to use different CSR tests. If all produce the same result, it is clear which point pattern type it is. However, if they differ, the interpretation is that the point pattern type is unspecified. When the task is to test for CSR, this might be a sufficient solution, albeit not for characterizing point patterns. We have to take into account different definitions of clustered and

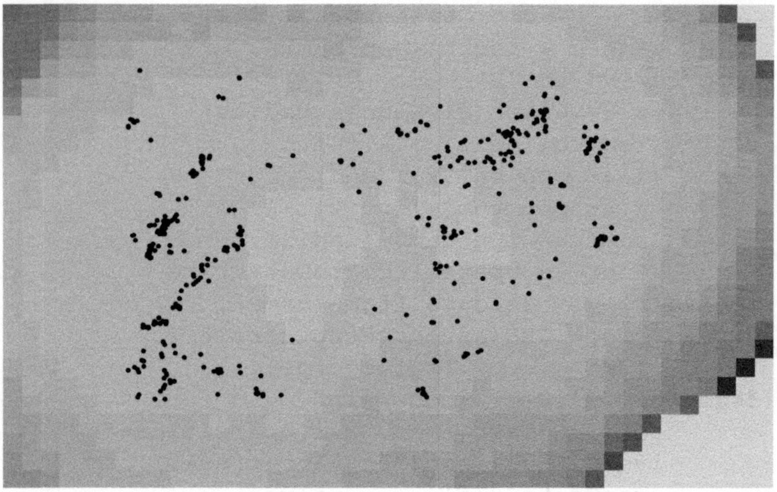

Fig. 7.9 Bronze Age barrows, G-function, moving window

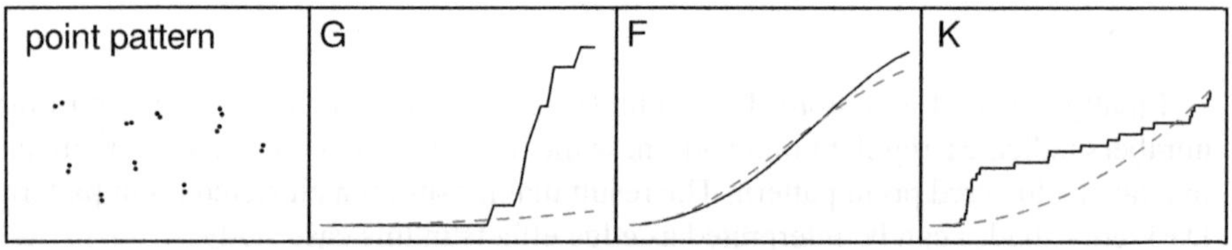

Fig. 7.10 Complicated point pattern with G-, F- and K-function. *Dashed line*: theoretical curve for CSR; *solid line*: empirical curve

regular point patterns and the different sensitivity of different functions. The three functions form a good basis for characterizing different variants of point patterns. In particular, complicated point patterns require at least these three functions. Four examples of complicated point patterns will exemplify this.

Our first example is a random pattern of point pairs (Fig. 7.10). The G-function shows a steep step at the beginning of the curve, since the regular distance between the points of a pair indicates a regular pattern. In detail, the steepness indicates the regular internal pattern of the clusters, indicated by the step above the theoretical curve. However the empty space F-function, however, sees the random pattern of the pairs. The K-function has the steep step at the beginning and then other distances, which increasingly tend towards randomness.

The next pattern is a regular distribution of regular clusters (Fig. 7.11). The G-function again has the steep step, which indicates the clusters with regular inner structure. The step begins at a certain distance and hence shows the regular inner structure of the clusters. By contrast, the F-function detects the clustered distribution of the clusters. This aspect can be seen in the K-function in the horizontal upper part of the curve.

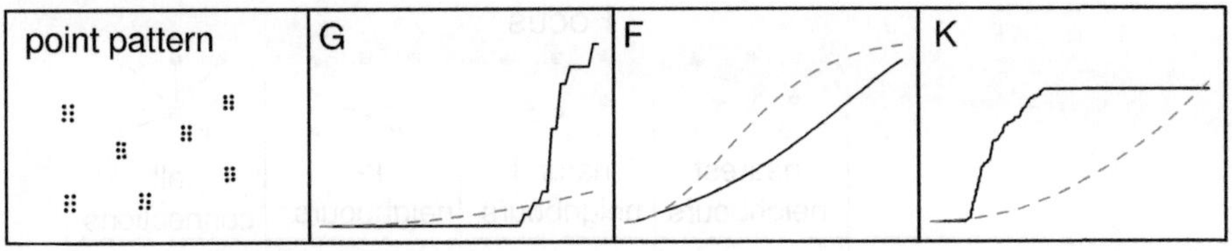

Fig. 7.11 Complicated point pattern with G-, F- and K-function. *Dashed line*: theoretical curve for CSR; *solid line*: empirical curve

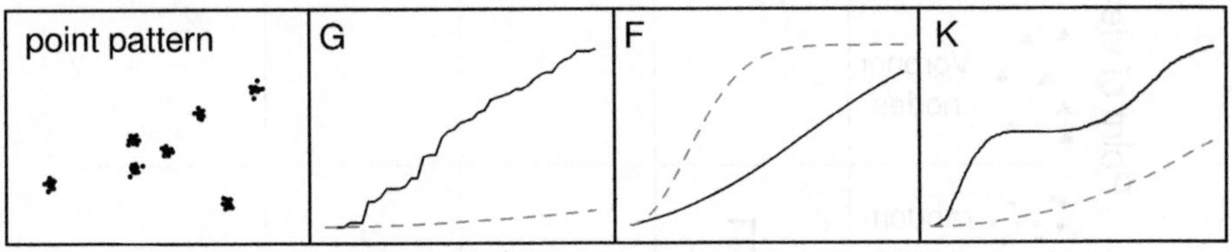

Fig. 7.12 Complicated point pattern with G-, F- and K-function. *Dashed line*: theoretical curve for CSR; *solid line*: empirical curve

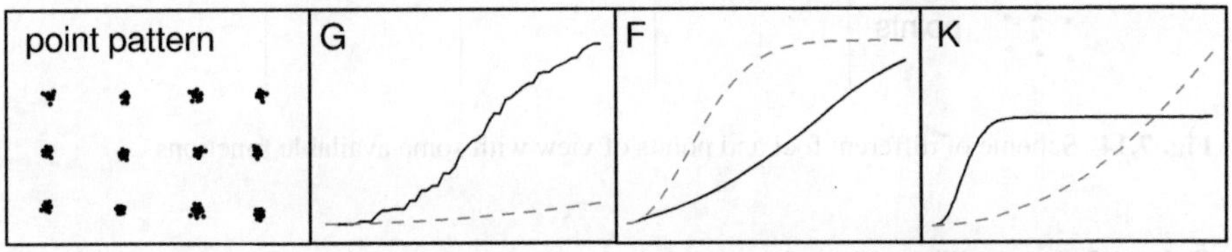

Fig. 7.13 Complicated point pattern with G-, F- and K-function. *Dashed line*: theoretical curve for CSR; *solid line*: empirical curve

A clustered pattern of clusters is shown in the third pattern (Fig. 7.12). The G- and F-function indicate the clustering. The G-function indicates the clustered inner structure of the groups of points, while the F-function is concerned with the clustered pattern of the clusters. The stepped shape of the K-function is caused by the fact that there are two types of clusters at two levels of organization.

Finally, we have a regular pattern of clustered clusters (Fig. 7.13). The G-function again indicates the inner clustering and the F-function seems to indicate a cluster of clusters. However, due to the dense clusters, the empirical curve has much higher distances than the same number of points would have for a random point pattern. This is why the F-function cannot detect the regular pattern of clusters. The same effect applies for the last example, where a wrong interpretation of F leads to the right result. The K-function expresses both effects. In the left part the small clusters are indicated and in the right part the regular pattern of clusters occurs.

A systematization of the point pattern characterization will enable us to better understand and interpret the results and develop additional functions (Fig. 7.14). In particular, we become aware of the missing functions. The functions used to characterize point patterns count the fraction of certain connections between points. Hence, the functions are controlled by two parameters.

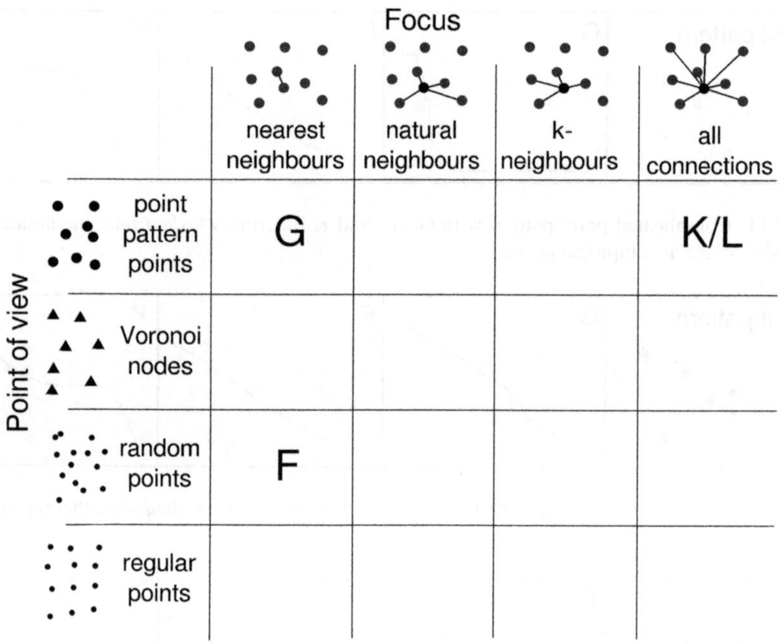

Fig. 7.14 Scheme of different foci and points of view with some available functions

Point of view The points from which the connection starts. This can be points of the point pattern, random points, a regular point grid, Voronoi nodes or any other group of points.

Focus The target points are the points from the point pattern. The focus defines which connections to target points are allowed. Nearest neighbours, natural neighbours, all points and all other rules are possible.

A point pattern is characterized by a combination of different functions that are able to detect specific configurations. A regular grid of clusters with random points is no longer an unspecific but rather a well-specified pattern.

7.4 Third-Order Properties

Finally, we turn briefly to third-order properties. The T-function is used for this test and it allows identifying interaction between point triples (Fig. 7.15).

```
> meg_env_t <- envelope(ppp_meg, fun =
+ Tstat, nrank = 2, nsim = 20)
> plot(meg_env_t)
```

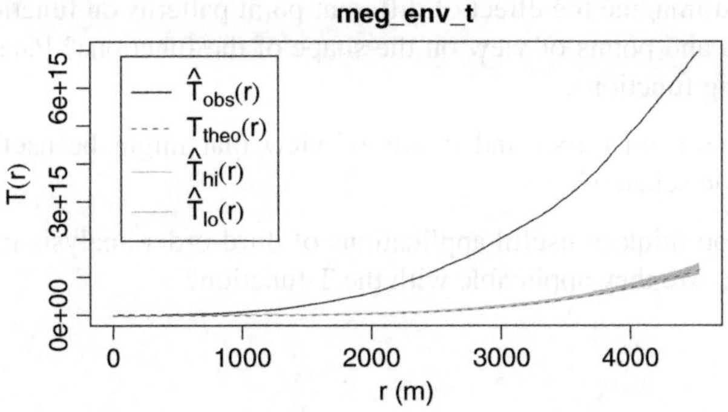

Fig. 7.15 Megaliths, CSR test, T-function (`ppa-Meg-t`)

7.5 Problems

7.1. Please take a distribution map of settlements and finds from the literature and think about different factors that might influence the location of the points.

7.2. Can you imagine a couple of different individual factors for the location of a settlement and a grave yard?

7.3. Please give some examples of factors of first-order properties.

7.4. Please explore the parameters of the point pattern simulation. Which point processes are possible? What effect on the result do different values of the parameters have?

7.5. Please apply the methods of second-order property analysis in this chapter to:

(a) different simulated point patterns; and
(b) the village point pattern.

7.6. Please apply the moving window technique with the F- and G-function on the same Bronze Age Barrow point pattern.

7.7. What would a G-, F-, and K-function look like for:

(a) a regular pattern of clusters where half of the clusters have a regular inner pattern and the other half a clustered inner pattern;
(b) a random pattern of clusters where half of the clusters has a regular inner pattern and the other half a clustered inner pattern.
(c) a point pattern with clusters with an internal clustered structure, whereby half of the clusters are ordered regularly and the other half are ordered clustered and
(d) a point pattern with clusters with an internal regular structure, whereby half of the clusters are ordered regularly and the other half are ordered clustered.

7.8. Please invent another complicated point pattern.

7.9. Can you imagine the effect of different point patterns on functions defined by different foci and points of view on the shape of the functions? Please concentrate on the missing functions.

7.10. Are there other foci and points of view that might be useful but are not included in the scheme?

7.11. Can you think of useful applications of third-order analysis in geography or archaeology? Are they applicable with the T-function?

References

1. Baddeley, A. (2008). *Analysing spatial point patterns in R*. Canberra: Csiro.
2. Baddeley, A., & Turner, R. (2005). Spatstat: an R package for analyzing spatial point patterns. *Journal of Statistical Software, 12*, 1–42.
3. Baddeley, A., Turner, R., Mateu, J., & Bevan, A. (2013). Hybrids of Gibbs point process models and their implementation. *Journal of Statistical Software, 55*, 1–43.
4. Baddeley, A. J., Møller, J., & Waagepetersen, R. (2000). Non- and semiparametric estimation of interaction in inhomogeneous point patterns. *Statistica Neerlandica, 54*, 329–350.
5. Besag, J. (1974). Spatial interaction and statistical analysis of lattice systems. *Journal of the Royal Statistical Society: Series B, 36*, 192–236.
6. Besag, J. (1975). Statistical analysis of non-lattice data. *The Statistican, 24*, 179–195.
7. Bevan, A. (2013). Models of settlement hierarchy based on partial evidence. *Journal of Archaeological Science, 40*, 2415–2427.
8. Bivand, R. S., Pebesma, E. J., & Gómez-Rubio, V. (2008). *Applied spatial data analysis with R*. New York: Springer.
9. Brundsdon, C., & Comber, L. (2015). *An introduction to R for spatial analysis and mapping*. Los Angeles: Sage.
10. Diggle, P. J. (2013). *Statistical analysis of spatial and spatio-temporal point patterns*, 3rd edn. Boca Raton: Chapman and Hall/CRC.
11. Gabriel, E., & Diggle, P. (2009). Second-order analysis of inhomogeneous spatio-temporal point process data. *Statistica Neerlandica, 63*, 43–51.
12. Getis, A., & Boots, B. (1978). *Models of spatial processes*. Cambridge: Cambridge University Press.
13. Hubbard, R., & Lindsay R. M. (2008). Why P values are not a useful measure of evidence in statistical significance testing. *Theory & Psychology, 18*, 69–88.
14. Illian, J., Penttinen, A., Stoxyan, H., & Stoyan, D. (2008). *Statistical analysis and modellig of spatial point patterns*. Chichester: Wiley.
15. Knitter, D., Nakoinz, O., Del Fabbro, R., Kohlmeyer, K., Schütt, B., & Meyer, M. (2014). The centrality of aleppo and its environs. *eTopoi, 3*, 107–127.
16. Knitter, D., & Nakoinz, O. (in press): Point pattern analysis as tool for digital geoarchaeology – A case study of megalithic graves in Schleswig-Holstein, Germany. In C. Siart, M. Forbirger & O. Bubenzer (Eds.), *Digital geoarchaeology. New techniques for interdisciplinary human-environmental research, Springer.*
17. Mayer, J., Schmidt, V., & Schweiggert, F. (2004). A unified framework for spatial stochastic models. *Simulation Modelling Practice and Theory, 12*, 307–326.
18. Møller, J., & Waagepetersen, R. P. (2004). *Statistical inverence and simulation for spatial point processes*. Boca Raton: Chapman & Hall/CRC.

19. Nakoinz, O. (2013). *Archäologische Kulturgeographie der ältereisenzeitlichen Zentralorte Südwestdeutschlands*. Universitätsforschung zur prähistorischen Archäologie, vol. 224. Bonn: Habelt.
20. Orton, C. (2004). Point pattern analysis revisted. *Archaeologia e Calcolatori, 15*, 299–315.
21. O'Sullivan, D., & Perry, G. L. W. (2013). *Spatial simulation: exploring pattern and process*. Chichester, West Sussex: John Wiley & Sons Inc.
22. Ripley, B. D. (1977). Modelling spatial patterns. *Journal of Royal Statistical Society, B 39*, 172–212.
23. Ripley, B. D. (1981). *Spatial statistics*. New York: Springer.
24. Thompson, B. (2006). A critique of p-values. *International Statistical Review, 74*, 1–14.

Chapter 8
Boundaries

8.1 Borders and Territoriality

Borders and territories are means of constructing and structuring space. In chapter one we discussed that spaces can be constructed by topologies that define connectedness and neighbourhood. Topological spaces provide the foundations of the metric spaces, which also define distances and serve as a basic means of orientation. Boundaries are a very important tool for the construction of topologies. They define something that distinguishes two entities. More specifically, borders distinguish territories. Accordingly, we can define (compare [13])

Definition 8.1. A **border** is a line or zone delimiting two spatial areas.

Definition 8.2. A **territory** is a bounded space with crisp borders assigned to something.

While the border implicitly defines certain spatial areas as entities that can be filled with meaning in a next step, the territory implicitly defines a border. Hence, borders and territories are closely coupled terms.

Despite the formal definition, territories are not simply geometrical objects; rather, they are elements of the social space [12, 13, 29, 41, 43, 45]. They are also a mapping of social structures and forming them. In this inter-relationship, territories are a self-stabilising object, institutionalised with a clear extent and boundary. Accordingly, territories tend to be persistent. The influences of territories are manifold [29]. They delimit different entities by contributing to the construction of the social space. Borders restrict interaction, working as friction for interaction. Furthermore, they support the establishment of certain rules of behaviour across the border.

The inter-relationship between territories and social space has a specific mechanism, rendering territories an important object in the discourse of power. A territory is not simply a patch of land or a tool for establishing differences between groups

O. Nakoinz, D. Knitter, *Modelling Human Behaviour in Landscapes*, Quantitative Archaeology and Archaeological Modelling, DOI 10.1007/978-3-319-29538-1_8

of people. When a territory is defined, a process of abstraction is set into motion, whereby people start to think that the territory is a homogeneous space. Sibley [36] calls this phenomenon the purification of space. On the one hand, this supports the formation of collective identities, whereby people deliberately behave according to the idea of a homogeneous space and they unconsciously adapt to each other in a unified interaction space. On the other hand, people are forced to adapt, given that singularities and the unusual behaviour of minorities are smoothed out by different scales of suppression, force and influence. Nonetheless besides the adaptive phenomena, a society in a certain territory can also disintegrate due to certain inner or external social forces. The persistence of territories in such cases—as well as the heterogeneous nature of some territories right at the beginning of the territorial definition—leads to a consistent system. This is what Agnew [1, 2] called the territorial trap. The behaviour is influenced by the imagination of a homogeneous territory, which may lead to wrong decisions. If a territory is defined, people tend to behave as if it were a homogeneous territory.

The general term of territory includes overlapping territories and animal territories [16]. The things connected with the delimited spatial area can be subsistence areas, interaction areas, areas of social activities or identities, areas of ethnics or power, economic areas and areas of shared ideas and cultural traits. When we speak about territoriality [12], we refer to a much more restricted version of territories, which are exclusively assigned to something and restricted to political territories. Political geography is concerned with the issue of territoriality [19]. In case of territoriality, land and space become a valuable commodity, even if the main task of defining a territory is to obtain, legitimate or preserve power. In this sense, Elden [7] describes territories as a political technology, although he rejects the concept of territoriality. While the border—despite being an essential part of the definition—appears as periphery in the case of many territories, in the case of territoriality it seems to be the opposite: the border seems to be the most impart thing and is strongly defended. This is a shift in esteem not concerning the entity to which the territory is assigned but rather the territory itself. Territoriality emerges if one or both of the following are assumed:

- the land, its resources and strategic location; and
- the territory as a unifying object that supports power.

Based upon these considerations, we can establish a ranking of different degrees of territorialisation:

1. no organisation of spatial areas;
2. fields without borders that assign a value to each place;
3. territories with crisp borders; and
4. territoriality with exclusive political territories.

This list makes it clear that these things are different, although in practice it is not uncommon to deduce one from the other. If we deduce a territory from territoriality, this is a correct inference. We can even deduce fields from territories if we accept a field with a non-continuous surface. However, a field that has spatial auto-correlation does not imply territories and territories do not imply territoriality. In particular, the last inference is a serious problem. We have to consider that territories have been used in a certain way. But simply, we cannot assume territories and territoriality; rather, we have to prove that they have existed. Neither is an important place is sufficient to deduce a territory nor is a border sufficient to deduce territoriality, although both observations can be a good starting point for further research. Theoretical modelling replaces empirical research although it can help to understand the details. If we model borders and territories, we must be aware that the existence of territories and territoriality in particular cases is not self-evident. The same can be said about aspects connected with the territory. Territories need not to be connected to political ethnic entity and not to cultural groups. In this context, we have to consider criticism about territorial approaches [37, 43].

8.2 Boundaries of Cultural Areas

In archaeology, the analysis of cultural areas is traditionally an important issue. The general concept is that cultural traits tend to concentrate in certain areas and they allow to delimiting cultural areas. The question concerning how to interpret such cultural areas is answered in many different ways. The idea that cultural areas are connected with a certain ethnic unit and that different environments and mental conditions lead to different cultures dates back to Herder [15]. This concept was further developed in ethnology—for example, by Tylor [42] and Frobenius [10]—and passed on to archaeology, where Kossinna [21] and Childe [3] made extensive use of it. This concept perceives cultural areas as a kind of tribal territories. However, this concept has attracted certain critiques (e.g. [17, 26]). Other researchers such as Clarke [4] interpret cultures as a mere classification unit, while Lüning [23] interprets cultures as an area of validity for chronologies. Nakoinz [24, 25, 27] interprets cultural areas as interaction spaces inside which the degree of interaction is greater than to outside locations. This leads to a cultural adaptation of the members of a culture. The empirical work in psycholinguistics concerning alignment in dialogue supports this concept [11, 30].

However, what is culture? Thus far, we have used the term but not defined it, as is often the case in archaeology. Now we want to offer a definition, provided by Hansen [14, 39]:

Definition 8.3. Culture covers standardisations that are valid in collectives.

This definition connects standardisations—which is something in common, a shared knowledge, cultural trait or tradition—with a group of people, the collective. This definition makes no statements about the content of culture or ideal states of culture; rather, it is a formal definition that covers many other existing definitions [22]. These properties of the definition allow applying it in many disciplines, particularly in archaeology. Standardisations are indicated by archaeological finds and building structures. We do not need to know the content of the standardisations. The opportunity to investigate standardisations with formal analysis suits archaeology very well, given that we can delimit and characterise cultures, even if we do not know what exactly the common knowledge is.

This definition is compatible—but not limited to—the interpretation of culture as interaction space. Cultures that are not spatially bound are in existence and become increasingly important in the archaeological discourse although they are excluded here owing to the spatial focus of this book. The focus lies on spatially delimited cultures that correspond formally but not in interpretation with the traditional archaeological cultures.

An important difference from the traditional archaeological cultures is that even a single standardisation with a corresponding collective can be a culture. Moreover, sets of standardisations are also possible. According to the definition from Hansen, cultures form a kind of poly-hierarchy, whereby certain sets of standardisations can be derived from different other ones. The question is not which cultures existed, but rather which are the most important ones for the archaeological interpretation. Among the important ones, cultures that correspond with the traditional archaeological concept—in the sense that they are spatially bound and possess crisp borders—are certainly dominant ones. However, we cannot detect such cultures with single diagnostic types; rather, we have to include the whole material into the analysis. The distribution of the archaeological types can allow the reconstruction of borders. If the borders for most of the types are located at the same place, only then can we speak of an archaeological culture with a border that was important to the people [25]. Here, we observe a distinct shift in the concept: traditional archaeological cultures were defined by the distribution of types in a certain area, whereas the new concept shifts the definition of cultures to a kind of cultural space populated with indicators for standardisations such as cultural traits. Here, we can find sets of types that commonly occur together. The test, if those sets of types are distributed in a limited area and hence show spatial borders, indicates spatially bound cultures and proofs that we have found a cultural unit and not a random combination of types. If the same combination of finds occurs in many nearby places, then it is not by chance but rather it maps a real phenomenon. If the distribution is heterogeneous, then a real phenomenon is still possible, although we lack the verification. For this approach, not only the presence of types but also the relative quantity matters.

To summarise, the new concept is a generalisation that connects to other disciplines such as cultural studies and defines cultures in a cultural space. The mapping to the geographical space simply serves the purposes of filtering spatial aspects and verifying the phenomenon.

Despite the extensive discussion concerning the term of culture there are three main reasons for delimiting cultural spaces:

- identifying interaction areas for culture historic interpretation;
- delimiting areas where chronologies are valid and
- delimiting areas for future research.

These reasons are not touched by problematic interpretations of culture, since "interaction" is the most common component in the different approaches. Although more in-depth interpretations may be more exciting and are indeed possible, the interaction space concept set us on common ground and even this abstract and general concepts lead to the emergence of important knowledge. Nonetheless, in any case we have to be cautious: although every individual has culture and belongs to many cultures, we cannot assume that archaeological cultures exist in a certain case; rather, we have to prove it based upon empirical evidence. Indeed, even if they exist, cultural territories with crisp borders also have to be proven. In some cases, a continuous model of cultural space is more appropriate, while for some purposes network approaches are more advisable. Based upon these considerations, we will judge the empirical boundary models as being the most important, and thus we continue with these models.

8.3 Empirical Boundary Models

Finding empirical boundaries is mainly a problem of archaeological evidence. Borders can be defined and marked in different ways:

- virtual lines defined by their relationship to topographic features, such as "in front of the forest";
- natural lines, such as river;
- lines that are marked by natural objects and are re-interpreted as symbols, such as certain trees;
- lines marked with symbols, such as poles or stones and
- monumental lines, such as dykes.

Some of these marks are obvious such as dykes [5, 25, 39]. They may mark areas on very different scales, but they are mainly visible. In the case of ditches, they can be seen as once comparable obvious. However, most ditches are longer visible and hence the problem is finding them. A more serious problem is the symbols, given that one has to know the code; otherwise, the markings remain meaningless. In addition to the problem of the border marks, the border itself can have different characterisations; for instance, borders can be lines or border zones. The marks do not allays indicate the nature of the border.

In practice an indirect approach complements the investigation of border marks, attempting to establish differences between the two sides of the border. To a certain degree, this approach is based upon the homogeneity hypothesis of territories, albeit in a weak form. The assumption is that the mean of the characteristic parameters differs inside and outside a territory and that the variance is sufficiently small to recognise the differences. Usually the presence of artefact types is used as a parameter, although building structures and monuments are also valuable evidence for this purpose. We will use our monuments and villages data sets to exemplify some methods. It is important to bear in mind that one of the main assumptions of

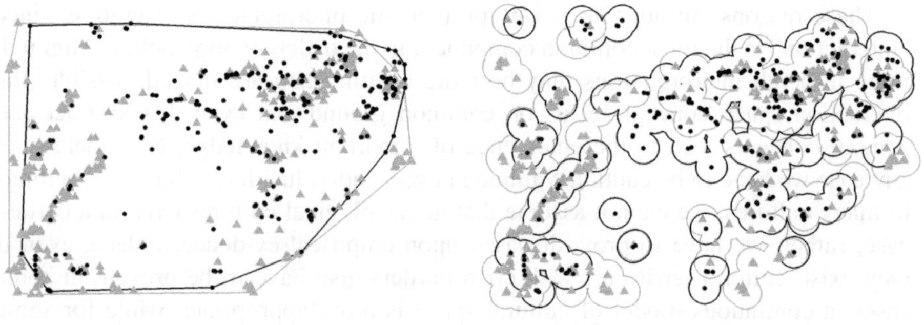

Fig. 8.1 Monuments, convex hull and buffer. *Black*: megalithic tombs; *grey*: bronze age barrows

landscape archaeological approaches is not given, namely the simultaneity of the sites. Since the reader is already familiar with our data, it seems more advisable to use this data than prepare a proper set of data for this purpose. The reader can obtain an extensive data set for analysing cultural areas at: http://www.johanna-mestorf-academy.uni-kiel.de/wordpress/data-exchange-platform/shkr/ [26].

The traditional approach is to draw a line around the find spots of a certain type, whereas a formalised version is to produce a convex hull around the points (Fig. 8.1). This method connects the outer points without producing "bays".

```
> library(spatstat)
> ch_meg <- convexhull(ppp_meg)
> ch_tum <- convexhull(ppp_tum)
> plot(ch_tum, border="grey", main="")
> plot(ch_meg, add=TRUE)
> points(ppp_tum$x, ppp_tum$y, pch=17, cex=0.6,
+   col="grey")
> points(ppp_meg$x, ppp_meg$y, pch=16, cex=0.4)
```

Of course, this method has some disadvantages; for instance, outlier has a very strong influence on the result. Moreover, concave parts and holes in the distribution are not properly mapped. Drawing the line exactly through the points does not seem useful, since the points mark the inner area of the territory. A buffer may solve at least some of these problems.

```
> buf_tum <- dilation(ppp_tum, 1000, polygonal=TRUE,
+   tight=F)
> buf_meg <- dilation(ppp_meg, 1000, polygonal=TRUE,
+   tight=F)
> plot(buf_tum, border="grey", main="")
> plot(buf_meg, add=TRUE)
> points(ppp_tum$x, ppp_tum$y, pch=17, cex=0.6,
+   col="grey")
> points(ppp_meg$x, ppp_meg$y, pch=16, cex=0.4)
```

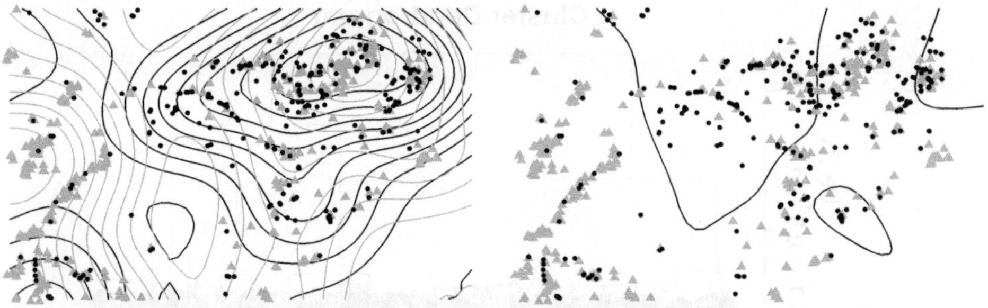

Fig. 8.2 Monuments, natural breaks contour lines and zero contour line. *Black*: megalithic tombs; *grey*: bronze age barrows

Using point density will produce more natural results. We have to calculate contour-lines to find the border, but how do we find the right contour line? We can search for natural breaks (Fig. 8.2).

```
> library("classInt")
> nb_meg <- classIntervals(dens_samp@data$meg, style =
+ "fisher", dataPrecision = NULL)
> nb_tum <- classIntervals(dens_samp@data$tum, style =
+   "fisher", dataPrecision = NULL)
> contour(sgdf_meg_dens, add=F, method = "edge", levels
+   = nb_meg$brks, drawlabels = F)
> contour(sgdf_tum_dens, add=T, method = "edge", levels
+   = nb_tum$brks, drawlabels = F, col="grey")
> points(ppp_tum$x, ppp_tum$y, pch=17, cex=0.6,
+   col="grey")
> points(ppp_meg$x, ppp_meg$y, pch=16, cex=0.4)
```

We can pick out the contour line with the highest gradient of sites. This is called the ideal contour line and seems to be the most characteristic delimitation [46].

Now it becomes obvious that both types have different core areas of distribution: something that we already know from the previous chapters. If we can establish the relation between the density of the two types, a proper border between both areas should be visible. The density values are optimal for comparing different point distributions. We can try a very simple approach by subtracting one density from the other, whereby the zero-value marks the border between the dominance of the two types. In this case, the contour lines respects both of the density data sets.

```
> ddif <- sgdf_meg_dens
> ddif@data$v <- sgdf_meg_dens$v - sgdf_tum_dens$v
```

The difference contour line approach is a good method for only two variables, although it is not applicable for more than two variables. The next approach is a cluster analysis [8, 20, 26, 33, 38] (Fig. 8.3); referring to many different methods with the common task grouping objects based upon their similarity. Generating four

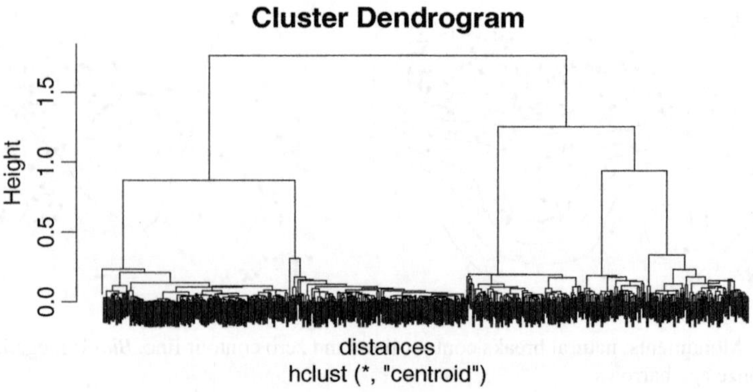

Fig. 8.3 Monuments and villages, dendrogram of a hierarchical cluster analysis

classes with only three variables is a little audacious but may work under special conditions. The first step is to obtain the data. We need a data frame where the columns are observations of different variables: in our case, the density values of different types. The rows are objects, which have to be grouped. Here, again we use the random sample points from chapter seven. To avoid the number of points rather than the relation influencing the result, we can normalise the values.

```
> dens_samp2 <- dens_samp[,1:3]
> dens_samp2@data[,1] <- dens_samp2@data[,1]
+ / max(dens_samp2@data[,1])
> dens_samp2@data[,2] <- dens_samp2@data[,2]
+ / max(dens_samp2@data[,2])
> dens_samp2@data[,3] <- dens_samp2@data[,3]
+ / max(dens_samp2@data[,3])
```

The definition of the groups is based upon the distance between objects, which has to be minimal; accordingly, we have to define a distance. The metric has to consider the type of data and the structure of data. In our case, the Euclidean distance is a good choice and can be applied in the feature space to the vectors of density values.

Subsequently, we have to decide which cluster algorithm is the right one. The cluster algorithm undertakes the clustering by grouping the objects. The idea is that the groups have maximal dissimilarities (distances in the feature space) to other clusters and minimal dissimilarities within the cluster. Put simply, the cluster algorithm informs us which elements belong together. Hierarchical cluster analysis produces a hierarchy of objects whereby step by step all objects are merged into clusters. This method allows plotting dendrograms and provides a good insight into the structure of the data, although it is perhaps a little confusing with large amounts of data. No details are visible but at least we can distinguish four or five main groups. The technique of producing a reduced dendrogram only with the most important clusters is described elsewhere [26].

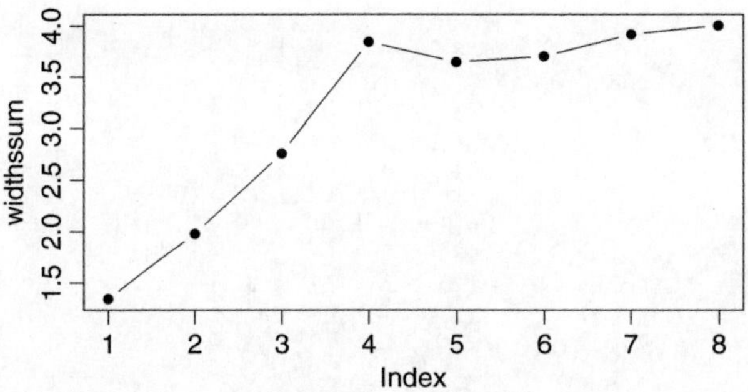

Fig. 8.4 Monuments and villages, silhouette width, PAM cluster analysis

```
> distances <- dist(dens_samp2@data,
+ method = "euclidean")
> hclust(distances, method="centroid")
Call:
hclust(d = distances, method = "centroid")
Cluster method   : centroid
Distance         : euclidean
Number of objects: 500
> hc <- hclust(distances, method="centroid")
> plot(hc)
```

Partitioning methods divide the objects into a certain number of clusters with minimal internal variance. We use the PAM algorithm (partitioning around medoids [20]). When using partitioning methods, we have to decide about the number of clusters. The hierarchical cluster analysis showed us that four or five natural groups are likely. We now apply the silhouette width, which is a quality measure for clusters [34]. Here, we find that four is a good choice (Fig. 8.4).

```
> library("cluster")
> widthssum <- c(
+     sum(pam(dens_samp2@data, 2, metric = "euclidean")
+ $silinfo$clus.avg.widths),
+     sum(pam(dens_samp2@data, 3, metric = "euclidean")
+ $silinfo$clus.avg.widths),
+     sum(pam(dens_samp2@data, 4, metric = "euclidean")
+ $silinfo$clus.avg.widths),
+     sum(pam(dens_samp2@data, 5, metric = "euclidean")
+ $silinfo$clus.avg.widths),
+     sum(pam(dens_samp2@data, 6, metric = "euclidean")
+ $silinfo$clus.avg.widths),
+     sum(pam(dens_samp2@data, 7, metric = "euclidean")
+ $silinfo$clus.avg.widths),
+     sum(pam(dens_samp2@data, 8, metric = "euclidean")
```

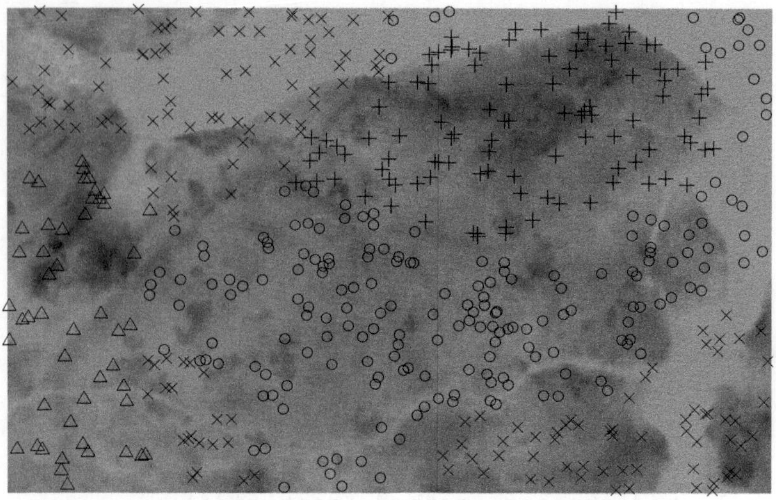

Fig. 8.5 Monuments and villages, cluster analysis. The symbols indicate the cluster to which the random sample points are assigned. Background: elevation; symbols: four clusters

```
+ $silinfo$clus.avg.widths),
+      sum(pam(dens_samp2@data, 9, metric = "euclidean")
+ $silinfo$clus.avg.widths))
> plot(widthssum, type ="b", pch=16)
```

Our final step is to apply the PAM cluster analysis to produce four clusters and plot the result with different signatures (Fig. 8.5). We could force more spatial closeness by including the coordinates in the cluster analysis, although this is not advisable, since the spatial distribution is an external validation of the results.

```
> library("cluster")
> dens_samp_clus <- pam(dens_samp2@data, 4,
+ metric = "euclidean")
> dens_samp2@data <- cbind(dens_samp2@data,
+ dens_samp_clus$clustering)
> names(dens_samp2)[names(dens_samp2) ==
+ 'dens_samp_clus$clustering'] <- 'clus'
> image(sgdf_srtm, ccol = gray.colors(20, start =
+ 0.8, end = 0.2))
> points(dens_samp, pch=dens_samp2@data$clus)
```

The aim of the cluster analysis is to assign the random sample points to four clusters. The symbols of the random points indicate the clusters and hence show the areas of specific combinations of the quantity of some types. We could also use regular sample points for this purpose and we could interpolate the values to make the border more visible. Since the identification numbers of the clusters are not real numeric values but rather simply names for the clusters, we should avoid numerical interpolation. This would be a proper application for a Thiessen polygon interpolation. The Voronoi cells with the same cluster name would be filled with the same colour, thus enhancing the visualisation without altering the content.

In our case, the interpretation of the results has to consider that the different types are from different times. The clusters are not something visible to the prehistoric people. In our case, the cluster maps certain patches of a cultural landscape with specific combinations of certain sites. The groups map the dominance of single types and include their quantities. Let us take a look at the characteristic density values of the first two clusters, which is the mean of the values of all members of a cluster:

```
> clus1 <- c(mean(dens_samp@data[dens_samp_clus$
+ clustering==1, 1]),
+               mean(dens_samp@data[dens_samp_clus$
+ clustering==1, 2]),
+               mean(dens_samp@data[dens_samp_clus$
+ clustering==1, 3]))
> clus2 <- c(mean(dens_samp@data[dens_samp_clus$
+ clustering==2, 1]),
+              mean(dens_samp@data[dens_samp_clus$
+ clustering==2, 2]),
+              mean(dens_samp@data[dens_samp_clus$
+ clustering==2, 3]))
> clus1
[1] 7.456359e-07 8.228024e-07 5.354327e-08
> clus2
[1] 1.017885e-06 1.661745e-06 2.120614e-08
```

The vectors clust1 and clust2 comprise the mean density values of all members of a cluster. We find specific density values for each cluster. Obviously the quantities of the different point types matter and it is not about simply the presence and absence of megaliths, burial mounds and villages.

We now return to one-type datasets. Another concept to analyse such data is to calculate density clusters that assign points to other points with higher density values. The result is nothing but a spatial dendrogram of hierarchical cluster analysis of spatial data. In contrast to the previous cluster analysis, spatial information is now involved. First we prepare the variables and calculate the distance matrix. The point pattern object dpd contains the density values. We insert empty variables, which are used to store the information about a connected point. Subsequently, we produce the distance matrix dpd.m.

```
> dpd <- ppp_meg
> dpd$d <- density(ppp_meg, 1000, edge=TRUE, at="points")
> k <- 1
> s <- -20000000
> dpd$id <- seq(along=dpd$x); dpd$v_id <- 0; dpd$v_x <- 0
dpd$v_y <- 0
+    dpd$v_d <- 0; dpd$dist <- 0; dpd$e <- 0
> dpd.d <- dist(cbind(dpd$x,dpd$y),upper = T)
> dpd.m <- as.matrix(dpd.d)
```

The search for the connections is undertaken in a loop. For each connection of points, a certain score is calculated and stored in dpd.e. This score e is

$$e = a - kb \tag{8.1}$$

where a is the density difference, k a weighting factor and b the spatial distance. Subsequently, the point with the highest score is selected as connection, if there is a higher score.

```
> maxd <- max(dpd$d)
> maxm <- max(dpd.m)
> dpd$d <- dpd$d * maxm / maxd
> dpd.e <- dpd.m
> for (i in seq(along=dpd$d)){
+    dpd.e[i,] <- (dpd$d - dpd$d[i]) - (k * dpd.m[i,])
+    w <-max(dpd.e[i,])
+    wi <- which(dpd.e[i,] == w)
+    if (i == wi | w < s)    {dpd$v_id[i] <- 0}
+    else                    {dpd$v_id[i] <- wi}
+    }
> dpd$v_id
  [1] 163 163  10  10  18  13  13  13  13   0   0   0
  ...
```

Afterwards the variables are filled with details on the connections.

```
> for (i in seq(along=dpd$d))    {
+    if (dpd$v_id[i] > 0)  {
+        dpd$v_x[i] <- dpd$x[dpd$v_id[i]]
+        dpd$v_y[i] <- dpd$y[dpd$v_id[i]]
+        dpd$v_d[i] <- dpd$d[dpd$v_id[i]]
+        dpd$dist[i]<- dpd.m[i,dpd$v_id[i]]
+        dpd$e[i]   <- dpd.e[i,dpd$v_id[i]]
+        }
>     else {
+        dpd$v_x[i] <- dpd$x[i]
+        dpd$v_y[i] <- dpd$y[i]
+        dpd$v_d[i] <- dpd$d[i]
+        }
+    }
> dpd
planar point pattern: 267 points
window: rectangle = [3550736, 3579036] x [6022467, 6040567] m
```

We now have to produce an object that we can plot and export to a file. A SpatialLines object is a complex object that has to be built in several steps.

```
> LinesList <- list()
> for(i in seq(along=dpd$id)) {
```

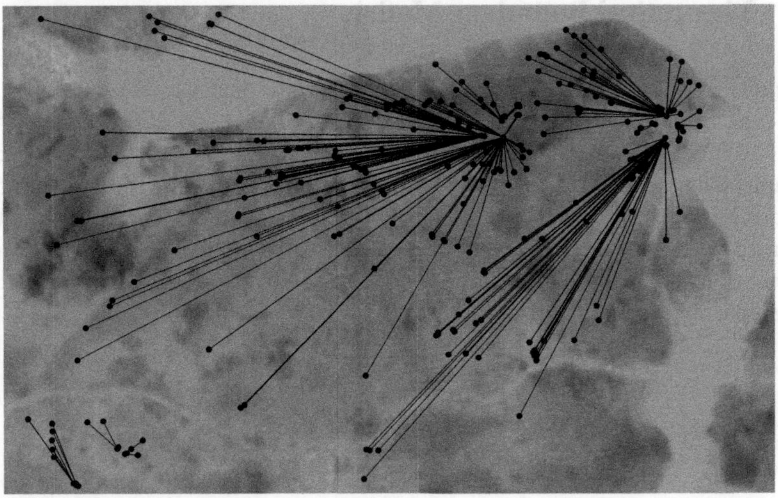

Fig. 8.6 Megaliths, density cluster

```
+      m <- matrix(data = c(dpd$x[i],dpd$v_x[i],dpd$y[i],
+     dpd$v_y[i]), nrow=2, ncol=2)
+      L <- Line(m)
+      LL <- list(L)
+      name  <- paste("connection", dpd$id,"_", dpd$v_id,
+     sep="")
+      LLL <- Lines(LL, ID = name[i])
+      LinesList[length(LinesList)+1] <- LLL
+      }
> sl <- SpatialLines(LinesList, proj4string = CRS(crs1))
```

Finally, we plot the result where each point is connected to another point with higher density in an acceptable distance if this is possible (Fig. 8.6). Put simply, each point is connected to another point with the highest density and within the shortest distance. Some clusters with density centres at data points emerge. This is a kind of spatial clustering where simply the structure of the point pattern is used. In addition to the distances between the points, this approach uses the density values and hence more information on the point pattern structure. Isolated points between two clusters—outliers—can become a centre in traditional coordinate clustering approaches, although this is not possible with the density cluster approach.

Some additional methods of boundary analysis are described by Jacquez et al. [18], dealing with data available as fields. Among others, they address moving split windows, spatially constrained clustering and fuzzy set modelling.

8.4 Theoretical Boundary Models

We now come to theoretical models. It is obvious that we can use topographic elements, elevation, rivers, etc. as markers for possible and useful borders. Mathematical models have to start with data. In most cases, the data reflects the centres of supposed cultural areas. A very common method is the aforementioned method of Voronoi graph or Thiessen polygons [31, 35, 40, 44]. The idea is that the border is drawn where the distance between two centres is equal. The first step is to gain information about centres. Accordingly, we start with calculating a new density map and preparing the variables.

```
> library(spatstat)
> bb    <- bbox(sgdf_srtm)
> win   <- owin(xrange=c(bb[1,1],bb[1,2]), yrange=
+ c(bb[2,1],bb[2,2]), unitname="m")
> tum_dens <- density(ppp_tum, kernel="gaussian",
+ sigma=1000, dimyx=c(36,56), w=win,  edge=TRUE, at="pixels")
> library(maptools)
> sgdf_tum_dens       <- as.SpatialGridDataFrame.im(tum_dens)
> ras <- sgdf_tum_dens
> r <- 5000
> ras@data$v[which(is.na(ras@data$v))] <- 0
> m <- max(ras@data$v)
> s <- m / 10
> indmax  <- c()
> indplan <- c()
```

The next step is a loop over all grid cells, whereby we use a moving window technique. In a window around each cell it is tested whether the centre is the maximum or at least equal to the other cells.

```
> for (i in seq(along=ras@data$v))  {
+     x <- coordinates(ras)[i,1]
+     y <- coordinates(ras)[i,2]
+     z <- ras@data$v[i]
+     indx <- which((coordinates(ras)[,1] > x - r) &
+    (coordinates(ras)[,1] < x + r))
+     indy <- which((coordinates(ras)[,2] > y - r) &
+    (coordinates(ras)[,2] < y + r))
+     indxy <-intersect(indx,indy)
+     if (max(ras@data[indxy,1]) == z & z > s)
+        {indmax[length(indmax)+1]    <- i}
+     if (sd(ras@data[indxy,1]) == 0)
+        {indplan[length(indplan)+1] <- i}
+     rm(indx)
+     rm(indy)
+     rm(indxy)
+     }
```

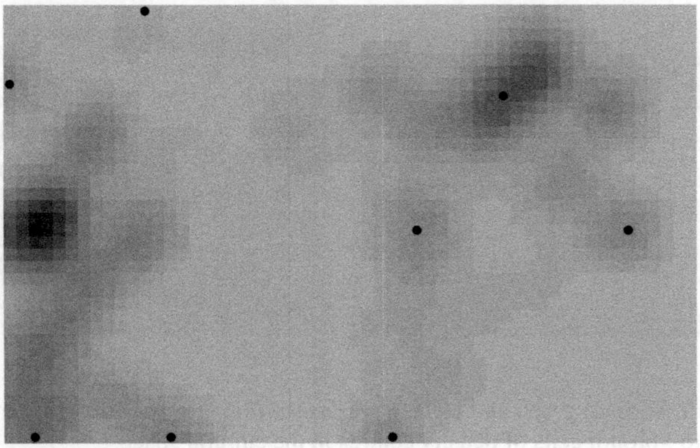

Fig. 8.7 Tumuli, local density centres

We now determine the coordinates of the detected points.

```
> mn <- length(indmax)
> mx <- coordinates(ras)[indmax,1]
> my <- coordinates(ras)[indmax,2]
> mx2 <- coordinates(ras)[indplan,1]
> my2 <- coordinates(ras)[indplan,2]
> mz <- ras@data[indmax,1]
> maxima <- data.frame(cbind(mx,my,mz))
```

Finally, we plot the result (Fig. 8.7). For our smooth density map, we only obtain a few local centres. A reduction of the bandwidth would produce a greater number of centres, up to the number of points.

Having the density centres, we can calculate and plot the Voronoi graph. In the course of the structural density calculation, we used the package "tripack" to calculate the Voronoi graph, now we are using the package "deldir". Indeed, the two packages have different data structures.

```
> library(deldir)
> try <- deldir(maxima[,1],maxima[,2],plot=TRUE,wl='te')
```

Rather than geographical distances we can use cultural distances. The cultural space is spanned by the cultural traits which are the archaeological types. The border is drawn where the cultural distances to two centres is equal. We can calculate for each raster cell which is the nearest centre in the cultural space. Since something should be left to you, we only calculate for our random sample points. First, we have to prepare our variables.

```
> cent <- data.frame(cbind(id=seq(1:length(maxima[,1])),
+ x=maxima[,1],y=maxima[,2],meg=0, tum=0))
> coordinates(cent)=~x+y
> proj4string(cent)   <- CRS(as.character(crs1))
```

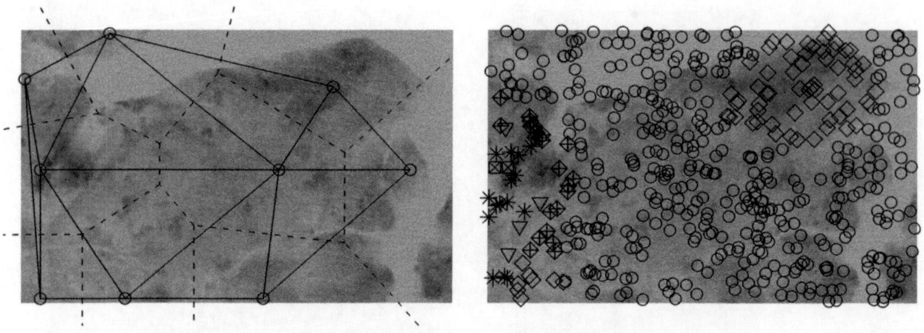

Fig. 8.8 Tumuli, Voronoi graph and Delaunay (*dashed line*) graph of density centres and random point assigned to Voronoi cells of density centres in the cultural space

```
> cent_meg  <- overlay(x=sgdf_meg_dens, y=cent)
> cent_tum  <- overlay(x=sgdf_tum_dens, y=cent)
> cent@data$meg <- cent_meg@data$v
> cent@data$tum <- cent_tum@data$v
> dens_samp@data <- cbind(dens_samp@data,cent=0)
```

A loop is used to determine the centre with the most likely density values, which is archived by calculating the cultural distance. The plot shows the reference centre for each sample point (Fig. 8.8).

```
> for(i in seq(along=(dens_samp@data$cent))) {
+     d1 <- sqrt((dens_samp@data$meg[i] -
+       cent@data$meg[1])^2 + (dens_samp@data$tum[i]
+         - cent@data$tum[1])^2)
+     d2 <- sqrt((dens_samp@data$meg[i] -
+       cent@data$meg[2])^2 + (dens_samp@data$tum[i]
+         - cent@data$tum[2])^2)
+     d3 <- sqrt((dens_samp@data$meg[i] -
+       cent@data$meg[3])^2 + (dens_samp@data$tum[i]
+         - cent@data$tum[3])^2)
+     d4 <- sqrt((dens_samp@data$meg[i] -
+       cent@data$meg[4])^2 + (dens_samp@data$tum[i]
+         - cent@data$tum[4])^2)
+     d5 <- sqrt((dens_samp@data$meg[i] -
+       cent@data$meg[5])^2 + (dens_samp@data$tum[i]
+         - cent@data$tum[5])^2)
+     d6 <- sqrt((dens_samp@data$meg[i] -
+       cent@data$meg[6])^2 + (dens_samp@data$tum[i]
+         - cent@data$tum[6])^2)
+     d7 <- sqrt((dens_samp@data$meg[i] -
+       cent@data$meg[7])^2 + (dens_samp@data$tum[i]
+         - cent@data$tum[7])^2)
```

```
+       d8 <- sqrt((dens_samp@data$meg[i] -
+         cent@data$meg[8])^2 + (dens_samp@data$tum[i]
+           - cent@data$tum[8])^2)
+       d8 <- sqrt((dens_samp@data$meg[i] -
+         cent@data$meg[8])^2 + (dens_samp@data$tum[i]
+           - cent@data$tum[8])^2)
+       d <- c(d1,d2,d3,d4,d5,d6,d7,d8,d9)
+       mindist <- min(d1,d2,d3,d4,d5,d6,d7,d8,d9)
+       id  <- which(d == mindist)
+       dens_samp@data$cent[i] <- id
+       }
> plot(dens_samp, pch=dens_samp@data$cent)
```

In principle, we could use each available space where distances are defined. Economic spaces can be used with cost distance calculations, which represent transportation costs. We will pick up this concept in the networks section. Here the map is simply plotted (Fig. 8.9).

One disadvantage of Voronoi graphs is that all points have the same influence on the result. The point in the North–East of our example may come from a much smaller settlement than the other points; accordingly, we should weight this point lower than the other points to obtain a smaller territory, which we will do in Chap. 9.

Weighted Voronoi graphs have been described by Fetter [9], Okabe et. al. [28] and are known in archaeology under the term "X-tent model", introduced by Renfrew and Level [31, 32, 35]. A new implementation in GIS has been developed by Ducke and Kroefges [6].

Here, we will provide a generalised formula for weighed Voronoi graphs. Φ is the influence of a centre on a point in the area. We have several variables to control the result.

$$\Phi = \alpha_s\left(t_\alpha \alpha_d + |t_a - 1|\right) - \gamma_s\left(t_\gamma \gamma_d + |t_\gamma - 1|\right)\psi\left(\sqrt{\left(x_z - x_p\right)^2 + \left(y_z - y_p\right)}\right) \tag{8.2}$$

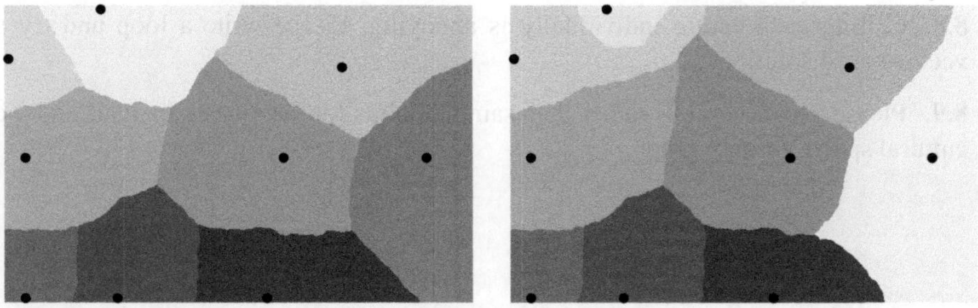

Fig. 8.9 Ordinary (*left*) and weighted (*right*) Voronoi graph of density centres in the economical space

α_s static additive weight
α_d dynamic additive weight, possibly different for each centre
γ_s static multiplicative weight
γ_d dynamic multiplicative weight, possibly different for each centre
t_α index for dynamic ($t = 1$) or static ($t = 0$)
t_γ index for multiplicative weight ($t = 1$) or static ($t = 0$)
ψ function manipulating the distance between the points (can include least cost analysis)
x_z geographical East of centre
y_z geographical North of centre
x_p geographical East of affected point
y_p geographical North of affected point

While this is a nice concept, we have to find empirical models that can be compared to the elaborated weighted Voronoi models. The empirical models need to be sufficient to validate the configuration of the many parameters in these models. In any case study, one should carefully consider whether this applies.

8.5 Problems

8.1. Can you imagine examples for the territorial trap?

8.2. Please develop an algorithm for the ideal contour line approach.

8.3. Please develop a loop version of the silhouette width graph code.

8.4. Please describe the algorithm of density cluster analysis in detail.

8.5. Please try density cluster analysis with different parameters.

8.6. Re-run the cluster analysis with other numbers of classes and compare the results.

8.7. Please compare the data structures of tripack and deldir Voronoi objects using the str() command.

8.8. Calling each centre individually is annoying. Please write a loop and try a vector-based solution.

8.9. Please use raster cells rather than sample points for the cluster analysis and the cultural space Voronoi graph.

References

1. Agnew, J. (1994). The territorial trap: The geographical assumptions of international relations theory. *Review of International Political Economy, 1*, 53–80.
2. Agnew, J. (2010). Still trapped in territory? *Geopolitics, 15*, 779–784.
3. Childe, V. G. (1925). *The dawn of European civilization*. London: K. Paul.
4. Clarke, D. L. (1968). *Analytical archaeology*. London: Methuen.
5. Dobat, A. S. (2009). Danevirke - a linear earthwork in the province of Schleswig (North Germany). In M. Segschneider (Ed.), *Ringwälle und verwandte Strukturen des ersten Jahrtausends n.Chr. an Nord- und Ostsee: Internationales Symposium Föhr 2005* (pp. 137–158). Neumünster: Wachholtz Verlag.
6. Ducke, B., & Kroefges, P. C. (2008). From points to areas: Constructing territories from archaeological site patterns using an enhanced Xtent model. In A. Posluschny, K. Lambers & I. Herzog (Eds.), *Layers of perception. Proceedings of the 35th International Conference on Computer Applications and Quantitative Methods in Archaeology (CAA). Berlin, Germany*, April 2–6, 2007. Kolloquien zur Vor- und Frühgeschichte (Vol. 10, pp. 245–251). Bonn: Habelt.
7. Elden, S. (2010). Land, terrain, territory. *Progress in Human Geography, 34*, 799–817.
8. Everitt, B. S., Landau, S., Leese, M., & Stahl, D. (2011). *Cluster analysis*. Chichester: Wiley.
9. Fetter, F. A. (1924). The economic law of market areas. *The Quarterly Journal of Economics, 38*(3), 520–529.
10. Frobenius, L. (1904). *Geographische Kulturkunde*. Leipzig: Brandstetter.
11. Garrod, S., & Pickering, M. J. (2009). Joint action, interactive alignment, and dialog. *Topics in Cognitive Science, 1*, 292–304.
12. Gold, J. R. (1982). Territoriality and human spatial behaviour. *Progress in Human Geography, 44*, 44–67.
13. Haggett, P. (1965). *Locational analysis in human geography*. London: Arnold.
14. Hansen, K. P. (2003). *Kultur und Kulturwissenschaft*. Tübingen/Basel: A. Francke.
15. Herder, J. G. (1774). *Auch eine Philosophie der Geschichte zur Bildung der Menschheit*. Riga: Hartknoch,
16. Howard, E. (1920). *Territory in bird life*. London: John Murray.
17. Jacob-Friesenm, K. H. (1928). *Grundfragen der Urgeschichtsforschung*. Hannover: Helwingsche Verlagsbuchhandlung.
18. Jacquez, G. M., Maruca, S., & Fortin, M.-J. (2000). From fields to objects: A review of geographic boundary analysis. *Journal of Geographical Systems, 2*, 221–241.
19. Johnston, R. (2001). Out of the 'moribund backwater': Territory and territoriality in political geography. *Political Geography, 20*, 677–693.
20. Kaufman, L., & Rousseeuw, P. J. (1990). *Finding groups in data. An introduction to cluster analysis*. Hoboken: Wiley.
21. Kossinna, G. (1911). *Die Herkunft der Germanen. Zur Methode der Siedlungsarchäologie: Vol. 6. Mannus-Bibliothek*. Würzburg: Kabitzsch.
22. Kroeber, A. L., & Kluckhohn, C. (1952). *Culture. A critical review of concepts and definitions*. Cambridge: Harvard University Press.
23. Lüning, J. (1972). Zum Kulturbegriff im Neolithikum. *Prähistorische Zeitschrift, 47*, 145–173.
24. Nakoinz, O. (2003). Dämme in Hügelgräberfeldern der Westeifel und des Hunsrücks. Diskussion und Katalog. *Archäologisches Korrespondenzblatt, 33*, 87–91.
25. Nakoinz, O. (2005). *Studien zur räumlichen Abgrenzung und Strukturierung der älteren Hunsrück-Eifel-Kultur: Vol. 118. Universitätsforschung zur Prähistorischen Archäologie*. Bonn: Habelt.
26. Nakoinz, O. (2013). *Archäologische Kulturgeographie der ältereisenzeitlichen Zentralorte Südwestdeutschlands: Vol. 224. Universitätsforschung zur Prähistorischen Archäologie*. Bonn: Habelt.

27. Nakoinz, O. (2014). Fingerprinting iron age communities in South-West-Germany and an integrative theory of culture. In C. Popa & S. Stoddart (Hrsg.), *Fingerprinting the iron age* (pp. 187–199). Oxford: Oxbow Books.
28. Okabe, A., Boots, B., Sugihara, K., & Chiu, S. N. (2000). *Spatial tessellations*. Chichester: Wiley.
29. Paasi, A. (2003). Region and place: Regional identity in question. *Progress in Human Geography, 28*, 475–485.
30. Pickering, M. J., & Garrod, S. (2006). Alignment as the basis for successful communication. *Research on Language and Computation, 2–3*, 203–228.
31. Redhouse, D. I., & Stoddart, S. (2011). Mapping Etruscan state formation. In N. Terrenato & D. C. Haggis (Eds.), *State formation in Italy and Greece. Questioning the Neoevolutionist Paradigm* (pp. 162–78). Oxford: Oxbow.
32. Renfrew, C., & Level, E. V. (1979). Exploring dominance: Predicting polities from centers. In C. Renfrew & K. L. Cooke (Eds.), *Transformations. Mathematical approaches to cultural change* (pp. 145–167). New York: Academic Press.
33. Romesburg, H. C. (1984). *Cluster analysis for researchers*. Raleigh: Lulu Press.
34. Rousseeuw, P. J. (1987). Silhouettes: A graphical aid to the interpretation and validation of cluster analysis. *Computational and Applied Mathematics, 20*, 53–65.
35. Scarry, J., & Payne, C. (1986). Mississippian polities in the fort Walton area: A model generated from the Renfrew-level Xtent algorithm. *Southeastern Archaeology, 5*(2), 79–90.
36. Sibley, D. (1988). Purification of space. *Environment and Planning D: Society and Space, 6*, 409–421.
37. Smith, M. (2005). Networks, territories, and the cartography of ancient states. *Annals of the Association of American Geographers, 95*, 832–849.
38. Sneath, P. H. A., & Sokal, R. R. (1973). *Numerical taxonomy. The principles and practice of numerical classification*. San Francisco: Freeman and Company.
39. Spratt, D. (1987). Neuere britische Forschungen zu prähistorischen Grenzen und Territorien. *Praehistorische Zeitschrift, 62*, 113–145.
40. Thiessen, A. H. (1911). Precipitation averages for large areas. *Monthly Weather Review, 39*, 1082–1084.
41. Tringham, R. (1972). Territorial demarcation of prehistoric settlements. In P. J. Ucko, R. Tringham & G. W. Dimbleby (Eds.), *Man, settlement and urbanism*. Gloucester: Duckworth.
42. Tylor, E. B. (1871). *Primitive culture*. London: John Murray.
43. Van Valkenburg, P., & Osborne, J. F. (2013). Home turf: Archaeology, territoriality, and politics. *Archaeological Papers of the American Anthropological Association, 22*, 1–27.
44. Voronoi, G. (1907). Nouvelles applications des paramètres continus àă la théorie des formes quadratiques. *Journal für die Reine und Angewandte Mathematik, 133*, 97–178.
45. Zierdt, M. (2009). Raum entsteht durch Grenzen oder: Topische und chorische Betrachtungsweise in der Geographie. In R. Kath & A.-K. Rieger (Eds.), *Raum - Landschaft - Territorium*. Wiesbaden: Dr. L. Reichert Verlag.
46. Zimmermann, A., Hilpert, J., & Wendt, K. P. (2009). Estimations of population density for selected periods between the Neolithic and AD 1800. In J. Steel & S. Shennan (Eds.), *Demography and cultural macroevolution. Human Biology, 81*(2), 357–380 [Special issue].

Chapter 9
Networks

9.1 Networks and Transportation Systems

At present *network analysis* [6, 38] is a fashionable term. In the same way as with the term "model", beyond the fashionable term network analysis offers a valuable conceptual framework and a useful toolbox for various types of analysis. Network analysis has two main branches [1]: the most fashionable at present is *social network analysis*, which dates back to the 1930s and became an important topic of social sciences in the 1970s [18, 22, 33, 44, 53]; and while certain parts of the *geographical network analysis* have a far longer tradition, this branch was developed into an important sub-discipline of geography in the 1960s [19–21, 40, 46] and is mainly concerned with road networks, transportation and exchange networks.

The common ground of both branches is the methodological foundation on graph theory (Sect. 1.6.3; [13]). All relevant elements in the real world are mapped with points/nodes and lines/edges. For this purpose, a metric space is not necessary but a topological space is required. The space in which the object of investigation is placed has to offer a measure of neighbourhood or connectivity. A measure of similarity or distance is useful for characterising the edges but not essential to the concept. For spatial graphs such as neighbourhood graphs, we can say that the graph is a model of the network structure. In addition to the graph, the network includes geographical locations, which can be point characteristics in the graph, but no basic properties. The spatial network is a model of the structure of the spatial system, which also contains traffic. In a network, traffic or the usage of the connections in general is a mere characterisation of the connections.

In general we can say that network analysis:

- focuses on the relationship between elements;
- provides a standard model concerning how to describe systems of relationships based upon graph theory;

O. Nakoinz, D. Knitter, *Modelling Human Behaviour in Landscapes*, Quantitative Archaeology and Archaeological Modelling, DOI 10.1007/978-3-319-29538-1_9

- excludes other aspects such as borders and areas; and
- provides techniques for analysing networks.

In archaeology, both branches are in use although a certain focus on social network analysis at present cannot be denied [7, 8, 11, 17, 27, 28, 35, 45]. Nonetheless, network analysis in archaeology is a fast-growing and promising approach.

The two main branches of network analysis differ in the characterisation of nodes and edges. Nodes in social network analysis can be individuals as well as groups of various size and definitions, while geographic network analysis uses places such as villages, sites and regions. For example, archaeological finds can be used in both branches. The edges represent interaction between the nodes (see Chap. 10 for interaction models). The relations can be established using different proxies for interaction:

- direct proxies for interaction (e.g. imports or citations);
- similarities between nodes; and
- the manifestation of connections (e.g. roads).

Many proxies simply allow establishing certain probabilities of connections. Let us take as an example a certain type of find that was produced at a certain place. There is a connection with a certain degree of probability between the production site and the find spot. We also imagine that the different sites where such a find occurred belonged to a network of interacting villages, although those connections are less probable.

Due to the focus of this book, we concentrate on geographical networks and particularly transportation networks. This will provide us with some methods that are also useful for social network analysis. Although we will concentrate on transportation, social aspects are not entirely out of focus, given that there is a strong interrelationship between transportation, society and the economy. In fact, we have two interrelated systems: the system of interaction and the system of transportation. The system of interaction involves the relationships between people and can be analysed in social network analysis. The system of transportation comprises of the roads and the traffic. It is obvious that the wish to interact is the cause of traffic and traffic is the cause of maintaining a road system. Upon first glance, the road system seems to hold minor importance; however, if we recognise the interrelationships between the different systems, our estimation will change. Usually society is assumed to be the most important research topic. In archaeology, our sources about society and interaction between people are very limited. In our case, we have no direct information about the interaction between people. However, if we are able to reconstruct the road system or at least obtain some empirical information about it, we can learn something about the system of interaction and society. Nonetheless, there is no simple mapping of both the systems. The interactions are canalised by the road system and cultural economic and social conditions also influence the system of interaction. The system of interaction induces modifications of the system of transportation, which is also influenced by natural conditions. We will benefit from the close interrelationship of the different systems. In this chapter, we deal with the

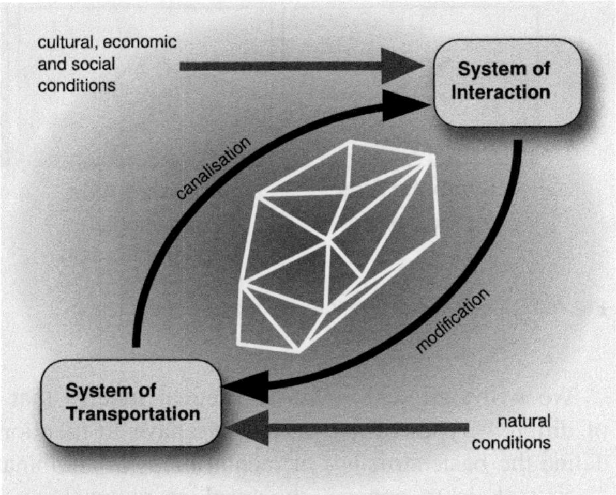

Fig. 9.1 Interrelationship of the system of interaction and the system of transportation

system of transportation, which is thought to be a proxy for the system of interaction and the social system. In the next chapter we will deal with the system of interaction itself. Both of the sources and concepts are complementary and have to be combined for a full picture (Fig. 9.1).

The analysis of the transport systems can be sub-divided into three levels of scale.

1. On the *local level*, the focus lies on the exact location of the pathways.
2. On the *regional level*, it is questioned which points are connected and which are not
3. On the *supra-regional level*, the objective is to investigate the main communication axes.

The different levels represent complementary approaches with different methods or at least a different application of methods. Each level is focused on a certain aspect. The combination leads to a much better understanding of the transport system than single analysis.

9.2 Supra-Regional Level

Due to the heterogeneous topic and the geographical scale, the description of the supra-regional level is rather cursory; although some remarks might help to understand the concept. This level of analysis is focused on the axes of communication, which are an abstraction from roads and sites. Here, the preferred connections between different areas or regions are addressed. These axes play an important role in mental maps and the spatial understanding of the world.

Fig. 9.2 Scheme of different types of axis of orientation

We will start with some theoretical models that are a kind of classification of different types of axes. First, we have to mention *axes of orientation*, which define the basic structure of mental maps in combination with important borders. Their task is to connect the local or regional social, cultural and metaphysic environment and topography to the meaningful outside world, whether imagined or real (Fig. 9.2). Symbolic axes are directions to mythical places like Mekka or Rom. Continental axes also belong to this category. Indicated axes are directions to magic or meaningful topographic signs (e.g. Fujiyama). Iconic axes can be visible roads or rivers.

While axes of orientation mainly hold mental importance and do not need to correlate with interaction, axes of exchange and movement are concerned with the actual interaction. These axes map where people usually move or communicate. The connection between the Mediterranean and Central Europe in the Iron Age as well as the Silk Road belongs to this category.

The empirical models of communication axes are a certain problem: how can we identify magic places or symbolic directions based upon only archaeological sources? Theoretical considerations and hermeneutic argumentations dominate this topic. Proving axes of orientation is rather difficult, although a remarkable exception is the analysis of continental axes of orientation [43]. Since the gene flow seems correlated to the continental axes, the axes appear to play an important role in the actual movement of people.

The analysis of exchange axes and movement are a rewarding object for quantitative analysis. For example, the analysis of cultural areas (see Chap. 8) can reveal axes of communication [37]. Furthermore, the spatial analysis of import finds can be very useful. The quantity of imports from different directions can be quantified and compared for different sites and regions [51].

9.3 Regional Level

The connection of sites is focussed on a regional level. The actual route does not matter, but rather whether two sites are connected. Graph theory and in particular neighbourhood graphs are a tool designed for exactly this purpose. Neighbourhood graphs allow constructing theoretical models. Two sites are connected if certain requirements of the spatial properties of the sites are fulfilled. We can interpret neighbourhood graphs as well as many other graphs as a kind of double structure. The sites are points in a geographical, metric space, whereby the properties in this space determine, whether two points are connected. If a connection is valid, an edge between the two points in a topological space is defined. In this step, the graph emerges, containing topological information only. The edges are defined, but not the location of the notes. Finally, we transfer the edges back to the geographical space and plot them on a geographical map. Alternatively, we can say that we produce a spatial constrained plot of the graph. This interpretation is sometimes more helpful for the understanding than the traditional one, where connections are drawn in a metric space directly.

There are different neighbourhood graphs [2, 10, 12, 32, 47–50, 52] which differ in the rules for valid connections. The most basic graph emerges when we connect all nodes to each other, whereby every site is connected to every other one. This might be an appropriate graph for mapping the quantified similarities or interactions of the sites but not for a transportation network. A road passing a village by some metres to reach an other village behind the first one seems ridiculous: wouldn't we go to the first village and proceed to the next one? A graph that realises this idea by connecting all natural neighbours is the Delaunay graph, which reduces all point combinations to all possible or appropriate connections. Since crossings are not allowed, the preferred compact form of three-angles ensures that no nearly parallel connections are made if avoidable. The rules for constructing edges (Fig. 9.3) in the Delaunay graph are based upon three-angles. The lines of the three-angles are valid if no other point is located inside the circle drawn through the three points. Nonetheless, the Delaunay graph still has many connections that do not seem very likely or suitable. Some other graphs are sub-graphs of the Delaunay graph that optimise the system and they are constructed according to similar rules.

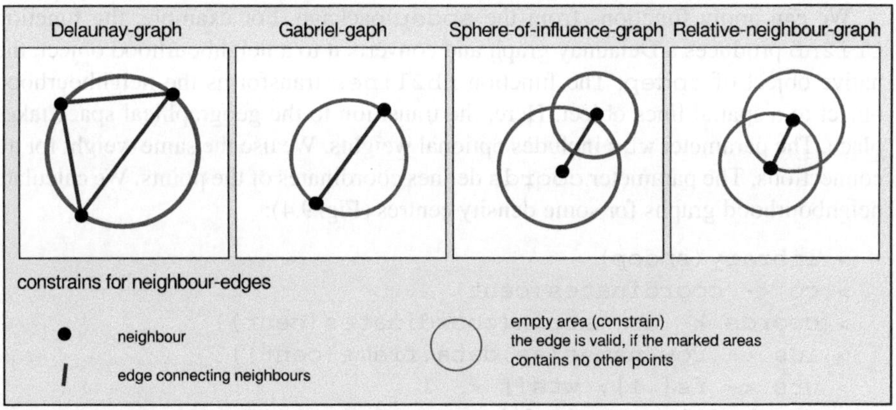

Fig. 9.3 Scheme of some construction rules of neighbourhood graphs

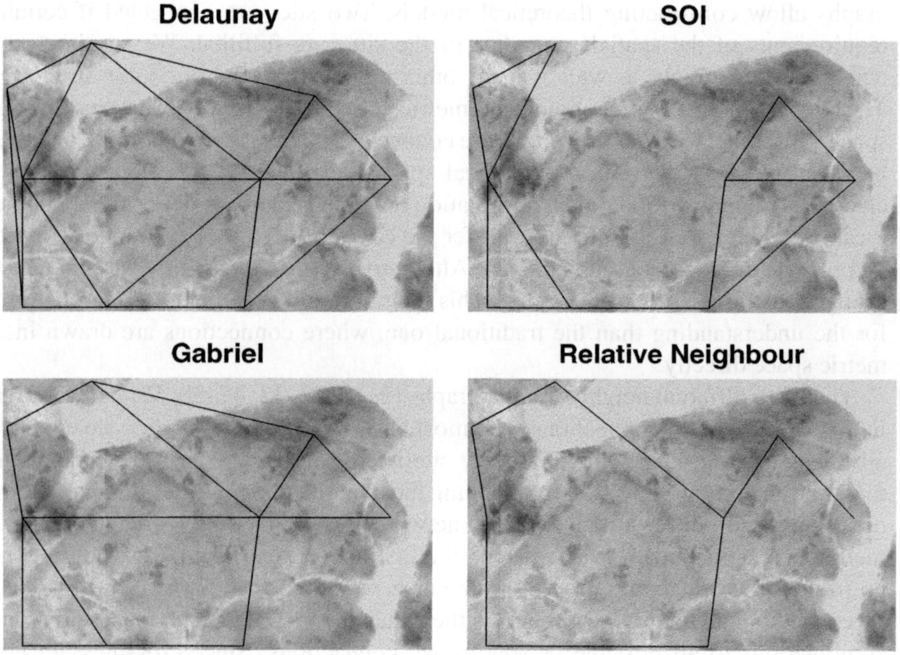

Fig. 9.4 Neighbourhood graphs for density centres

The Gabriel graph works with a circle of minimal diameter drawn through just two points. The sphere-of-influence graph (SOI) uses two circles where the diameter is determined by surrounding points. In this graph, the constraint is that the circles have to intersect. The relative-neighbour graph is similar, although the diameters of the circles are determined by the distance between the two points. These graphs tell us which connections would be useful in an optimised system.

We can apply functions from the `spdep` package. For example, the function `tri2nb` produces a Delaunay graph and converts it to a neighbourhood object, the native object of `spdep`. The function `nb2lines` transforms the neighbourhood object to a spatial lines object. Here, the transition to the geographical space takes place. The parameter `wts` includes optional weights. We use the same weight for all connections. The parameter `coords` defines coordinates of the points. We calculate neighbourhood graphs for some density centres (Fig. 9.4):

```
> library(spdep)
> co <- coordinates(cent)
> coords <- as.matrix(coordinates(cent))
> ids <- row.names(as.data.frame(cent))
> wts <- fs[,1]; wts[] <- 1
> fs_nb_del <- tri2nb(co, row.names=ids)
> del <- nb2lines(fs_nb_del, wts=wts, coords=coords,
```

```
+        proj4string =
+     CRS(as.character(crs1)))
> fs_nb_soi <- graph2nb(soi.graph(fs_nb_del, co),
+        row.names=ids)
> soi <- nb2lines(fs_nb_soi, wts=wts, coords=coords,
+        proj4string =
+     CRS(as.character(crs1)))
> fs_nb_gabriel <- graph2nb(gabrielneigh(co),
+        row.names=ids)
> gabriel <- nb2lines(fs_nb_gabriel, wts=wts,
+        coords=coords, proj4string =
+     CRS(as.character(crs1)))
> fs_nb_relative <- graph2nb(relativeneigh(co),
+        row.names=ids)
> relative <- nb2lines(fs_nb_relativ, wts=wts,
+        coords=coords, proj4string =
+     CRS(as.character(crs1)))
> par(mfrow=c(2,2))
> image(sgdf_srtm, col = gray.colors(25, start =
+        0.97, end = 0.4))
> lines(del)
> image(sgdf_srtm, col = gray.colors(25, start =
+        0.97, end = 0.4))
> lines(soi)
> image(sgdf_srtm, col = gray.colors(25, start =
+        0.97, end = 0.4))
> lines(gabriel)
> image(sgdf_srtm, col = gray.colors(25, start =
+        0.97, end = 0.4))
> lines(relative)
> par(mfrow=c(1,1))
```

Empirical based graphs on the regional level can be obtained by calculating similarities between sites. If the similarity is higher than a certain threshold, then a connection is drawn. The similarities can also be used to weight the edges. Nonetheless, a threshold should be used to exclude many connections from the all-to-all graph—i.e. a graph where all nodes are connected with each other—with negligible similarities. Another solution would be to reconstruct the regional connections based upon the local pathways, if these are reconstructed or observed.

9.4 Local Level

Now we turn to the local level, which investigates the actual routes of the connections of the regional level. On this level the straight lines from the regional level can turn into curves. The important information is not whether but rather how the sites are connected. On this level, the spatial information becomes more important because the graph with topological information is sometimes used as tool rather than being interpreted as a result.

It is useful to consider different types of routes. Unmarked tracks can be routes on the water where one has to decide for the exact route, which is not marked by usage but is nevertheless well defined. Pathways are marked by usage. The traveller—who produces the marks by usage—has to decide for the route but does not need not to care for other things. In the case of roads, the constructor and user are different, the constructor defines the route and has to maintain the road, whereas the user has to decide whether to use it. The three basic types of routes have decreasing requirements of navigation competence for the user and an increasing effort of maintaining the way. In addition, the decision for the route is based upon different parameters. Which is the most efficient route? Is there already a route that can be used? How much does it cost to build and maintain the road?

We start with empirical models. Here, we can apply the same neighbourhood graphs like on the regional level. However this time we apply them as a pattern recognition tool on the monuments. The general ideas is that the monuments occur along the ways. In this case, monuments can be used as proxies for the pathways.

There is a discussion concerning whether monuments are located along ways or borders ([5, 188–192]; Fig. 9.5). This question is not easy to decide. Furthermore, it is possible that pathways and borders are partly located at the same line. The theoretical model of Voronoi and Delaunay graph is an optimisation of the spatial system according to certain parameters that do not need to apply to prehistoric cases. In the area of our case study which is the Southern part of Jutland, the traditional interpretation as pathway-indicators [34] remains still an option. Therefore we assume that the monuments are located along pathways and do not exclude the border interpretation at the same time. Our task is to find lines in the point pattern of monuments, which we will interpret as pathways. Neighbourhood graphs have

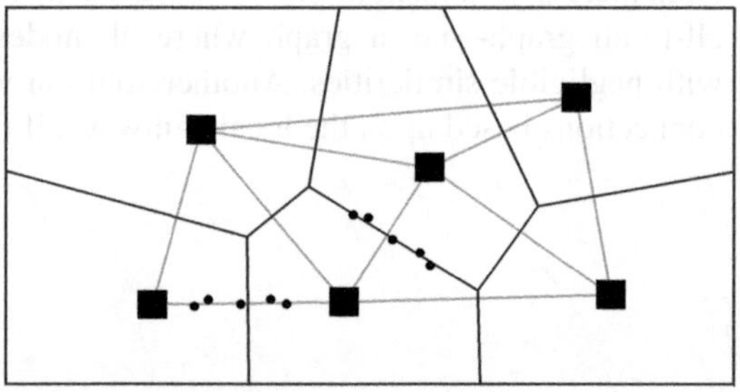

Fig. 9.5 Scheme of monuments along borders and pathways

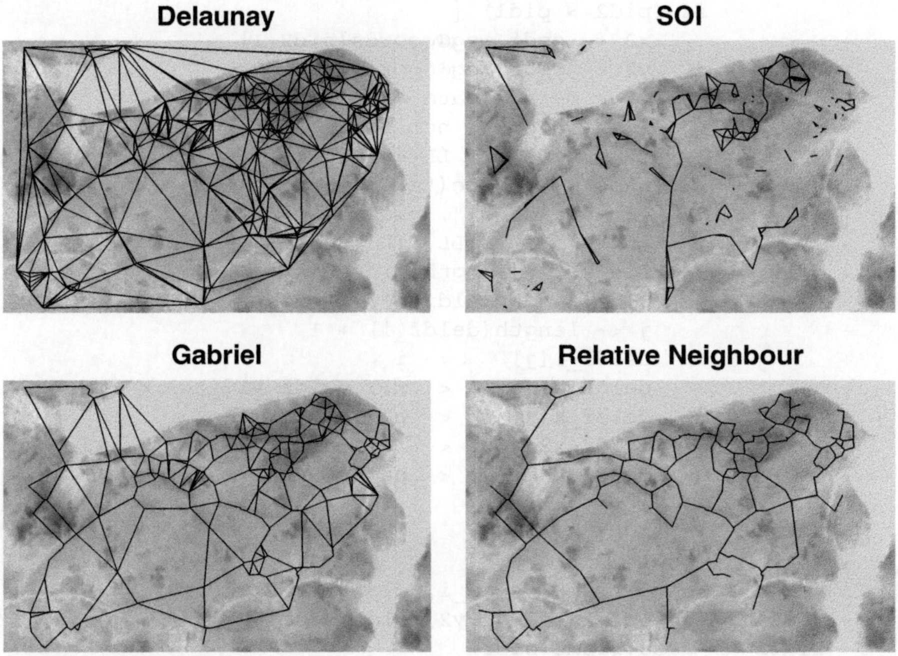

Fig. 9.6 Neighbourhood graphs of monuments

been developed as a pattern recognition tool and as such they will be applied here. We apply the neighbourhood graphs to the monuments data set (Fig. 9.6).

The first graph is again the Delaunay graph, which is produced by the `tri.mesh` function of the `tripack` package. The function `neighbours` transforms the graph into a neighbourhood object. Subsequently, we create a `SpatialLinesDataFrame` and export the results to a shapefile and a csv file. Incidentally, we provide a useful code fragment that can be adapted to export different types of graphs.

```
> library(rgdal)
> library(tripack)
> fsd <- tri.mesh(spdf_meg, duplicate = 'remove')
> fsnn <- neighbours(fsd)
> LinesList <- list()
> sldf <- c(); deldf_i <- c(); deldf_x1 <- c()
> deldf_y1 <- c(); deldf_k  <- c()
> deldf_x2 <- c(); deldf_y2 <- c()
> deldf_name <- c()
> for(i in seq(along=spdf_meg@coords[,1])) {
+   pid1 <- i
+   x1 <- spdf_meg@coords[i,1]; y1 <- spdf_meg@coords[i,2]
+   for(k in seq(along=(fsnn[i][[1]]))) {
+       pid2 <- fsnn[[i]][k]
```

```
+           if (pid2 > pid1) {
+               x2 <- spdf_meg@coords[pid2,1]
+               y2 <- spdf_meg@coords[pid2,2]
+               m <- matrix(data = c(x1,x2,y1,y2),
+                     nrow=2, ncol=2)
+               L <- Line(m); LL <- list(L)
+               name  <- paste("edge", "_",
+                     pid1,"_", pid2, sep="")
+               LLL <- Lines(LL, ID = name)
+               LinesList[length(LinesList)+1] <- LLL
+               sldf[length(sldf)+1] <- name
+               j <- length(deldf_i) + 1
+               deldf_i[j]     <- i
+               deldf_x1[j]    <- x1; deldf_y1[j]    <- y1
+               deldf_k[j]     <- pid2
+               deldf_x2[j]    <- x2; deldf_y2[j]    <- y2
+               deldf_name[j] <- name
+               }
+           }
+       }
> deldf <- data.frame(deldf_i,deldf_x1,deldf_y1,
+   deldf_k,deldf_x2,deldf_y2,deldf_name)
> sldf2 <- data.frame(sldf)
> sl <- SpatialLines(LinesList, proj4string =
+   CRS(as.character(crs1)))
> sdf <- SpatialLinesDataFrame(sl, sldf2,
+   match.ID = FALSE)
> writeOGR(sdf, "./5result", "delaunay_meg", driver=
+ "ESRI Shapefile", overwrite_layer=TRUE)
> write(rbind(deldf_i,deldf_x1,deldf_y1,deldf_k,
+ deldf_x2,deldf_y2,deldf_name), file
+ = "./5result/delaunay_meg.csv", ncolumns = 7, sep =
+  ";")
```

The Delaunay graph is obviously not useful for detecting linear structures in point patterns because there are too many connections, whereas the SOI-graph is not useful because there are too few connections and thus many isolated areas. The Gabriel graph is much better. The most convincing reconstruction of linear structures produces the relative neighbourhood graph, which is the best choice for this type of pattern recognition.

The neighbourhood graphs already discussed define neighbourhoods based upon the structure of the point pattern, which is useful for many purposes. However, there is another type of neighbourhood graphs which is less useful in general but can contribute to reveal hidden patterns in point patterns, namely metric neighbourhood graphs (Fig. 9.7). These graphs connect neighbours based upon distances, whereby the point with the smallest distance is the nearest neighbour. In this case, the neighbourhood degree k is 1. In general, the neighbourhood degree is the rank

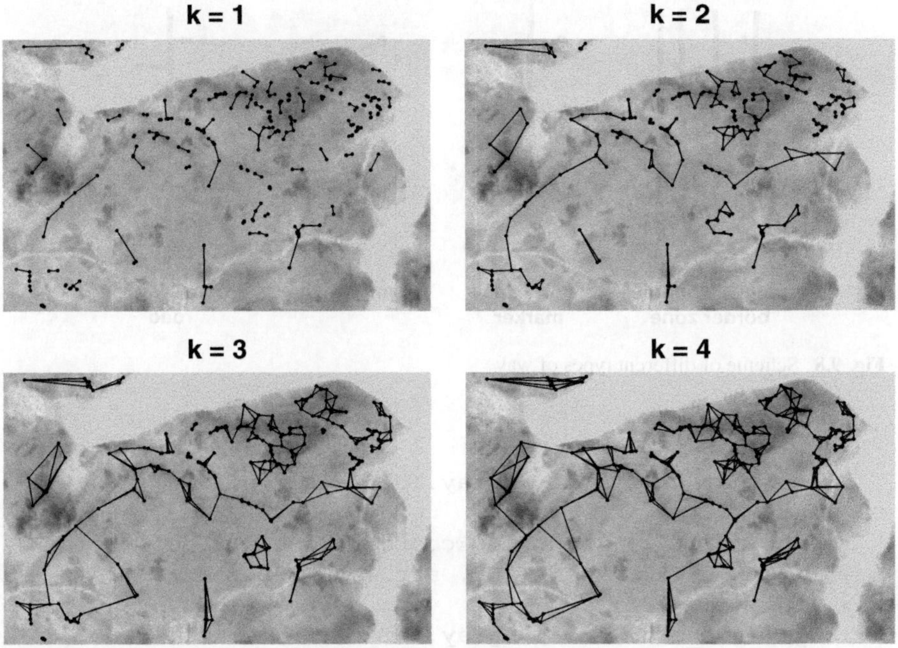

Fig. 9.7 Metric neighbourhood graphs of degree 1–4 of density centres

of the increasing distances. Metric neighbourhood graphs are usually plotted for neighbourhood degrees from one up to a certain number. The spdep package provides the knn2nb function to calculate metric neighbourhood graphs.

```
> nb_k1 <- knn2nb(knearneigh(spdf_meg@coords, k=1),
+   row.names=ids)
> nb_k2 <- knn2nb(knearneigh(spdf_meg@coords, k=2),
+   row.names=ids)
> nb_k3 <- knn2nb(knearneigh(spdf_meg@coords, k=3),
+   row.names=ids)
> nb_k4 <- knn2nb(knearneigh(spdf_meg@coords, k=4),
+   row.names=ids)
> par(mfrow=c(2,2))
image(sgdf_srtm, col = gray.colors(25, start =  0.97,
+ end = 0.4)
> plot.nb(nb_k1, spdf_meg@coords, pch= 16, col="black",
+   points=TRUE, add=TRUE, arrows=FALSE, cex=0.4)
> title("k = 1")
image(sgdf_srtm, col = gray.colors(25, start =  0.97,
+ end = 0.4))
> plot.nb(nb_k2, spdf_meg@coords,  pch= 16, col="black",
+   points=TRUE, add=TRUE, arrows=FALSE, cex=0.4)
```

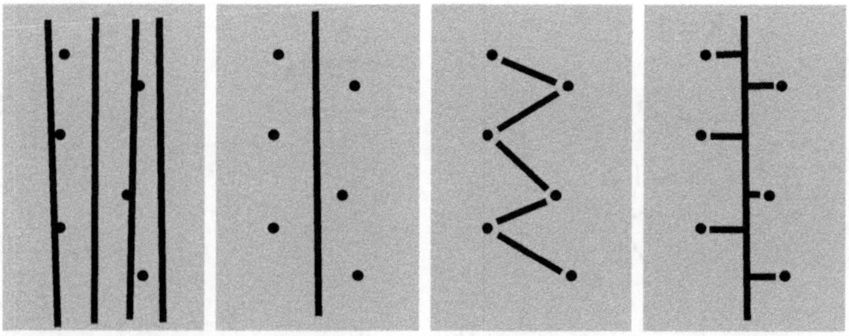

Fig. 9.8 Scheme of different types of way

```
> title("k = 2")
image(sgdf_srtm, col = gray.colors(25, start =   0.97,
+ end = 0.4))
> plot.nb(nb_k3, spdf_meg@coords,  pch= 16, col="black",
+   points=TRUE, add=TRUE, arrows=FALSE, cex=0.4)
> title("k = 3")
image(sgdf_srtm, col = gray.colors(25, start =   0.97,
+ end = 0.4))
> plot.nb(nb_k4, spdf_meg@coords,  pch= 16, col="black",
+   points=TRUE, add=TRUE, arrows=FALSE, cex=0.4)
> title("k = 4")
> par(mfrow=c(1,1))
```

The neighbourhood graph approach has one disadvantage, namely that the lines pass through the points. The basic assumption is that the monuments are located directly beside the pathway. Even if the monuments are indicators for the pathway, this is a very strong assumption. Other configurations are possible, where the line is near the points. We can have pathway bundles, fuzzy lines and pass ways to the main road (Fig. 9.8).

An approximative approach is necessary to deal with the other configurations, which can be based upon the density calculations. The idea is to extract lines in the area with the highest density of monuments as the most likely location of the ways. The ridges of the "density mountains" are those lines (Fig. 9.9).

We already calculated the density in Chap. 4. We will take the existing calculation, although the ridge detection is very sensitive to different bandwidth values in the kernel density estimation. Now we have to calculate the ridges. For this purpose, we employ the *Peucker–Douglas algorithm* [41], which is a moving window technique. Now, we apply this approach to our data (Fig. 9.10):

```
> ras_ridges <- sgdf_tum_dens
> ras        <- sgdf_tum_dens
> cols <- sgdf_tum_dens@grid@cells.dim[1]
```

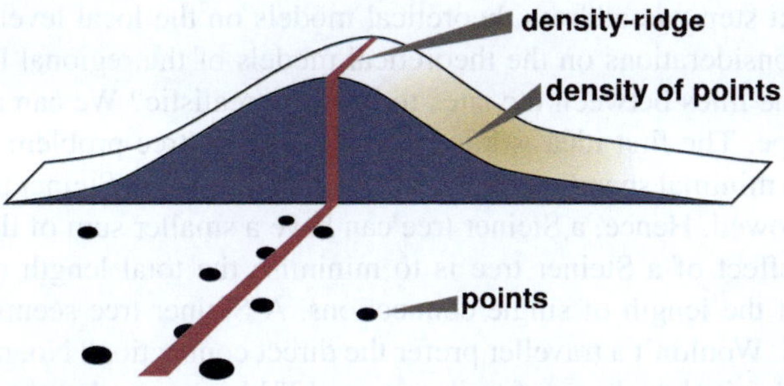

Fig. 9.9 Scheme of the density ridge method

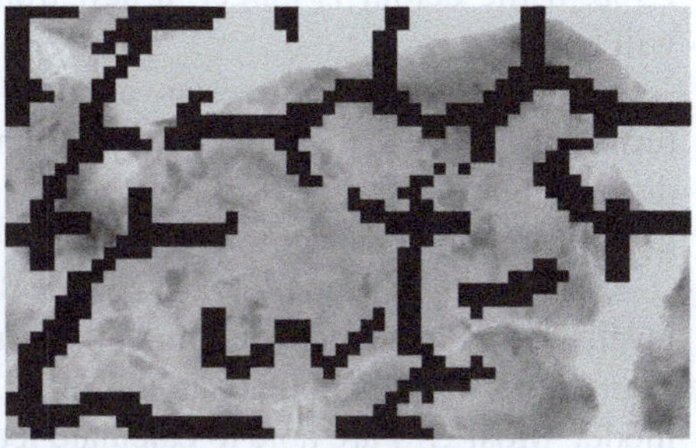

Fig. 9.10 Density ridges of the burial mound density

```
> ras_ridges@data$v <- 1
> ras@data$v[is.na(ras@data$v)] <- 1000000000
>
> for (i in 1:(length(ras@data$v)-(2*cols)-2)) {
+       ind <- c(i,i+1,i+2,i+cols,i+cols+1,i+cols
+ +2,i+(2*cols),i+(2*cols)+1,i+(2*cols)+2)
+       ind_min1 <- which(ras@data$v[ind]==
+ min(ras@data$v[ind]))
+       ind_min2 <-ind[ind_min1]
+       ras_ridges@data$v[ind_min2] <- 0}
> par( mai = c(0, 0, 0, 0))
> image(sgdf_srtm, col = gray.colors(25, start =
+ 0.97, end = 0.4))
> image(ras_ridges, col = gray.colors(2, start =
+ 0.3, end = 0.7), zlim=c(1,1), add=TRUE)
```

This method can be improved in three points:

- use a dynamical kernel where the bandwidth is adapted to a certain degree to the density of points, which will produce more details in dense areas;
- run the calculation in a loop and add points on the ridge to the data after each step, which will amplify the pattern and produce a sharper ridge structure; and
- connect the branches by using the related neighbourhood graph, which will produce a connected pathway system.

In the next step, we address theoretical models on the local level. We will start with some considerations on the theoretical models of the regional level. How can we modify the lines between the sites to be more realistic? We can add points and alter the shape. The first idea is known as the Steiner tree problem [42], which is similar to the minimal spanning tree. The difference is that in Steiner trees additional nodes are allowed. Hence, a Steiner tree can have a smaller sum of the length of all edges. The effect of a Steiner tree is to minimise the total length of the network at the cost of the length of single connections. A Steiner tree seems to favour the road builders. Wouldn't a traveller prefer the direct connection? No, not necessarily, given that empirical analyses of trail systems [23] have revealed that people prefer to use existing trails, albeit not at all costs. The threshold for detours is at about 25 %: if the detour is longer, a new trail will emerge; otherwise, the existing one will be used.

Nonetheless, Steiner trees are a minimisation of the total network length. Now we turn to minimise the length of single connections. Here, we do not use the Euclidean distance but rather the effort of using the path. Obstacles, slope, the condition of the ground and other aspects are parameters that should be considered.

Least cost path models [24, 26, 31, 36, 54] are theoretical models on the local level. The path is calculated that allows reaching point b from point a at minimum effort. The main parameter is the relief, which is available as a digital elevation model. Most GIS are able to calculate least cost path analysis but R allows the easy integration in a broader research framework. First, we have to prepare the variables. We use the SRTM elevation model and the density centres.

```
> library(raster)
> library(gdistance)
> ras <- raster(sgdf_srtm)
> nz <- 8   # neighbourhood number: 4,8,16
> projection(ras) <- crs1
> ras <- focal(ras, w=matrix(1/9,nrow=3,ncol=3),
+   NAonly=TRUE)
> plot(ras, col = gray.colors(25, start = 0.to reach97,
+   end = 0.4))
> starts <- cbind(cent@coords[,1],cent@coords[,2])
```

The next step is to prepare some cost functions (Fig. 9.11; [25]) that set the relief parameters—particularly the slope—in relation to the costs. We define some cost functions according to the literature [25]. In addition, we define an auxiliary function for the difference in altitude.

```
> # Tobler1993 velocity
> tobler1993a <- function(s){6 * exp(-3.5 *
+   abs(s + 0.05))}       # km/h
> tobler1993b <- function(s){0.36 * exp(-3.5 *
+   abs(s + 0.05))}    # m/min
> # Minetti2002 metabolic costs J/(kg*m) walking
> minetti2002w <- function(s){(280.5 * s^5 - 58.7 *
```

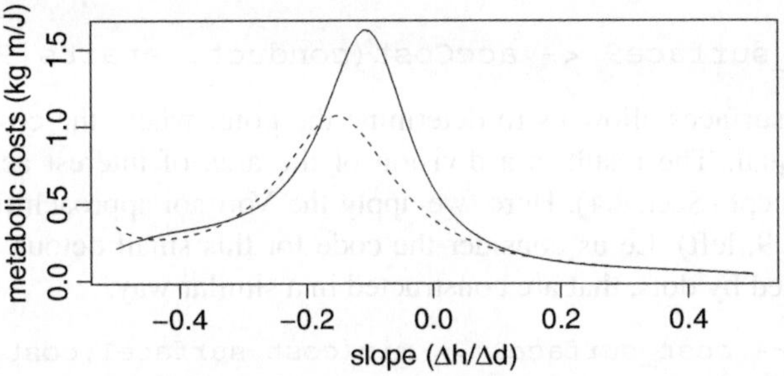

Fig. 9.11 Inverse cost functions (*solid line*: herzog2012wi; *broken line*: minetti2002wi)

```
+    s^4 - 76.8 * s^3 + 51.9 * s^2 + 19.6 * s + 2.5)}
> minetti2002wi <- function(s){1/(280.5 * s^5 -
+    58.7 * s^4 - 76.8 * s^3 + 51.9 * s^2 + 19.6 * s + 2.5)}
> # Herzog2012 metabolic costs J/(kg*m) walking
> herzog2012_w <- function(s){(1337.8 * s^6 +
+    278.19 * s^5 - 517.39 * s^4 - 78.199 * s^3
+    + 93.419 * s^2 + 19.825 * s + 1.64)}
> herzog2012_wi <- function(s){1/(1337.8 * s^6 +
+    278.19 * s^5 - 517.39 * s^4 - 78.199 *
+    s^3 + 93.419 * s^2 + 19.825 * s + 1.64)}
> # auxiliary function
> hdiff <- function(x){x[2]-x[1]}
```

The cost functions define the effort of moving a certain distance based upon the values of a certain parameter; for instance, the slope. Usual units are speed or energy consumption. Since gdistance works with conductivity rather than the more usual approach using costs, we need inverse cost functions.

The next step is to compute a *transitional object* hd that contains the transitions between grid cells such as differences in altitude. The geoCorrection function divides hd by the distance and results in the slope. Applying an inverse cost function, we derive the conductivity.

```
> hd <- transition(ras,hdiff,nz,symm=TRUE)
> slope <- geoCorrection(hd,scl=FALSE)
> adj <- adjacent(x=ras, cells=1:ncell(ras),
+    direction=nz)
> cost <- slope
> cost[adj] <- herzog2012_wi(slope[adj])
> conduct <- geoCorrection(cost, scl=FALSE)
```

Now we can compute the cost surface for each centre. The cost surface is a grid that contains for each point the cost for moving to the centre.

```
> cost_surface1 <- accCost(conduct, starts[1,])
> cost_surface2 <- accCost(conduct, starts[2,])
```

```
...
> cost_surface9 <- accCost(conduct, starts[9,])
```

The cost surfaces allow us to determine the point where the cost to reach two centres is equal. The result is a division of the area of interest according to the Voronoi concept (Sect. 8.4). Here, we apply the Voronoi approach in an economic space (Fig. 8.9, left). Le us consider the code for this small detour. We skip some lines, indicated by dots, that are constructed in a similar way.

```
> csm1 <- cost_surface1 == min(cost_surface1,cost_surface2,
+ cost_surface3,cost_surface4,cost_surface5,cost_surface6,
+ cost_surface7,cost_surface8,cost_surface9)
> csm2 <- cost_surface2 == min(cost_surface1,cost_surface2,
+ cost_surface3,cost_surface4,cost_surface5,cost_surface6,
+ cost_surface7,cost_surface8,cost_surface9)
> df <- data.frame(id=c(0,1), v=c(0,2))
> csm2 <- subs(x=csm2, y=df)
...
> csm9 <- cost_surface9 == > min(cost_surface1,cost_surface2,
+ cost_surface3,cost_surface4,cost_surface5,cost_surface6,
+ cost_surface7,cost_surface8,cost_surface9)
> df <- data.frame(id=c(0,1), v=c(0,9))
> csm9 <- subs(csm9, df)
> csm.a <- csm1 + csm2 + csm3 + csm4 + csm5 + csm6 + csm7
+ + csm8 + csm9
```

It is very easy to apply a weighting of centres, namely we simply have to manipulate the cost surface grids by addition or multiplication (Fig. 8.9, right). The important code fragment for the weighted Voronoi approach in an economic space can be found in the first line, where the costs to reach centre one are weighted twice:

```
> cost_surface1b <- cost_surface1 * 2.5
> cost_surface6b <- cost_surface6 * 0.7
> csm1 <- cost_surface1b == min(cost_surface1b,cost_surface2,
+ cost_surface3,cost_surface4,cost_surface5,cost_surface6b,
+ cost_surface7,cost_surface8,cost_surface9)
> csm2 <- cost_surface2 == min(cost_surface1b,cost_surface2,
+ cost_surface3,cost_surface4,cost_surface5,cost_surface6b,
+ cost_surface7,cost_surface8,cost_surface9)
> df <- data.frame(id=c(0,1), v=c(0,2))
> csm2 <- subs(x=csm2, y=df)
...
> csm6 <- cost_surface6b == min(cost_surface1b,cost_surface2,
+ cost_surface3,cost_surface4,cost_surface5,cost_surface6b,
+ cost_surface7,cost_surface8,cost_surface9)
> df <- data.frame(id=c(0,1), v=c(0,6))
> csm6 <- subs(csm6, df)
...
> csm9 <- cost_surface9 == min(cost_surface1b,cost_surface2,
```

```
+ cost_surface3,cost_surface4,cost_surface5,cost_surface6b,
+ cost_surface7,cost_surface8,cost_surface9)
> df <- data.frame(id=c(0,1), v=c(0,9))
> csm9 <- subs(csm9, df)
> csm.b <- csm1 + csm2 + csm3 + csm4 + csm5 + csm6 + csm7
+ + csm8 + csm9
```

Now we return to the least cost path analysis itself. The analysis begins with the definition of start- and end points. We will achieve this with the Delaunay graph, which produces natural neighbour connections.

```
> library(deldir)
> try <- deldir(starts[,1], starts[,2], plot=TRUE,
+   wl='tr')
> LinesList <- list()
> id <- seq(along=try$delsgs[,1])
> for(i in seq(along=try$delsgs[,1])) {
+     m <- matrix(data = c(try$delsgs[i,1],
+           try$delsgs[i,3],try$delsgs[i,2],
+    try$delsgs[i,4]), nrow=2, ncol=2)
+    L <- Line(m)
+    LL <- list(L)
+    name  <- paste("edge", "_", try$delsgs[i,5],"_",
+         try$delsgs[i,6], sep="")
+    LLL <- Lines(LL, ID = name)
+    LinesList[length(LinesList)+1] <-LLL
+ }
> deldf2 <- data.frame(try$delsgs[,5], try$delsgs[,1],
+      try$delsgs[,2], try$delsgs[,6],
+    try$delsgs[,3], try$delsgs[,4], paste("edge", "_",
+      try$delsgs[,5],"_"),
+    try$delsgs[,6], sep="")
> cols <- c("a","b","c","d","e","f","g","h")
> colnames(deldf2) <- cols
> sl <- SpatialLines(LinesList, proj4string =
+ CRS(as.character(crs1))
> starts2 <- SpatialLinesDataFrame(sl, deldf2,
+   match.ID = FALSE)
```

Now we can undertake the least cost path analysis for each connection.

```
> for(i in 1:length(starts2[,1])){
+     i1 <- i*2-1
+     i2 <- i*2
+    s <- SpatialPoints(cbind(starts2@data$b[i],
+ starts2@data$c[i]))
+    z <- SpatialPoints(cbind(starts2@data$e[i],
+ starts2@data$f[i]))
```

```
+         sz <- shortestPath(conduct, s, z,
+           output="SpatialLines")
+         zs <- shortestPath(conduct, z, s,
+           output="SpatialLines")
+         sz@lines[[1]]@ID <- as.character(i1)
+         zs@lines[[1]]@ID <- as.character(i2)
+         if(i==1){sdf <-rbind(sz,zs)}
+         if(i>1){sdf <- rbind(sdf,sz,zs,
+           makeUniqueIDs = TRUE)}
+         if(i==1){df <- cbind(c(1,2), c("sz","zs"),
+           c(starts2@data$g[i]))}
+         if(i>1){df <- cbind(c(df[,1],i1,i2),
+           c(df[,2],"sz","zs"), c(df[,3],
+               starts2@data$g[i],starts2@data$g[i]))}
+ }
> lcp_df <- as.data.frame(df)
> lcp_sldf <- SpatialLinesDataFrame(sdf,lcp_df,
+           match.ID = FALSE)
```

The result is a network of the paths that allows moving from one node of the network to another with the minimum effort defined by a certain set of parameters (Fig. 9.12, left). Perhaps there is a second and third optimal path. The classical least cost path analysis assumes that the traveller possesses perfect knowledge of the area and always makes absolute rational decisions, although in practice this is not realistic. A second optimal path may be in use because there are very small differences to the optimal path and the second one seems best. A certain degree of randomness should be taken into account and not one path but rather the likeliness of a path for all points in the area should be the result (Fig. 9.12, right). The `passage` function from the `gdistance` package allows this [14]. The variable `theta` controls the degree of randomness.

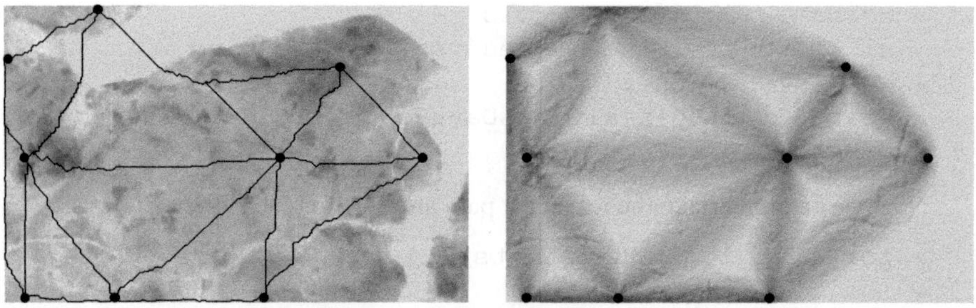

Fig. 9.12 *Left*: Least cost path analysis; the *line* indicates the least cost path. *Right*: Least cost path analysis with random walk; the *grey shade* indicated the number of random walks crossing a grid cell

```
> path <-ras
> path[] <- 0
> for(i in 1:length(starts2[,1])){
+    s <- SpatialPoints(cbind(starts2@data$b[i],
+         starts2@data$c[i]))
+    z <- SpatialPoints(cbind(starts2@data$e[i],
+        starts2@data$f[i]))
+    path <- max(path, passage(conduct, s, z,
+         theta=0.0001, totalNet="total"))}
>  plot(path, col=gray.colors(80, start=0.9, end=0.1,
+ gamma=0.2))
>  points(SpatialPoints(cbind(starts2@data$b,starts2@
+ data$c)), pch=16, cex=0.8)
```

We can calculate different least cost models using different parameters of preference. Which model fits best to the observed points that are assumed to be near the pathway? We could use the mean distance of the monuments to the pathway network as an inverse validation parameter. A better choice is to use the least cost model with random walk. For each cell, we know the likeliness for a pathway to cross the cell. The mean value of those values sampled at the monument's location is a rather good validation parameter: the higher the value, the better the fit. Let us assume that `path2` is the result of the passage calculation, where we do not use the topography but rather the density of megaliths as attractors.

```
> pathn_topo <- extract(path, spdf_meg)
> pathn_tumdens <- extract(path2, spdf_meg)
> mean(pathn_topo)
[1] 0.119158
> mean(pathn_tumdens)
[1] 0.2800619
```

Obviously, the megalith-attractor model is the better choice for modelling the pathways between the tumulus density centres. This is understandable, since we know that both types of monuments prefer high elevation values. A more detailed analysis of the monuments in this area reveals details of the parameters that determine the location of pathways. In fact, this area shows a preference of pathways with good visibility in the Bronze Age [36], which is not the case in the Neolithic Age. Accordingly, we can deduce that security and the visibility of potential enemies mattered in the Bronze Age. Hence, least cost path analysis can tell us much about society.

9.5 Characterising Elements in Networks and Networks

There are several coefficients for characterising transportation networks [39]. Here, we use centrality coefficients from social network analysis [16]. Centrality is one of the most important characteristics of networks. In the case of transportation networks, the most likely vital points in the system can be detected (Fig. 9.13). These calculations are theoretical models since empirical models need evidence of centrality. Centrality coefficients only show centrality potential because they are based upon the structure of the network rather than the actual interaction. First, we construct the Delaunay graph as an `igraph` object.

```
> library(igraph)
> library(spdep)
> ids <- row.names(as.data.frame(spdf_meg))
> meg_nb_del <- tri2nb(spdf_meg, row.names=ids)
> m <- nb2mat(meg_nb_del)
> g <- graph.adjacency(m, mode="lower", weighted=T)
> g <- set.vertex.attribute(g, "x", index=V(g),
+   coordinates(spdf_meg)[,1])
> g <- set.vertex.attribute(g, "y", index=V(g),
+   coordinates(spdf_meg)[,2])
```

Subsequently, we add the distances as edge weight.

```
> dpd  <- deldf
> dist <- sqrt((dpd[2] - dpd[5])^2 + (dpd[3] - dpd[6])^2 )
> dist2 <- dist^2
```

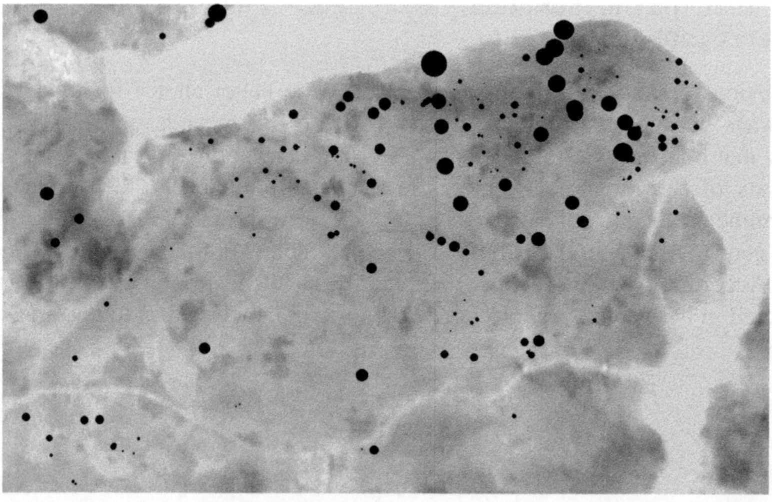

Fig. 9.13 Betweenness centrality of megaliths; the larger the *circle*, the higher its centrality

```
> dimnames(dist) <- list(NULL,"dist")
> dimnames(dist2) <- list(NULL,"dist2")
> dpd$dist   <- dist
> dpd$dist2  <- dist2
> g          <- set.edge.attribute(g, "distance2",
+ index=E(g), dist2)
> E(g)$weight <- dist
```

Finally, we calculate the centrality indices [3, 4, 15, 29, 30] and produce a spatial data frame that we can plot.

```
> c.degree <- degree(g, v=V(g))
> c.closness <- closeness(g, v=V(g))
> c.betweenness <- betweenness(g, v=V(g))
> c.bonacich.power <- bonpow(g, nodes=V(g))
>
> ctab <- data.frame(cbind(id = V(g)+1, x = fs[,1],
+   y = fs[,2], degree=c.degree, closness=c.closness,
+   betweenness=c.betweenness, bpower=c.bonacich.power))
> coordinates(ctab)=~x+y
> proj4string(ctab)  <- CRS(as.character(crs1))
> image(sgdf_srtm, col = gray.colors(25, start =
+   0.97, end = 0.4))
> points(ctab, pch=16, cex=sqrt(ctab$betweenness)/50)
```

If we find that places with a high betweenness centrality actually show indications of importance, then we can deduce that centrality in the sense of betweenness was important to the people. Betweenness measures the number of transit interactions at one point and hence the control of interaction. Degree is a measure for the number of direct interaction partners and closeness for the mean distance to all other members of the network. Bonacich's power centrality attempts to reflect a generalisation of the other measures.

9.6 Problems

9.1. Please compare area-based approaches (Chap. 8) with network-based approaches. What advantages and disadvantages can you find for both approaches?

9.2. Do you know other examples for axes of orientation?

9.3. Do you know or can you invent other neighbourhood graphs?

9.4. What is your opinion about the border/pathway problem? Do monuments mark borders, pathways, both or nothing and why do you think so?

9.5. Please re-run the least cost path analysis using additional parameters.

9.6. How can we validate the lcp models?

9.7. Please develop the algorithm for the local empirical model.

9.8. Why is the relative neighbour graph for monuments an empirical model?

9.9. Re-run the analysis with density centres from a KDE with smaller bandwidth.

References

1. Barthélemy, M. (2014). Discussion: Social and spatial networks. *Nouvelles de l'archéologie, 135*, 51–61.
2. Bivand, R. S., Pebesma, E. J., & Gómez-Rubio, V. (2008). *Applied spatial data analysis with R*. New York: Springer.
3. Bonacich, P. (1987). Power and centrality: A family of measures. *American Journal of Sociology, 92*, 1170–1182.
4. Borgatti, S. P. (2005). Centrality and network flow. *Social Networks, 27*, 55–71.
5. Bourgeois, Q. (2013). *Monuments on the Horizon. The formation of the barrow landscape throughout the 3rd and 2nd millennium BC*. Leiden: Sidestone Press.
6. Brandes, U., Robins, G., McCranie, A., & Wasserman, S. (2013). What is network science? *Network Science, 1*, 1–15.
7. Brughmans, T. (2010). Connecting the dots: Towards archaeological network analysis. *Oxford Journal of Archaeology, 29*, 277–303.
8. Brughmans, T. (2013). Thinking through networks: A review of formal network methods in archaeology. *Journal of Archaeological Method and Theory, 20*, 623–662.
9. Brughmans, T., Keay, S., & Earl, G. P. (2013). Understanding inter-settlement visibility in Iron Age and Roman Southern Spain with exponential random graph models for visibility networks. *Journal of Archaeological Method and Theory, 22*, 1–32.
10. Chen, G., Gould, R. J., Jacobson, M. S., Schelp, R. H., & West, D. A. (1992). A characterization of influence graphs of a prescribed graph. *Vishwa International Journal of Graph Theory, 1*, 77–81.
11. Collar, A., Coward, F., Brughmans, T., & Mills, B. J. (2015). Networks in archaeology: Phenomena, abstraction, representation. *Journal of Archaeological Method and Theory, 22*, 1–32.
12. Delaunay, B. N. (1934). Sur la sphère vide. *Bulletin of the Academy of Sciences of the USSR, 7*(6), 793–800.
13. Diestel, R. (2000). *Graph theory*. New York: Springer.
14. van Etten, J. (2015). R Package gdistance: Distances and routes on geographical grids. *Journal of Statistical Software, 10*, 1–22.
15. Freeman, L. C. (1977). A set of measures of centrality based on betweenness. *Sociometry, 40*, 35–41.
16. Freeman, L. C. (1978/1979). Centrality in social networks - conceptual clarification. *Social Networks, 1*, 215–239.
17. Fulminante, F. (2014). The network approach: Tool or paradigm? *Archaeological Review from Cambridge, 29*, 167–178.
18. Granovetter, M. S. (1973). The strength of weak ties. *The American Journal of Sociology, 78*, 1360–1380.
19. Haggett, P. (1965). *Locational analysis in human geography*. London: Arnold.
20. Haggett, P. (1970). Network models in geography. In R. J. Chorley & P. Haggett (Eds.), *Integrated models in geography* (pp. 609–668). London: Methuen.
21. Haggett, P., & Chorley, R. J. (1969). *Network analysis in geography*. London: Arnold.

22. Hanneman, R. A., & Riddle, M. (2005). *Introduction to social network methods*. University of California, Riverside, Department of Sociology, Riverside, CA: Digitalpublikation. http://faculty.ucr.edu/~hanneman/nettext/.Cited18Feb2014.
23. Helbing, D., Keltsch, J., & Molnár, P. (1997). Modelling the evolution of human trail systems. *Nature, 388*, 47–50.
24. Herzog, I. (2013). Theory and practice of cost functions. In F. Contreras, M. Farjas & F. J. Melero (Eds.), *Fusion of cultures. Proceedings of the 38th Annual Conference on Computer Applications and Quantitative Methods in Archaeology, Granada, Spain*, April 2010. BAR International Series, Vol. 2494. (pp. 375–382).
25. Herzog, I. (2013). Potential and limits of optimal path analysis. In A. Bevan & M. Lake (Eds.), *Computational approaches to archaeological spaces* (pp. 179–211). Walnut Creek, CA: Left Coast Press.
26. Herzog, I. (2014). Least-cost paths - some methodological issues. *Internet Archaeology, 36*. http://dx.doi.org/10.11141/ia.36.5.
27. Knappett, C. (2011). *An archaeology of interaction: Network perspectives on material culture and society*. Oxford: Oxford University Press.
28. Knappett, C. (Ed.). (2013). Network analysis in archaeology: New approaches to regional interaction. Oxford: Oxford University Press
29. Koschützki, D., Lehmann, K. A., Peeters, L., Richter, S., Tenfelde-Podehl, D., & Zlotowski, O. (2005). Centrality indices. In U. Brandes & T. Erlebach (Eds.), *Network analysis* (pp. 16–61). Berlin: Springer.
30. Koschützki, D., Lehmann, K. A., Tenfelde-Podehl D., & Zlotowski, O. (2005). Advanced centrality concepts. In U. Brandes & Erlebach, T. (Eds.), *Network analysis* (pp. 83–111). Berlin: Springer.
31. Llobera, M. (2000). Understanding movement: A pilot model towards the sociology of movement. In G. Lock (Ed.), *Beyond the Map. Archaeology and Spatial Technologies* (pp. 65–84). Amsterdam, Berlin, Oxford, Tokyo, Washington DC: IOS Press.
32. Michael, T. S., & Quint, T. (1999). Sphere of influence graphs in general metric spaces. *Mathematical and Computer Modelling, 29*, 45–53.
33. Moreno, J. L. (1934). *Who shall survive*? Washington, DC: Nervous and Mental Disease Publishing Company.
34. Müller, S. (1904). Vei og Bygd i Sten- og Bronzealdern. *Aarbøger for Nordisk oldkyndighed og historie, 1904*, 1–64.
35. Müller, U. (2012). Networks of towns' networks of periphery? Some relations between the North European Medieval town and its hinterland. In S. Brather, U. Müller & H. Steuer (Eds.), *Raumbildung durch Netzwerke? Der Ostseeraum zwischen Wikingerzeit un Spaetmittelalter aus archaeologischer und geschichtswissenschaftlicher Perspektive* (pp. 55–78). Bonn: Dr. Rudolf Habelt GmbH.
36. Nakoinz, O. (2012). Ausgewählte Parameter der Lage von Wegen und Monumenten als Proxy für soziale Prozesse prähistorischer Gesellschaften. In M. Hinz & J. Müller (Eds.), *Siedlung, Grabenwerk, Großsteingrab. Studien zu Gesellschaft, Wirtschaft und Umwelt der Trichterbechergruppen im nördlichen Mitteleuropa: Vol. 2. Frühe Monumentalität und soziale Differenzierung* (pp. 445–456). Bonn: Habelt.
37. Nakoinz, O. (2013). *Archäologische Kulturgeographie der ältereisenzeitlichen Zentralorte Südwestdeutschlands: Vol. 224. Universitätsforschung zur Prähistorischen Archäologie*. Bonn: Habelt.
38. Newman, M. E. J. (2010). *Networks: An introduction*. Oxford: Oxford University Press.
39. Nuhn, H., & Hesse, M. (2006). *Verkehrsgeographie*. Paderborn: Schöningh.
40. Ortúzar, J. de D., & Willumsen, L. G. (2011). *Modelling transport*. Chichester: Wiley.
41. Peuker, T. K., & Douglas, D. H. (1975). Detection of surface-specific points by local parallel processing of discrete terrain elevation data. *Computer Graphics and Image Processing, 4*, 375–387.
42. Prömel, H. J., & Steger, S. (2002). *The Steiner tree problem. A tour through graphs, algorithms, and complexity*. Braunschweig: Vieweg.

43. Ramachandran, S., & Rosenberg, N. A. (2011). A test of the influence of continental axes of orientation on pattern sof human gene flow. *American Journal of Physical Anthropology, 146*, 515–529.
44. Scott, J. (1991). *Social network analysis: A handbook*. London: Sage.
45. Sindbæk, S. M. (2007). Networks and nodal points: The emergence of towns in early viking age Scandinavia. *Antiquity, 81*, 119–132.
46. Taaffe, E. J., Gauthier, H. L., & O'Kelly, M. E. (1973). *Geography of transportation*. Upper Saddle River: Prentice Hall.
47. Toussaint, G. T. (1980). Pattern recognition and geometric complexity. In *Proceedings of the 5th International Conference on Pattern Recognition* (pp. 1324–1347). Miami Beach, FL.
48. Toussaint, G. T. (1980). The relative neighborhood graph of a finite planar set. *Pattern Recognition, 12*, 261–268.
49. Toussaint, G. T. (1981). Computational geometric problems in pattern recognition. In J. Kittler (Ed.), *Pattern recognition theory and applications* (pp. 73–91). Oxford: NATO Advanced Study Institute, Oxford University Press.
50. Toussaint, G. T. (2014). The sphere of influence graph: Theory and applications. *International Journal of Information Technology & Computer Science, 14*, 2091–1610.
51. Tremblay-Cormier, L. (2014). Le mobilier métallique méditerranéen comme témoin des échanges àă longue distance entre Rhin et Rhôe, du 10ème au 5ème siècle avant notre ère. In P. Barral, J.-P. Guillaumet, M.-J. Roulière-Lambert, M. Saracino & D. Vitali (Eds.), *Les Celtes en Italie*, May 2012 (pp. 297–309). Verone, Italy: Société archéologique de l'Est.
52. Urquhart, R. B. (1980). Algorithms for computation of relative neighborhood graph. *Electronics Letters, 16*, 556–557.
53. Wasserman, S., & Faust, K. (1994). *Social network analysis: Methods and applications.* Cambridge: Cambridge University Press, pp. 58–143.
54. White, D. A., & Surface-Evans, S. (Eds.). (2012). *Lest cost analysis of social landscapes*. Ann Arbor: The University of Uta Press.

Chapter 10
Interaction

10.1 Interaction

A brief introduction into the concept and term of "interaction" will serve the purpose to understand the integration of different phenomena and high potential of interpretation of this concept. The reader will make connections to other chapters of this book and case studies from literature.

10.1.1 Interaction as a Key Term

Interaction is certainly one of the most important aspects of human behaviour [24, 26], as one of the main drivers of historical, economic, social and cultural processes. At the same time, interaction is an abstract concept used in many disciplines. The concept covers all types of contacts between individuals and groups, as well as human–nature interaction. The disciplinary variations considerably differ and hence it is not easy to provide a universal definition; nonetheless, the following definition may serve our purpose:

Definition 10.1. Interaction is the joint action of at least two interaction partners.

Interaction hence requires the actions of two partners that are related in some aspect. The action can be to join forces to reach a common task, exchange something to serve complementary needs or fight each other. We can distinguish between positive and negative interaction, the exchange of material and immaterial goods and other types of behaviour that refer to each other. While the range of different types of interaction is obviously very wide, the abstract concept of interaction offers a framework to deal with different types of interaction in a similar way.

O. Nakoinz, D. Knitter, *Modelling Human Behaviour in Landscapes*, Quantitative Archaeology and Archaeological Modelling, DOI 10.1007/978-3-319-29538-1_10

Communication is a very special type of interaction. Accordingly, we can define:

Definition 10.2. Communication is the exchange of information.

This is a very good example of interaction, whereby the first interaction partner acts by sending some information and the second partner receives and interprets the information. Without sending—deliberately or otherwise—and receiving and interpreting, there is no interaction. Both partners need to be involved: while they may have different intentions, different expectations and different motivations both need to participate in the interaction process. If the second partner refuses to react to the impetus produced by the first partner, there is no interaction but rather simply action. However, communication is usually part of a human interaction process, accompanying the other types. Aside from the mechanical reaction to simple stimuli, the reaction is based upon the interpretation of certain signs. Interaction processes usually involve many steps of interpretation, whereby the first and the second partner change roles in an alternating way.

In this volume, we have a special interest in *spatial* interaction. We can define:

Definition 10.3. Spatial Interaction connects different locations by the means of moving people, goods or knowledge between the locations.

In pre-modern times, the movement of people can be presumed for all remote interaction processes. Whether the realisation of this movement matters depends on the focus of the intended interaction model. For example, we can look at the interaction between two villages and abstract from the many steps in the interaction process, which can include down-the-line exchange as well as the visit of one interaction partner in the other's village. Other interaction models can be interested in the difference between the two different modes of exchange.

10.1.2 Interaction in Different Disciplines

In order to explore the different types of interaction we will summarise some interaction concepts. In Chap. 2, the gravity law was mentioned. In physics, the forces that have an effect on other particles—for instance, gravity, electromagnetism or nuclear forces—are object to interaction analysis. Fields describing forces are called potentials; for example, magnetic potential. Potentials with parameters that are meaningful (for instance, Paris potential) are distinguished from those potentials with parameters simply used to calibrate the potential to the observations (for instance, Hamada–Johnston potential). In ecology, interaction between subsystems of the ecosystem is addressed. Human–nature interaction is one of the main ecological topics, usually leading to very complex interaction models. The complexity of these models arises from the interaction of many elements, which also holds true for climate models.

After mentioning some interaction concepts in science, we are moving to humanities. The symbolic interactionism from Blumer—based on the work of

Mead—describes modes of social interaction [1]. Symbols enable people to judge situations and adjust their behaviour towards other people. Here, we have the explicit combination of communication and action. Parsons [27] states that the interaction of people is determined by the role of people. In psychology, the temporal and causal processes of interaction in dyades or groups is addressed [8]. In ethnology, exchange is subject to interaction studies, such as Malinowski's [22] exchange of gifts. Polanyi's [28] concept of the market leads to an economy where the interaction between producer and consumer bears a certain moment.

We have already described some concepts in geography in Chap. 2. In geography, the interaction in dependence of distance is addressed. The authors addressing interaction include Christaller [3], Daudé [5], Fetter [10], Fotheringham [11], Haggett [15], Hägerstrand [16], Isard [19], Ravenstein [29, 30], Steward [36], Stouffer [37], Wilson [43] and Zipf [44].

In archaeology, migration is an important topic connected to interaction, since the movement of people is one means of interaction. Here, we only mention the work of Burmeister [2] and Rouse [33], although various authors have addressed exchange; indeed, some collected volumes provide an impression of this field of research [9, 17]. The investigation of communication and transportation [34] and of interaction networks [21, 35] is a more recent trend in archaeological interaction analysis. The analysis of cultural areas as interaction spaces and cultural borders as interaction obstacles [20, 25] represents a field of quantitative applications. The research on distance dependent interaction with distance diagrams and distance decay functions [24, 26, 31] and applying the gravity model [6, 7, 32] is also notable.

10.1.3 Parameters of Interaction

The main purpose of interaction models is to map the dependence of interaction on different, independent parameters. These parameters are mostly distances of some kind. First, we have to mention geographical distances, which are represented by Euclidean distances of coordinates on projected maps (see Chap. 1). Geographical distances are the most commonly used distance type. Furthermore, we can use cultural distances (Chap. 8) and economic distances (Chap. 9). The distance in use determines the interpretation of the results. From a spatial perspective economic distances are more useful than geographical distances, since they map the effort to move the distance between the two interaction partners. Geographical distances are usually used as a proxy for economical distances and in some cases they prove a good proxy in a comparative analysis of two different models [24]. Furthermore, the comparison of empirical and theoretical models with different distances can help to estimate which distance type is most significant.

In addition to distance—which is a property of the relation between two interaction partners—features of the nodes also influence the interaction. For example, gravity models include the size or mass of the interaction partners: the larger a node or village or the more important a person, the more attractive it is for interaction.

Mixed models—involving different distances and features of nodes—are most likely to fit best to reality. In this case, we use the whole cultural landscape with all its cultural, economic, religious and social levels of meaning, as well as the natural parameters of landscape as parameters that are attracting or frictions for movements. Whether these complicated models are useful depends on the research question: if we are interested in the relationship of transport and interaction or social distances and interaction, we would certainly prefer simple models.

10.1.4 Measuring Interaction

In the previous section, we discussed the independent parameters, whereas now we turn to the dependent parameter, which is interaction itself. Particularly in an archaeological context, it is very difficult to quantify the interaction itself by counting the interaction processes; instead, we use interaction proxies. We can distinguish between two basic categories of interaction proxies. The first category is *movement indicators*. These indicators do not represent the interaction itself, but rather the means of spatial interaction, the movement of people, objects and ideas. The movement of people—migration in general—and travelling people—tradesmen, travelling craftsmen, people living in the transhumance system—can be detected by associated objects or human remains. In particular, isotope analysis can identify foreign individuals and in some cases it is able to highlight possible areas of origin. Isotope analysis and chemical analysis can also help to determine the provenance of objects. A more traditional yet still very important method is to identify foreign goods and imports using typology, although this has some limitations. In the case of rather general shapes, it is very difficult to identify non-local types. In short distance exchange, the objects often belong to the same types and hence are not identifiable. Typology is also used to detect the exchange of ideas. Here, a more thorough analysis is necessary: we have to show that the type of an object, its shape and hence its idea has a foreign origin, but not its material. If an idea spreads over an area, the new type is locally produced according to a general template. Local variations may help to establish the spread of ideas. Infrastructure like a road system also indicates a certain degree of interaction, since the road is used to move people and objects.

The *interaction effect indicators* is based on the idea that interaction leads to an adaptation of the interaction partner to each other [12]. In this case, the similarity of the interaction partners and the inverse cultural distance of the partners can be used as interaction proxies. However, what about the endeavour to stand out and distinguish from the others in border regions? This is a special case, since some effects superimpose each other. First, the transboundary interaction leads to an adaptation, which is the formation of a common symbology. Different signs of this symbolic language are used to distinguish the different groups, whereby the groups indicated by the different signs have a higher internal interaction than with other groups. Put simply, a certain degree of interaction is a precondition for developing distinct and not simply different groups that already have or attain higher internal interaction. It is difficult to detect the transboundary common symbology because the signs belonging to this language occur separated. A high intensity or density of different distinct symbols itself indicates a level of interaction that is not visible in the other sources. These effects should be considered in the analysis, although we will not explore this topic in further detail.

10.2 Empirical Interaction Models

10.2.1 Indicators and Characterisations

As mentioned above, borders, territories and networks indicate interaction and provide us with more specific information about the interaction processes. Chapters 2 and 9 present some methods in these fields of research. Another indicator of interaction is the CSR tests presented in Chap. 7. In the case of second-order properties, it is assumed that the interaction between the points influences the location of the points. Attraction and repulsion are interactive effects that can be shown with CSR tests if complete spatial randomness has to be rejected.

Another indicator of interaction or interaction processes is a test for auto-correlation. Let us assume that some points are characterised by the density of megaliths. According to the aforementioned ideas, the more similar the density values, the more likely the interaction between the two points. With a survey of the similarity of neighbouring points, we can explore whether the degree of interaction in the system has to be estimated as rather high or low. This is archived by a test for auto-correlation, like Moran's `I` test [4, 23, 40]. Moran's `I` coefficient is

$$I = \frac{N}{\sum_i \sum_j w_{ij}} \frac{\sum_i \sum_j w_{ij}(X_i - \bar{X})(X_j - \bar{X})}{\sum_i (X_i - \bar{X})^2} \tag{10.1}$$

We apply the test to the empty circle nodes from Chap. 4. For the calculation of `I`, we first determine the natural neighbours, which will be used for the comparison of values. Subsequently, the `moran.test` function will do the rest.

```
> library(spdep)
> voro_nb_del <- tri2nb(coordinates(fs_vd_spdf), row.names=
+ row.names(as.data.frame(fs_vd_spdf)))
> moran.test(fs_vd_spdf@data$fs_vd, nb2listw(voro_nb_del,
+ style="W"))
Moran's I test under randomisation
data:  fs_vd_spdf@data$fs_vd
weights: nb2listw(voro_nb_del, style = "W")
Moran I statistic standard deviate = 24.6373, p-value <
+ 2.2e-16
alternative hypothesis: greater
sample estimates:
```

```
Moran I statistic       Expectation          Variance
     0.6473760460     -0.0020202020      0.0006947563
```

The value of `0.64` indicates a certain auto-correlation. In our case, this shows that we can interpolate the values (see Chap. 5) rather than an actual interaction. Applied to the presence of certain types of sites, this could indicate interaction. The value `0` would mean no interaction and negative values would indicate negative interaction.

10.2.2 Distance Diagrams

Distance diagrams are one of the most simple—yet very effective—tools to explore interaction. An interaction proxy is plotted against a certain distance. As previously mentioned, we can use geographical, economic, cultural and any other distances. However, distance and interaction proxy are not the only aspects that control the result and interpretation of the distance diagrams. Similar to the generalised point pattern characterisation, we can decide for different foci and points of view (see Chap. 7), each of which can use fixed, selected and all points. Fixed points allow a result that is literally fixed on a map, thus making it easy to identify the influence of different topographic features, as well as different organisational structures on interaction. The usage of all points allows focusing on the effect of absolute distances on the interaction to identify distance thresholds (Table 10.1).

We will discuss and apply some of the nine types of distance diagrams. We are using the megalith density centres as viewpoints and assume that the megalith density is a characteristic parameter that allows calculating cultural distances as inverse interaction proxies. Although this is an idealised example, it will show principles of the approach very clearly and can be adapted to any kind of data which allow the determination of distances. Where we use simple differences in our example, one has to apply a distance function such as the Euclidean distance. The results from a research project and based on an extensive database are published elsewhere [24, 26].

Table 10.1 Type codes, names and examples of different types of distance diagrams (dd)

	Fixed focus	Selected focus	All focused
Fixed viewpoint	dd1 fixed profile dd, similarity profiles	dd2 fixed sector dd	dd3 fixed multi-focal dd, fall-off curve
Selected viewpoints	dd4 selected profiles dd	dd5 selected sector dd	dd6 selected multi-focal dd
All viewpoints	dd7 aggregated profile dd	dd8 aggregated sector dd	dd9 aggregated multi-focal dd, variogram

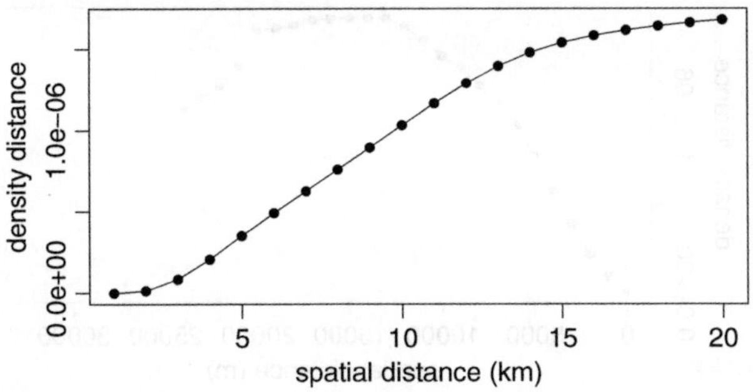

Fig. 10.1 Interaction model dd1

Profile distance diagrams are the type with the most distinct reference to specific locations and their properties. Each point in the diagram corresponds to a certain location. We start with the density maximum and look westwards (Fig. 10.1).

```
> spoints <- data.frame(cbind(x=(-seq(20:1)*1000)
+ + 3571203, y=rep(6036796, 20)))
> coordinates(spoints)=~x+y
> proj4string(spoints)  <- CRS(as.character(crs1))
> i_kde <- extract(raster(sgdf_meg_dens), spoints)
> mdistance <- i_kde[1] - i_kde
> plot(mdistance, col="black", pch=16, xlab="spatial
+ distance (km)", ylab= "density distance")
> lines(mdistance,lty=1,col="black")
```

As expected, the density distances are increasing with the spatial distance which indicates decreasing interaction.

The next distance diagram version is `dd3`, which uses all focal points. If the location of production is chosen as the viewpoint, this is nothing but a classical empirical *fall-off curve*. The curve looks different, since we use cultural distances rather than finding counts that are used for fall-off curves. Here, some preparations are helpful. We prepare a `matrix` for interim results, a `dataframe` for results and some regular sample points that we use to sample the megalith density map.

```
> dist <- seq(from=0, to=33000, by=1000)
> cdist <- id <- 1:length(dist)
> dresult <- cbind(id, dist, cdist[] <- 0)
> samppt   <- spsample(sgdf_srtm, 500,  type="regular")
> i_kde <- extract(raster(sgdf_meg_dens), samppt)
> ref_kde <- extract(raster(sgdf_meg_dens), cbind(3571203,
+ 6036796))
> dmat <- matrix(1:length(dist)*length(sgdf_meg_dens@data$v),
+ nrow=length(dist), ncol=length(sgdf_meg_dens@data$v))
> dmat[] <- as.double(dmat[] <-NA)
```

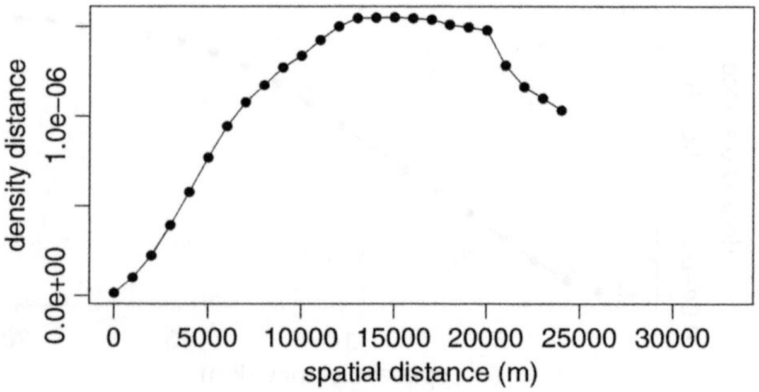

Fig. 10.2 Interaction model dd3

```
> mmean <- function (x) {mean(x, na.rm=TRUE)}
> edist <-function(x1,x2,y1,y2) {sqrt((x1 - x2)^2 + (y1 -
+ y2)^2)}
```

Now, we calculate the distances in a loop and subsequently aggregate them into the result `dataframe`. The results are as expected and the decreasing part on the right corresponds to the density centre in the South–West corner of the area (Fig. 10.2).

```
> for (i in seq_along(samppt@coords[,1])) {
+      x1 <- 3571203; y1 <- 6036796
+      x2 <- samppt@coords[i,1]; y2 <- samppt@coords[i,2]
+      sdist <-edist(x1,x2,y1,y2)
+      dind <- floor(sdist/1000) + 1
+      dmat[dind,i] <- abs(i_kde[i] - ref_kde)
+      }
> dresult[,3] <-  apply(dmat, 1, mmean)
> plot(x=dresult[,2], y=dresult[,3], col="black", pch=16,
+ xlab="spatial distance (m)", ylab= "density distance")
> lines(x=dresult[,2], y=dresult[,3],lty=1,col="black")
```

The distance diagram version `dd2` (Fig. 10.3) is very similar to `dd3`. The only difference is a selection of the target points. We will distinguish the target points West and East of the viewpoint. We undertake a similar preparation and simply add an additional column in the result `dataframe`.

```
...
dresult <- cbind(id, dist, cdist[] <- 0, cdist2[] <- 0)
...
```

Subsequently we insert a condition for the selection of viewpoints and calculate the values for two conditions. Here is the code for the Eastern part of the area:

```
> for (i in seq_along(samppt@coords[,1])) {
+      x1 <- 3571203; y1 <- 6036796
+      x2 <- samppt@coords[i,1]; y2 <- samppt@coords[i,2]
```

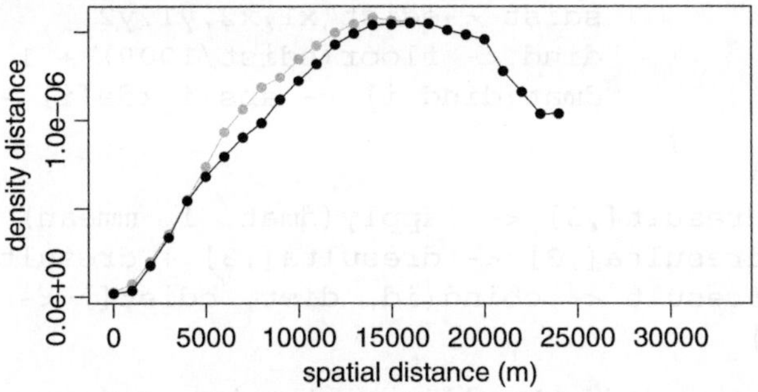

Fig. 10.3 Interaction model dd2. *Grey*: East; *black*: West

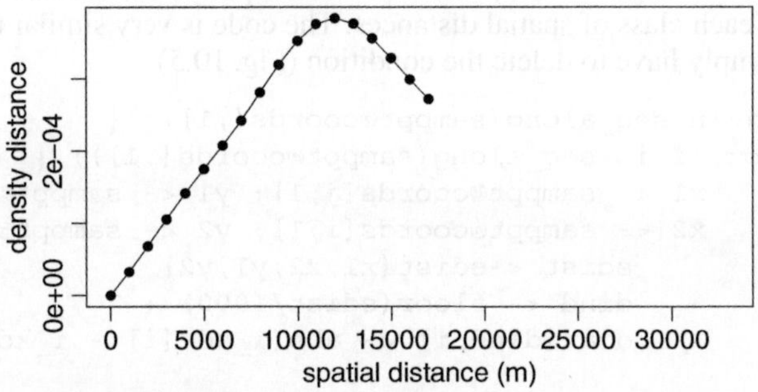

Fig. 10.4 Interaction model dd7

```
+       if (x1 < x2) {
+            sdist <-edist(x1,x2,y1,y2)
+            dind <- floor(sdist/1000) + 1
+            dmat[dind,i] <- abs(i_kde[i] - ref_kde) }
+ }
> dresult[,4] <-  apply(dmat, 1, mmean)
```

The result shows us differences in interacting to the West and East. In particular, this might be useful in border zones.

For the aggregated versions, we simply have to calculate the results in a loop across all viewpoints. Now, we use two result data frames: one for each internal loop and one for the aggregated result. All other steps in the preparation are the same as before. While dd2 looks from one point to all others that have coordinates higher or lower than the one from the viewpoint, dd7 looks from all points along a straight line (Fig. 10.4).

```
...
dresulta <- dresult
...
<- samppt@coords[i,1]; y2 <- samppt@coords[i,2]
+            if (x1 == x2 & y2 >= y1) {
```

```
+               sdist <-edist(x1,x2,y1,y2)
+               dind <- floor(sdist/1000) + 1
+               dmat[dind,i] <- abs(i_kde[i] - i_kde[j])
+         }
+     }
+     dresult[,3] <-  apply(dmat, 1, mmean)
+     dresulta[,3] <- dresulta[,3] + dresult[,3]
+     dresult <- cbind(id, dist, cdist[] <- 0)
+     }
```

Our final example is dd9 which is nothing but a variogram (see Chap. 5). The effect of topography is minimised in dd9. Here, distance thresholds take full effect. We are looking from all points to all other points and collect the differences in values for each class of spatial distances. The code is very similar to the previous model: we simply have to delete the condition (Fig. 10.5).

```
> for (j in seq_along(samppt@coords[,1])) {
+     for (i in seq_along(samppt@coords[,1])) {
+         x1 <- samppt@coords[j,1]; y1 <- samppt@coords[j,2]
+         x2 <- samppt@coords[i,1]; y2 <- samppt@coords[i,2]
+             sdist <-edist(x1,x2,y1,y2)
+             dind <- floor(sdist/1000) + 1
+             dmat[dind,i] <- abs(i_kde[i] - i_kde[j])
+     }
+     dresult[,3] <-  apply(dmat, 1, mmean)
+     dresulta[,3] <- dresulta[,3] + dresult[,3]
+     dresult <- cbind(id, dist, cdist[] <- 0)
+ }
```

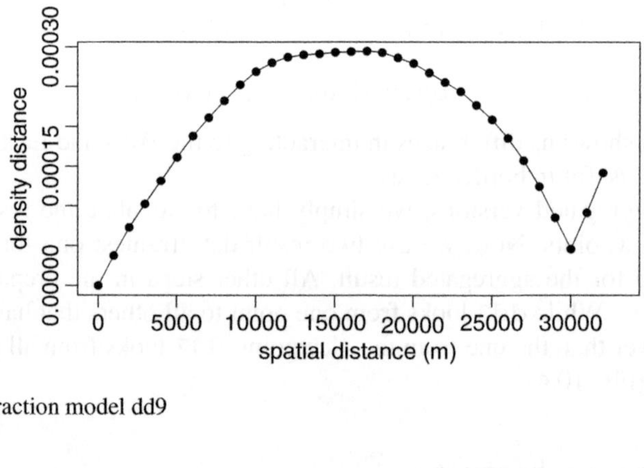

Fig. 10.5 Interaction model dd9

10.3 Theoretical Interaction Models

There are many theoretical interaction models that can be found in the literature. We will focus on distance decay functions and gravity models.

10.3.1 Distance Decay Functions

Tobler's first law of geography ([41, 42]; see Chap. 2) is a good starting point for discussing theoretical interaction models:

Everything is related to everything else, but near things are more related than distant things.

This means that the likeliness of interaction—which is a kind of being related—decreases with distance according to a monotone function. Realisations of this model are called *distance decay functions*. Although Tobler's first law covers many different functions, this is a valuable theoretical model, enabling us to compare the theoretical model with the data. If we find that the empirical distance diagrams include parts where the interaction is increasing with distance (remember: increasing interaction intensity = decreasing cultural distance), then this model does not apply, whereas if it is a law, it must. Accordingly the question emerges whether Tobler's first law is really a law.

From a traditional perspective, it seems that there is a difference between proper scientific laws like Newton's gravity law and Tobler's law. Scientific laws are supposed to be proven without doubt while it appears difficult to prove that Tobler's first law applies in all possible cases. However, if we remember that Newton's mechanics is considered to be an approximation for conditions of small velocity in modern physics, the difference shrinks. Tobler himself [42] points out that the famous physicist Feynman defines a scientific law as a guess about regularities of certain observable entities where the consequences of the guess agree with the observations. Accordingly, a law is not inherent in nature but depends on observations; thus, a law is a tool to describe regularities in observations rather than the nature of nature.

In our context, the usage of Tobler's first law as a simple theoretical model that applies in general or not does not seem an appropriate approach. We will benefit from using the heuristic potential of Tobler's first law as law. We do not suggest that Tobler's first law is always right, but we assume that this law is valid in a heuristic application. Now, the question is not whether Tobler's first law as a theoretical model agrees with empirical data, but rather how we can define distance an interaction to make the law agree with the observations. Let us explain this with an example and assume that we have a fixed profile distance diagram `dd1` with an anomaly. In the middle part, there is a strong decrease in interaction, followed by a strong increase. This would force us to reject the theoretical model. However, if we assume that the theoretical model as law is right, then we have to explain the anomaly in a way that agrees with the law. For example, we can find topographic features like mountains that work as friction for movements and hence hamper interaction. Using economical distances rather than geographical ones would transform the observations in a way that the theoretical model is more agreeable. The distance diagram can tell us even more, whereby we can distinguish a step from a peak. A step would mean that we have a certain friction of movement, but that people reach the points after the obstacle by overcoming the obstacle. By contrast, a peak would mean that people preferred another way that does not correspond to the profile to reach the target with less effort. We could adapt the profile to the least cost path, which would make the empirical model fit better to the theoretical model. Using this approach, we can learn much about the conditions of interaction. One advantage of this approach is that a detailed theoretical model is not necessary; rather, we can use Tobler's rather general first law of geography. This is equal to using different sophisticated theoretical models that involve inhomogeneous space and similar aspects but require fewer assumptions.

A general scheme of some anomalies in distance diagrams can help to find interpretations of the curves in the diagrams. We can distinguish steps from peak, skips, and waves (Fig. 10.6).

In particular, we have to consider different types of distances. Geographical, economic and cultural distances can be applied. The distance can be calculated in the plain and a network, such as a road system. The wave distance diagram can emerge in distribution systems with relay stations, as well as in cases where the profile cuts the road system at several points.

The interpretation of aggregated distance diagrams is different, since it is not fixed on the map. Distances themselves dominate the interpretations. A simple scheme will visualise possible interpretations for `dd9` distance diagrams (Fig. 10.7).

In section 1, a steep slope allows two interpretations, which depend on the scale of analysis and the data: first, the location within the distances of section one is in

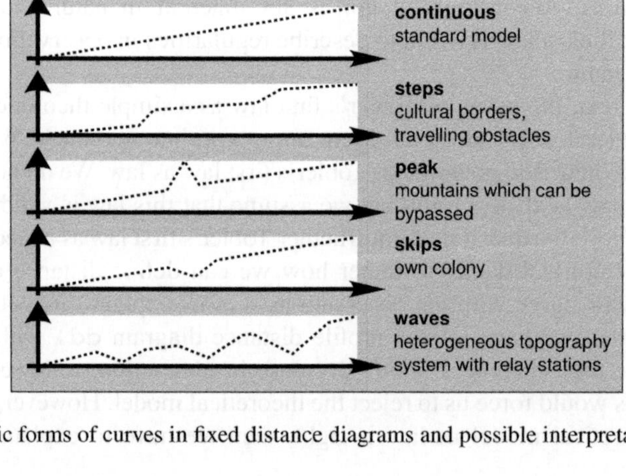

Fig. 10.6 Basic forms of curves in fixed distance diagrams and possible interpretations

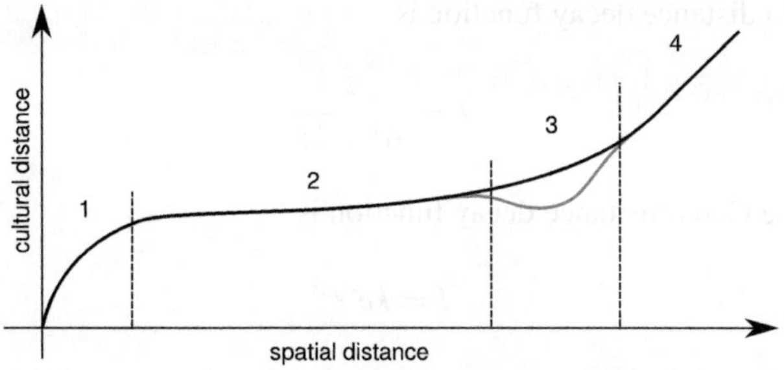

Fig. 10.7 Scheme of an agglomerative distance diagram with characteristic sections

the direct sphere of influence of the centre and hence the cultural distances are rather small; and second, the step indicates a natural variation of data. The next village—the nearest neighbour and related to the center—shows a variation of cultural traits due to the selectivity of data. However since the level of variation is similar in all directions while the cultural distance between the neighbours is at the same level, a step emerges. In this case, a curve meeting the axis not at zero but rather at a higher value might be more appropriate. This would indicate a certain standard deviation similar to the nugget effect in variograms.

In section 2 we find a slow yet monotonic increase of the cultural distances according to Tobler's first law. In section 3, the end of the usual distance range is pronounced by a skip, which indicates that people are aware of the distance threshold marked by the border between sections 3 and 4. People can try to optimise their travels by going up to the distance threshold. Section 4 represents a distance that is not travelled in daily life. The distance threshold is a very characteristic value influenced by cultural practice as well as the means of transportation. Hence the comparison of distance thresholds for different regions can be meaningful.

Distance decay functions are more specific theoretical models used for the comparison with empirical *fall-off curves* [31]. The distance decay diagrams are similar to the distance diagrams, although they simply use an interaction proxy rather than an inverse interaction proxy. Among the functions usually used as distance decay functions, a power function, an exponential function, a Gauss function and a Pareto function are frequently used [13, 14, 18, 19, 38, 39]. The three functions use two parameters that control the result. Although the symbol is similar, the interpretation of the parameters might differ. The values of these parameters have to be determined empirically. The power distance decay function is

$$I = \frac{k}{d^j} \tag{10.2}$$

The exponential distance decay function is

$$I = ke^{-jd} \tag{10.3}$$

The Pareto distance decay function is

$$I = \frac{k}{(d+k)^j} \tag{10.4}$$

Finally, the Gauss distance decay function is

$$I = ke^{-jd^2} \tag{10.5}$$

Here, k and j are simply parameters that determine the exact shape of the curves. For the calculation, we first define the functions as `ddecay1`, `ddecay2` and `ddecay3`, set the parameter and subsequently plot the curves with the `matplot` and `lines` commands.

```
> ddecay1 <- function (d, k, j) {i <- k/d^j; return(i)}
> ddecay2 <- function (d, k, j) {i <- k*2.718282^(-j*d);
+ return(i)}
> ddecay3 <- function (d, k, j) {i <- (k/(d+k)^j);
+ return(i)}
> ddecay4 <- function (d, k, j) {i <- k*2.718282^(-j*(d^2);
+ return(i)}
> k <- 3
> j <- 3
> xval <- seq(0,1,0.01)
> matplot(xval, ddecay1(xval, k, j)*0.00005, ylim=c(0,1),
+ type="l", xlab=expression(paste("distance")),
+ ylab="interaction")
> lines(xval, ddecay2(xval, k, j)*0.3, type="l", lty=2)
> lines(xval, ddecay3(xval*10, k, j)*9, type="l", lty=3)
> lines(xval, ddecay4(xval*10, k, j)*0.2, type="l",
+ lty=4)
> legend("topright", legend =c("power", "exponential",
+ "Pareto","Gauss"), lty=c(1,2,3,4))
```

Renfrew [31] proposed the idea that the different distance decay functions (Fig. 10.8) can be interpreted in a specific way. For example, he interprets empirical fall-off curves that fit to a Gaussian distance decay function as random walk, while exponential distance decay is interpreted as down-the-line exchange. The success of this approach depends on the quality of the data and other influences on the interaction intensity. The decision concerning which distance decay function fits best to the data requires high-quality data and minor influences by topography. The approach with less specific theoretical models seems more promising with medium—and low-quality data and heterogeneous topography.

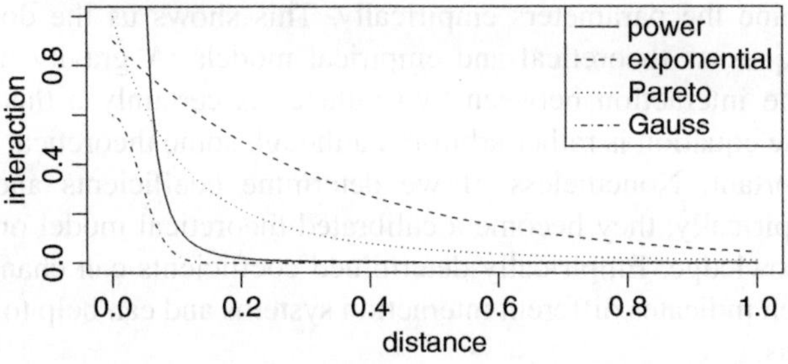

Fig. 10.8 Different distance decay functions

10.3.2 Gravity Models

The distance diagrams and distance decay functions deal with distances only. Additional information like topography and cultural aspects of the space between the points can be included in the distances. Properties of the points like population size are not adequately mirrored in the distances. Gravity approaches are a simple solution to implement point properties (refer to Chap. 2 and the beginning of this chapter). The classical gravity equation with m_1 and m_2 for the masses and g for the gravity constant is

$$F = g\frac{m_1 m_2}{d^2} \tag{10.6}$$

The processes for which we are looking can have different mechanisms than physical gravity. A generalisation can be useful to fit the curve to the observations, which is achieved by allowing different exponents. In addition, we apply the names of our previous coefficients.

$$I = k\frac{m_1 m_2}{d^j} \tag{10.7}$$

In fact, the gravity equation comprises a distance decay term and a mass term:

$$I = k\frac{m_1 m_2}{d^j} = ke^{-jd} m_1 m_2 \tag{10.8}$$

Of course, we can use other distance decay terms, such as an exponential distance decay function, as follows:

$$I = ke^{-jd} m_1 m_2 \tag{10.9}$$

From a very simple equation with just a scaling factor, we have changed to more parameters, the exponent j and an interchangeable distance decay term. These modifications allow a better adaptation to the data, although they force us to determine the parameters empirically. This shows us the double nature of some techniques as theoretical and empirical models. A gravity model used for estimating the interaction between two villages is certainly a theoretical model. The use of the equation is rather arbitrary, although some theoretical considerations can be important. Nonetheless, if we determine coefficients and parts of the equation empirically, they become a calibrated theoretical model or a tool to gain empirical knowledge. Empirically determined coefficients can change in different regions, which indicates different interaction systems and can help to develop social interpretations.

Here, we give the code for a simple gravity model using Eq. (10.7). We will calculate the theoretical interaction between the natural neighbours of the density centres of the megalithic tombs. The density of the megaliths will be used as characterisation of the points. The density centres represent the villages for which we have no original data. The megalith density at these points represents the population. Despite making some assumptions that are questionable and have to be discussed in a real research project, we can use this as a simple example. The reader can develop more sophisticated models using the simple techniques presented here. First, we prepare a `dataframe` with the Delauny edges of the density centres.

```
> library(tripack)
> fsd <- tri.mesh(cent, duplicate = 'remove')
> fsnn <- neighbours(fsd)
> LinesList <- list()
> sldf <- c();deldf_i <- c();deldf_x1 <- c();deldf_y1 <-
+ c();deldf_k <- c();deldf_x2 <- c();deldf_y2 <- c();
+ deldf_name <- c();deldf_dens1 <- c();deldf_dens2 <- c()
> for(i in seq(along=cent@coords[,1])) {
+    pid1 <- i
+    x1 <- cent@coords[i,1]
+    y1 <- cent@coords[i,2]
+    dens1 <- cent@data$meg[i]
+    for(k in seq(along=(fsnn[i][[1]]))) {
+        pid2 <- fsnn[[i]][k]
+        if (pid2 > pid1) {
+            x2 <- cent@coords[pid2,1]
+            y2 <- cent@coords[pid2,2]
+            dens2 <- cent@data$meg[pid2]
+            m <- matrix(data = c(x1,x2,y1,y2), nrow=2,
+                 ncol=2)
+            L <- Line(m); LL <- list(L)
+            name  <- paste("edge", "_", pid1,"_", pid2,
+                sep="")
+            LLL <- Lines(LL, ID = name)
+            LinesList[length(LinesList)+1] <- LLL
+            sldf[length(sldf)+1] <- name
+            j <- length(deldf_i) + 1
+            deldf_i[j]      <- i
```

```
+             deldf_x1[j]    <- x1; deldf_y1[j]    <- y1
+             deldf_k[j]     <- pid2
+             deldf_x2[j]    <- x2; deldf_y2[j]    <- y2
+             deldf_name[j] <- name
+             deldf_dens1[j] <- dens1
+             deldf_dens2[j] <- dens2
+    }}}
> deldf_c <- data.frame(deldf_i,deldf_x1,deldf_y1,deldf_k,
+ deldf_x2,deldf_y2,deldf_name,deldf_dens1,deldf_dens2)
> dist  <- sqrt((deldf_c[2] - deldf_c[5])^2 + (deldf_c[3]
+ - deldf_c[6])^2 )
> dimnames(dist) <- list(NULL,"dist")
> deldf_c$dist    <- dist
```

Subsequently, we calculate the interaction with Eq. (10.7), where we set $k = 1$ and $j = 3$.

```
> inter <- deldf_c$deldf_dens1 * deldf_c$deldf_dens2 /
+ deldf_c$dist^2
> dimnames(inter) <- list(NULL, "inter")
> deldf_c$inter    <- inter * 1e+22
```

Actually, it is done. Since interaction is an important parameter for network analysis, we produce an `igraph` object, a graph weighted by interaction.

```
> library(igraph)
> library(spdep)
> co <- coordinates(cent)
> coords=as.matrix(coordinates(cent))
> ids <- row.names(as.data.frame(cent))
> meg_cent_nb_del <- tri2nb(coordinates(cent), row.names=ids)
> m <- nb2mat(meg_cent_nb_del)
> g <- graph.adjacency(m, mode="lower", weighted=T)
> g <- set.vertex.attribute(g, "x", index=V(g),
+ coordinates(cent)[,1])
> g <- set.vertex.attribute(g, "y", index=V(g),
+ coordinates(cent)[,2])
> g <- set.vertex.attribute(g, "dens", index=V(g),
+ cent@data$meg)
> g <- set.edge.attribute(g, "distance2", index=E(g),
+ deldf_c$dist)
> g <- set.edge.attribute(g, "inter", index=E(g),
+ deldf_c$inter)
> E(g)$weight <- deldf_c$inter
> plot(g, edge.width=sqrt(deldf_c$inter), layout =
+ coordinates(cent))
```

We will not print this plot, although the reader will find that the graph is not located on a map. For geographical network analysis, a `SpatialLines` object has some advantages. Both plots use the root of the interaction to scale the values in a decent range for the line width (Fig. 10.9).

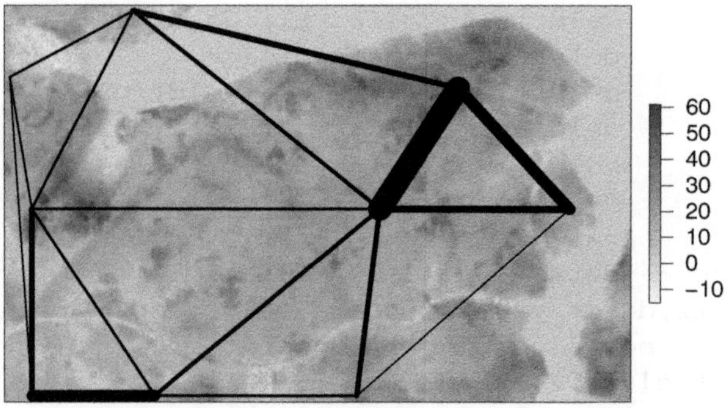

Fig. 10.9 Gravity model of megalith density centres

```
> LinesList <- list()
> for(i in seq(along=deldf_c[,1])) {
+     pid1 <- i
+     x1 <- deldf_c$deldf_x1[i]; x1 <- deldf_c$deldf_y1[i]
+     x2 <- deldf_c$deldf_x2[i]; y2 <- deldf_c$deldf_y2[i]
+     m <- matrix(data = c(x1,x2,y1,y2), nrow=2, ncol=2)
+     L <- Line(m); LL <- list(L)
+     LLL <- Lines(LL, ID = deldf_name[i])
+     LinesList[length(LinesList)+1] <- LLL
+     }
> sl <- SpatialLines(LinesList, proj4string =
+ CRS(as.character(crs1)))
> sdf_inter_meg_cent <- SpatialLinesDataFrame(sl, deldf_c,
+ match.ID = FALSE)
> plot(raster(sgdf_srtm), col = gray.colors(25, start =
+ 0.97, end = 0.4))
> for (i in 1:length(sdf_inter_meg_cent@data$inter)){
> lines(sdf_inter_meg_cent[i,], lwd=sqrt(sdf_inter_meg_cent@
+ data$inter[i]))}
```

10.4 Problems

10.1. Do you know additional factors which influence interaction.

10.2. Please apply several types of distance graphs to our case study.

10.3. Try to fit a theoretical curve to the empirical data (refer to Chap. 5 for regression methods).

10.4. Do you know other interaction models than the gravity model, which can be transferred from other disciplines to archaeology?

References

1. Blumer, H. (1969). *Symbolic interactionism; perspective and method*. Eaglewood Cliffs: Prentice-Hall.
2. Burmeister, S. (2000). Archaeology and migration: Approaches to an archaeological proof of migration. *Current Anthropology, 41*, 539–567.
3. Christaller, W. (1933). *Die Zentralen Orte in Süddeutschland*. Jena: Fischer.
4. Cliff, A. D., & Ord, J. K. (1973). *Spatial autocorrelation*. London: Pion.
5. Daudé, E. (2004). Apports de la simulation multi-agents à l'étude des processus de diffusion, Cybergeo. *Revue européenne de géographie, 255*. http://cybergeo.revues.org/3835; doi: 10.4000/cybergeo.3835
6. Diachenko, A. (2013). Settlement growth as a fractal. Jungsteinsite. *Journal of Neolithic Archaeology, 15*, 88–105.
7. Diachenko, A., & Menotti, F. (2012). The gravity model: Monitoring the formation and development of the Tripolye culture giant-settlements in Ukraine. *Journal of Archaeological Science, 39*, 2810–2817.
8. Dunn, J. (1993). Social interaction, relationships, and the development of causal discourse and conflict management. *European Journal of Psychology of Education, 111*, 391–401.
9. Earle, T. K., & Ericson, J. E. (Eds.) (1977). *Exchange systems in prehistory*. New York: Academic Press.
10. Fetter, F. A. (1924). The economic law of market areas. *Quarterly Journal of Economics, 38*, 520–529.
11. Fotheringham, A. S., & O'Kelly, M. E. (1989). *Spatial interaction models: Formulations and applications*. Dordrecht: Kluver.
12. Garrod, S., & Pickering, M. J. (2009). Joint action, interactive alignment, and dialog. *Topics Cognitive Science, 1*, 292–304.
13. Getis, A. (1991). Spatial interaction and spatial autocorrelation: A cross-product approach. *Environment and Planning A, 23*, 1269–1277.
14. Getis, A., & Ord, J. K. (1992). The analysis of spatial association by use of distance statistics. *Geographical Analysis, 24*, 189–206.
15. Haggett, P., & Chorley, R. J. (1969). *Network analysis in geography*. London: Arnold.
16. Hägerstrand, T. (1967). *Innovation diffusion as a spatial process*. Chicago: University of Chicago Press.
17. Hårdh, B., Larsson, L., Olausson, D., & Petré, R. (1988). *Trade and exchange in prehistory. Studies in honour of Berta Stjernquist: Vol. 16. Acta Archaeologica Lundensia*. Lund: Lunds Universitets Historiska Museum.
18. Harris, B. (1964). A note on the probability of interaction at a distance. *Journal of Regional Science, 5/2*, 31–35.
19. Isard, W. (1998). Gravity and spatial interaction models. In: W. Isard, I. J. Azis, M. P. Drennan, R. E. Miller, S. Saltzman & E. Thorbecke (Eds.), *Methods of interregional and regional analysis* (pp. 243–279). Aldershot/Brookfield/Singapore/Sydney: Ashgate.
20. Kimes, T., Haselgrove, C., & Hodder, I. (1982). A method for identification of the location of regional cultural boundaries. *Journal of Anthropological Archaeology, 1*, 113–131.
21. Knappett, C., Evans, T., & Rivers, R. (2008). Modelling maritime interaction in the Aegean bronze age. *Antiquity, 82*, 1009–1024.
22. Mallinowski, B. (1922). *Argonauts of the Western Pacific. An account of native enterprise and adventure in the archipelagoes of Melanesian New Guinea*. London: Routledge and Kegan Paul Ltd.
23. Moran, P. A. P. (1950). Notes on continuous stochastic phenomena. *Biometrika, 37*, 17–23.
24. Nakoinz, O. (2013). Models of interaction and economical archaeology. *Metalla, 20/2*, 107–115.

25. Nakoinz, O. (2013). *Archäologische Kulturgeographie der ältereisenzeitlichen Zentralorte Südwestdeutschlands: Vol. 224. Universitätsforschung zur Prähistorischen Archäologie*. Bonn: Habelt.
26. Nakoinz, O. (2014). Räumliche Interaktionsmodelle in der Archäologie. *Prähistorische Zeitschr, 88*, 225–256.
27. Parsons, T. (1937). *Structure of social action*. New York: McGraw Hill.
28. Polanyi, K. (1944). *The great transformation*. New York: Farrar and Rinehart.
29. Ravenstein, E. G. (1885). The laws of migration. *Journal of the Royal Statistical Society, 48*, 167–235.
30. Ravenstein, E. G. (1889). The laws of migration. *Journal of the Royal Statistical Society, 52*, 241–305.
31. Renfrew, C. (1977). Alternative models for exchange and spatial distribution. In T. E. Earle & J. E. Ericson (Eds.), *Exchange systems in prehistory* (pp. 71–90). New York: Academic Press.
32. Renfrew, C. & Level, E. V. (1979). Exploring dominance: predicting polities from centers. In C. Renfrew & K. L. Cooke (Hrsg.), *Transformations. Mathematical approaches to cultural change* (pp. 145–167). New York: Academic Press.
33. Rouse, I. (1986). *Migrations in prehistory: Inferring population movement from cultural remains*. New Haven: Yale University Press.
34. Salač, V. (2002). Kommunikationswege, Handel und das Ende der Oppidazivilisation. In: C. Dobiat, S. Sievers & T. Stöllner (Eds.), *Dürrnberg und Manching. Wirtschaftsarchäologie im ostkeltischen Raum: Vol. 7. Kolloquien Vor- und Frühgesch* (pp. 349–354) [Tagung Hallein 1998]. Bonn: Habelt.
35. Sindbœk, S. M. (2007). Networks and nodal points: The emergence of towns in early viking age Scandinavia. *Antiquity, 81*, 119–132.
36. Stewart, J. Q. (1948). Demographic gravitation: Evidence and applications. *Sociometry, 11*(1/2), 31–58.
37. Stouffer, S. A. (1940). Intervening opportunities: A theory relating to mobility and distance. *American Sociological Review, 5*, 845–867.
38. Taylor, P. J. (1971). Distance transformation and distance decay function. *Geographical Analysis, 3*, 221–238.
39. Taylor, P. J. (1983). Distance decay in spatial interactions. *Catmog, 2*, 3–35.
40. Tiefelsdorf, M. (2000). *Modelling spatial processes: The identification and analysis of spatial relationships in regression residuals by means of Moran's I*. Berlin: Springer.
41. Tobler, W. (1970). A computer movie simulating urban growth in the Detroit region. *Economic Geography, 46*, 234–240.
42. Tobler, W. (2004). On the first law of geography: A reply. *Annals of the Association of American Geographers, 94*, 304–310.
43. Wilson, A. G. (1978). Spatial interaction and settlement structure: Towards an explicit central place theory. In S. Karlqvist, L. Lundqvist, F. Snickars & J. W. Weibull (Eds.), *Spatial interaction theory and planning models* (pp. 137–156). Amsterdam: North-Holland.
44. Zipf, G. (1946). The PP/D hypothesis: On the intercity movement of persons. *American Sociological Review, 11*, 677–686.

Chapter 11
Landscape Perception

11.1 Changing the Point of View

Landscape is the cultural and natural environment in which we live, which we shape with our behaviour and which sets constraints to our behaviour, although it is also a certain piece of space that we perceive. Perception is not just part of an aesthetic process of admiring a beautiful landscape; rather, it is the basis of furnishing parts of the space with meaning and establishing the landscape. Landscape can be characterised as perceived space (see Chap. 1; [2, 9, 15]).

In most parts of this book, we apply an etic, scientific, formalised term of landscape. We assume perfect and objective knowledge, while the ancient people who lived in the landscape that we are investigating may not have been aware of the characterisations that we make. Certainly, we can presume that there are significant structures that are closely connected to people's behaviour, resulting from unconscious and unintended actions. The meaning of elements in etic landscapes is constructed by the scientists' definitions. This term of landscape has some disadvantages, two of which are mentioned below.

1. Source filters lead to incorrect data which produce wrong models.
2. The people who live in the investigated landscape and whose perception actually establishes the landscape that we aim to investigate are not involved in our characterisation of the landscape.

The last problem can be solved with the emic term of landscape, understanding landscape as a perceived space. In this type of landscape people are aware of the landscape characterisation. They furnish the landscape with meaning by narratives based upon perception. However, this term of landscape is subjective and also encounters some problems:

O. Nakoinz, D. Knitter, *Modelling Human Behaviour in Landscapes*, Quantitative Archaeology and Archaeological Modelling, DOI 10.1007/978-3-319-29538-1_11

1. There may be imagined elements in the landscapes that do not correspond with real elements.
2. This type of landscape is only a cognitive structure and it depends on who is perceiving the landscape. This means that there is not only one landscape corresponding with a certain part of the geographical space, but rather a multitude.

The second problem can be solved with the etic term of landscape, although this chapter is dedicated to the emic term of landscape. Since this term is subjective and cognitive, empirical models are rather difficult. We focus on theoretical models of landscape perception, which are nothing but a hypothesis concerning how people might have perceived the landscape.

We will distinguish two types of perception: *sensual perception* and *cognitive perception*. Sensual perception deals with the question *what is visible?* Landscape reconstruction and viewshed analysis are applications connected to this type of perception. Cognitive perception deals with the question *what emerges in the mind?* Fuzzy classifications and cognitive maps are methods belonging to this type of perception. Before we start with these methods connected to the two types of perception, we will address coordinate systems as manifestations of the point of view in landscape perception.

The crucial point in this chapter is to change the point of view from an etic perspective to an emic perspective. We leave the distant point of view and step to the position of prehistoric actors. This change can be expressed by a transformation of the coordinate system, whereby we will transform the coordinates to a polar system with the centre at the observer's viewpoint.

```
> trans.pol <- function(a, b=c(0,0)){
+ x    <- a[1]
+ y    <- a[2]
+ xt   <- b[1]
+ yt   <- b[2]
+ r <- (((x-xt)^2)+((y-yt)^2))^0.5
+      if ((x-xt) >= 0 & (y-yt) >= 0)  phi <- atan((y-yt)/
+ (x-xt))
+      if ((x-xt) < 0  & (y-yt) >= 0)  phi <- atan((y-yt)/
+ (x-xt))  + pi
+      if ((x-xt) < 0  & (y-yt) < 0)   phi <- atan((y-yt)/
+ (x-xt))  - pi
+      if ((x-xt) >= 0 & (y-yt) < 0)   phi <- atan((y-yt)/
+ (x-xt))  + 2 * pi
+ return(c(r, phi))
+ }
> trans.cartes <- function(a, b=c(0,0)){
+ r    <- a[1]
+ phi  <- a[2]
+ xt   <- b[1]
+ yt   <- b[2]
```

```
+ x      <- r*cos(phi) + xt
+ y      <- r*sin(phi) + yt
+ return(c(x, y))
+ }
> a <- c(3559376, 6027178)
> b <- c(3564474, 6032765)
> c <- trans.pol(a,b)
> c
[1] 7563.344036    -2.310461
> trans.cartes(c,b)
[1] 3559376 6027178
```

11.2 Sensual Perception

What was visible from a certain point of view? This is one of the most pressing questions in the topic of ancient sensual perception. At the geographical scale of landscapes, this is addressed by the viewshed approach [5, 13, 16, 18, 20]. Viewshed analyses are usually grid-based and they calculate whether a certain grid cell is visible from a certain point of view. It is assumed that the one thing that can prevent visibility is an elevated part of the earth cutting the line of sight (Fig. 11.1).

For the analysis, we need to supply a digital elevation model, a point of view, the height of the eye above the surface at the point of view, as well as the target height. The algorithm calculates whether there is anything at the view-line between the view-point and target-point. The algorithm should consider that the general surface of the earth is not a plain but rather an ellipsoid. If the algorithm simply considered the elevation values from the digital elevation model—which is referenced to the ellipsoid surface—the result could be incorrect.

We could develop the algorithm in R since the principle is rather simple, although we prefer to show that R can be connected to other software. The advantage of this approach is that specialised software uses optimised algorithms in fast implementations. In this book, we generally prefer the slower R-based versions for

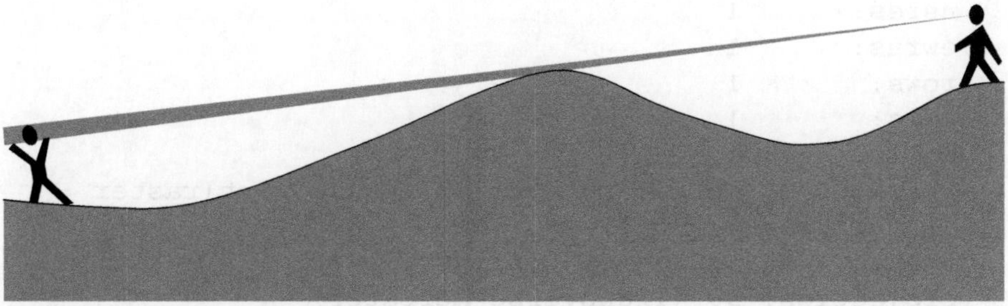

Fig. 11.1 Visibility

didactic reasons. The specialised software that we use here is the open source GIS system GRASS (https://grass.osgeo.org/). For the currently stable version GRASS 7, we need the R-package spgrass7:

```
> install.packages("spgrass7", repos="http://R-Forge.
+ R-project.org")
> library(rgdal)
> library(spgrass7)
```

The package spgrass7 needs to set up the environment, which defines the place, where the GRASS software can be found, and the place, where the GRASS database should be stored:

```
> loc <-  initGRASS("/usr/lib/grass70",home=tempdir(),
+ mapset = "PERMANENT", override = TRUE)
```

Subsequently, we can check the location and define it according to our data:

```
> execGRASS("g.proj", flags = c("p"))
XY location (unprojected)
> execGRASS("g.proj", flags = c("c"), parameters =
+ list(proj4=crs1))
```

Now, we can load our digital elevation model from R to GRASS, show the raster parameter and adjust the region's resolution:

```
> writeRAST(x = sgdf_srtm, vname = "dem")
> execGRASS("g.list", type = "rast")
dem
> execGRASS("g.region", flags = c("p"))
projection: 99 (Transverse Mercator)
zone:       0
datum:      ** unknown (default: WGS84) **
ellipsoid:  wgs84
north:      1
south:      0
west:       0
east:       1
nsres:      1
ewres:      1
rows:       1
cols:       1
cells:      1
> execGRASS("g.region", parameters = list(raster =
+ "dem",res = "50"))
> execGRASS("g.region", flags = c("p"))
projection: 99 (Transverse Mercator)
zone:       0
datum:      ** unknown (default: WGS84) **
```

```
ellipsoid:  wgs84
north:      6040566.6406
south:      6022466.6406
west:       3550736.1482
east:       3579036.1482
nsres:      50
ewres:      50
rows:       362
cols:       566
cells:      204892
```

After the preparation, we are ready to run the viewshed analysis. First, we explore the parameters that are required in GRASS for a viewshed analysis. We simply call the GRASS `r.viewshed` command with `parseGRASS` and receive some help:

```
> parseGRASS('r.viewshed')
Command: r.viewshed
Description: Computes the viewshed of a point on an
+ elevation raster map.
Keywords: Default format: NULL (invisible), vertical
+ angle wrt viewpoint (visible).
Parameters:
  name: input, type: string, required: yes, multiple: no
  keydesc: name, keydesc_count: 1
 [Name of input elevation raster map]
  name: output, type: string, required: yes, multiple: no
  keydesc: name, keydesc_count: 1
 [Name der Ausgabe-Rasterkarte]
  name: coordinates, type: float, required: yes,
  + multiple: no
  keydesc: east,north, keydesc_count: 2
 [Coordinates of viewing position]
  name: observer_elevation, type: float, required:
  + no, multiple: no
  default: 1.75
  keydesc: value, keydesc_count: 1
 [Viewing elevation above the ground]
  name: target_elevation, type: float, required:
  + no, multiple: no
  default: 0.0
  keydesc: value, keydesc_count: 1
 [Offset for target elevation above the ground]
  name: max_distance, type: float, required: no,
  + multiple: no
  default: -1
  keydesc: value, keydesc_count: 1
 [Maximum visibility radius. By default infinity (-1)]
  name: refraction_coeff, type: float, required: no,
  + multiple: no
```

```
  default: 0.14286
[Refraction coefficient]
  name: memory, type: integer, required: no, multiple: no
  default: 500
  keydesc: value, keydesc_count: 1
[Verwendete SpeichergröSSe in MB]
  name: directory, type: string, required: no, multiple: no
[Directory to hold temporary files (they can be large)]
Flags:
  name: c [Consider the curvature of the earth (current
  + ellipsoid)] {FALSE}
  name: r [Consider the effect of atmospheric refraction]
  + {FALSE}
  name: b [Output format is invisible = 0, visible = 1]
  + {FALSE}
  name: e [Output format is invisible = NULL, else current
  + elev - viewpoint_elev] {FALSE}
  name: overwrite [Ausgabedateien dürfen bereits existierende
  + Dateien Überschreiben.] {FALSE}
  name: help [Print usage summary] {FALSE}
  name: verbose [Ausführlicher Ausgabemodus] {FALSE}
  name: quiet [Schweigsamer Ausgabemodus] {FALSE}
```

We now fill in the parameters and run the `r.viewshed` command again with `execGRASS`. Since we do not give the height of viewer and target, the default values of 1.75 m and 0.0 m are used. One of the megaliths is used as the viewer's location.

```
> co.meg <- spdf_meg@coords
> execGRASS("r.viewshed", flags = c("overwrite","b"),
+ parameters = list(input = "dem",output = "view.meg",
+ coordinates = co.meg[160,]))
Computing events...
Computing visibility...
Writing output raster map...
> single.viewshed <- readRAST("view.meg")
Exporting raster as integer values (bytes=4)
```

The result is a map, indicating whether a grid cell is visible from the viewpoint or not. We now want to produce a map showing from how many monuments and villages a grid cell is visible:

```
> dem <- readRAST(vname = "dem")
> co.meg <- cbind(spdf_meg@coords[,1][spdf_meg@coords[,1]
+ >dem@bbox[1,1] & spdf_meg@coords[,1]<dem@bbox[1,2]],
+ spdf_meg@coords[,2][spdf_meg@coords[,2]>dem@bbox[2,1]
+ & spdf_meg@coords[,1]<dem@bbox[2,2]])
> co.tum <- cbind(spdf_tum@coords[,1][spdf_tum@coords[,1]
+ >dem@bbox[1,1] & spdf_tum@coords[,1]<dem@bbox[1,2]],
+ spdf_tum@coords[,2][spdf_tum@coords[,2]>dem@bbox[2,1]
```

```
+ & spdf_tum@coords[,1]<dem@bbox[2,2]])
> co.vil <- cbind(spdf_vil@coords[,1][spdf_vil@coords[,1]
+ >dem@bbox[1,1] & spdf_vil@coords[,1]<dem@bbox[1,2]],
+ spdf_vil@coords[,2][spdf_vil@coords[,2]>dem@bbox[2,1]
+ & spdf_vil@coords[,1]<dem@bbox[2,2]])
+ cum.view.meg <- raster(dem)
+ cum.view.tum <- raster(dem)
+ cum.view.vil <- raster(dem)
+ cum.view     <- raster(dem)
+ for (i in seq(1, length(co.meg[,1]))) {
+    execGRASS("r.viewshed"
+              ,flags = c("overwrite","b")
+              ,parameters = list(input = "dem",output =
+ "view.meg",coordinates = co.meg[i,])
+    )
+    viewshed <- readRAST("view.meg")
+    if (i==1) cum.view.meg <- raster(viewshed)
+    else  cum.view.meg <- raster(viewshed) + cum.view.meg
+    cat("iteration ", i, " of ", length(co.meg[,1]),"\n")
+}
+ for (i in seq(1, length(co.tum[,1]))) {
+    execGRASS("r.viewshed"
+              ,flags = c("overwrite","b")
+              ,parameters = list(input = "dem",output =
+        "view.tum",coordinates = co.tum[i,])
+    )
+    viewshed <- readRAST("view.tum")
+    if (i==1) cum.view.tum <- raster(viewshed)
+    else  cum.view.tum <- raster(viewshed) + cum.view.tum
+    cat("iteration ", i, " of ", length(co.tum[,1]),"\n")
+}
+ for (i in seq(1, length(co.vil[,1]))) {
+    execGRASS("r.viewshed"
+              ,flags = c("overwrite","b")
+              ,parameters = list(input = "dem",output =
+ "view.vil",coordinates = co.vil[i,])
+    )
+    viewshed <- readRAST("view.vil")
+    if (i==1) cum.view.vil <- raster(viewshed)
+    else cum.view.vil <- raster(viewshed) + cum.view.vil
+    cat("iteration", i, " of ", length(co.vil[,1]),"\n")
+ }
```

Having calculated the cumulative viewshed for megaliths, tumuli and villages, we now combine the results and plot all four maps (Fig. 11.2):

```
+ cum.view <- cum.view.meg+cum.view.tum+cum.view.vil
+ cum.view.b <- brick(cum.view.meg, cum.view.tum,
+ cum.view.vil, cum.view)
+ plot(cum.view.b, col = grey(20:0/30))
```

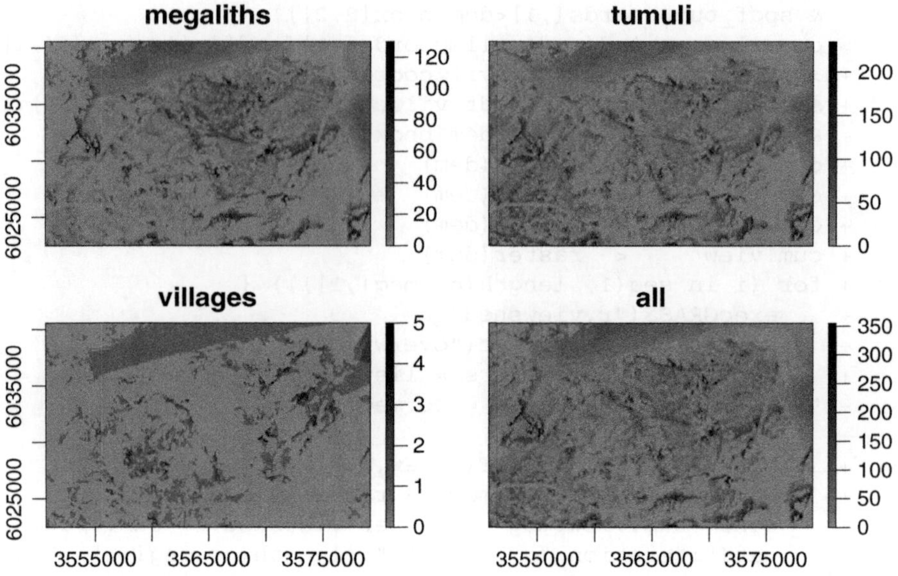

Fig. 11.2 Cumulated viewsheds from megalith, burial mounds, villages and all point of views; the *grey shade* indicates the number of points from which the area of a grid cell is visible

There are parameters that have not been considered; for instance, the vegetation—such as trees—can cut the line of sight, while the size contrast of that targets needs to be sufficient. Accordingly, the viewshed does not show what was visible, but rather what was not visible. Grid cells that are marked as not visible are in no cases visible, although the visibility of grid cells marked as visible can be prevented by different effects. Although this is a serious limitation of the interpretation, view-shed analysis helps to gain a certain impression of the ancient visibility.

11.3 Cognitive Perception

In this section, we deal with the product of cognitive processes. We apply two approaches, first categorising observations and construction mental maps. Since categorising is a main cognitive technique in data processing, we can be sure that ancient people categorised what they saw. However, we cannot be certain that people imagined space as maps and from the bird's eye perspective; for instance, it is possible simply to remember the sequence of landmarks while moving in the landscape. Hence, a cognitive map is a theoretical model of how people could have imagined space, if they have used the concept of maps. Cognitive maps are very useful, when we use another formulation, reflecting the translation of a spatial imagination into a concept with which we are familiar. Cognitive maps are very useful for comparing emic and etic approaches of landscape research.

11.3.1 Fuzzy Categories

Categorising our observations is not only a very essential technique in science, but also in everyday life. Categorising is a basic cognitive technique [3, 6, 10, 12]. Categorisations usually are not arbitrary but rather they are based upon similar features. Thresholds can be used to delimit categories; for instance, we could set a threshold between high and low altitude in our research at a value of 20 m. This threshold might be useful for scientific purposes, although in everyday life "high" and "low" depend on the context. In low areas, it might be necessary to distinguish really "low" areas below 5 m from "high" areas above 5 m. We can solve this problem with

1. a classification hierarchy; or
2. definitions that adapt to the context.

The second solution is very frequently used in everyday life and means, that there is no fixed threshold. We can formalise this idea with the fuzzy set approach [11, 21, 22], which is based upon the idea that linguistic variables such as "low" or "high" are not distinguished by a certain threshold. The definition of the two classes are membership functions, defining degrees of membership to both categories (Fig. 11.3):

```
> memb.low <- function(x){
+     y <- 12.53 * dnorm(x, mean=5, sd=5)
+     return(y)}
> memb.high <- function(x){
+     y <- 12.53 * dnorm(x, mean=15, sd=5)
+     return(y)}
> seq1 <- seq(0,20,0.1)
> mlow <- memb.low(seq1)
> mhigh <- memb.high(seq1)
> matplot(seq1, mlow, type="l", lty=1, ylab="membership
+ degree", xlab="Time")
> matplot(seq1, mhigh, type="l", lty=2, ylab="membership
+ degree", xlab="Time", add=T)
```

Our membership functions are not perfect. Usually, all possible values should be recognised in the same way and hence the sum of all membership functions should be 1; otherwise, certain values are suppressed and others amplified, which can produce serious biases. Please note that all membership degrees have to be between 0 and 1.

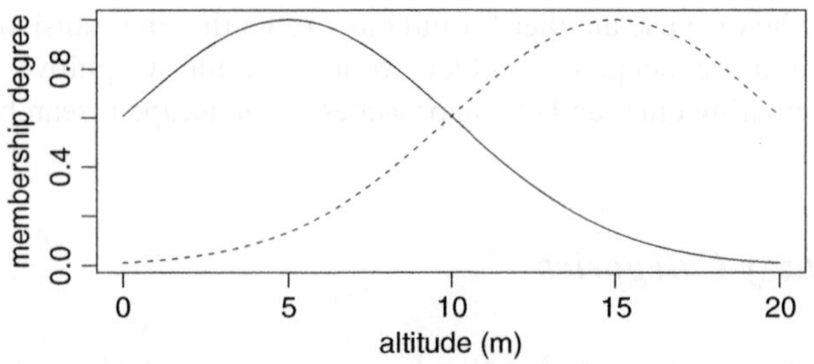

Fig. 11.3 Membership functions of low and high (*dashed*) altitude

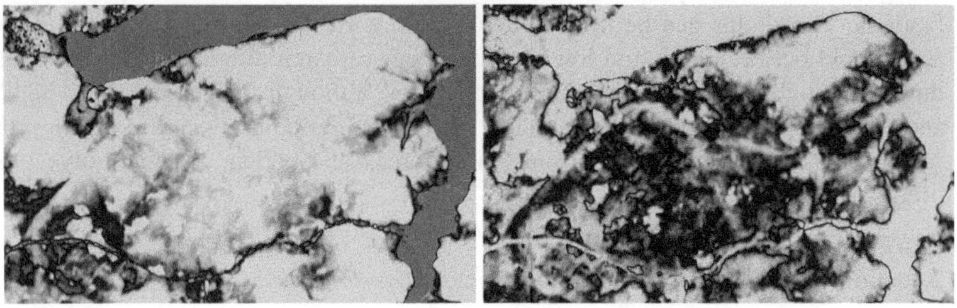

Fig. 11.4 Membership degree for class "low" (*left*) and "high" (*right*). The darker the colour, the higher the membership degree

The membership degree of certain altitude values indicates the degree to which altitude is judged as high or low. We can apply the membership functions to the srtm grid and obtain maps of the membership degree for each grid cell of the two classes (Fig. 11.4):

```
> sgdf_srtm_low <- sgdf_srtm_high <- sgdf_srtm
> sgdf_srtm_low@data[,1] <- memb.low(sgdf_srtm@data[,1])
> sgdf_srtm_high@data[,1] <- memb.high(sgdf_srtm@data[,1])
> par(mfcol=c(1,2), mai = c(0, 0, 0, 0))
> image(sgdf_srtm_low, col = gray.colors(25,
+ start = 0.90, end = 0.2))
> image(sgdf_srtm_high, col = gray.colors(25,
+ start = 0.90, end = 0.2))
> par(mfcol=c(1,1))
```

The process of turning a numerical variable into a linguistic one is called fuzzyfication. The linguistic variables can be used for inferences and combinations, which are rather intuitive. Subsequently, a defuzzification transforms the result back into numeric variables. Fuzzy approaches are used in archaeology for different purposes [1, 8, 14, 17, 18].

11.3.2 Cognitive Maps

It is possible to manipulate maps in such a way that they fit to our cognitive maps. We simply have to define how topographic features appear in our mind and apply some techniques to reproduce the result. However, if we try to do so, some difficulties appear. The first problem lies in describing our cognitive maps. Shemyakin [19] describes two types of cognitive maps.

1. **Route maps** are a tool to memorise spatial relationships based upon movement, whereby a chain of landmarks defines spatial relationships.
2. **Survey maps** are tools to map the topological relationship of objects.

Although a dominance of route maps in young ages and survey maps in older ages of people is assumed, the parallel usage of both is evident. We focus on survey maps in this section. The next problem is how to proof the result. This is difficult for our own cognitive maps and rather impossible if those, whose cognitive maps we aim to reconstruct cannot tell us about their cognitive maps because they lived thousands of years ago in an age without writing. Finally, the individual cognitive maps may differ considerably. Is the reconstruction of cognitive maps useless? No, because even if a proper validation of the cognitive maps is not possible, there are some hints about the dominance and relationship of different parameters. Moreover, reconstructed cognitive maps are a useful heuristic tool for understanding the relationship of parameters and the effect of processes. If the meaning and significance of sites change, cognitive maps can offer us an impression concerning how this can affect the perception of landscape. Hence, we have to be aware that cognitive maps reflect our perception of ancient landscapes rather than the perception of ancient people. Nonetheless, they are still closer to the ancient perception compared with etic models.

There are three important aspects of reconstructed cognitive maps, namely maps

- take a certain point of view;
- manipulate locations by changing distances and angles and
- manipulate the significance of elements.

Again, we use a very simple example. First a point of view in the working area is defined:

```
> vp <- c(3565015, 6030963)
```

We now have to populate our map. The megalithic tombs would be an obvious choice, although we decide for the density centres of megaliths due to the smaller number. In fact, it would be useful to use both. We would know all megaliths in our vicinity but in remote areas we would remember agglomerations and necropolis rather than single monuments. Some monuments may have a certain significance to us, whereby they would seem to be nearer and thus dominate our cognitive map. In the reconstructed cognitive map, density centres with high density values are marked with larger symbols and they are moved towards the viewpoint. In addition, we assume that there are axes of orientation that structure the landscape. All density centres tend to move slightly towards the axes to simplify the reference of the point's location with axes of orientation.

We prepare a data frame of density centres with original, relative polar and new Cartesian coordinates. Here, the coordinate transformation functions are used. Subsequently, we apply the manipulations of distances and angles, before transforming the coordinates back to Cartesian ones. Finally, we produce a `SpatialPointsDataFrame` with all information:

```
> cm_denspt <- data.frame(coordinates(cent_meg),
+ 10000000 * over(cent_meg, sgdf_meg_dens),
+ r=0, phi=0, r2=0, phi2=0, x2=0, y2=0)
> tp2 <- function(a,b) trans.pol(a,vp)
> cm_pc <- apply(cm_denspt[,1:2], 1, tp2)
> cm_denspt[,4] <- cm_pc[1,]
> cm_denspt[,5] <- cm_pc[2,]
> cm_denspt[,6] <- cm_denspt[,4] / (0.9 * cm_denspt[,3]^0.2)
> cm_denspt[which(cm_denspt[,5] < pi & cm_denspt[,5] > 0),7]
+ <- cm_denspt[which(cm_denspt[,5] < pi &
+ cm_denspt[,5] > 0),5] * 0.95
> cm_denspt[which(cm_denspt[,5] > pi),7] <- 2 * pi -
+ (2 * pi - cm_denspt[which(cm_denspt[,5] > pi),5]) * 0.95
> cm_denspt[which(cm_denspt[,5] > -pi & cm_denspt[,5] <
+ 0),7] <- cm_denspt[which(cm_denspt[,5] > -pi &
+ cm_denspt[,5] < 0),5] * 0.95
> tc2 <- function(a,b)  trans.cartes (a,vp)
> cm_cc <- apply(cm_denspt[,6:7], 1, tc2)
> cm_denspt[,8] <- cm_cc[1,]
> cm_denspt[,9] <- cm_cc[2,]
> cm_despt2 <- SpatialPointsDataFrame(cbind(cm_cc[1,],
+ cm_cc[2,]), cm_denspt, proj4string =
+ CRS(as.character(crs1)))
```

We have now conducted all manipulations of the main topographic objects and we can plot the result (Fig. 11.5). The result is not very convincing since we have not considered that the manipulation of the main topographic elements might affect the other map content. The elevation map should also be distorted according to the applied manipulations. We will try different approaches to produce this result.

The first approach is very simple: we produce grids with the x and y coordinates as z-variables, where we put the new coordinates of the density centres at the original places of the density centres. Subsequently, an interpolation of the values indicates the new position of all grid cells. The three grids for x, y, and elevation are converted to one data frame. Here, we have to consider `NA` values.

```
> grid_x <- gstat::idw(x2~1, cm_despt2, newdata=sgdf_srtm,
+ nmax=12, maxdist=20000, idp=4.0)
[inverse distance weighted interpolation]
> grid_y <- gstat::idw(y2~1, cm_despt2, newdata=sgdf_srtm,
+ nmax=12, maxdist=20000, idp=4.0)
```

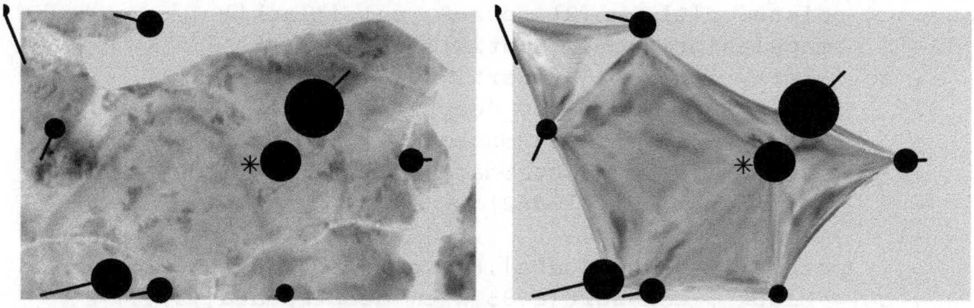

Fig. 11.5 Cognitive maps. *Left*: modified density centres on original elevation. *Right*: modified density centres on distorted elevation (interpolation approach). The *star* is the point of view while the point size indicates the local density of monuments

```
[inverse distance weighted interpolation]
> cm_spdf <- data.frame(x=grid_x@data[,1], y=grid_y@data
+ [,1], z=sgdf_srtm@data[,1])
> cm_spdf <- cm_spdf[intersect(intersect(which(!is.na(
+ cm_spdf[,1])), which(!is.na(cm_spdf[,2]))), which(
+ !is.na(cm_spdf[,3]))),]
> coordinates(cm_spdf)  = ~x+y
> proj4string(cm_spdf)  <- CRS(as.character(crs1))
```

The data frame—which is actually a `SpatialPointsDataFrame`—is used to produce a grid by interpolation.

```
> library(gstat)
> vt3    <- variogram(cm_spdf@data$z ~ 1, cm_spdf)
> v.fit3 <- fit.variogram(vt3, vgm(1, "Mat", 5000, 1))
> vgrid_cm <- krige(cm_spdf@data$z ~ 1, cm_spdf,
+ newdata=sgdf_srtm, v.fit3, nmin = 4, maxdist = 200,
+ nmax = 15)
[using ordinary kriging]
> vgrid_cm <- raster(grid_cm)
> vgrid_cm[is.na(grid_cm)] <- 0
```

The final step is to plot the results. Here, we draw lines between the original and new point of the density centres to indicate the manipulations. The code for plotting the first two cognitive maps side by side (Fig. 11.5) is detailed below:

```
> par(mfcol=c(1,2), mai = c(0, 0, 0, 0))
>     image(sgdf_srtm, col = gray.colors(25, start = 0.97,
+ end = 0.1))
>     for (i in 1:length(cm_despt2@data[,1])) {
+         xl <- c(cm_despt2@data[i,1], cm_despt2@data[i,8])
+         yl <- c(cm_despt2@data[i,2], cm_despt2@data[i,9])
+         lines(xl,yl, lwd=2)
+     }
>     points(cm_despt2@data[,8], cm_despt2@data[,9], pch=16,
+ col='black', cex=sqrt(1.35 * cm_despt2@data[,3]))
```

```
>    points(vp[1], vp[2], pch=8, col='black')
>    image(as(grid_cm, 'SpatialGridDataFrame'),
+ col = gray.colors(25, start = 0.97, end = 0.1))
>    for (i in 1:length(cm_despt2@data[,1])) {
+        xl <- c(cm_despt2@data[i,1], cm_despt2@data[i,8])
+        yl <- c(cm_despt2@data[i,2], cm_despt2@data[i,9])
+        lines(xl,yl, lwd=2)
+    }
>    points(cm_despt2@data[,8], cm_despt2@data[,9], pch=16,
+ col='black', cex=sqrt(1.35 * cm_despt2@data[,3]))
>    points(vp[1], vp[2], pch=8, col='black')
> par(mfcol=c(1,1))
```

The result has rather strong distortions, suggesting that perhaps we can produce better results. We can try a six-parameter affine transformation, which is used in rubber sheeting [4, 212–216]. This approach uses some points where both coordinates are known and a set of equations to calculate the new coordinates. The new coordinates u and v are

$$u = \beta_0 x + \beta_1 y + \beta_2 \tag{11.1}$$

$$v = \beta_3 x + \beta_4 y + \beta_5 \tag{11.2}$$

The coefficients use p and q as fixed terms and involve n as the number of points, x_i and y_i as original coordinates of certain points, $\bar{x}_i$ and $\bar{y}_i$ as the mean value of the coordinates and u_i and v_i as new coordinates.

$$p = \frac{\sum_{i=1}^{n}((x_i - \bar{x}_i)(y_i - \bar{y}_i))}{\sum_{i=1}^{n}(y_i - \bar{y}_i)^2} \tag{11.3}$$

$$q = \frac{\sum_{i=1}^{n}((x_i - \bar{x}_i)(y_i - \bar{y}_i))}{\sum_{i=1}^{n}(x_i - \bar{x}_i)^2} \tag{11.4}$$

$$\beta_1 = \frac{\sum_{i=1}^{n}((y_i - \bar{y}_i)(u_i - x_i)) - q\sum_{i=1}^{n}((x_i - \bar{x}_i)(u_i - x_i))}{\sum_{i=1}^{n}(y_i - \bar{y}_i)^2 - q\sum_{i=1}^{n}((x_i - \bar{x}_i)(y_i - \bar{y}_i))} \tag{11.5}$$

$$\beta_3 = \frac{\sum_{i=1}^{n}((x_i - \bar{x}_i)(v_i - y_i)) - p\sum_{i=1}^{n}((y_i - \bar{y}_i)(v_i - y_i))}{\sum_{i=1}^{n}(x_i - \bar{x}_i)^2 - p\sum_{i=1}^{n}((y_i - \bar{y}_i)(x_i - \bar{x}_i))} \tag{11.6}$$

$$\beta_4 = 1 - p\beta_3 \frac{\sum_{i=1}^{n}((y_i - \bar{y}_i)(v_i - y_i))}{\sum_{i=1}^{n}(y_i - \bar{y}_i)^2} \tag{11.7}$$

$$\beta_0 = 1 - q\beta_1 \frac{\sum_{i=1}^{n}((x_i - \bar{x}_i)(u_i - x_i))}{\sum_{i=1}^{n}(x_i - \bar{x}_i)^2} \tag{11.8}$$

$$\beta_2 = \frac{1}{n}\sum_{i=1}^{n}(u_i - x_i) + \bar{x} - \beta_0\bar{x} + \beta_1\bar{y} \tag{11.9}$$

$$\beta_5 = \frac{1}{n}\sum_{i=1}^{n}(v_i - y_i) + \bar{y} - \beta_4\bar{y} + \beta_3\bar{x} \tag{11.10}$$

To apply this, we have to prepare a dataframe with all relevant coordinates of the density points and the elevation values and calculate the coefficients:

```
> srtm <- data.frame(x=coordinates(sgdf_srtm)[,1],
+ y=coordinates(sgdf_srtm)[,2], z=sgdf_srtm@data[,1], u=0,
+ v=0)
> cmdf <- cbind(x=cm_denspt[,1], y=cm_denspt[,2],
+ u=cm_denspt[,8], v=cm_denspt[,9])
> n <- length(cmdf[,1])
> p <- sum((cmdf[,1] - mean(cmdf[,1])) * (cmdf[,2] -
+ mean(cmdf[,2]))) / sum((cmdf[,2] - mean(cmdf[,2]))^2)
> q <- sum((cmdf[,1] - mean(cmdf[,1])) * (cmdf[,2] -
+ mean(cmdf[,2]))) / sum((cmdf[,1] - mean(cmdf[,1]))^2)
> b1 <- (sum((cmdf[,2] - mean(cmdf[,2])) * (cmdf[,3] -
+ cmdf[,1])) - q * sum((cmdf[,1] - mean(cmdf[,1]))
+ * (cmdf[,3] - cmdf[,1]))) / (sum((cmdf[,2] -
+ mean(cmdf[,2]))^2) - q * sum((cmdf[,1] -
+ mean(cmdf[,1])) * (cmdf[,2] - mean(cmdf[,2]))))
> b3 <- (sum((cmdf[,1] - mean(cmdf[,1])) * (cmdf[,4] -
+ cmdf[,2])) - p * sum((cmdf[,2] - mean(cmdf[,2]))
+ * (cmdf[,4] - cmdf[,2]))) / (sum((cmdf[,1] -
+ mean(cmdf[,1]))^2) - p* sum((cmdf[,2] -
+ mean(cmdf[,2])) * (cmdf[,1] - mean(cmdf[,1]))))
```

```
> b4 <- 1 - p * b3 + sum((cmdf[,2] - mean(cmdf[,2]))
+ * (cmdf[,4] - cmdf[,2])) / sum((cmdf[,2] -
+ mean(cmdf[,2]))^2)
> b0 <- 1 - q * b1 + sum((cmdf[,1] - mean(cmdf[,1]))
+ * (cmdf[,3] - cmdf[,1])) / sum((cmdf[,1] -
+ mean(cmdf[,1]))^2)
> b2 <- (1/n) * sum(cmdf[,3]-cmdf[,1]) + mean(cmdf[,1])
+ - b0 * mean(cmdf[,1]) - b1 * mean(cmdf[,2])
> b5 <- (1/n) * sum(cmdf[,4]-cmdf[,2]) + mean(cmdf[,2])
+ - b4 * mean(cmdf[,2]) - b3 * mean(cmdf[,1])
```

We can now define coordinate transformation functions and apply them with `apply`:

```
> trans.x <- function(x) u <- b0*x[1] +b1*x[2] + b2
> trans.y <- function(x) u <- b3*x[1] +b4*x[2] + b5
> srtm[,4] <- apply(srtm[,1:2], 1, trans.x)
> srtm[,5] <- apply(srtm[,1:2], 1, trans.y)
```

Finally, we produce a `SpatialPointsDataFrame` and use this to generate a raster with the `rasterise` function.

```
> coordinates(srtm) = ~u+v
> proj4string(srtm) <- CRS(as.character(crs1))
> cm_raster <- rasterize(srtm, raster(sgdf_srtm),
+ field='z', update=TRUE, proj4string =
+ CRS(as.character(crs1)))
```

The result (Fig. 11.6) looks much more convincing, although this approach also has some disadvantages. If we use many points to control the transformation, the result is rather more approximative than exact, since the six-parameter transformation cannot adapt to any detail. One solution is to cut the map into several parts and apply transformations for any part separately. A Delaunay triangulation of the reference points is the optimal structure to achieve this [7]. Inside the Delaunay cells, we use the same transformation algorithm.

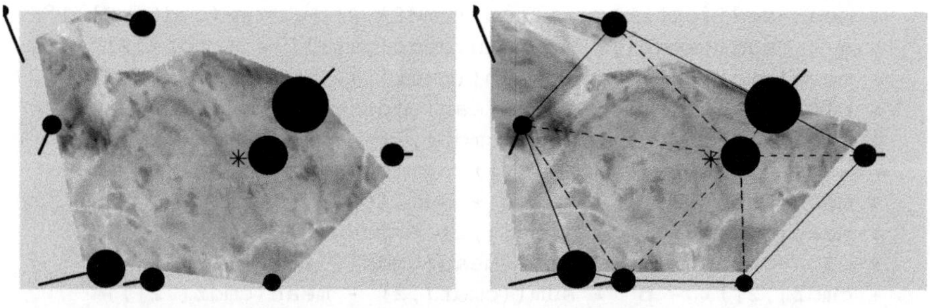

Fig. 11.6 Cognitive maps. *Left*: modified density centres on distorted elevation (simple rubber sheet approach). *Right*: modified density centres on distorted elevation (Delaunay rubber sheet approach). The star is the point of view while the point size indicates the local density of monuments

First, we need some preparations, including the calculation of the Delaunay graph and the definition of the transformation functions. We use the `spatstat` package for the Delaunay calculation because this package—in contrast to the `deldir` package, for instance—does not simply return the edges, but rather the complete triangles.

```
> sgdf <- sgdf_srtm
> sgdf@data[,1]  <- 0
> srtm <- data.frame(x=coordinates(sgdf_srtm)[,1],
+ y=coordinates(sgdf_srtm)[,2], z=sgdf_srtm@data[,1],
+ u=0, v=0)
> library(spatstat)
> cm_pp <- ppp(cm_denspt[,1], cm_denspt[,2],
+ window=owin(c(bb[1,1],bb[1,2]),c(bb[2,1],bb[2,2])))
> cm_del <- delaunay(cm_pp)
> cm_pp2 <- ppp(cm_denspt[,8], cm_denspt[,9],
+ window=owin(c(bb[1,1],bb[1,2]),c(bb[2,1],bb[2,2])))
Warnmeldung:
In ppp(cm_denspt[, 8], cm_denspt[, 9], window =
+ owin(c(bb[1, 1],  :
  1 point was rejected as lying outside the
     specified window
> cm_del2 <- delaunay(cm_pp2)
> trans.x <- function(x) u <- b0*x[1] +b1*x[2] + b2
> trans.y <- function(x) u <- b3*x[1] +b4*x[2] + b5
```

Subsequently, we apply the transformation for all Delaunay cells in a loop:

```
> for (i in 1:cm_del$n)   {
+      x1 <- tiles(cm_del)[[i]]$bdry[[1]][[1]][1]
+      y1 <- tiles(cm_del)[[i]]$bdry[[1]][[2]][1]
+      x2 <- tiles(cm_del)[[i]]$bdry[[1]][[1]][2]
+      y2 <-tiles(cm_del)[[i]]$bdry[[1]][[2]][2]
+      x3 <-tiles(cm_del)[[i]]$bdry[[1]][[1]][3]
+      y3 <- tiles(cm_del)[[i]]$bdry[[1]][[2]][3]
+      u1 <- cm_despt2@data[which(cm_despt2@data[,1] == x1),
+ 8][1]
+      v1 <- cm_despt2@data[which(cm_despt2@data[,2] == y1),
+ 9][1]
+      u2 <- cm_despt2@data[which(cm_despt2@data[,1] == x2),
+ 8][1]
+      v2 <- cm_despt2@data[which(cm_despt2@data[,2] == y2),
+ 9][1]
+      u3 <- cm_despt2@data[which(cm_despt2@data[,1] == x3),
+ 8][1]
+      v3 <- cm_despt2@data[which(cm_despt2@data[,2] == y3),
+ 9][1]
+      cmdf <- cbind(x=c(x1,x2,x3), y=c(y1,y2,y3),
+ u=c(u1,u2,u3), v=c(v1,v2,v3))
```

```
+     n <- length(cmdf[,1])
+     p <- sum((cmdf[,1] - mean(cmdf[,1])) * (cmdf[,2]
+ - mean(cmdf[,2]))) / sum((cmdf[,2] -
+ mean(cmdf[,2]))^2)
+     q <- sum((cmdf[,1] - mean(cmdf[,1])) * (cmdf[,2]
+ - mean(cmdf[,2]))) / sum((cmdf[,1] - mean(cmdf[,1]))^2)
+     b1 <- (sum((cmdf[,2] - mean(cmdf[,2])) * (cmdf[,3]
+ - cmdf[,1])) - q * sum((cmdf[,1] - mean(cmdf[,1]))
+ * (cmdf[,3] - cmdf[,1]))) / (sum((cmdf[,2]
+ - mean(cmdf[,2]))^2) - q * sum((cmdf[,1]
+ - mean(cmdf[,1])) * (cmdf[,2] - mean(cmdf[,2]))))
+     b3 <- (sum((cmdf[,1] - mean(cmdf[,1])) * (cmdf[,4]
+ - cmdf[,2])) - p * sum((cmdf[,2] - mean(cmdf[,2]))
+ * (cmdf[,4] - cmdf[,2]))) / (sum((cmdf[,1]
+ - mean(cmdf[,1]))^2) - p * sum((cmdf[,2]
+ - mean(cmdf[,2])) * (cmdf[,1] - mean(cmdf[,1]))))
+     b4 <- 1 - p * b3 + sum((cmdf[,2] - mean(cmdf[,2]))
+ * (cmdf[,4] - cmdf[,2])) / sum((cmdf[,2]
+ - mean(cmdf[,2]))^2)
+     b0 <- 1 - q * b1 + sum((cmdf[,1] - mean(cmdf[,1]))
+ * (cmdf[,3] - cmdf[,1])) / sum((cmdf[,1]
+ - mean(cmdf[,1]))^2)
+     b2 <- (1/n) * sum(cmdf[,3]-cmdf[,1]) + mean(cmdf[,1])
+ - b0 * mean(cmdf[,1]) - b1 * mean(cmdf[,2])
+     b5 <- (1/n) * sum(cmdf[,4]-cmdf[,2]) + mean(cmdf[,2])
+ - b4 * mean(cmdf[,2]) - b3 * mean(cmdf[,1])
+     cm_ind <- which(inside.owin(srtm[,1], srtm[,2],
+ tiles(cm_del)[[i]]) == T)
+     srtm[cm_ind,4] <- apply(srtm[cm_ind,1:2], 1, trans.x)
+     srtm[cm_ind,5] <- apply(srtm[cm_ind,1:2], 1, trans.y)
+     }
```

Finally, again we produce a `SpatialPointsDataFrame` and `rasterize` the result (Fig. 11.6). With the substitution of `NA` and `0` values and the focal function—which applies a moving window calculation for missing values—we remove some computational artefacts:

```
> coordinates(srtm) = ~u+v
> proj4string(srtm) <- CRS(as.character(crs1))
> cm_raster2 <- rasterize(srtm, raster(sgdf), field='z',
+ update=TRUE, proj4string = CRS(as.character(crs1)))
> cm_raster2[which(getValues(cm_raster2) == 0)] <- NA
> cm_raster2 <- focal(cm_raster2, w= matrix(rep(1,25),
+ nrow=5), na.rm=TRUE, mean, NAonly=TRUE)
> cm_raster2[is.na(cm_raster2)] <- 0
```

In our example, we used rather poor information to produce the cognitive map. In a proper set-up of a cognitive map reconstruction we would base the space distortion on information about cultural distances, leastcost distances, viewsheds, borders and routes and settlement sizes. The cognitive map reconstruction is a kind of simulation with which we will deal in the next chapter.

11.4 Problems

11.1. Why would certain view conditions be important to ancient people?

11.2. Do you think that it is possible to include vegetation information in viewshed analysis?

11.3. Please plot the sum of the two membership functions.

11.4. Please find some decent membership functions with the sum of 1.

11.5. How could we manage to verify a fuzzy classification?

11.6. Please describe your cognitive map of your hometown.

11.7. Why do we use polar coordinates to manipulate the density centres' locations?

11.8. Can you explain the missing values at the margin of the cognitive maps?

11.9. What other information could we use for cognitive map reconstruction?

References

1. Baxter, M. (2009). Archaeological data analysis and fuzzy clustering. *Archaeometry, 51*, 1035–1054.
2. Bender, B. (1993). Introduction: Landscapes - meaning and action. In B. Bender (Ed.), *Landscape: Politics and perspectives* (pp. 1–18). Oxford: Berg.
3. Burleigh, T. J., & Schoenherr, J. R. (2015). A reappraisal of the uncanny valley: Categorical perception or frequency-based sensitization? *Frontiers in Psychology, 5*, 1488.
4. Clarke, K. C. (1995). *Analytical and computer cartography*. Upper Saddle River: Prentice Hall.
5. Conolly, J., & Lake, M. (2006). *Geographical information systems in archaeology*. Cambridge: Cambridge University Press.
6. Estes, W. K. (1994). *Classification and cognition*. New York: Oxford University Press.
7. Gillman, D. W. (1985). Triangulations for rubber-sheeting. In *Auto-Carto Proceedings of the International Symposium on Computer-Assisted Cartography*. Falls Church: American Society of Photogrammetry.
8. Hermon, S., & Niccolucci, F. (2002). Estimating subjectivity of typologists and typological classification with fuzzy logic. *Archeologia e Calcolatori, 13*, 217–232.
9. Ingold, T. (2000). *The perception of the environment: Essays on livelihood, dwelling and skill.* Routledge: London.
10. Kruschke, J. K. (2005). Category learning. In K. Lamberts, & L. Goldstone (Eds.), *Handbook of cognition* (pp. 183–201). London: Sage.
11. Knitter, D., & Nakoinz, O. (in press): Point pattern analysis as tool for digital geoarchaeology – A case study of megalithic graves in Schleswig-Holstein, Germany. In C. Siart, M. Forbirger & O. Bubenzer (Eds.), Digital Geoarchaeology. *New Techniques for Interdisciplinary Human-Environmental Research*, Springer.
12. Lamberts, K., & Shanks, D. R. (Eds.). (1997). *Knowledge, concepts and categories*. Cambridge, Mass.: MIT Press.

13. van Leusen, M. (2004). Visibility and the landscape. An exploration of GIS modelling techniques? In K. Fischer Ausserer, W. Böner, M. Goriany & L. Karlhuber-Vöckl (Eds.), *Entering the past: The e-way into the four dimensions of cultural heritage. Proceedings of the 31st CAA Conference*, Vienna, Austria, April 2003. BAR International Series (Vol. 1227, pp. 1–15). Oxford: British Archaeological Reports.
14. Machálek, T., Cimler, R., Olševičová, K., & Danielisová, A. (2013). Fuzzy methods in land use modeling for archaeology. In H. Vojackova (Ed.), *Proceedings of the 31st International Conference Mathematical Methods in Economics* (pp. 552–557). Jihlava: College of Polytechnics Jihlava.
15. Meier, T. (2012). 'Landscape', 'environment' and a vision of interdisciplinarity. In S. Kluiving & E. Guttmann-Bond (Eds.), *Landscape archaeology between art and science* (pp. 503–514). Amsterdam: Amsterdam University Press.
16. Nakoinz, O. (2006). Kommunikation und Kontrolle zur Wikingerzeit in der Kieler Bucht - Ein Beitrag zur Methode der Sichtanalyse. *Archéologie in Schleswig, 11*, 95–103.
17. Nakoinz, O. (2012). Datierungskodierung und chronologische Inferenz - Techniken zum Umgang mit unscharfen chronologischen Informationen. *Praehistorische Zeitschrift, 87*, 189–207.
18. Rášová, A. (2014). Fuzzy viewshed, probable viewshed, and their use in the analysis of prehistoric monuments placement in Western Slovakia. In J. Huerta, S. Schade & C. Granell (Eds.), *Connecting a digital Europe through location and place* (AGILE Digital Editions). Cham: Springer. http://repositori.uji.es/xmlui/handle/10234/99490.
19. Shemyakin, F. N. (1961). Orientation in space. *Psychological Science in the USSR, 1*, 186–255.
20. Wheatley, D., & Gillings, M. (2002). *Spatial technology and archaeology: The archaeological applications of GIS*. London: CRC Press.
21. Zadeh, L. A. (1965). Fuzzy sets. *Information and Control, 8*, 338–353.
22. Zadeh, L. A. (2006). Generalized theory of uncertainty (GTU)-principal concepts and ideas. *Computational Statistics and Data Analysis, 51*, 15–46.

Chapter 12
Simulations

12.1 Definitions and Random Numbers

Simulations are an important modelling approach used in many disciplines. Examples from geography [9, 18] and archaeology [2, 3, 10, 11, 17, 20, 21] show a wide range of approaches. In this chapter, it is hardly possible to touch upon the topic comprehensively, although we offer some ideas about basic approaches with a focus on stochastic techniques. Before proceeding into detail, it is necessary to discuss the term 'simulation', before the second part of this section is dedicated to random numbers.

12.1.1 Definitions

Sometimes the term simulation is used in the context of modelling. Since the term 'simulation' can be used as a synonym for 'modelling' and for a special type of models this term is rather confusing. We can define:

Definition 12.1. A **simulation** is a process in which a theoretical model is used for generating artificial data used to make a pseudo-empirical model.

Simulation in this sense is not a synonym for modelling, but rather a specific modelling procedure. The idea is to use well-known rules, which is nothing but a theoretical model to produce artificial data. There are two differences from simple theoretical models. First, in a simulation, the theoretical model is used to produce data. The generation of data that have the same characteristics as empirical data is the main part of a simulation. After we have produced pseudo-empirical data, we use them in an empirical model, just in the same way as we would do with real empirical observations. This model can range between simple visualisations and rather complicated analyses.

O. Nakoinz, D. Knitter, *Modelling Human Behaviour in Landscapes*, Quantitative Archaeology and Archaeological Modelling, DOI 10.1007/978-3-319-29538-1_12

Simulations are used to analyse and understand the outcome of well-defined processes and they are particularly useful when it is difficult to predict the result for certain process parameters and settings. For instance, complex processes with features like a butterfly effect, non-linear relations and emergence are cases where simulations are very helpful. Simulations are a common tool for studying the influence of different parameters on the result of a theoretical model. This is important when our theoretical models are rather general and cannot be directly compared with empirical models. In this case, simulations show what would happen, if parameters changed. This helps us to rule out certain theoretical models, even if a perfect match between theoretical and empirical models is not possible.

A classification of simulations can have a focus on producing or using artificial data.

- S1: Models with a dominant empirical modelling component
  - 3D simulations
  - Visualisations of the outcome of theoretical models
- S2: Models with complicated or complex theoretical models
  - Non-linear interrelationships
  - Differential equations
  - Predator–prey models
- S3: Models where the rules of the theoretical models are partly undefined or unknown
  - Random numbers
  - Monte Carlo simulations
  - Point processes

The first type (S1) has a focus on using the artificial data for visualisation. A 3D elevation model is an example of this type. The data are based upon measurements but can be artificial in the sense that the values for most points used in the simulation are interpolated, even with a dense net of measured points. However, the more important component of these theoretical models is the visualisation rules, given that the most effort in these simulations is engaged in visualisation. The next step is to include more theoretical assumptions; for instance, we could extend our example by including the reconstruction of buildings. In this case, many parts of the building are guessed and not indicated by archaeological evidence. With this example, we are approaching the border to those simulations with a focus on theoretical models. If there are complex interrelationships, differential equations can be employed. While we know all the rules of the theoretical model, due to the complexity a simple prediction is not possible. The calculation of interrelated populations is an example of this type of simulations. Finally, cases with uncertainty and random components have to be mentioned. Here, the prediction is also not possible and random numbers help to produce data of different scenarios.

12.1.2 Random Numbers

Random numbers—used to introduce randomness in simulations—are numbers that cannot be predicted—in principle. The process of taking random numbers is thought to be something like dicing. True random number generators are based upon the measurement of real random events or noise and they are offered by hardware-based generators and some services (for instance, www.random.org). In practice—and in R—pseudo-random numbers are usually used. In this case, there is a pre-calculated list of numbers or an ad-hoc calculation using well-defined equations. Drawing a random number means picking one number out of the list.

In R, the function `runif` generates random numbers. In the example, we want 11 numbers between 10 and 25:

```
> r1 <- runif(11, 10, 25)
> r1
 [1] 10.23130 20.28426 19.97188 14.55902 16.54916 20.27554
 + 18.77722 11.26316 14.84382 16.39823 10.72193
> r2 <- runif(11, 10, 25)
> r2
 [1] 17.68780 14.97107 18.07993 11.26686 23.99934 15.47418
 + 21.50804 19.60076 23.05224 12.53369 19.47359
```

We see that both runs produce different results, which is the result that we expect from random number generation. Since this function uses pseudo-random numbers, the numbers are predictable if we set a certain starting point for the random number generator with `set.seed`, whereby we obtain the same result, which can be useful for reproducible results:

```
> set.seed(444)
> r3 <- runif(11, 10, 25)
> r3
 [1] 12.52080 12.77653 15.84529 15.48235 10.73310 18.65206
 + 18.39157 10.84036 22.73591 14.24675 14.56461
> set.seed(444)
> r4<- runif(11, 10, 25)
> r4
 [1] 12.52080 12.77653 15.84529 15.48235 10.73310 18.65206
 + 18.39157 10.84036 22.73591 14.24675 14.56461
```

The system produces floating-point numbers. If we want integers, we can of course use the `floor` function.

```
> set.seed(444)
> r5 <- runif(11, 10, 25)
> r5 <- floor(r5)
> r5
 [1] 12 12 15 15 10 18 18 10 22 14 14
```

Another way to obtain integers is the sample function. Here, we draw 11 integers from the sequence from 10 to 25:

```
> set.seed(444)
> r6 <- sample(10:25,11)
> r6
 [1] 12 25 15 14 10 16 23 21 20 11 17
```

It is also possible to allow multiple tokens by replacing the drawn numbers:

```
> set.seed(444)
> r7<- sample(10:25, 11, replace=T)
> r7
 [1] 12 12 16 15 10 19 18 10 23 14 14
```

These integer numbers can be used to obtain random samples from any vectors; for instance, vectors with text:

```
> set.seed(444)
> vt <- c("a","b","c","d")
> r8<- sample(1:4, 11, replace=T)
> vt[r8]
 [1] "a" "a" "b" "b" "a" "c" "c" "a" "d" "b" "b"
```

It is easier to apply the sample function directly to the text vector:

```
> set.seed(444)
> sample(vt, 11, replace=T)
 [1] "a" "a" "b" "b" "a" "c" "c" "a" "d" "b" "b"
```

Let us return to the runif function. This function produces random numbers, where all possible numbers have the same probability occurring in the sample. The random numbers have a uniform distribution. A histogram of the random numbers shows the distribution (Fig. 12.1). In case of 25 numbers, the empirical distribution is not very helpful:

```
> set.seed(444)
> r9 <- runif(25, 10, 25)
> hist(r9, breaks=10:26, col="grey")
```

In case of 25000 numbers the result looks much more like a uniform distribution:

```
> set.seed(444)
> r10 <- runif(25000, 10, 25)
> hist(r10, breaks=10:26, col="grey")
```

In addition to the uniform distribution many more distributions are implemented; for example, the normal distribution or Gaussian distribution:

```
> set.seed(444)
> r11 <- rnorm(25000, 10, 25)
> hist(r11[r11 > 10 & r11 < 25], breaks=10:25, col="grey",
+ main="Histogram of r11", xlab="r11")
```

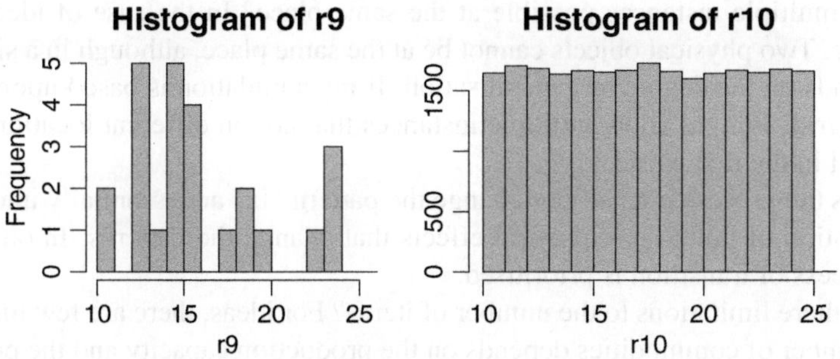

Fig. 12.1 Histogram of two sets of random numbers

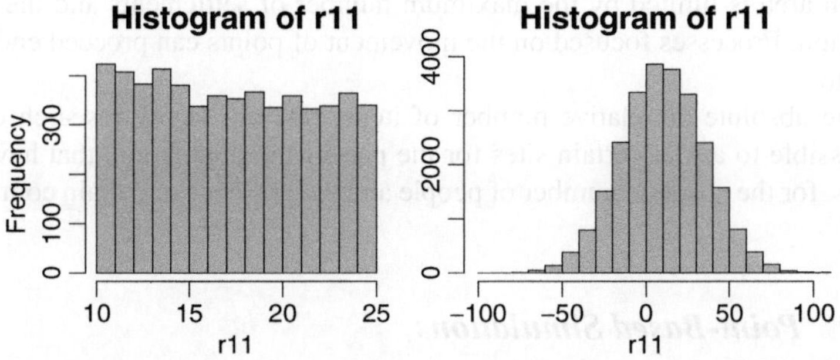

Fig. 12.2 Histogram of a set of random numbers

Here, we need to exclude some values with a restriction to the index `[r11 > 10 & r11 < 25]]`. The histogram does not look much like a normal distribution, although we can zoom out by removing the pre-defined breaks (Fig. 12.2):

```
> hist(r11, col="grey", main="Histogram of r11", xlab="r11")
```

Subsequently, a proper normal distribution is visible. Obviously, the parameters of `rnorm` are not the same as for `runif`. The second parameter is the mean, while the third one is the standard deviation.

12.2 Spatial Simulation Examples

12.2.1 Preliminary Considerations

Classical topics of spatial simulations are simulations of location and movement of sites, people, commodities and ideas. Processes are often simulated with an iterative approach. Before we start with some simple simulations, some points have to be considered.

Are multiple instances possible at the same place? In the case of ideas, this is possible. Two physical objects cannot be at the same place, although in a simulation it depends on the degree of generalisation. If my simulation is based upon a coarse spatial grid, I might allow multiple instances that are on different locations on one grid cell in the real world.

Does the process intensify or change the pattern? If I am essentially interested in the location of points, I will avoid effects that change the patterns. In other cases, the process of transition is prioritised.

Are there limitations to the number of items? For ideas, there are few limitations. The number of commodities depends on the production capacity and the population depends on the carrying capacity and biological reproducibility.

Is the process limited or unlimited? A point process producing settlements in a certain area is limited by the maximum number of settlements and the maximal population. Processes focused on the movement of points can proceed endlessly, in principle.

Is the absolute or relative number of items relevant to my research question? It is possible to ask at certain sites for the part of the population, that have certain features, for the absolute number of people and the presence of certain commodities.

12.2.2 Point-Based Simulations

Here, we try some simulations of point processes to produce point patterns [1, 13, 14]. The first idea is to use random numbers as coordinates. We try this in our research area:

```
> x1 <- bbox(sgdf_srtm)[1,1]; x2 <- bbox(sgdf_srtm)[1,2]
> y1 <- bbox(sgdf_srtm)[2,1]; y2 <- bbox(sgdf_srtm)[2,2]
> xs1 <-  runif(100, x1, x2)
> ys1 <-  runif(100, y1, y2)
> spdf_rpp1 <- SpatialPointsDataFrame(cbind(xs1,ys1),
+ as.data.frame(cbind(xs1,ys1)), proj4string=CRS
+ (as.character(crs1)))
```

In this example, submerged points are possible since we have not restricted the points to land. We can also imagine a point process, where points emerge from a certain location and spread over the landscape. Some commodities could be produced at the centre. According to the general interaction models, it is more likely to find the commodities near the centre. If the spatial distribution is a normal distribution, then we can use `rnorm`:

```
> xs2 <-  rnorm(100, mean(c(x1, x2)), 4000)
> ys2 <-  rnorm(100, mean(c(y1, y2)), 2000)
> spdf_rpp2 <- SpatialPointsDataFrame(cbind(xs2,ys2),
+ as.data.frame(cbind(xs2,ys2)), proj4string=CRS
+ (as.character(crs1)))
```

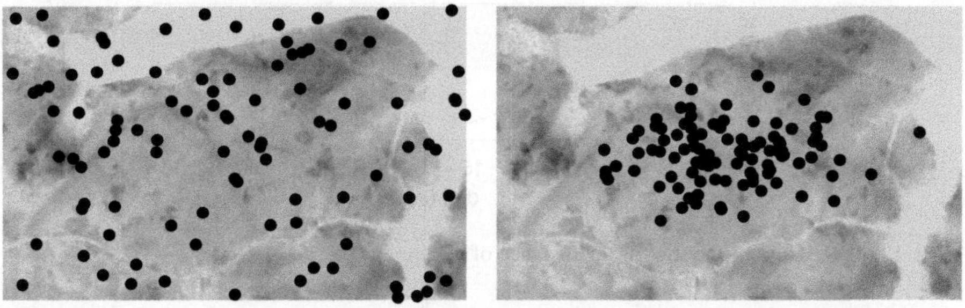

Fig. 12.3 Simulated point processes with uniform and normal random coordinates

Here, we use two different values for the standard deviation, which results in an oval-shaped distribution (Fig. 12.3).

In the next simulation points with high altitude are preferred. For this purpose, we prepare a raster with relative altitude values with a minimum at zero and a maximum at one. Additionally, we prepare some variables:

```
> xs3 <- c(); ys3 <- c()
> rel_srtm <- sgdf_srtm
> rel_srtm@data[is.na(rel_srtm@data)] <- 0
> rel_srtm@data[,1] <- rel_srtm@data[,1] /
+ max(rel_srtm@data[,1])
> rel_srtm <- raster(rel_srtm)
> i <- 0
> set.seed(555)
```

Subsequently, we produce points in a loop until we have 100 points. In each step, we generate random coordinates and an additional random number `rn`, after which we extract the relative altitude at the random coordinates. If the sum of the relative altitude and random number exceeds one, then the point is transferred to the `xs3` and `ys3` coordinates list. All coordinates are possible, although high altitudes are preferred.

```
> while (i < 101) {
+     xs <-  runif(1, x1, x2)
+     ys <-  runif(1, y1, y2)
+     rn <-  runif(1,  0,  1)
+     rp_alt <- extract(rel_srtm,
+ SpatialPoints(cbind(xs,ys)), proj4string=CRS(
+ as.character(crs1)))
+     if ((rp_alt + rn) > 1) {
+         i <- i + 1
+         xs3[i] <- xs
+         ys3[i] <- ys
+         }
```

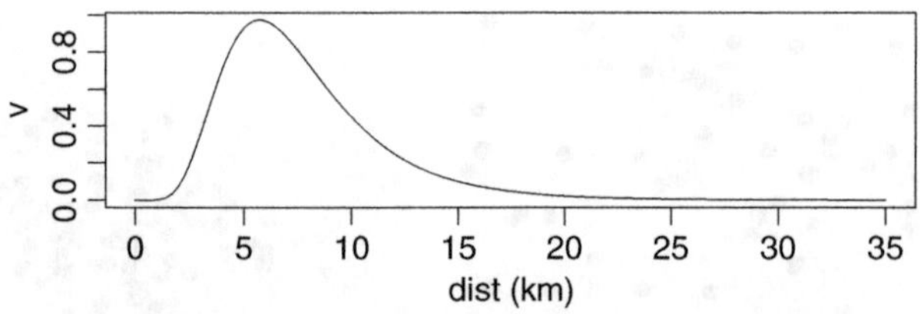

Fig. 12.4 Weighting function for the distance of new points

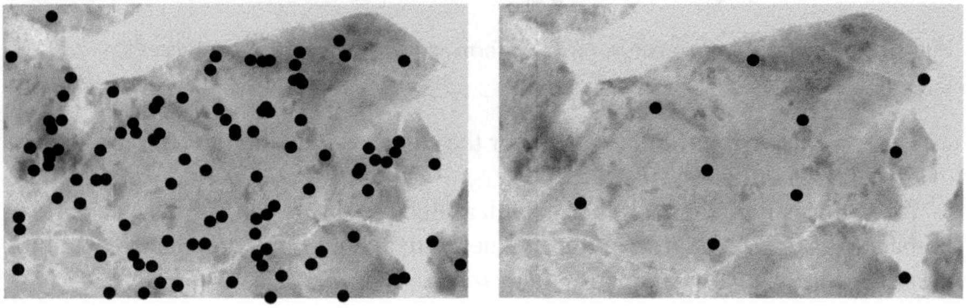

Fig. 12.5 Simulated point process with the preference of high altitude and certain distances to other points

```
+       }
> spdf_rpp3 <- SpatialPointsDataFrame(cbind(xs3,ys3),
+ as.data.frame(cbind(xs3,ys3)), proj4string=
+ CRS(as.character(crs1)))
```

We now want to consider interaction with other points. New points shall prefer a certain distance to other points. We apply a similar technique, but instead of relative altitude we use the weighted distance. The weighting function is based upon the Fisher distribution (Fig. 12.4):

The algorithm calculates and weights all distances and uses these values for the decision concerning which random points are allowed to remain in the random point pattern (Fig. 12.5).

```
> set.seed(333)
> xs4 <- c( runif(1, x1, x2)); ys4 <- c(runif(1, y1, y2))
> edist <- function(a){sqrt((a[1] - a[3])^2 + (a[2] -
+ a[4])^ 2)}
> i <- 0
> set.seed(555)
> while (i < 10) {
+     xs <-  runif(1, x1, x2)
+     ys <-   runif(1, y1, y2)
+     rn <-  runif(1,  0,  1)
+     rdf <- data.frame(xs4,ys4,xs,ys)
+     dmin <- min(edist(rdf))
```

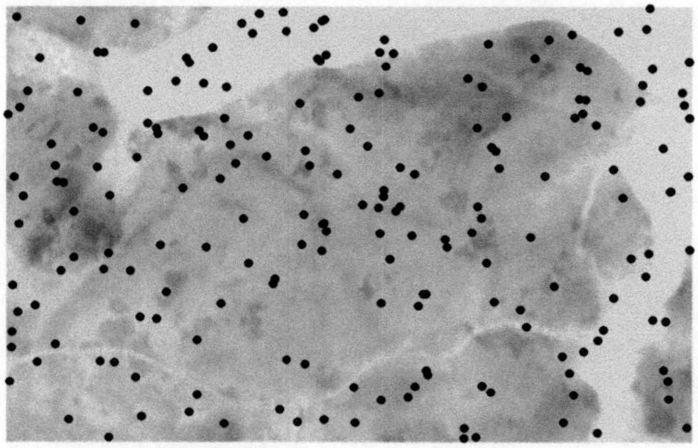

Fig. 12.6 Simulated Strauss point process

```
+       dval <- df(dmin/7000, 20, 20)
+       if ((dval + rn) > 1.5) {
+           i <- i + 1
+           xs4[i] <- xs
+           ys4[i] <- ys
+       }
+ }
> spdf_rpp4 <- SpatialPointsDataFrame(cbind(xs4,ys4),
+ as.data.frame(cbind(xs4,ys4)), proj4string=
+ CRS(as.character(crs1)))
```

The R-package `spatstat` allows simulating some pre-defined point processes. Our example simulates a *Strauss* process (Fig. 12.6). The parameters of this process are compiled in a `list`-object and forwarded to the `rmh`-function, which applies the simulation. Lists are suitable objects for the storage of different types of data and hence a good solution to store parameters for certain functions. Please refer to Chap. 7 for further details about point pattern processes.

```
> library(spatstat)
> ppspec <- list(cif="strauss",par=list(beta=2,gamma=0.2,
+ r=0.7), w=c(bb[1,1],bb[1,2],bb[2,1],bb[2,2]))
> ppsim <- rmh(model=ppspec,start=list(n.start=200),
+ control=list(nrep=10,nverb=5))
> plot(ppsim)
```

12.2.3 Grid-Based Simulations

In grid-based models, we observe the characteristics of different grid cells. The grid cells can represent the presence of a certain attribute, the population, the degree of saturation of a certain property, etc. The iterative process steps through all grid cells

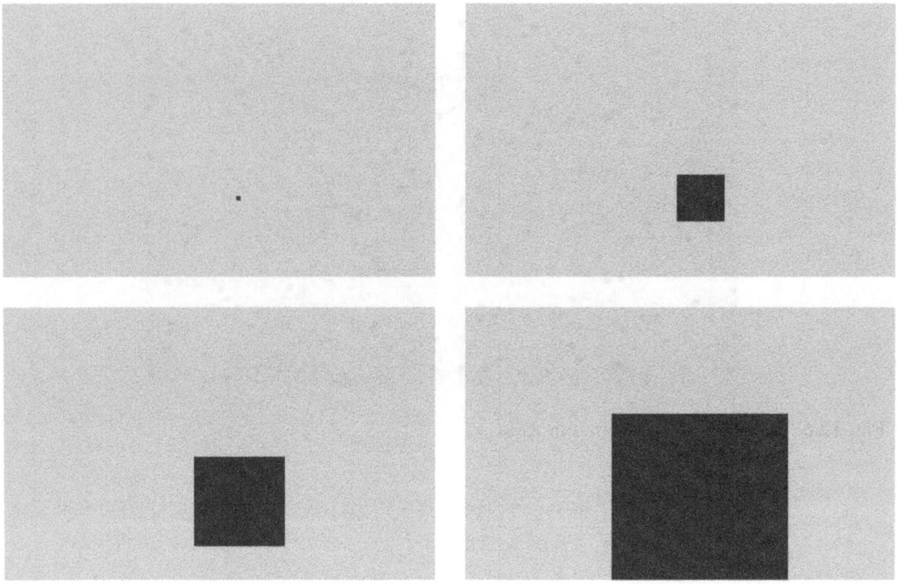

Fig. 12.7 Simple grid-based spread model

that can influence each other. In the case of cellular automata [6, 7, 15], the grid values depend on the values of surrounding grid cells. Usually the values 0 and 1 or dead and alive are used. We try to model the distribution of ideas or innovations with a grid-based model (Fig. 12.7). We distinguish between idea present (*1*) and idea absent (*0*). The innovation starts at a certain point. We use a simple moving window approach and set every grid cell to the maximum of all cells from the neighbourhood. If there is one *1* in the neighbourhood, that cell will obtain the value *1*.

```
> gt = GridTopology(cellcentre.offset=c(x1,y1),
+ cellsize=c(2500,2500),cells=c(100, 64))
> gt = SpatialGrid(gt, proj4string=CRS(as.character(crs1)))
> df <- data.frame(coordinates(gt))
> df[,1] <- 0
> cgrid1 <- SpatialGridDataFrame(gt, df, proj4string =
+ CRS(as.character(crs1)))
> cgrid1@data[4555,1] <- 1
> cgrid0 <- cgrid1
> cgrid2 <- cgrid1
> for (j in 1: 21){
+     for (i in (1:length(coordinates(cgrid1)[,1]))) {
+         gx1 <- coordinates(cgrid1)[i,1]
+         gy1 <- coordinates(cgrid1)[i,2]
+         rdf <- data.frame(coordinates(cgrid1)[,1],
+ coordinates(cgrid1)[,2],gx1,gy1)
+         ddist <- edist(rdf)
+         nind  <- which(ddist < 3600)
```

```
+          cgrid2@data[i,1] <- max(cgrid1@data[nind,1])
+        }
+      cgrid1 <- cgrid2
+      if (j==5)  {cgrid5   <- cgrid2}
+      if (j==10) {cgrid10  <- cgrid2}
+      if (j==20) {cgrid20  <- cgrid2}
+ }
```

The result is not a surprise. The maps of different steps show that a continuous spread takes place. This result does not show fancy patterns like *Conway's game of life*, although it is at least archaeologically interpretable. An improvement would be to include obstacles (Fig. 12.8). Here, we define a short line of grid cells that cannot change the values. Instead of an artificial line, we also could involve real topographic features. For the visualisation, we add an obstacle layer, where the lines are marked with 2 and the obstacle occurs in black.

```
> gt = GridTopology(cellcentre.offset=c(x1,y1),cellsize=
+ c(2500,2500),cells=c(100, 64))
> gt = SpatialGrid(gt, proj4string=CRS(as.character(crs1)))
> df <- data.frame(coordinates(gt))
> df[,1] <- 0
> cgrid1 <- SpatialGridDataFrame(gt, df, proj4string =
+ CRS(as.character(crs1)))
> cgridx <- cgrid1
> cgrid1@data[4555,1] <- 1
```

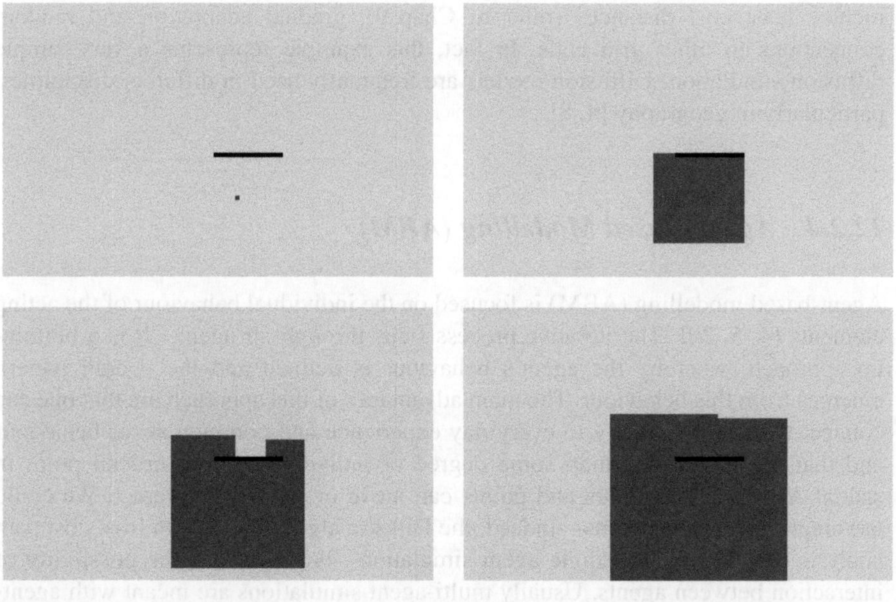

Fig. 12.8 Simple grid based spread model with an obstacle (*black*)

```
> cgridx@data[3550:3565,1] <- 2
> image(cgrid1, col=c("grey", "black"))
> cgrid0 <- cgrid1
> for (j in 1: 21){
+     for (i in (1:length(coordinates(cgrid1)[,1]))) {
+         gx1 <- coordinates(cgrid1)[i,1]
+         gy1 <- coordinates(cgrid1)[i,2]
+         rdf <- data.frame(coordinates(cgrid1)[,1],
+ coordinates(cgrid1)[,2],gx1,gy1)
+         ddist <- edist(rdf)
+         nind <- which(ddist < 3600)
+         cgrid2@data[i,1] <- max(cgrid1@data[nind,1])
+     }
+     cgrid2@data[3550:3565,1] <- 0
+     cgrid1 <- cgrid2
+     if (j==10) {cgrid10  <- cgrid2}
+     if (j==15) {cgrid15  <- cgrid2}
+     if (j==20) {cgrid20  <- cgrid2}
+ }
> cgrid0@data[,1]  <- cgrid0@data[,1]  + cgridx@data[,1]
> cgrid10@data[,1] <- cgrid10@data[,1] + cgridx@data[,1]
> cgrid15@data[,1] <- cgrid15@data[,1] + cgridx@data[,1]
> cgrid20@data[,1] <- cgrid20@data[,1] + cgridx@data[,1]
```

The result is that an obstacle produces a certain type of shadow, which is different from a light shadow with the present algorithm. The circumvention of mountains in the spread of innovations can show similar patterns. Further improvements could include least cost distances (refer to Chap. 9), gradual adaptation and random connections to other grid cells. In fact, this example represents a very simple diffusion simulation. Diffusion models are frequently used in different disciplines, particularly in geography [4, 8].

12.2.4 Agent-Based Modelling (ABM)

Agent-based modelling (ABM) is focused on the individual behaviour of the acting elements [4, 5, 20]. The iterative process steps through all agents. It is a bottom-up approach, whereby the agent's behaviour is defined and the overall pattern emerges from this behaviour. The main advantages of this approach are that one can connect the agents directly to every day experience and common sense behaviour and that the model can map some degree of individuality. The crucial point in spatial ABMs is that actors and points can move or jump and interact. We could use single agent simulations—indeed, the Dijkstra algorithm used in least cost path analysis can be called a single agent simulation—but then lack the possibility of interaction between agents. Usually multi-agent simulations are meant with agent-based models. The interaction of agents in an iterative process forms the basis for complex systems characterised by non-linear behaviour, the emergence of new structures, path dependency and other features. Agent-based models of complex systems are very useful, while in the case of agent-based models of simple systems one would sometimes prefer analytical models.

There are specialised software packages available, as well as `R` packages that connect to this software, or apply ABM algorithms on their own. The program NetLogo with the connection package `rnetlogo` and the `R package simecol` are examples. R is not optimised for simulations, but offers a flexible framework for different applications [12, 16, 19].

We try a simple agent-based model in which three types of agents with different behaviour search for an optimal location. In each loop, the agents are offered a new location. Based upon some parameters, they decide whether to move to the new one or not. The parameters are agent density, altitude, soil quality, distance to pathway and distance to the new location.

- Type a agent
  - prefers short distance moves
  - prefers high altitude
  - demands high soil quality
  - prefers low density areas
  - prefers short distances to pathways
- Type b agent
  - prefers medium distance moves
  - prefers low altitudes
  - no soil quality preferences
  - prefers rather high density areas
  - prefers short distances to pathways
- Type c agent
  - prefers long distance moves
  - no altitude preferences
  - no soil quality preferences
  - prefers rather high density areas
  - demands short distances to pathways

For the realisation of the model, we do not use one of the sophisticated ABM software packages; rather, we undertake a simple model by hand. The basic principle is an iteration in which each agent acts according to some rules. In our model, the agents simply decide for a new location or not. Before we start the loop that conducts the iteration, we have to prepare and set some variables. We start with the number of iterations and some spatial grids. In principle, the agents are free to move wherever the random numbers allow. We introduce some simple restrictions. We use grids of the same grid topology for some parameters. The agents' locations are just a reference to a grid cell. A maximum of one agent is allowed for each grid cell.

```
> n <- 50
> gt = GridTopology(cellcentre.offset=c(x1,y1),cellsize=
+ c(500,500),cells=c(56, 36))
> gt = SpatialGrid(gt, proj4string=CRS(as.character(crs1)))
> abmpt <- SpatialPoints(gt)
> proj4string(abmpt)  <- CRS(as.character(crs1))
> cn <- length(abmpt@coords[,1])
> abm_alt <- SpatialGridDataFrame(gt, data.frame(extract
+ (rel_srtm, abmpt)), proj4string = CRS(as.character(crs1)))
> abm_path <- SpatialGridDataFrame(gt, over(abmpt, as(path,
+ 'SpatialGridDataFrame')), proj4string =
+ CRS(as.character(crs1)))
> abm_path@data[,1] <- abm_path@data[,1] /
+ max(abm_path@data[,1])
> abm_soil <- abm_path
> abm_soil@data[,1] <- 1
```

The next step is to prepare a dataframe of the agents:

```
> abm <- data.frame(id=1:70, type=0, gc1=0, gc2=0, dist=0,
+ dens1=0, dens2=0, densa1=0, densa2=0, alt1=0, alt2=0,
+ soil1=0, soil2=0, path1=0, path2=0, eval1=0, eval2=0)
> abm[,2] <- c(rep("a",30),rep("b",30),rep("c",10))
> abm[,3] <- sample(1:cn, 70)
```

We need some functions for different purposes. First, we define distance, Gaussian weighing and kernel density functions. Note that the density values of this function are relative to fit our needs. Subsequently, we define some evaluation functions that turn different parameter values in evaluations ranging from zero to one. These functions control the agent's behaviour.

```
> edist2  <- function(x){sqrt((x[1] - x[3])^2 + ((x[2] -
+ x[4])^2))}
> gau1   <- function(x, sd){dnorm(edist2(x), mean=0, sd=sd)}
> kde <- function(pp,grid,sd1){
>     grid2 <- grid
+     for (i in seq(along=grid2@data[,1])){
+         pdist <- cbind(coordinates(grid2)[i,1],
+ coordinates(grid2)[i,2],pp[,1],pp[,2])
+         grid2@data[i,1]<- sum(apply(
+   pdist,1,gau1,sd=sd1))}
+     grid2@data[,1] <- grid2@data[,1] /
+   max(grid2@data[,1])
+     return(grid2)}
> fline <- function(x,x1,x2,y1,y2) {
+     m <- (y2-y1) / (x2-x1)
+     b <- (y2 - x2*(y2-y1) / (x2-x1))
+     y <- m*x + b
+     return(y)}
> fdist_a <- function(x){
```

```
+     if (x<0.2)  {y <- fline(x,0,0.2,0,1)}
+     else        {y <- fline(x,0.2,1,1,0)}
+     return(y)}
> fdist_b <- function(x){
+     if (x<0.5)   {y <- fline(x,0,0.5,0,1)}
+     else         {y <- fline(x,0.5,1,1,0)}
+     return(y)}
> fdist_c <- function(x){
+     if (x<0.9)  {y <- fline(x,0,0.9,0,1)}
+     else        {y <- fline(x,0.9,1,1,0)}
+     return(y)}
> falt_a <- function(x){
+     if (x<0.7)   {y <- fline(x,0,0.7,0.2,1)}
+     else         {y <- fline(x,0.7,1,1,0.2)}
+     return(y)}
> falt_b <- function(x){
+     if (x<0.3)   {y <- fline(x,0,0.3,0.2,1)}
+     else         {y <- fline(x,0.3,1,1,0.2)}
+     return(y)}
> falt_c <- function(x){y=0.5
+     return(y)}
> fsoil_a <- function(x){
+     y <- fline(x,0,1,0,1)
+     return(y)}
> fsoil_b <- function(x){y=0.5
+     return(y)}
> fsoil_c <- function(x){y=0.5
+     return(y)}
> fdens_a <- function(x){
+     if (x<0.3)   {y <- fline(x,0,0.3,0,1)}
+     else         {y <- fline(x,0.3,1,1,0)}
+     return(y)}
> fdens <- function(x){
+     if (x<0.7)   {y <- fline(x,0,0.7,0,1)}
+     else         {y <- fline(x,0.7,1,1,0)}
+     return(y)}
> fpath_c <- function(x){
+     y <- fline(x,0,1,1,0)
+     return(y)}
> fpath <- function(x){
+     y <- fline(x,0,1,1,0.5)
+     return(y)}
```

Since we want to compare the initial distribution of agents with a result after some iterations, we draw some maps:

```
> sp_a1 <- SpatialPoints(coordinates(abm_alt)
+ [abm[which(abm[,2]=="a"),3],], proj4string
+ = CRS(as.character(crs1)))
> sp_b1 <- SpatialPoints(coordinates(abm_alt)
```

```
+ [abm[which(abm[,2]=="b"),3],], proj4string
+ = CRS(as.character(crs1)))
> sp_c1 <- SpatialPoints(coordinates(abm_alt)
+ [abm[which(abm[,2]=="c"),3],], proj4string
+ = CRS(as.character(crs1)))
```

We can now start the loop. First, we set the random locations, although we avoid multiple agents on the same grid cell. The random numbers are unique and agents are allowed to stay where they are. Therefore, the set of new locations offered to the agents is not allowed to have an intersection with the old locations. Subsequently, we calculate the density maps and sample the maps for the old and new locations of the agents. The next step is to weight the parameters and aggregate the single values to a validation value. Thereafter, type a agents reduce the soil quality at their location. Finally, the agents move to the new locations if the new one has a better validation score.

```
> for (i in 1:n) {
+     abm[,4] <- sample(1:cn, 70)
+     while (length(intersect(abm[,3],abm[,4])) > 0) {
+      abm[,4] <- sample(1:cn, 70)  }
+     kde_all <- kde(coordinates(abm_alt)[abm[,3],], abm_alt,
+ 2000)
+     kde_a <- kde(coordinates(abm_alt)[abm[which(abm[,2]
+ =="a"),3],], abm_alt, 2000)
+     kde_all2 <- kde(coordinates(abm_alt)[abm[,4],],
+ abm_alt, 2000)
+     kde_a2 <- kde(coordinates(abm_alt)[abm[which(abm[,2]
+ =="a"),4],], abm_alt, 2000)
+     abm[,5] <-  apply(cbind(coordinates(abm_alt)[abm[,3],],
+  coordinates(abm_alt)[abm[,4],]),1,  edist2) / 34000
+     abm[,6] <- kde_all@data[abm[,3],1]
+     abm[,7] <- kde_all2@data[abm[,3],1]
+     abm[,8] <- kde_a@data[abm[,3],1]
+     abm[,9] <- kde_a2@data[abm[,3],1]
+     abm[,10] <- abm_alt@data[abm[,3],1]
+     abm[,11] <- abm_alt@data[abm[,4],1]
+     abm[,12] <- abm_soil@data[abm[,3],1]
+     abm[,13] <- abm_soil@data[abm[,4],1]
+     abm[,14] <- abm_path@data[abm[,3],1]
+     abm[,15] <- abm_path@data[abm[,4],1]
+     abm[which(abm[,2]=="a"),5]  <- apply(data.frame
+ (abm[which(abm[,2]=="a"),5]),  1, fdist_a)
+     abm[which(abm[,2]=="a"),6]  <- apply(data.frame
+ (abm[which(abm[,2]=="a"),6]),  1, fdens)
+     abm[which(abm[,2]=="a"),7]  <- apply(data.frame
+ (abm[which(abm[,2]=="a"),7]),  1, fdens)
+     abm[which(abm[,2]=="a"),8]  <- apply(data.frame
+ (abm[which(abm[,2]=="a"),8]),  1, fdens_a)
+     abm[which(abm[,2]=="a"),9]  <- apply(data.frame
```

```
+ (abm[which(abm[,2]=="a"),9]), 1, fdens_a)
+     abm[which(abm[,2]=="a"),10] <- apply(data.frame
+ (abm[which(abm[,2]=="a"),10]), 1, falt_a)
+     abm[which(abm[,2]=="a"),11] <- apply(data.frame
+ (abm[which(abm[,2]=="a"),11]), 1, falt_a)
+     abm[which(abm[,2]=="a"),12] <- apply(data.frame
+ (abm[which(abm[,2]=="a"),12]), 1, fsoil_a)
+     abm[which(abm[,2]=="a"),13] <- apply(data.frame
+ (abm[which(abm[,2]=="a"),13]), 1, fsoil_a)
+     abm[which(abm[,2]=="a"),14] <- apply(data.frame
+ (abm[which(abm[,2]=="a"),14]), 1, fpath)
+     abm[which(abm[,2]=="a"),15] <- apply(data.frame
+ (abm[which(abm[,2]=="a"),15]), 1, fpath)
+     abm[which(abm[,2]=="b"),5]  <- apply(data.frame
+ (abm[which(abm[,2]=="b"),5]),  1, fdist_b)
+     abm[which(abm[,2]=="b"),6]  <- apply(data.frame
+ (abm[which(abm[,2]=="b"),6]),  1, fdens)
+     abm[which(abm[,2]=="b"),7]  <- apply(data.frame
+ (abm[which(abm[,2]=="b"),7]),  1, fdens)
+     abm[which(abm[,2]=="b"),8]  <- apply(data.frame
+ (abm[which(abm[,2]=="b"),8]),  1, fdens)
+     abm[which(abm[,2]=="b"),9]  <- apply(data.frame
+ (abm[which(abm[,2]=="b"),9]),  1, fdens)
+     abm[which(abm[,2]=="b"),10] <- apply(data.frame
+ (abm[which(abm[,2]=="b"),10]), 1, falt_b)
+     abm[which(abm[,2]=="b"),11] <- apply(data.frame
+ (abm[which(abm[,2]=="b"),11]), 1, falt_b)
+     abm[which(abm[,2]=="b"),12] <- apply(data.frame
+ (abm[which(abm[,2]=="b"),12]), 1, fsoil_b)
+     abm[which(abm[,2]=="b"),13] <- apply(data.frame
+ (abm[which(abm[,2]=="b"),13]), 1, fsoil_b)
+     abm[which(abm[,2]=="b"),14] <- apply(data.frame
+ (abm[which(abm[,2]=="b"),14]), 1, fpath)
+     abm[which(abm[,2]=="b"),15] <- apply(data.frame
+ (abm[which(abm[,2]=="b"),15]), 1, fpath)
+     abm[which(abm[,2]=="c"),5]  <- apply(data.frame
+ (abm[which(abm[,2]=="c"),5]),  1, fdist_c)
+     abm[which(abm[,2]=="c"),6]  <- apply(data.frame
+ (abm[which(abm[,2]=="c"),6]),  1, fdens)
+     abm[which(abm[,2]=="c"),7]  <- apply(data.frame
+ (abm[which(abm[,2]=="c"),7]),  1, fdens)
+     abm[which(abm[,2]=="c"),8]  <- apply(data.frame
+ (abm[which(abm[,2]=="c"),8]),  1, fdens)
+     abm[which(abm[,2]=="c"),9]  <- apply(data.frame
+ (abm[which(abm[,2]=="c"),9]),  1, fdens)
+     abm[which(abm[,2]=="c"),10] <- apply(data.frame
+ (abm[which(abm[,2]=="c"),10]), 1, falt_c)
+     abm[which(abm[,2]=="c"),11] <- apply(data.frame
+ (abm[which(abm[,2]=="c"),11]), 1, falt_c)
+     abm[which(abm[,2]=="c"),12] <- apply(data.frame
```

```
+ (abm[which(abm[,2]=="c"),12]), 1, fsoil_c)
+     abm[which(abm[,2]=="c"),13] <- apply(data.frame
+ (abm[which(abm[,2]=="c"),13]), 1, fsoil_c)
+     abm[which(abm[,2]=="c"),14] <- apply(data.frame
+ (abm[which(abm[,2]=="c"),14]), 1, fpath_c)
+     abm[which(abm[,2]=="c"),15] <- apply(data.frame
+ (abm[which(abm[,2]=="c"),15]), 1, fpath_c)
+     abm[,16] <- apply(data.frame(abm[,6],abm[,10],
+ abm[,12],abm[,14]), 1, sum)
+     abm[,17] <- apply(data.frame(abm[,5],abm[,7],
+ abm[,11],abm[,13],abm[,15]), 1, sum)
+     abm[which(abm[,2]=="a"),16]  <- abm[which
+ (abm[,2]=="a"),16] + abm[which(abm[,2]=="a"), 8]
+     abm[which(abm[,2]=="a"),17]  <- abm[which(abm[,2]
+ =="a"),16] + abm[which(abm[,2]=="a"), 9]
+     abm_soil@data[abm[,3],1] <- abm_soil@data[
+ abm[,3],1] * 0.9
+     for (j in 1:length(abm[,3])) {if(abm[j,17]
+ <abm[j,16]) {abm[j,3] <- abm[j,4]}}
+ }
```

Finally, we prepare a second map and plot both maps side by side:

```
> sp_a1 <- SpatialPoints(coordinates(abm_alt)[abm[which(
+ abm[,2]=="a"),3],], proj4string = CRS(as.character(crs1)))
> sp_b1 <- SpatialPoints(coordinates(abm_alt)[abm[which(
+ abm[,2]=="b"),3],], proj4string = CRS(as.character(crs1)))
> sp_c1 <- SpatialPoints(coordinates(abm_alt)[abm[which(
+ abm[,2]=="c"),3],], proj4string = CRS(as.character(crs1)))
> par(mfcol=c(1,2), mai = c(0, 0, 0, 0))
> image(sgdf_srtm, col = gray.colors(25, start = 0.97,
+ end = 0.4))
> points(sp_a, pch=15, col="black", cex=0.5)
> points(sp_b, pch=19, col="black", cex=0.5)
> points(sp_c, pch=17, col="black", cex=0.5)
> image(sgdf_srtm, col = gray.colors(25, start = 0.97,
+ end = 0.4))
> points(sp_a1, pch=15, col="black", cex=0.5)
> points(sp_b1, pch=19, col="black", cex=0.5)
> points(sp_c1, pch=17, col="black", cex=0.5)
> par(mfcol=c(1,1))
```

The maps show the initial pattern and the pattern after the simulation (Fig. 12.9). The specific pattern helps us to understand the effect of certain set of behaviour rules. It is possible and useful to collect some aggregated information for each iterative step and plot the result as a curve, which allows studying the system state during certain processes. For instance, the emergence and disappearance of agglomerations can be studied with agglomeration indices.

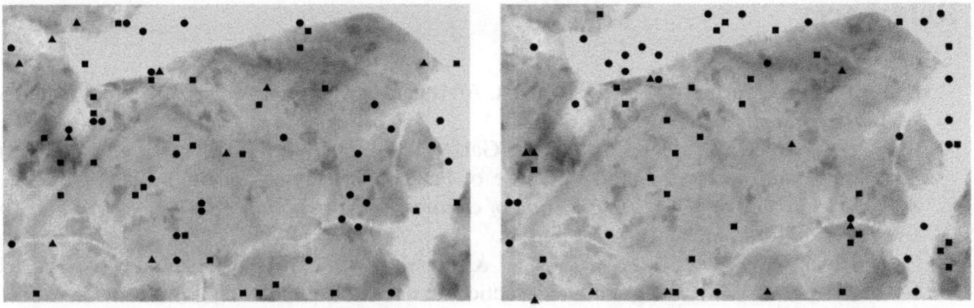

Fig. 12.9 Agent-based model: location of the agents after 50 loops

12.3 Problems

12.1. For what purpose do we need true random numbers?

12.2. Why is setting a seed for random number generation useful and when should it be used?

12.3. Can you imagine other basic point processes? Can you implement this process as a simulation?

12.4. Please find archaeological applications for cellular automata.

12.5. Here are some problems for our agent-based model:

(a) Please plot some weighting functions.
(b) Why is this an agent-based model given that we are using grids?
(c) How can we interpret the agents: individuals, communities, households?
(d) How can we restrict the agents to land?
(e) How can we explain the resulting pattern?
(f) Which behaviour rules are visible in the result and which are not?
(g) Are second order properties—i. e. interaction—involved in the model?
(h) How can we implement soil regeneration?
(i) How can we implement the collection of an agglomeration index?
(j) How could we implement trade between the agents?
(k) Can you find some improvements?
(l) Is this model useful? What does it explain in particular?

12.6. What drives you to conduct research? Which processes are troubling you? Develop a simple simulation for your favourite topic and explore which aspects of the topic are enlightened by the simulation.

References

1. Baddeley, A., & Turner, R. (2005). Spatstat: An R package for analyzing spatial point patterns. *Journal of Statistical Software, 12*, 1–42.
2. Barceló, J., Cuesta J., Del Castillo, F., Galán, J., Mameli, L., Miguel, F., et al. (2013). Simulating prehistoric ethnicity: The case of Patagonian Hunter-Gatherers. In F. Contreras & F. J. Melero (Eds.), *CAA 2010: Fusion of cultures, bar international series* (Vol. S2494, pp. 137–144). Oxford: ArcheoPress.
3. Danielisová, A., Olševičová, K., Cimler, R., & Machálek, T. (2015). Understanding the iron age economy: sustainability of agricultural practices under stable population growth. In G. Wurzer, K. Kowarik & H. Reschreiter (Eds.), *Agent-based Modeling and simulation in archaeology* (pp. 183–216). New York: Springer.
4. Daudé, E. (2004) Apports de la simulation multi-agents à l'étude des processus de diffusion. *Cybergeo: Revue Europenne de Gographie, 255*, 15. http://cybergeo.revues.org/3835; doi: 10.4000/cybergeo.3835.
5. Epstein, J. M. (1999). Agent-based computational models and generative social science. *Complexity, 4*(5), 41–60.
6. Fonstad, M. A. (2006). Cellular automata as analysis and synthesis engines at the geomorphol-ogyecology interface. *Geomorphology, 77*, 217–234 (2006).
7. Gardner, M. (1970). Mathematical Games the fantastic combinations of John Conway's new solitaire game "life". *Scientific American, 223*, 120–123.
8. Hägerstrand, T. (1967). *Innovation diffusion as a spatial process*. Chicago: University of Chicago Press.
9. Hepppenstall, A. J., Crooks, A. T., See, L. M., & Batty, M. (Eds.). (2012). *Agent-based models of geographical systems*. New York: Springer.
10. Kohler, T. A., & Gumerman, G. J. (2000). *Dynamics in human and primate societies: Agent-based modeling of social and spatial processes*. Oxford: Oxbow.
11. Lake, M. W. (2014). Trends in archaeological simulation. *Journal of Archaeological Method and Theory, 21*, 258–287.
12. Mayer, J., Schmidt, V., & Schweiggert, F. (2004). A unified framework for spatial stochastic models. *Simulation Modelling Practice and Theory, 12*, 307–326.
13. Møller, J., & Waagepetersen, R. P. (2004). *Statistical inference and simulation for spatial point processes*. Boca Raton: Chapman & Hall/CRC.
14. O'Sullivan, D., & Perry, G. L. W. (2013). *Spatial simulation: Exploring pattern and process*. Chichester: Wiley.
15. Packard, N. H., & Wolfram, S. (1985). Two-dimensional cellular automata. *Journal of Statistical Physics, 38*, 901–946.
16. Petzoldt, T., & Rinke, K. (2007). Simecol: An object-oriented framework for ecological modeling in R.İ *Journal of Statistical Software, 22*(9), 1–31.
17. Premo, L. S. (2008). Exploring behavioral terra incognita with archaeological agent-based models. In B. Frischer & A. Dakouri-Hild (Eds.), *Beyond illustration: 2D and 3D technologies as tools of discovery in archaeology. British Archaeological Reports International Series* (pp. 46–138). Oxford: ArchaeoPress.
18. Tobler, W. (1970). A computer movie simulating urban growth in the Detroit region. *Economic Geography, 46*(2), 234–240.
19. Velten, K. (2009). *Mathematical modeling and simulation*. Weinheim: VLC.
20. Wurzer, G., Kowarik, K., & Reschreiter, H. (Eds.). (2015). *Agent-based modeling and simulation in archaeology*. New York: Springer.
21. Zubrow, E. (1981). Simulation as a heuristic device in archaeology. In J. A. Sabloff (Ed.), *Simulations in archaeology* (pp. 143–188). Albuquerque: University of New Mexico Press.

Index

O. Nakoinz, D. Knitter, *Modelling Human Behaviour in Landscapes*, Quantitative Archaeology and Archaeological Modelling, DOI 10.1007/978-3-319-29538-1

9783319295367